Syntheses of Higher Education Research

Also available from Bloomsbury

Higher Education Research, Malcolm Tight

Reflective Teaching in Higher Education, Paul Ashwin with David Boud, Susanna Calkins, Kelly Coate, Fiona Hallett, Gregory Light, Kathy Luckett, Jan McArthur, Iain McLaren, Monica McLean, Velda McCune, Katarina Mårtensson and Michelle Tooher

Transforming University Education A Manifesto, Paul Ashwin

Changing Higher Education for a Changing World, edited by Claire Callender, William Locke and Simon Marginson

The Roma In European Higher Education: Recasting Identities, Re-Imagining Futures, edited by Louise Morley, Andrzej Mirga and Nadir Redzepi

Scholarly Leadership in Higher Education: An Intellectual History of James Bryan Conant, Wayne J. Urban

Locating Social Justice in Higher Education Research, edited By Jan Mcarthur and Paul Ashwin

Exploring Consensual Leadership in Higher Education: Co-Operation, Collaboration and Partnership, edited by Lynne Gornall, Brychan Thomas and Lucy Sweetman

Leadership For Sustainability in Higher Education, by Janet Haddock-Fraser, Peter Rands and Stephen Scoffham

Academics' International Teaching Journeys: Personal Narratives of Transitions in Higher Education, edited by Anesa Hosein, Namrata Rao, Chloe Shu-Hua Yeh and Ian M. Kinchin

Socially Just Pedagogies: Posthumanist, Feminist and Materialist Perspectives in Higher Education, edited by Rosi Braidotti, Vivienne Bozalek, Tamara Shefer and Michalinos Zembylas

Leadership In Higher Education from a Transrelational Perspective, Christopher M. Branson, Maureen Marra, Margaret Franken and Dawn Penney

Syntheses of Higher Education Research

What We Know

Malcolm Tight

BLOOMSBURY ACADEMIC
LONDON • NEW YORK • OXFORD • NEW DELHI • SYDNEY

BLOOMSBURY ACADEMIC
Bloomsbury Publishing Plc
50 Bedford Square, London, WC1B 3DP, UK
1385 Broadway, New York, NY 10018, USA

BLOOMSBURY, BLOOMSBURY ACADEMIC and the Diana logo are
trademarks of Bloomsbury Publishing Plc

First published in Great Britain 2021

Copyright © Malcolm Tight

Malcolm Tight has asserted his right under the Copyright, Designs and Patents Act,
1988, to be identified as Author of this work.

Cover design: Charlotte James
Cover image © lasagnaforone/ iStock

All rights reserved. No part of this publication may be reproduced or
transmitted in any form or by any means, electronic or mechanical,
including photocopying, recording, or any information storage or retrieval system,
without prior permission in writing from the publishers.

Bloomsbury Publishing Plc does not have any control over, or responsibility for,
any third-party websites referred to or in this book. All internet addresses given in this
book were correct at the time of going to press. The author and publisher regret
any inconvenience caused if addresses have changed or sites have ceased to exist,
but can accept no responsibility for any such changes.

A catalogue record for this book is available from the British Library.

Library of Congress Cataloging-in-Publication Data
Names: Tight, Malcolm, author.
Title: Syntheses of higher education research :
what we know / Malcolm Tight.
Description: London ; New York : Bloomsbury Academic, 2020. | Includes
bibliographical references and index.
Identifiers: LCCN 2020033894 (print) | LCCN 2020033895 (ebook) | ISBN
9781350128736 (hardback) | ISBN 9781350128729 (paperback) | ISBN
9781350128743 (ebook) | ISBN 9781350128750 (epub)
Subjects: LCSH: Education, Higher–Research. | Education, Higher–Evaluation.
Classification: LCC LB2326.3 .T54 2020 (print) | LCC LB2326.3 (ebook) | DDC 378.0072–dc23
LC record available at https://lccn.loc.gov/2020033894
LC ebook record available at https://lccn.loc.gov/2020033895

ISBN:	HB:	978-1-3501-2873-6
	PB:	978-1-3501-2872-9
	ePDF:	978-1-3501-2874-3
	eBook:	978-1-3501-2875-0

Typeset by Integra Software Services Pvt. Ltd.
Printed and bound in Great Britain

To find out more about our authors and books visit www.bloomsbury.com
and sign up for our newsletters.

Contents

List of Illustrations — vi

Part one Overview — 1

1. Introduction — 3
2. Research syntheses — 9
3. Research syntheses in higher education — 23

Part two Analyses — 35

4. Teaching and learning — 37
5. Course design – types of instruction — 51
6. Course design – types of learning — 67
7. Course design – distance, online and e-learning — 81
8. Course design – curriculum — 103
9. Course design – assessment — 119
10. Course design – outcomes — 133
11. The student experience — 155
12. Quality — 177
13. System policy — 193
14. Institutional management — 203
15. Academic work — 215
16. Knowledge and research — 225

Part three Conclusion — 231

17. Conclusion — 233

References — 238
Index — 278

Illustrations

Tables

1	Numbers of Syntheses by Theme	28
2	Percentages of Syntheses and Articles Compared	30
3	Types of Syntheses by Date	31
4	Types of Syntheses by Source	32
5	Numbers of Syntheses by Sub-Theme for Course Design	33

Box

1	Varieties of Research Synthesis	10

Part one

Overview

The first part of this book contains three chapters.

Chapter 1 provides an introduction to what the book is about and what it contains: the identification and examination of syntheses of higher education research. Taken together, these provide a highly useful guide to what we know, and conversely what we don't know, about higher education.

Chapter 2 examines the nature of research syntheses: systematic reviews, meta-analyses and substantive literature reviews. It discusses what they are, what they do and how they are applied in practice.

Chapter 3 identifies, and provides an overview of, the syntheses that have been carried out of higher education research to date. These are then examined in more detail in the thirteen chapters in part two of the book.

Together, these three chapters provide an overview of, and introduction to, the book as a whole.

Chapter 1
Introduction

This book identifies, discusses and interrogates the many syntheses of higher education research that have been carried out to date, and published in the English language, across the globe.

Research syntheses take a number of forms. Historically, the most common has been the literature review, normally undertaken as part of a larger study to set out – usually selectively – the relevant research that has been done on the topic in question. Literature reviews may also be undertaken as stand-alone exercises, however, when they may be more thorough and comprehensive in their approach to the literature. At some point literature reviews shade into what are now more commonly known as systematic reviews.

Systematic reviews and meta-analyses are – qualitative and quantitative respectively – means of synthesizing the research studies that have been carried out on a particular topic (e.g. learning approaches, peer assessment, the research/teaching nexus). They comprise the bulk of research syntheses and aim to identify, assess and summarize all of the research that has been carried out and published on a particular topic.

As well as comprehensive literature reviews, systematic reviews and meta-analyses, there are some other studies which may qualify as research syntheses. The most obvious are in the form of what are essentially textbooks, focusing on a particular topic or field and embodying substantive and critical reviews of the relevant academic literature. There are a number of these that focus on higher education research.

Most research studies – of higher education as well as other areas – are relatively small scale, and their findings can vary, but, as the evidence builds up, research syntheses enable a summary or overview to be made to see what general lessons can be learnt. By drawing the lessons from all of these exercises together in one place, this book provides an invaluable source of information on what we know about higher education and how it works. By implication, it also indicates what we don't know and where, in particular, further research might most fruitfully be directed.

The third wave

The recent growth in the numbers of systematic reviews and meta-analyses of higher education research (see Chapter 3) may be seen as a 'third wave' in the development of higher education and higher education research.

The first wave was the expansion of higher education itself, transforming – in a relatively short time period, a matter of a few decades – from a system that served only an elite portion of the population to one offering mass participation and, beyond that, to providing higher educational opportunities for everyone in society who wished to make use of them (and, increasingly, to use them on more than one occasion). This latter position is now the norm, or at least the aspiration, in all developed and many developing countries around the world.

The second wave – somewhat lagging behind the development of higher education itself – was the growth of higher education research. As higher education expanded, interest in researching it naturally grew. In part, this was driven by personal interest; those working within the higher education sector noticed changes that were underway, had their own ideas about them and conducted some small-scale research to provide evidence. But there was also a drive from above; those funding higher education became more concerned that their money was being well spent, while those running higher education institutions wanted to ensure they were doing so effectively, and to compare their performance and practice with other institutions (i.e. through benchmarking).

The third wave – again with a time lag built in – came as the volume of higher education research built up. As more and more research studies were completed on a growing range of topics – albeit most of them small scale and local in nature – the need to compare their findings grew. How well did a particular innovation in the design or delivery of the curriculum work in different countries, institutions and disciplines?

Hence the contemporary interest in systematic reviews, meta-analyses and other syntheses of higher education research. These syntheses seek to identify all of the relevant published studies on a given theme or at least all of those in a particular language and/or published in a given time period. They then summarize or synthesize their findings to try and reach more general conclusions.

The fourth wave, by implication, will involve improvements in both higher education and higher education research, as the lessons from research in the form of systematic reviews and meta-analyses are taken on board. In the future, therefore, in what we might term the fifth wave, higher education research will most likely be much more targeted – on what we don't know or don't know enough about – while still maintaining some space for purely interest-driven research.

What this book contains

This book contains seventeen chapters, organized into three parts, and an extensive list of references. Following this introductory chapter, the first substantive chapter (Chapter 2) discusses the nature of systematic reviews, meta-analyses and other forms of research syntheses, their history, the different kinds of data sources that they use, how they are carried out, and their strengths and weaknesses. Existing syntheses of higher education research published in the English language – which form the basis for the analysis in the remainder of the book – are then identified and discussed in Chapter 3.

The main part of the book, part two, consists of thirteen chapters – Chapters 4 to 16 – which examine in detail the syntheses that have been carried out in different areas of higher education research. Eight areas or themes are used to organize the discussion: teaching and learning, course design, the student experience, quality, system policy, institutional management, academic work, knowledge and research.

These areas or themes are, of course, to some extent arbitrary, but they provide a system for analysing higher education research that I have developed and applied over the last twenty years and which has been taken up and used by other researchers worldwide. There are also, and again of course, inevitably overlaps between the areas or themes, but these will be dealt with in the book through the use of cross-referencing.

As will become apparent as you look and read through the book, the volume of research, and hence the numbers of systematic reviews, meta-analyses and other research syntheses that have been carried out and published, varies between areas and themes. Course design, in particular, has been a very popular topic for research and then research synthesis.

To make the text more manageable, therefore, the syntheses that have been carried out into research into course design are discussed in six themed chapters (Chapters 5 to 10). These focus on, successively, types of instruction; types of learning; distance, online and e-learning; curriculum; assessment; and outcomes. This explains, of course, why the eight areas or themes require thirteen chapters to discuss.

One other key point is that, in practice, as discussed in Chapter 2, the terminology of research syntheses has been applied in varied ways, both historically and contemporarily. Most significantly, as has already been pointed out, systematic reviews are on the same spectrum as, and hence overlap with, literature reviews.

Indeed, some literature reviews – which I shall call substantive literature reviews – are as comprehensive as systematic reviews, even though their authors do not identify them as such (the term 'systematic review' has only recently gained general acceptance). A number of these have, therefore, been included in the analyses, because to exclude them would have been wasteful.

A final chapter (Chapter 17), in part three, offers some general conclusions from the analyses, as much in terms of what they do not cover as what they do, and looks forward to what the future may bring.

How the book was compiled

This book forms part of a continuing project which I have been conducting over the last two decades, aiming to chart the changing state of higher education research worldwide. The project has to date resulted in the publication of three major books (Tight 2003, 2012a,

2019a) and a series of journal articles and book chapters (Tight 2004, 2006, 2007, 2008, 2009a, 2009b, 2011a, 2012b, 2012c, 2013, 2014a, 2014b, 2014c, 2014d, 2015a, 2015b, 2015c, 2015d, 2015e, 2016a, 2016b, 2018a, 2018b, 2019b, 2020, forthcoming a).

The methodology used in this research – though I was not initially aware that it had this label – has been chiefly that of systematic review, though it also involves elements of meta-analysis. In the current book this methodology is applied to systematic reviews and meta-analyses. In other words, in this book I am conducting a systematic review of systematic reviews and meta-analyses of higher education research to try to produce a comprehensive, overall picture.

Search engines – principally Scopus, Google Scholar and World of Science – and keywords – 'higher education', 'university', 'college', 'systematic review', 'meta-analysis', 'literature review' and a range of words reflecting the different themes or areas of research identified – have been employed to identify relevant published work in the English language. Different search engines were used because none of them are wholly comprehensive, and each has a particular coverage and historical reach. The items identified through the searches were then accessed, read and – where relevant – incorporated in the analysis. The references included in each item were also checked for further research syntheses that had not been identified through the search engines.

While the book takes an explicitly international focus, it has to be acknowledged that confining attention to English language publications does impose some limitations. A great deal of higher education research – and resultant systematic reviews and meta-analysis – is published in Arabic, Chinese, French, German, Portuguese, Russian, Spanish and other languages. While it is increasingly true that the best researchers seek to publish their work in English – as the current academic lingua franca – some syntheses will undoubtedly have been missed because of this language limitation.

It is also the case, of course, that, despite assiduous and repeated searches, some relevant English language systematic reviews and meta-analyses will have been missed. This might be due to their age or relatively obscure publication but is more likely a consequence of the increasing volume of academic publication, year by year, across the board. More and more systematic reviews and meta-analyses are being carried out and published with each succeeding year.

In a few cases I was unable to obtain a copy of a published systematic review or meta-analysis. In some other cases, while I was able to obtain copies, I decided that the systematic review or meta-analysis was not of the requisite quality for inclusion in this book (e.g. their coverage was poor, their scope was too narrow or their approach was unclear).

The focus has been on published systematic reviews, meta-analyses and other research syntheses, as this should ensure some level of quality assurance through the review process normally required for publication. The vast majority of the research syntheses identified and referred to are, therefore, in the form of refereed journal articles. Reports produced for reputable academic, governmental or other organizations have also been included, as have a few books and edited book chapters.

Unpublished syntheses, chiefly student theses and dissertations, and unpublished conference papers have largely been excluded. Many of these, where they are of the requisite quality, later appear as publications.

I would be grateful to hear of any important systematic reviews, substantive literature reviews or meta-analyses of higher education research that I have missed, particularly the older and more obscure. I will then endeavour to incorporate these, along with new systematic reviews and meta-analyses as they appear, in subsequent editions of this book.

How to use this book

A book of this nature lends itself to being used in a variety of ways. It is unlikely, however, that many readers will choose to read it literally from cover to cover.

Fellow higher education researchers, whether new to the field or more experienced, should be able to readily focus on particular topics of interest to them, using the index and/or contents pages to navigate speedily to the relevant pages. Published systematic reviews, meta-analyses and research syntheses are a very useful means for accessing specialist literatures, so identifying and obtaining copies of any that are relevant to your current research is likely to be helpful.

Alternatively, those following a course on higher education or higher education research might fruitfully use a number of the chapters – and potentially the whole book – as a guide to studying particular topics or themes in more detail. Remember, of course, that what is not in this book may be of more interest than what is, because it has not been researched or at least not been researched so much that it has produced a research synthesis.

Policymakers and practitioners should find the book useful in summarizing what we already know about higher education, which is quite a lot. Funders might be interested to discover which areas or aspects of higher education have, so far, been under-researched, so as to target funds in those directions.

Hopefully, all users of the book will find it both easy to navigate and read, as I have endeavoured to write it in an accessible and readable style. All specialist terms or 'jargon', where it has been necessary to use them, have been explained in everyday language. Linkages have been made between related studies or topics discussed in different chapters. The conclusions reached by particular studies have been drawn out, considered and compared with those of other relevant studies.

However you use the book, I hope that you will find it helpful and stimulating.

Chapter 2
Research syntheses

Introduction

This chapter discusses the nature of research syntheses, while the following chapter examines how they have been applied to higher education research studies. A careful reading of these two chapters should give you an overview and understanding of how and why these methods are used and what they have to contribute to our understanding of the research field.

This chapter starts by reviewing the variety of research syntheses and the terminology in use for describing them. This, like in many areas of research, is diverse and potentially confusing.

The meanings of systematic reviews and meta-analyses, as they are used in this book, are then clarified. The origins, development and practical application of these parallel techniques are examined. Like all research methodologies, systematic reviews and meta-analyses have been the subject of critique, so their strengths and weaknesses are discussed. Finally, some conclusions are provided.

The varieties of research synthesis

In practice, many terms are in use for research syntheses, with some authors recognizing a considerable variety of forms (this is not uncommon in academic research). In some cases, the same terms are used to refer to different approaches or processes, while, in others, alternative terms are used to refer to what is essentially the same approach. It is easy, therefore, to become rather confused; hence, once the varieties have been discussed, I will set out a simple typology for research syntheses, as used in the remainder of this book.

To start with a relatively simple typology, Oliver and Tripney (2017) identify three different approaches to what they term systematic reviewing (by which they mean all research syntheses) or 'analyses of multiple studies': for testing hypotheses, for generating theory and for exploring theory. This is an interesting typology, as it emphasizes the purpose rather than the methodology of the research synthesis.

Oliver and Tripney then relate this distinction to the qualitative/quantitative research spectrum:

> Between these two extremes of syntheses that build theory from qualitative studies and syntheses that test theory with quantitative studies, are mixed methods syntheses that explore theories and assumptions. These reviews start with an existing framework or theory to direct the initial search for evidence and progress by amending the initial framework or theory in light of emerging evidence.
>
> (p. 467)

The first of these 'extremes' (i.e. building theory from qualitative studies) could also be termed systematic reviews, and the second (testing theory with quantitative studies) meta-analyses, while the third might involve elements of both.

It does seem rather too simple a distinction, however, to view systematic reviews/qualitative research as being all about building theory, while meta-analyses/quantitative research is solely concerned with testing theory. Each may seek to do both of these things, suggesting that they more typically take the form of 'mixed methods syntheses' between the two 'extremes' identified.

Other researchers recognize both a wider range of research synthesis methods, and some confusion and overlap in the usage of terminology. Three examples of such typologies are given in Box 1, illustrating some of the range and potential confusion. While Arksey and O'Malley (2005) recognize seven varieties of research synthesis, and Suri and Clarke (2009) come up with six, Grant and Booth (2009) identify an impressive fourteen different forms.

Box 1: Varieties of Research Synthesis

Arksey and O'Malley (2005)

1. (full) systematic review
2. meta-analysis
3. rapid review
4. (traditional) literature review
5. narrative review
6. research synthesis
7. structured review

Suri and Clarke (2009)

1. *Statistical research syntheses* ... such as meta-analysis and best-evidence synthesis.
2. *Systematic reviews* ... emphasizes a priori protocols, comprehensive searches, transparency to reduce biases, and the involvement of stakeholders in the review process.

3. *Qualitative research syntheses* … various formally proposed individual methods for synthesizing qualitative research.
4. *Qualitative syntheses of qualitative and quantitative research* …
5. *Critical impetus in reviewing research* … discussions on a range of critical issues associated with the production and use of research syntheses …
6. *Exemplary syntheses*: explicit critiques or taxonomies of published syntheses. (p. 397; emphases in original)

Grant and Booth (2009)

1. critical review
2. literature review
3. mapping review/systematic map
4. meta-analysis
5. mixed studies review/mixed methods review
6. overview
7. qualitative systematic review/qualitative evidence synthesis
8. rapid review
9. scoping review
10. state-of-the-art review
11. systematic review
12. systematic search and review
13. systematized review
14. umbrella review

Perhaps significantly, all three typologies identify as one of their types both systematic reviews and meta-analyses. These may be regarded as the most prominent contemporary forms of research synthesis, with systematic reviews taking a primarily qualitative approach and meta-analyses a primarily quantitative approach.

However, even here there is potential confusion. Thus, meta-analysis is seen by Suri and Clarke as just one kind of statistical research synthesis, and Grant and Booth recognize more than one kind of systematic review. Arksey and O'Malley and Grant and Booth also identify both literature reviews and rapid reviews as types of research synthesis. Beyond this, though, the categorizations diverge, with each term suffixed with 'review' or 'synthesis' and prefaced with such typically academic words as critical, exemplary, mapping, scoping, state-of-the art, structured or umbrella.

The three pairs of authors identified are not to be particularly blamed for this state of affairs, however, though they might be accused of missing an opportunity to clarify and simplify matters. Arguably, their classifications simply reflect their reading of the relevant research literature. Thus, Arksey and O'Malley (2005) argue that the

> rapid growth in undertaking reviews of the literature has resulted in a plethora of terminology to describe approaches that, despite their different names, share certain essential characteristics, namely, collecting, evaluating and presenting the available

research evidence ... There do not appear to be any consistent definitions of these different review 'animals', with the result that researchers may use labels loosely. For instance, there is a risk that reviews defined by their authors as 'systematic' may not all adopt the same high standards in terms of protection against bias and the quality assessment for the selection of primary research. On this basis the correct label would be 'literature review' and not 'systematic review'.

(p. 20)

Grant and Booth (2009), working in a health sciences context, also stress the lack of consistent terminology and agreed methodology:

> [W]hilst labels may supply a pragmatic 'shorthand' for authors, there are frequent inconsistencies or overlaps between the descriptions of nominally different review types. Currently, there is no internationally agreed set of discrete, coherent and mutually exclusive review types.
>
> (p. 104)

The reference to a lack of 'internationally agreed' set of terms is a common refrain in the social sciences. While it is probably unrealistic to expect this in a rapidly growing and contested field, we might expect to move towards greater agreement as the field matures.

We may also, though, critique elements of the work of these authors. Grant and Booth only briefly describe how they arrived at their categorization, so much rests on the authors' perceived expertise:

> After initial scoping searches of the literature, the authors drew on their combined experience of 26 years of having worked with both the theory and practice of reviews in multifarious guises to examine the vocabulary used in the published literature, unpublished documents and other source material. The purpose was to determine the prevalent terminology; a process known as literary warrant. From this, common review types and their associated key attributes were identified and mapped against a Search, Appraisal, Synthesis and Analysis (SALSA) framework. Each review type was analysed, its characteristics were described and its perceived strengths and weaknesses were outlined. An example of each type of review was identified and selected, primarily for its usefulness in illustrating review characteristics.
>
> (p. 93)

Some of the examples given could, however, be accommodated under more than one of the categories identified.

Suri and Clarke's (2009) six-fold categorization may be criticized on the grounds that while the first two categories seem fairly clear – i.e. systematic reviews and meta-analyses – the other four categories appear to be rather more specialist and/or overlapping. How different are 'qualitative research syntheses' and 'qualitative syntheses of qualitative and quantitative research'? How common are 'exemplary syntheses', and is 'critical impetus in reviewing research' simply methodological discussion?

Suri and Clarke go on, however, to usefully propose 'three general guiding principles for a quality research synthesis: informed subjectivity and reflexivity, purposefully informed selective inclusivity, and audience-appropriate transparency' (p. 408). In short, they emphasize the practical or pragmatic issues involved in carrying out a research synthesis, recognizing that some selectivity may be necessary in what is reviewed and that the end result should never be viewed as an 'objective' analysis.

With no internationally accepted terminology, nor any obvious mechanism available for agreeing one in the foreseeable future, it remains the case that, as with many fields of educational and social research, varied terminologies are in use, particularly where systematic reviews are concerned. Thus, in addition to the terms already identified, you may come across

- focused mapping reviews and syntheses (Bradbury-Jones et al 2019a),
- integrative reviews (Kornhaber et al 2016, Torraco 2005, Whittemore and Knafl 2005),
- narrative literature reviews (Juntunen and Lehenkari 2019),
- scoping literature reviews (Arksey and O'Malley 2005, Armstrong et al 2011, Virtanen et al 2017),
- systematic literature reviews (Safipour, Wenneberg and Habsiabdic 2017),
- systematic quantitative literature reviews (Horta et al 2015),
- meta-ethnographies (Noblitt 1988),
- interpretative meta-ethnographies (Savin-Baden and Major 2007, Savin-Baden, McFarland and Savin-Baden 2008) and
- bibliometric analysis (Huang et al 2019).

It is as if any combination of a limited group of words may be spun together in a huge variety of ways, resulting in a multitude of similar sounding terms. However, while all of the authors referenced doubtless can, and usually do, spell out exactly how their form of research synthesis differs from some (if not all) of the others identified, the differences between many of these terms and practices are not that great. A simpler approach is possible.

The terminology used in this book

The chief distinction made in this book is between systematic reviews and meta-analyses as the main forms of research synthesis. However, a further distinction, partly historical in usage, needs to be made between systematic reviews and literature reviews. The former distinction is discussed in this section, the latter in the following one.

Systematic reviews and meta-analyses are parallel techniques or methodologies. They have the same underlying purpose and follow a similar, but by no means identical, process. The key difference between them is that, while systematic reviews focus on qualitative findings, meta-analyses focus on quantitative findings (Littell, Corcoran and

Pillai 2008). Their usefulness and applicability vary, therefore, with the nature of the data that is available and with the researcher's preferences and intentions.

Systematic reviews seek to identify and critically review everything – or, at least, everything that is available and accessible – that has been written and published on a particular topic. They then aim to synthesize all of the research to date on the topic selected. Because of their comprehensive coverage, they are extremely valuable to the interested reader, even though the detail given on individual sources may not be extensive.

Meta-analyses also seek to identify and assess everything that has been written and published on a particular topic but focus on those items published that report quantitative findings. These quantitative findings are then amalgamated, bearing in mind the different sample sizes, to provide an overall result (termed the effect size) for whatever is the focus of the analysis. The underlying idea is that, while twenty, thirty or fifty quantitative studies of a particular issue will each individually be of interest, a single, combined quantitative synthesis of all of their results will have much more power and generalizability.

Systematic reviews and meta-analyses may be conducted together (e.g. Frajerman et al 2019, Gegenfurtner and Ebner 2019, Reyes et al 2019, Richardson, Abraham and Bond 2012, Schudde and Brown 2019, Severiens and Ten Dam 1994, Winzer et al 2018, Xu et al 2019: all of which are discussed in this book). There are even systematic reviews of meta-analyses (e.g. Schneider and Preckel 2017), which this book is also an example of (as well as, of course, systematically reviewing systematic reviews). Systematic reviews may also be employed in combination with other methodologies, such as citation network analysis (Colicchia, Creazza and Strozzi 2017) and narrative synthesis (Pino and Mortari 2014).

In this book I, therefore, will make the simple, twofold distinction between systematic reviews and meta-analyses in terms of their emphasis as follows:

A *systematic review* provides a mainly qualitative overview of a research field.
A *meta-analysis* aims to offer a quantitative summary of the findings on a particular topic.

As well as being simple, this distinction has the advantage of highlighting the two terms in most widespread usage. All of the other terms that have been identified will be treated as synonyms, variants or subsets of these two basic types of research synthesis.

Systematic reviews and literature reviews

There is a close relationship between the literature review and the systematic review, such that the former shade into the latter and may also be worthy of close consideration (e.g. Kehm and Teichler 2007). Indeed, sometimes the terms are used interchangeably, or are combined, as in systematic literature review.

This is largely because the term 'systematic review', and the processes associated with it, has only come into widespread use (at least in the social sciences generally) relatively recently. Thus, a number of older literature reviews have the characteristics of systematic reviews, and this is even true of some that have been published only recently.

It is probably simplest to regard systematic reviews as being part of the literature review 'family', but as rather more ambitious than most literature reviews. On the 'literature review spectrum', systematic reviews are at one end, with the kind of relatively brief literature reviews that are found in most academic articles at the other end.

> Traditional literature reviews typically present research findings relating to a topic of interest. They summarise what is known on a topic. They tend to provide details on the studies that they consider without explaining the criteria used to identify and include those studies or why certain studies are described and discussed while others are not. Potentially relevant studies may not have been included because the review author was unaware of them or, being aware of them, decided for reasons unspecified not to include them. If the process of identifying and including studies is not explicit, it is not possible to assess the appropriateness of such decisions or whether they were applied in a consistent and rigorous manner.
>
> (Gough, Oliver and Thomas 2017, p. 5)

There are, in other words, differences of scope, thoroughness and transparency between literature reviews and systematic reviews.

That said, however, there is still an overlap between literature reviews and systematic reviews. Some authors carry out literature reviews in much the same way as others approach systematic reviews (see the next section). It seems sensible, therefore, to include such comprehensive or substantive literature reviews in with systematic reviews, and that is the practice that has been adopted in this book.

Systematic reviews in practice

The methodology of systematic reviews was first developed and popularized in health care research, where their promise has been highly extolled as one of the main techniques underlying evidence-based practice:

> Systematic reviews have several advantages over other types of research that have led to them being regarded as particularly important tools for decision-makers. Systematic reviews take precedence over other types of research in many hierarchies of evidence, as it inherently makes sense for decisions to be based on the totality of evidence rather than a single study. Moreover, they can generally be conducted more quickly than new primary research and, as a result, may be attractive to policy-makers required to make a rapid response to a new policy issue.
>
> (Bunn et al 2015, p. 1)

Bunn et al go on to note, however, that their usage by policymakers is not as high as might be expected, possibly partly because of a lack of familiarity with the methodology.

Systematic reviews have only latterly been adopted in the social sciences more generally (Bearman et al 2012) and then rather too slowly for some. They have not, however, always been welcomed, as, for example, in the case of educational research, where their usage has become bundled into the ongoing, and highly critical, debate on evidence-based practice (see e.g. Light and Pillemer 1982, Maclure 2005, Thomas and Pring 2004, Wrigley 2018).

Unsurprisingly – given what has already been revealed about the diversity of terms used for research syntheses – systematic reviews have been defined in rather divergent ways. Here are two somewhat contrasting definitions:

> A systematic review differs from a traditional narrative review in that its methods are explicit and open to scrutiny. It seeks to identify *all* the available evidence with respect to a given theme. Systematic reviews have the advantage of including all the studies in a field (sometimes positive and negative studies), so the reader can judge using the *totality* of evidence.
>
> (Torgerson 2003, p. 6, emphases in original)

> We ... define a systematic review as a review with a clear stated purpose, a question, a defined search approach, stating inclusion and exclusion criteria, producing a qualitative appraisal of articles.
>
> (Jesson, Matheson and Lacey 2011, p. 12)

Thus, while Torgerson emphasizes 'all' and 'totality', Jesson, Matheson and Lacey simply stress the systematic nature of the review. The difference between this approach and that of a literature review (or a traditional narrative review, as Torgerson calls it), particularly if the literature review is carried out in a systematic fashion while not seeking to encompass the totality of the literature on the particular topic, is unclear. Yet, as we have already argued, systematic reviews and literature reviews are on the same spectrum and must, therefore, elide into each other at some point.

Torgerson's definition seems to me, however, to be clearer and hence preferable. I would, though, differ from her in arguing that, even in a more limited literature review, the methods used to select the literature and compile the review should be 'explicit and open to scrutiny'.

Torgerson goes further in identifying nine aims for a systematic review:

(i) to address a specific (well-focused, relevant) question;
(ii) to search for, locate and collate the results of the research in a systematic way;
(iii) to reduce bias at all stages of the review (publication, selection and other forms of bias);
(iv) to appraise the quality of the research in the light of the research question;
(v) to synthesize the results of the review in an explicit way;
(vi) to make the knowledge base more accessible;
(vii) to identify gaps; to place new proposals in the context of existing knowledge;
(viii) to propose a future research agenda; to make recommendations;
(ix) to present all stages of the review in the final report to enable critical appraisal and replication.

(2003, pp. 7–8)

This adds a number of important features to what you might expect from a basic literature review, while also including some things that a competent literature review would be expected to deliver. Thus, the aims of reducing bias, in part by examining all relevant research, and then by carefully appraising quality, are of key importance. The end result of producing an accessible and transparent synthesis of the research field, clearly presented in a report, is also paramount.

However, the proposed use of the systematic review to identify knowledge gaps and propose a future research agenda is something that a literature review might also attempt. This might be particularly so in the context of an academic thesis or dissertation, where the literature review frequently leads on to the identification of the research questions.

Conversely, the identification of knowledge gaps and a future research agenda might not be part of the aims of a systematic review, which could serve simply to synthesize the knowledge in a particular field or topic. It would then be left to others to identify knowledge gaps and/or generate future research agendas.

Published systematic reviews tend to follow a similar format: databases and search engines are specified, the date limiters are given, language restrictions are set out and the keywords used in the search are listed. The stages involved in getting from the initial list of publications identified down to a more focused set for analysis are rehearsed and often set out in diagrammatic form. In some fields, notably medicine and health care, there are also published guidelines for carrying out systematic reviews (and meta-analyses): e.g. the Preferred Reporting Items for Systematic Reviews and Meta-Analyses (PRISMA: see Moher et al 2009). There are also journals that specialize in publishing systematic reviews (see Chapter 3).

The underlying idea is that anyone reading a published systematic review, so long as they have access to the databases and search engines specified, should be able to replicate, extend and/or update the reviews produced. In this way, systematic reviews serve as a record of the state of research on a particular topic at a given time, a record which may be returned to again and again. As Chapters 4 to 16 make clear, this is what has happened over the years with popular topics for research.

Meta-analyses in practice

Glass (1976; see also Tipton, Pustejovsky and Ahmadi 2019) usefully outlines the origins of meta-analysis, while also helpfully distinguishing it from what he terms primary analysis and secondary analysis:

> *Primary analysis* is the original analysis of data in a research study ... *Secondary analysis* is the re-analysis of data for the purpose of answering the original research question with better statistical techniques, or answering new questions with old data ... Meta-analysis refers to the analysis of analyses. I use it to refer to the statistical analysis of a large collection of analysis results from individual studies for the purpose of integrating the findings.
>
> (p. 3)

The primary/secondary/meta-distinction might also, of course, be applied to qualitative research. It is also analogous to the distinction made between primary, secondary and tertiary data and analysis in documentary research (Tight 2019c).

Jesson, Matheson and Lacey (2011) offer a very similar definition to that of Glass: 'Meta-analysis is a statistical technique which has been developed to combine quantitative results obtained from independent studies that have been published' (p. 129). Cooper (2010), while noting that terms like 'systematic review', 'research synthesis' and 'meta-analysis' are often used interchangeably, concurs, restricting meta-analysis to 'the quantitative procedures used to statistically combine the results of studies' (p. 6).

The stages involved in a meta-analysis are similar to those involved in a systematic review, as it is equally important to identify all of the studies on the topic concerned and then to assess their quality before carrying out the actual analysis. The key difference is that a meta-analysis aims at a quantitative synthesis of the results of all of the studies identified, rather than a qualitative summary or categorization:

> Meta-analysis permits summary of studies' results and is designed for scenarios in which the primary studies' raw data are not available. The meta-analytic process involves summarizing the results of each study using an effect size (ES), calculating an overall average across studies of the resulting ESs, and exploring study- and sample-related sources of possible heterogeneity in the ESs. The overall average ES provides a single best estimate of the overall effect of interest to the meta-analyst.
>
> (Beretvas 2010, p. 255)

The ability to carry out a meta-analysis without access to the raw data of the studies being analysed, using just the summary results, is particularly convenient, saving a great deal of time.

There are a number of ways, of varying degrees of complexity, in which meta-analyses may be carried out. Cooper (2010), for example, recognizes seven main stages: formulating the problem, searching the literature, gathering information from studies, evaluating the quality of studies, analysing and integrating the outcomes of studies, interpreting the evidence, and presenting the results. The similarity between these stages, at least in their abstract form, and those encountered in systematic reviews seems obvious (cf. the earlier quotation from Torgerson (2003)).

Software is, of course, available to do the number crunching. The basic method involves identifying the effect sizes (a measure of the difference between the experimental and control groups) reported by each study and then combining these in an average effect size, with the studies weighted in accordance with their sample sizes (Borenstein et al 2009). A simpler, but much criticized, method, referred to as vote counting, involves counting the numbers of positive, negative and null results from the studies identified. Whatever method is used, however, it is important to consider the variability of the results as well as their average or overall tendency.

Like systematic reviews, meta-analyses tend to be reported in a fairly standardized or formulaic way. They don't have to be that large in scope; obviously it depends upon the number of quantitative studies of the topic of interest that have been carried out, but it is not unusual (as we shall see in this book) to find meta-analyses based on fewer than fifty studies. Meta-analyses should, therefore, be within the scope of most competent researchers, providing you have access to the necessary software and an understanding of what you are doing.

Some researchers have, however, gone much further. For example, Hattie (2009) synthesized over 800 meta-analyses 'which encompassed 52,637 studies, and provided 146,142 effect sizes about the influence of some program, policy, or innovation on academic achievement in school' (p. 15). This was truly a major piece of research, which took up a substantial part of one man's academic career. This book is, of course, attempting to do something similar – albeit on a somewhat smaller scale, but incorporating systematic reviews as well as meta-analyses – for the narrower field of higher education research.

In a more limited, but still extensive, study, Schneider and Preckel (2017) carried out a systematic review of thirty-eight meta-analyses which had investigated the impact on student achievement of various practices in higher education. Their study, and the meta-analyses they considered, is reviewed further in this book (see Chapter 10). This kind of approach has also been adopted in other disciplines or fields. For example, moving away from meta-analyses, Kitchenham et al (2009) presented a systematic literature review of twenty systematic reviews of software engineering.

Strengths and weaknesses

Of course, gathering together and synthesizing the existing studies on a particular topic does not guarantee excellent and informative results. For a start, there may simply be insufficient studies that have been carried out and published on the topic in question. But useful syntheses can be done on relatively small numbers of studies, and quite a few of those referred to in this book involved less than ten.

There are always, of course, quality issues involved in assessing the studies concerned (Hallinger 2013), both in terms of the quality of the studies being analysed and the quality of the synthesis performed. Among these issues is that of reporting bias (Dawson and Dawson 2016): the tendency to overlook, ignore or leave out studies that do not reflect the view of the person carrying out the analysis. This is, of course, an issue for all research and is difficult to detect unless more than one synthesis of the research on the topic involved has been carried out, or the reader themselves is very knowledgeable about the topic.

A related issue, but less often referred to, is what might be termed the positivity bias. In higher education research, and educational research, it is the case that studies that get published very commonly report successful developments, experiments or innovations. There are fairly obvious reasons for this: individual researchers, their colleagues and their host institutions are unlikely to want to publicize their failure (even though this might be equally as interesting and informative as success).

Educational innovations also have a tendency to be successful, at least in the short term (which is all that the great majority of published studies consider), because the students and/or academics involved can see that someone is trying to improve their experience, which they appreciate, even if it doesn't work. This effect is known by various names in the research literature: Hawthorne, Dr Fox, etc. Hattie explains it in the following way:

> Innovation ... was a theme underlying most of these positive effects. That is, a constant and deliberate attempt to improve the quality of learning on behalf of the system, the principal, and the teacher, typically related to improved achievement. The implementation of innovations probably captures the enthusiasm of the teacher implementing the innovation and the excitement of the students attempting something innovative. Often this has been explained as an experimental artifact in terms of a Hawthorne effect. However, another reason is that when teachers introduce innovation there can be a heightened attention to what is making a difference and what is not, and it is this attention to what is not working that can make the difference – feedback to the teacher about the effect of their actions!
>
> (2009, p. 12)

This also raises the issue of how long innovation can be sustained: by an individual teacher, course team, department or institution. We may live in a time when 'continuous quality improvement' is a mantra, but in practice this is unrealistic in an activity like higher education. So how long does the success of a particular innovation last, and what happens between innovations?

The positivity presented by the published research literature has to be viewed with a critical eye, therefore. Articles may report developments or innovations which only worked after many attempts and then in carefully controlled and monitored circumstances. They may not work (so well) in other institutions or circumstances or over the longer term.

Another key issue with research syntheses is the provision of sufficient methodological detail (again, this is an issue for all research). Systematic reviews and meta-analyses need to be carried out carefully, thoroughly and transparently (Abrami, Cohen and d'Apollonia 1988, Bowman 2012, Denson and Seltzer 2011, Fitz-Gibbon 1985, Rosenthal and DiMatteo 2001, Stanley 2001).

The search criteria used, the databases and/or other sources (e.g. books, journals, reports, theses) searched should be specified, as should the time period and languages of publication covered. This should then enable other researchers to repeat and check, and, more importantly, update and/or extend, the analysis at a later date.

For systematic reviews, there is a particular need to carry out a deep rather than a superficial reading (Kilburn, Nind and Wiles 2014). The analyst needs to ask themselves what may be missing as well as what is there. Similarly, for meta-analyses, it is critically important that the quality of the quantitative analysis carried out in the individual studies identified is assessed and that the meta-analysis itself is completed accurately.

It should be stressed, therefore, that the referencing of a systematic review or meta-analysis in this book should not be taken as an absolute guarantee of its quality. As all of those referenced have either been published in refereed academic journals, or by reputable academic organizations, this can, however, be taken as some indication of their having met at least basic quality thresholds. But it is possible that I may have missed or misinterpreted something in my reading and analysis of particular studies.

Done well, the key strength of systematic reviews and meta-analyses is the way in which they provide a succinct summary or synthesis of the research findings on a particular topic. Implicit in that statement, however, is an indication of their key weakness; they are only a summary or synthesis. It is inherent in the practice of research synthesis that it reduces the variety of experience. Variety should also be both celebrated and researched. Understanding what we know, or what works, should also include an understanding of the circumstances in which it works or works best.

To understand any topic more comprehensively, therefore, one will always have to go back to the individual studies that have been analysed and/or carry out some more research of one's own. Fortunately, as well as providing a summary of the existing studies on a topic, research syntheses also offer a guide to these studies and where they can be found.

Conclusion

Research syntheses – systematic reviews, substantive literature reviews and meta-analyses – are of growing importance within higher education research. In many cases their results are complementary, allowing a bringing together of the quantitative and qualitative conclusions from the available research.

A key problem – for policymakers and researchers alike – is that most people are not sufficiently proficient with, or interested in, both qualitative and quantitative research. This is a general problem which needs addressing, as there is no acceptable reason why most educated people should not be able to handle and recognize the value of both.

Research syntheses like systematic reviews and meta-analyses are equally valuable for highlighting what we know and what we don't know. Our understanding of the former, however, needs to be qualified by a recognition of the circumstances and conditions of what we know. Our appreciation of the latter should assist us in determining where research efforts might be targeted in the future.

Chapter 3
Research syntheses in higher education

Introduction

Having introduced the general strategy behind research syntheses, with a particular focus on systematic reviews and meta-analyses, in the previous chapter (Chapter 2), this chapter looks at how these techniques have been applied to higher education research. First, the data sources used in syntheses of higher education research – principally databases and journals – are considered. The different ways in which syntheses are focused – generically on higher education research as a whole, on particular countries and/or disciplines or, most commonly, on a specific topic – are then discussed.

The remainder of the chapter examines the research syntheses – systematic reviews, literature reviews, meta-analyses and combinations of these – of higher education research that have been identified for, and which are interrogated in, this book. In all, a total of 515 such research syntheses have been identified, which represents a substantial source of information on what we know, and what we don't know, from higher education research.

Among the issues considered are

- the trends in publication over time;
- the balance between systematic reviews, literature reviews and meta-analyses;
- the journals involved in publishing these syntheses;
- where the researchers carrying out these syntheses are located and
- the popularity of different themes and topics.

Some conclusions are then drawn.

Data sources

The two main data sources used for conducting syntheses of higher education research – and other subject areas, whether the syntheses are systematic reviews, literature reviews or meta-analyses – are academic journals (or publications more generally) and databases. Nowadays, of course, with journals widely available online, these two sources overlap.

The traditional approach to research synthesis would have involved the interrogation of printed copies of selected academic journals and/or books in a university library or a number of university libraries. The comprehensiveness of any research synthesis undertaken would have been constrained by what was available within one's own university library, other libraries that one could get access to, and by what was available through the inter-library loan system.

Databases were available, but only in printed form, and typically with a national focus, such as the Educational Resources Information Center (ERIC) in the United States or the British Education Index in the UK. Under such circumstances, research syntheses could rarely aim to be fully comprehensive, often remained restricted to national 'silos', and might completely miss important authors, studies and/or publications.

With the advent of the internet, of course, almost all research syntheses are now carried out using online resources. The growth and multiplication of online databases have greatly facilitated the conduct of systematic reviews, literature reviews and meta-analyses. While the researcher is still somewhat constrained by what is available in and through their library – through hard copies and online versions of journals and books – it is much easier to identify what has been published on any particular topic and then to chase particular items down if they cannot be readily obtained.

Journals

Analyses of journal output may focus on a single journal or encompass a limited or larger number of journals. Single journal analyses are often done by the editors themselves, perhaps at a significant milestone in the journal's life, to review or showcase the journal's contribution. For example, in the context of higher education, Dobson (2009) examined the *Journal of Higher Education Policy and Management*, Huisman (2008) discussed *Higher Education Policy*, Harvey and Williams (2010a, 2010b) analysed *Quality in Higher Education*, Lloyd and Bahr (2016) reviewed the *Journal of Learning Design*, Ross (1992) and Calma and Davies (2017) considered *Higher Education*, and Tight (2011b) and Calma and Davies (2015) assessed *Studies in Higher Education*. In other cases, the analysis may be carried out by researchers who are not the editor of the journal concerned; for example, Volkwein, Carbone and Volkwein (1988) looked at *Research in Higher Education*.

Other authors have conducted comparative analyses of the outputs of a limited number of higher education journals, particularly, but not exclusively, in the American context (e.g. Budd 1990, Budd and Magnusson 2010, Donaldson and Townsend 2007,

Haggis 2009, Hart and Metcalfe 2010), and often focusing on a particular topic or theme. For example, Haggis looked at student learning research, while Hart and Metcalfe focused on feminist research. In the American context, it is not uncommon to focus on the three US-based journals that are regarded as the most influential: the *Journal of Higher Education, Research in Higher Education* and the *Review of Higher Education*.

One American author, Silverman (1982), took a slightly unusual approach, certainly for the time, in examining the articles published in 1975 and 1980 in three higher education journals 'of special interest' – the *Journal of Higher Education, Higher Education* and *Research in Higher Education* – including one international journal, *Higher Education*, as well as two key American ones. Three years later, he (Silverman 1985) published a citation study of 1,103 articles published in eight 'core' journals – the three previously identified, plus *College and University, Educational Record, Journal of College Student Personnel, Liberal Education* and *Review of Higher Education* (all US-based) – over the 1975–81 period.

More recent analyses of the output of multiple journals include Kosmutzky and Krucken's (2014) examination of 4,095 articles published in eight higher education journals over the period 1992–2012, focusing on international comparative research. Then there are my own analyses of the output of seventeen higher education journals in 2000 (406 articles) and of fifteen journals for 2000 and 2010 (388 and 567 articles, respectively: Tight 2003, 2012a).

Databases

Nowadays, however, the tendency is to make use of the increasing numbers of online databases. These databases vary in their coverage of academic journals but allow the researcher to search all of the journals (as well as books, book chapters, reports and other publications) they cover or only selected ones. Thus, Jung and Horta (2013) used the Scopus database to identify 514 English language articles on higher education published in thirty-eight 'core identifiable journals' (p. 404) between 1980 and 2012 that had at least one author based in Asia. Later, Kim, Horta and Jung (2017) examined 349 articles on higher education published in the period 1980–2013 that had authors based in Hong Kong, Japan, China or Malaysia.

Kuzhabekhova, Hendel and Chapman (2015) used the Web of Science database to identify and analyse 2,302 publications on higher education over the period 2002–11 that were not focused on the United States. Moving away from English language publications, Chen and Hu (2012) used Chinese databases to explore the growth of the field of higher education research in China over the previous thirty years. Taking a broader perspective, Huang et al (2019) analysed all of the articles published in twenty-four education journals (including two specifically higher education journals, *Higher Education* and *Studies in Higher Education*) over the period between 2000 and 2017 to chart the evolution of topics in educational research.

The research underlying this book has made particular use of three databases or search engines – Google Scholar, Scopus and the Web of Science – to identify research syntheses of higher education for further examination.

Of course, sources other than journals and publication databases may be used to carry out systematic reviews and meta-analyses of higher education research. In an early example, Kellams (1975) analysed a sample of 279 (from 1,130) abstracts held in an inventory of current higher education research in the United States and Canada. More recently, Forsberg and Geschwind (2016) analysed a database of 399 doctoral theses on higher education completed between 2000 and 2013 to study the state of Swedish higher education research.

Study focus

Systematic reviews, literature reviews and meta-analyses vary in their ambition and focus. Some, which I will term generic, seek to analyse the entirety of, in this case, higher education research (though some limits are usually set, such as language and date), while others focus on a particular country, discipline or topic. Generic studies, and those focused on a country or discipline, tend to be systematic reviews, while studies of particular topics are more likely to be meta-analyses.

We will discuss and exemplify each type in turn.

Generic studies

My own work (2003, 2012a) offers an example of a generic approach to reviewing higher education research, though limited in restricting itself to the output of selected English language journals in selected years. The former book analysed the output of seventeen higher education journals published outside of North America for the year 2000. The latter publication was more comprehensive, examining the output of fifteen leading higher education journals based in the United States, Europe and Australasia for the years 2000 and 2010. This enabled elements of both comparative and longitudinal analysis to be incorporated.

The latter book sought to provide an 'overview of contemporary higher education research' (2012a, p. 2) and a detailed examination of research issues and approaches in terms of eight empirically identified themes: teaching and learning, course design, the student experience, quality, system policy, institutional management, academic work, knowledge and research. These themes are employed again in the analysis presented in this book.

Country studies

Most of the published studies that have focused on higher education in one country have looked at the United States, or the United States plus Canada (i.e. North America). An early example is Kellams's work (1973, 1975). More recently, however, similar reviews have been carried out of the higher education research undertaken in other (large) countries, e.g. China (Chen and Hu 2012).

Other authors have carried out systematic reviews of higher education research in particular regions or groups of countries. The research by Horta and colleagues (Horta and Jung 2014, Horta, Jung and Yonezawa 2015, Jung and Horta 2013, Kim, Horta and Jung 2017) on the development of Asian higher education research is a notable recent example.

Discipline studies

Systematic reviews and meta-analyses of higher education in particular disciplines appear to be relatively rare (though they may also be more difficult to identify). Clearly, discipline-based studies of higher education are not themselves rare, though research into higher education varies in popularity between disciplines. It appears, rather, that discipline-based higher education researchers have mostly not yet got around to systematically reviewing or meta-analysing the results of this research.

Blair's (2015) study is one example of a disciplinary focus, examining research on teaching and learning in higher education in the discipline of political science and international relations. He examined the output of six journals published in the UK and the United States in 2012 (a total of seventy-three articles). In a second, rather different, example, Schmidt and Gunther (2016) provide a systematic review of public sector accounting research relating to the higher education sector.

Topic studies

Most systematic reviews and meta-analyses of higher education research are, however, more focused or less ambitious in their coverage, examining the output of research on a particular topic or issue (such as student retention, peer assessment or the research/teaching nexus). These are the prime focus of this book and will now be discussed in more depth.

Identified studies

In total, 515 syntheses of higher education research have been identified (see Table 1). These are made up of 280 systematic reviews, 60 substantive literature reviews (having much of the character of systematic reviews but not identified as such), 165 meta-analyses and 10 studies which used both systematic review and meta-analysis. Overall, therefore, there were about twice as many qualitative reviews (i.e. systematic reviews and literature reviews) as there were quantitative analyses (meta-analyses). These research syntheses have been categorized in Table 1 in terms of eight key issues or themes identified from my previous research (Tight 2003, 2012a).

These syntheses were identified using keyword searches on Scopus, Google Scholar and World of Science (final searches carried out on 1 January 2020). The keywords

Table 1 Numbers of Syntheses by Theme

Theme	Meta-Analyses	Systematic Reviews	Literature Reviews	Both MA and SR	Total
Teaching and learning	6	16	1	1	24 (4.7%)
Course design	114	133	36	6	289 (56.1%)
Student experience	11	51	2	3	67 (13.0%)
Quality	22	19	7	0	48 (9.3%)
System policy	2	9	9	0	20 (3.9%)
Institutional management	2	22	2	0	26 (5.0%)
Academic work	0	23	3	0	26 (5.0%)
Knowledge and research	8	7	0	0	15 (2.9%)
Total	165 (32.0%)	280 (54.4%)	60 (11.7%)	10 (1.9%)	515

used were 'systematic review' or 'meta-analysis' and 'higher education', 'university' or 'college', together with terms descriptive of the eight key issues or themes. The studies identified were then accessed and checked and, if they were systematic reviews, substantive literature reviews or meta-analyses of higher education research, allocated to one of the eight key themes or issues.

Other systematic reviews, substantive literature reviews and meta-analyses were added to the collection by checking references in the identified publications (this was particularly useful as the historical coverage of online databases is rather variable), following up leads and keeping a researcherly eye open at all times. Searches were carried out regularly to ensure that the latest published syntheses – often not yet allocated to a journal issue but published first online – were included before the delivery of this book to the publishers in February 2020.

It is important to note that, in a few cases, the research syntheses identified included studies of other levels or sectors of education alongside higher education. This is specifically noted in the chapters that follow when these studies are discussed. The position taken, both in these studies and in this book, is that – particularly as most such syntheses include studies of students in the final year(s) of secondary school (e.g. K-12) as well as those in higher education – the differences between the students being studied are not fundamental, so do not invalidate the results reached from the perspective of higher education research.

It is highly unlikely, of course, that every published systematic review, substantive literature review and meta-analysis focused on higher education research has been successfully identified. The decision was taken not to pursue research syntheses in the form of unpublished conference papers or research degree theses, on the grounds that the publication process ensured some quality checks and that many of these would in any case subsequently appear in published form. Some of the published research syntheses identified were, however, also rejected on grounds of insufficient quality or scope.

It is also the case, of course, that new systematic reviews and meta-analyses are being carried out all of the time, so we may expect the list to grow – and at an accelerating pace – year by year. Thus, there will be a need, assuming the demand is there, for further editions of this book.

However, the syntheses identified do represent a substantial systematic review of systematic reviews, substantive literature reviews and meta-analyses of the field at the present time.

Themes and kinds of syntheses

The data collected for Table 1 illustrate a number of interesting points. Perhaps the most important point is that systematic reviews, literature reviews and meta-analyses have been carried out on each of the eight key issues or themes in higher education research identified, with two exceptions. For academic work, no meta-analyses were identified (though there were twenty-three systematic reviews and three substantive literature reviews), while for knowledge and research, no literature reviews were found (though there were eight meta-analyses and seven systematic reviews).

One key theme, course design, accounted for just over half, 289 or 56.1 per cent, of all the studies identified. This theme – covering how teaching and learning in higher education are planned, delivered and evaluated – is clearly at the heart of higher education research and thus of syntheses of this research. When combined with the linked topics of teaching and learning (24 syntheses or 4.7 per cent) and the student experience (67 syntheses or 13.0 per cent), the first three topics accounted for nearly three-quarters, 73.8 per cent, of all the research syntheses identified. These three issues or themes might be collectively termed pedagogical research and are clearly both well researched and well synthesized.

But other topics or issues have also been the subject of significant numbers of systematic reviews or meta-analyses, even, somewhat surprisingly, knowledge and research (15 studies identified, 2.9 per cent of the total). Conversely, however, system policy is a theme that has been extensively researched and written about (Tight 2003, 2012a), but which has so far attracted a comparative paucity of research syntheses (just 20 studies, 3.9 per cent of the total).

It is interesting in this context to briefly compare the distribution of the research syntheses identified between the eight themes with the distribution found for the articles published in fifteen international higher education journals in 2010 and 2000 (Table 2; see Tight 2012a). We should be careful not to make too much of this comparison, because the journal samples are for specific dates and journals, while the research syntheses are for all dates and all journals, and include other forms of publication than journal articles.

Nevertheless, the sizes of the three samples are similar and the comparison of their spread is interesting. Thus, there appear to be relatively more published articles on the student experience, system policy, institutional management and academic work, but relatively more published research syntheses on course design and quality. Even when

Table 2 Percentages of Syntheses and Articles Compared

Theme	Syntheses	Articles 2010	Articles 2000
Teaching and learning	4.7	3.7	6.4
Course design	56.1	31.0	23.5
Student experience	13.0	24.0	21.4
Quality	9.3	7.2	6.4
System policy	3.9	9.5	15.2
Institutional management	5.0	9.3	12.6
Academic work	5.0	12.5	12.4
Knowledge and research	2.9	2.6	2.1
Sample size (n)	515	567	388

we combine the first three themes (teaching and learning, course design and the student experience) together as pedagogical research, the proportions of articles are significantly smaller, 51.3 per cent in 2000 and 58.7 per cent in 2010, than the proportion of research syntheses, 73.8 per cent.

There is a suggestion here, therefore, that the popularity of research syntheses varies to some extent between themes or perhaps among the researchers working on those themes. Or it could be that – with the two article samples suggesting an upward trend – carrying out research syntheses on course design topics has become more popular very recently.

Trends in publication

Table 3 illustrates trends in publication of the different types of syntheses of higher education research, plotting them decade by decade.

Clearly, most of the research syntheses identified are relatively recent; 350 of the 515 (69.1 per cent) date from 2010 or later. Indeed, there has been a recent explosion in the numbers being published, with only three of those identified dating from the 1960s, eight from the 1970s, thirty-six from the 1980s, thirty-six from the 1990s and seventy-six from the 2000s. Yet 44 were published in 2016 alone, 44 in 2017, 54 in 2018 and 108 in 2019, the last full year considered.

This is what you might expect, of course, as published research studies (and the number and size of outlets for their publication) have grown in numbers year on year, meaning that there has been a greater need and impetus to synthesize them. At the same time, the popularity of research synthesis as a strategy has evidently increased.

The balance between kinds of research syntheses has changed over time. Almost all of the earlier syntheses were meta-analyses, with the first relevant meta-analysis identified dating to 1962 and the first systematic review to 1976 (and the first substantive literature review to 1965). It was only in the mid-2010s that published systematic reviews consistently began to outnumber meta-analyses, but since then the former have

Table 3 Types of Syntheses by Date

Decade	Meta-Analyses	Systematic Reviews	Literature Reviews	Both MA and SR	Total
2020–		6			6 (1.2%)
2010s	69	234	37	9	350 (68.0%)
2000s	39	26	11		76 (14.8%)
1990s	19	7	9	1	36 (7.0%)
1980s	30	4	2		36 (7.0%)
1970s	7	1			8 (1.6%)
1960s	1		1		3 (0.6%)
Total	165	280	60	10	515

mushroomed. Of the 108 syntheses of higher education research published in 2019, 85 (or 79 per cent) were systematic reviews, 15 were meta-analyses, 3 were substantive literature reviews and 5 were a combination of meta-analysis and systematic review.

Journals of publication

It is clear that some journals are more likely to publish systematic reviews, substantive literature reviews and meta-analyses than others. Thus, the *Review of Educational Research* (a journal which explicitly welcomes these kinds of articles) has published forty-six (8.9 per cent) of the articles identified, while *Research in Higher Education* published sixteen, *Educational Research Review* sixteen, *Studies in Higher Education* fourteen, *Computers and Education* fourteen and *Higher Education* twelve. These 6 journals between them accounted for 118 (22.9 per cent) of the total identified.

Others of the articles included have, however, appeared in an extremely wide range of both educational and non-educational (e.g. economics, management, nursing, psychology) journals – over 250 journals in total. While the great majority of the syntheses identified were in the form of published journal articles, a minority were in the form of reports, books, book chapters and published conference proceedings.

Countries of authors

Table 4 shows the main countries or parts of the world in which the first authors of the syntheses identified were located. This analysis has only been done for first authors to keep it simple; where syntheses had multiple authors, they tended to be based in the same country (indeed, usually in the same institution), though they were some examples of truly international collaborations.

Unsurprisingly, given the focus on English language publications, the articles are mainly authored by researchers based in English-speaking countries. The United States

Table 4 Types of Syntheses by Source

Source	Meta-Analyses	Systematic Reviews	Literature Reviews	Both MA and SR	Total
USA	98	67	13	2	180 (35.0%)
UK	4	59	16	1	80 (15.5%)
Australia	7	33	7		47 (9.1%)
Canada	13	6	4	1	24 (4.7%)
Rest of Europe	22	80	9	5	116 (22.5%)
Rest of World	21	35	11	1	68 (13.2%)
Total	165	280	60	10	515

provided the first authors for 180 (35.0 per cent) of the syntheses identified, with the UK contributing 80 (15.5 per cent), Australia 47 (9.1 per cent) and Canada 24 (4.7 per cent). Indeed, if the other predominantly English-speaking countries of Ireland and New Zealand are added in, these six countries together provided the first authors for over two-thirds, 344 (66.8 per cent), of the articles identified.

This does mean, however, that nearly one-third of the articles identified were first authored by researchers from non-English-speaking countries, illustrating the importance of English as the current lingua franca of the academic world, in higher education research as elsewhere. Thus, Belgium, China, Germany, the Netherlands, Portugal, Spain and Sweden each provided the first authors for at least seven of the articles included.

First authorship was widely spread around the world, though dominated by the developed countries. Nineteen European countries accounted for 196 (38.1 per cent) of the articles, with 2 North American countries accounting for 204 (39.6 per cent), 2 Australasian countries for 53 (10.3 per cent), 20 Asian countries for 48 (9.3 per cent), four South American countries for 9 (1.7 per cent), 2 African countries for 3 (0.6 per cent) and the location of the authors of 4 articles unknown.

What is particularly interesting about Table 4, however, is how different parts of the world appear to favour different kinds of research syntheses. Thus, in the United States, the majority of the 180 research syntheses identified (98 or 54.4 per cent) were quantitative in nature, taking the form of meta-analyses. A similar pattern was observed for Canada, with thirteen out of twenty-four (or 54.2 per cent) of the syntheses identified in the form of meta-analyses.

In the rest of the world, however, the patterns are somewhat different, indeed reversed. To take the most extreme example, in the UK, seventy-five of the eighty syntheses identified (93.8 per cent) were qualitative in nature: i.e. systematic reviews or substantive literature reviews. In Australasia the qualitative proportion was 86.8 per cent, in the rest of Europe 76.7 per cent and in the rest of the world 67.6 per cent.

These patterns reflect the underlying methodological preferences of individual higher education researchers (and not just higher education researchers) in those countries and parts of the world. There is, then, something of a quantitative/qualitative divide between North America and the rest of the world (Shahjahan and Kezar 2013, Tight 2014b).

This has something to do with the earlier massification of higher education in North America and the earlier availability of large-scale quantitative datasets there. It is also related to the different training that higher education researchers receive in different systems (and thus reflects some underlying systematic preferences, at least at the present time). Looking ahead, however, with the increasingly widespread availability of both quantitative and qualitative data on higher education across the globe, it would be advantageous to see a more balanced methodological pattern developing.

Themes and sub-themes

As course design is such a dominant theme, it has been broken down into sub-themes in Table 5. This shows that one of the sub-themes included within the course design theme, distance, online and e-learning has more syntheses identified (69, 13.4 per cent of the total) than any of the other seven main themes. Another sub-theme – outcomes – also has more syntheses identified, 68 or 13.2 per cent of the total, as the next largest theme, the student experience (with 67 or 13.0 per cent).

Table 5 also indicates that, for the majority of the sub-themes identified (the exception being curriculum, where qualitative syntheses dominate), there are roughly equal numbers of meta-analyses and systematic reviews. For all of the six sub-themes identified – considered in more detail in Chapters 5 to 10 – there are healthy numbers of research syntheses to examine.

Specific topics

Within the eight broad themes, and the six sub-themes of course design, certain topics have attracted particular attention – most probably reflecting the volume of research studies – and been the subject of two or more systematic reviews and/or meta-analyses.

Table 5 Numbers of Syntheses by Sub-Theme for Course Design

Sub-Theme	Meta-Analyses	Systematic Reviews	Literature Reviews	Both MA and SR	Total
Types of instruction	23	15	4	1	43 (14.9%)
Types of learning	18	14	3	0	35 (12.1%)
Online learning	23	31	14	1	69 (23.9%)
Curriculum	5	27	4	1	37 (12.8%)
Assessment	14	18	5	0	37 (12.8%)
Outcomes	31	28	6	3	68 (23.5%)
Total	114 (39.7%)	133 (45.7%)	36 (12.4%)	6 (2.1%)	289

These repeated syntheses have been carried out with the aim of updating, extending and/or reconfirming the results of the earlier studies. They are discussed in more detail in the analysis chapters concerned.

Thus, within the teaching and learning theme, both approaches to learning and self-regulated learning have been the subject of multiple systematic reviews. The course design theme is, as already indicated, particularly well populated with studies: there have been two or more systematic reviews published on feedback, formative assessment, mobile learning, professional identity development and ubiquitous learning environments; and two or more meta-analyses on blended learning, critical thinking, distance education, peer assessment, self-assessment, and technology and learning. Interestingly, within the student experience theme, the topic of mental health prevention has also been the subject of multiple meta-analyses.

Even outside of these more popular research themes, however, some topics have attracted the repeated attention of systematic reviewers or meta-analysts. In the quality theme, quality management has been the subject of several systematic reviews, while student evaluation of teaching has been the focus of multiple meta-analyses. In academic work, academic (or faculty) development has been the subject of several systematic reviews. And in the knowledge and research theme, the research/teaching nexus topic has been the concern of multiple systematic reviews and meta-analyses.

Clearly, if the studies are there – whether qualitative or quantitative in nature – research synthesists are increasingly attracted to do their work, but not invariably so, as the relative paucity of syntheses on system policy demonstrates.

Scale

One other factor to note is that the scale of the research syntheses identified varies a great deal. At one extreme is a systematic review that identified 4,095 relevant studies (Kosmutzky and Krucken 2014), while there are another eight studies (six systematic reviews and two meta-analyses) which examined over 1,000 studies (Feldman and Newcomb 1969, Hallinger and Chatpinyakoop 2019, Kosmutzky and Putty 2016, Mayhew et al 2016, Pascarella and Terenzini 1991, Schmid et al 2014, Steinhardt et al 2017, Villano and Tran 2019). At the other are a number of syntheses which could only find less than ten. This is partly, of course, a reflection of the relative popularity of the research topic being synthesized, as well as the selectivity exercised by the synthesizers involved.

Conclusion

Systematic reviews and meta-analyses are of growing importance within higher education research. In many cases their results are complementary, bringing together the quantitative and qualitative conclusions from the available research. Research syntheses like these are equally valuable for highlighting what we know and what we don't know, i.e. where research efforts might be targeted in the future.

Part two

Analyses

The second, and major, part of this book contains thirteen chapters. These look successively at each of the eight major themes for higher education research that have been identified through my previous work (Tight 2003, 2012a, 2019a): teaching and learning, course design, the student experience, quality, system policy, institutional management, academic work, and knowledge and research.

However, course design has been far and away the most popular theme for research syntheses (and also research), accounting for over half of the total identified for this book (see Chapter 3, especially Tables 1 and 5). To avoid having one extremely long chapter, therefore, course design has been broken into six sub-themes – types of instruction; types of learning; distance, online and e-learning; curriculum; assessment; outcomes – which are examined in Chapters 5 to 10, respectively. Hence the need for thirteen chapters.

In each of the thirteen chapters the major topics that have been subject to research synthesis are identified and discussed. Where there have been a number of research syntheses, their findings are compared, with particular attention paid to changes over time. At the end of each chapter some conclusions about what we know (and what we don't know) are listed.

Part Two

Chapter 4
Teaching and learning

Introduction

This chapter focuses on syntheses of research into teaching and learning in higher education. Teaching and learning here are being interpreted in a relatively narrow way: i.e. as concerning the actions of teaching and learning or what teachers and learners do in order to teach and learn as part of their everyday activities.

The broader institutional and/or external contexts for teaching and learning are considered in the following chapters, which focus on course design (how courses are designed, delivered and assessed: Chapters 5 to 10) and the student experience (of higher education and all other aspects of their lives while they are students: Chapter 11).

There is much of close relevance to this chapter, therefore, in some of the following chapters, notably Chapters 5 (which considers types of instruction), 6 (types of learning) and 7 (distance, online and e-learning). Indeed, the inclusion of the word 'learning' in the titles of two of these chapters, and in the discussion throughout them, is indicative of the different ways in which this word is employed. Here, as indicated, the focus is on research into how students learn and how higher education teachers teach, while in the later chapters it is on how learning may be organized and delivered.

Given the relatively narrow interpretation of teaching and learning adopted for this chapter, it should not be surprising that relatively few research syntheses of the topic have been carried out. A total of twenty-four have been identified for this book, just under 5 per cent of the overall total. Most, sixteen, were systematic reviews, with six meta-analyses, one substantive literature review and one study which combined meta-analysis and systematic review.

There are a number of specialist higher education journals that focus on the issues dealt with in this chapter. They include *Active Learning in Higher Education*, the *Journal of College Teaching and Learning*, and three journals concentrating on the scholarship of teaching and learning: the *Canadian Journal of the Scholarship of Teaching and Learning*, the *International Journal of the Scholarship of Teaching and Learning*, and the *Journal of the Scholarship of Teaching and Learning*.

Syntheses of research into teaching and learning in higher education have taken a variety of strategies. In this chapter their discussion has been organized in terms of whether their focus is primarily on learning or primarily on teaching, though obviously the two processes are intimately related. In addition, and unusually for higher education research (which is not particularly known as yet for its methodological or theoretical innovation), there have been systematic reviews of the particular methodological approaches taken to, and/or developed for, researching teaching and learning, notably phenomenography.

Syntheses of learning research in higher education have notably focused on approaches to learning research, but also on cognate areas such as learning patterns and learning styles, as well as on issues such as self-regulated learning, and interdisciplinary and innovative learning (see also Chapter 6, which focuses on types of learning from the perspective of course design).

Syntheses of teaching research in higher education have focused on issues such as teaching excellence (see also the discussion of quality in Chapter 12) and the scholarship of teaching and learning.

Learning

Learning approaches, patterns and styles

Learning approaches, patterns and styles, and other cognate terms, are used to refer to related aspects of learning and have been developed by different researchers at different times and places. Care needs to be taken not to confuse these terms with each other or to elide them too closely together.

The basic idea underlying these terms is that different students – or the same student in different circumstances – learn in different ways. In any particular set of circumstances, some ways of learning are believed to be more effective. A key task for the teacher, therefore, is to be aware of the learning approaches, patterns and styles of their students, and to be able to guide them, through their teaching, to learn in more effective ways. This is not, of course, an easy task, particularly in an era of mass higher education.

Approaches to learning research – with its origins in Swedish, Australian and UK studies in the late 1960s and 1970s – have been one of the most popular strategies adopted for researching learning in higher education. Its key finding that students may adopt surface or deep approaches to learning, and various strategies in between, has been very influential in contemporary academic development and training (see Chapter 15). Not surprisingly, therefore, it – and related areas of research – has been the subject of a number of research syntheses.

Asikainen and Gijbels (2017) carried out a systematic review of research examining whether students' approaches to learning changed during their higher education, developing from more surface learning towards the deeper end of the spectrum. This is what you might expect, or at least hope for, if both teachers and students were working effectively.

Using the ERIC, PsycINFO and Web of Science databases, Asikainen and Gijbels identified forty-three relevant studies. They failed, however, to confirm the hoped-for development. They conclude that

> longitudinal research within the SAL [student approaches to learning] tradition, aiming to investigate how students change their approaches to learning at group level during higher education, is a 'dead end'. First of all, there is no clear theoretical or empirical foundation in the SAL tradition for the claim that students should develop deeper or lesser surface approaches to learning across different years ... Second, ignoring the contextual differences between different courses and study years within higher education is in contradiction to the theoretical assumption that students' approaches to learning change as a result of the individual characteristics of the learner and the characteristics of the context.
>
> (p. 230)

This is a fairly damning conclusion to draw with respect to the approaches to learning school of research and practice. It may be, as Asikainen and Gijbels's second point implies, that many students are able to employ either a deep or a surface learning approach in response to the particular demands being made upon them.

It is also commonly the case, as Asikainen and Gijbels suggest, that the programmes of study (e.g. a complete bachelor's degree) followed by students typically lack an overall teaching/learning plan, strategy or structure. Degree programmes are commonly divided into separate courses and/or modules – some compulsory, some optional or elective, such that each student will be following a somewhat different programme – taught by different teachers, who will come together to share their ideas only rarely. Expecting progression over time in approaches to learning in such a system is probably asking a lot.

Asikainen and Gijbels end by suggesting that other frameworks should be explored more alongside, or instead of, approaches to learning.

In a much earlier study, Severiens and Ten Dam (1994) examine the broader area of research into learning styles, incorporating approaches to learning research and focusing on gender differences. They provide both a narrative review and a meta-analysis of relevant research carried out since 1980, with the meta-analysis (n = 26) focusing on research using Kolb's Learning Styles Inventory (LSI) and Entwistle's Approaches to Studying Inventory (ASI). They used an 'onion' model of concentric layers to organize their analysis, recognizing that some aspects, or layers, of learning style were more malleable:

> In the inner layer a given learning style is viewed as a fairly fixed personality trait; it is not considered sensitive to variables within the educational system. In the outer layer though, theories assume external factors influence learning styles. The onion's middle layer contains learning style concepts that are considered more stable than those in the outer layer, but nevertheless subject to modification according to the learning context.
>
> (p. 489)

Severiens and Ten Dam found only modest gender differences:

> The most important concept in the inner layer of the onion model was the field (in)dependence dimension ... Apart from one study, none of the reviewed studies showed statistically significant gender differences. In most studies in the middle layer, Kolb's theory on experiential learning was used. In the narrative review heterogeneous results were found. Meta-analysing this instrument resulted in a small consistent gender difference: men showed a greater preference than women for the abstract conceptualisation mode of learning. In the outer layer a gender difference appeared on the scales for extrinsic motivation. This difference also appeared in the meta-analysis. In all these different settings, men were more often interested in the courses for the qualifications they offer. Women on the other hand, are more often interested in learning for learning's sake. In the narrative review the deep and surface dimension turned out to be slightly gender sensitive. In several studies, men showed more often a deep approach to learning, women more often a surface or reproducing approach to learning.
>
> (p. 498)

The slightly greater interest of men students in abstract conceptualization, extrinsic motivation and deep learning is interesting to know, but it is difficult to see how this might inform overall teaching and learning strategies.

Coffield et al's (2004) critical systematic review of the learning styles literature identified an extraordinary seventy-one different models, demonstrating the tendency of academic researchers to reinvent wheels rather than build upon existing studies. Of these, thirteen (on which they identified 351 articles) were designated as major models and explored further. Coffield et al's conclusions were rather mixed:

> This review examined in considerable detail 13 models of learning style and one of the most obvious conclusions is the marked variability in quality among them; they are not all alike nor of equal worth and it matters fundamentally which instrument is chosen. The evaluation ... showed that some of the best known and widely used instruments have such serious weaknesses (e.g. low reliability, poor validity and negligible impact on pedagogy) that we recommend that their use in research and in practice should be discontinued. On the other hand, other approaches emerged from our rigorous evaluation with fewer defects and, with certain reservations ... we suggest that they deserve to be researched further.
>
> (p. 138)

As with Asikainen and Gijbels's (2017) systematic review, this is a very critical judgement. Much disparate research on learning styles has clearly not got us very far in practical terms, though some hope is still held out.

Marambe, Vermunt and Boshuizen (2012) carried out a cross-cultural meta-analysis of three large-scale studies of what they termed learning patterns. These studies had been carried out in Indonesia, Sri Lanka and the Netherlands, in each case using the Inventory of Learning Styles (ILS) instrument, an updated version of the LSI explored by Severiens and Ten Dam. This cross-cultural study is particularly interesting for its focus on countries that are not commonly discussed in the English language literature. It set out to challenge the assumptions underlying the concept of the 'Asian learner', seen wrongly as someone overly concentrated on memorization in learning:

> Results showed most differences in student learning patterns between Asian and European students. However, many differences were identified between students from the two Asian countries as well. The Asian learner turned out to be a myth. Moreover, Sri Lankan students made the least use of memorising strategies of all groups. That Asian learners would have a propensity for rote learning turned out to be a myth as well. Some patterns of learning turned out to be universal and occurred in all groups, other patterns were found only among the Asian or the European students.
>
> (p. 299)

Considered rationally, of course, there is no reason to suppose that the idea of the 'Asian learner' would have any validity – as if all of those living in our most populous continent would behave in the same narrow way – but it is useful to have the evidence to dismiss this idea.

Self-regulated learning

Other research syntheses have focused on specific types of student learning, with self-regulated learning being a particular interest. This is hardly surprising because, like critical thinking (see Chapter 10), the ability of students to control and regulate their own learning behaviour is believed to be fundamental to success in higher education and working life.

Several recent relevant systematic reviews on the topic have been identified. Broadbent and Poon (2015) undertook a systematic review, over the period 2004–14, of studies of self-regulated learning in relation to academic achievement in online environments (see also Chapter 7), identifying twelve relevant studies. They concluded that

> [s]elf-regulated learning strategies of time management, metacognition, critical thinking, and effort regulation were found to have significant positive correlations with academic success in online settings, albeit these effect sizes were smaller than those found in the traditional classroom. In contrast, rehearsal, organization, and elaboration were found to be the least empirically supported SRL [self-regulated learning] strategy within the online environment, indicating that there is less benefit in these strategies for online learners.
>
> (p. 13)

Note the inclusion here of critical thinking as an element of self-regulated learning and also the notion that some self-regulated learning strategies would be more useful online than in the classroom and vice versa.

De Bruijn-Smolders et al (2016) took a similar focus, on effective self-regulatory learning processes, searching the databases ERIC, Scopus, PsycINFO, PubMed and Cinahl, and identifying ten relevant studies. They produced somewhat different, if overlapping, findings to Broadbent and Poon, noting that 'the current review indicates that the following SRPs [self-regulatory learning processes] constitute effective SRL in higher education, that is, SRL that benefits learning outcomes: metacognitive strategies, motivation, self-efficacy, handling task difficulty and demands, and resource management' (p. 154).

Roth, Ogrin and Schmitz (2016) examined self-report instruments designed to measure self-regulated learning. They searched PsycARTICLES, PSYNDEXplus Literature and Audiovisual Media, PsycINFO and Web of Science databases, focusing on 115 articles that used 9 different instruments. They noted the variations in the definitions of self-regulated learning being used and recommended further development and triangulation of instruments:

> In general, our systematic review illustrates the manifold work in the field of SRL research but also indicates that further development is desirable and certainly possible. For this reason, we encourage researchers to explore new approaches to assess SRL, combine them with the established and well-verified instruments from this review, and with that implement ... triangulation. Particularly useful and promising seems to be the combination of process- and component-oriented instruments as well as the development of qualitative standards. Likewise, future research should increasingly focus on integrated models that cover component and process aspects simultaneously.
>
> (p. 246)

Panadero, Klug and Järvelä (2016) also review the literature on the measurement of self-regulated learning, arguing that this has now entered a 'third wave':

> [T]he third wave ... is characterized by studies that use a combination of measurement + intervention, because the tool used for measurement is also part of an intervention to promote the regulation of learning ... it seems that the field of SRL has reached maturity where measures are not an 'external' artifact to evaluate the phenomena, but part of the SRL process itself.
>
> (pp. 732–3)

This is a much more positive conclusion than that reached by Roth, Ogrin and Schmitz (2016).

Jansen et al (2019) present a number of meta-analyses and carry out meta-analytic structural equation modelling (n = 126) to investigate the relationships between self-regulated learning interventions, activity and achievement (which are generally assumed to be positive and self-supporting). They came to rather more nuanced conclusions:

> With advanced statistical methods, we tested whether improvements in achievement after implementing an SRL intervention are mediated by SRL activity. We found evidence that the effect of SRL interventions on achievement is only partially mediated by SRL activity. Most of the effectiveness of SRL interventions for improving student achievement is thus not due to improvements in SRL, but due to other factors, contrary to common assumption. Furthermore, we provided insight into the factors that moderate each of the three studied relations in higher education. We have thereby shown that SRL interventions may have different effects on students' achievement and students' engagement in SRL activities. By combining mediation analysis with three

separate meta-analyses, this systematic review provides a thorough and complete synthesis of current SRL research in higher education, while opening new avenues for future exploration.

(p. 18)

Jansen et al identify time on task, cognitive activity and task motivation as factors effecting the effectiveness of self-regulated learning interventions that are worthy of further investigation.

Williams et al (2019), coming from a dental education background but with a generic intention, provide a contemporary systematic review of instruments designed to measure the ability to self-reflect, a quality clearly related to self-regulation. They identified 131 relevant articles, of which 18 were deemed to provide higher quality evidence: 'three broad types of instrument were identified, namely: rubrics (or scoring guides), self-reported scales and observed behaviour' (p. 389). However, they were unable to recommend 'a single most effective instrument' (p. 389).

In an earlier meta-analysis (n = 129), Symons and Johnson (1997) examine research on the self-reference effect (SRE) in memory, that is the idea that, if material is related to the self, it is more likely to be remembered. Their analysis identified

> self-referent encoding strategies yielding superior memory relative to both semantic and other referent encoding strategies. Consistent with theory and research that suggest self-reference (SR) produces both organized and elaborate processing, the SRE was smaller (a) when SR is compared with other-reference (OR) rather than semantic encoding and (b) when the comparison tasks promote both organization and elaboration. Thus, the SRE appears to result primarily because the self is a well-developed and often-used construct that promotes elaboration and organization of encoded information.
>
> (p. 371)

There is no denying, therefore, the importance of the individual or the self in effective learning.

Interdisciplinary and innovative learning

This final subsection on learning considers syntheses that have examined research on the related areas of interdisciplinary and innovative learning.

Interdisciplinarity, along with cognate ideas like trans-disciplinarity and cross-disciplinarity, has regularly been heralded as the way forward for learning and teaching (and research) in higher education. However, it has yet to really catch hold alongside, or instead of, the disciplinary and sub-disciplinary strengths of existing university departments.

Spelt et al (2009), a Dutch team, considered interdisciplinary teaching and learning in higher education. Taking the period 1992–2009, they searched ERIC and SCI, SSCI and AHCI (the science, social science, and arts and humanities citation indexes) through the Web of Science, ending up with thirteen relevant publications in their systematic review. They came up with three main findings:

> The first finding is that despite repeated acknowledgement of the lack of scientific research in the field of teaching and learning in interdisciplinary higher education, to date, such research has been limited and explorative. Second, the present review should be regarded as one of the first scientific studies to offer a clear and comprehensive view of the teaching and learning interdisciplinary thinking in interdisciplinary higher education. Third, the adopted outcome-based approach, consistent with the theory of Biggs, also appears to be innovative in interdisciplinary higher education presumably because interdisciplinary higher education is still being defined not in terms of what students gain in ability but in terms of its own pedagogical characteristics.
>
> (p. 375)

They concluded that 'while interdisciplinary higher education is commonly practiced nowadays, a surprisingly small body of theory has accumulated' (p. 376).

Savin-Baden and colleagues (Savin-Baden and Major 2007, Savin-Baden, McFarland and Savin-Baden 2008), a UK-based team, employed what they termed interpretative meta-ethnography, but I would term systematic review. Their focus was on what they termed innovative learning and teaching, which sounds like a broad formulation but seems to have been narrowly interpreted in practice.

The first of these studies examined the relationship between innovative approaches to learning and their impact on understanding of teaching. Though a total of fourteen databases were searched, they ended up with only six studies, three from the UK and three from the United States, four of which involved one of the authors of the systematic review. Perhaps unsurprisingly, they found that

> [f]aculty in these studies re-examined their understanding of their roles as the lecturer, of their students' role as learners, of the structures of their disciplines, and of their views of teaching. As participants reflected on their experiences, the combined effect of time, resources, support for risk-taking, and collegial discussion presented an unusual gateway for the transformation of their pedagogical stances, knowledge, and practice.
>
> (p. 849)

The second study focused on the factors that influence teaching and learning practices and thinking in higher education and concluded that

> issues of pedagogical stance, disjunction, learning spaces, agency, notions of improvement and communities of interest can help to locate overarching themes and hidden subtexts that are strong influences on areas of practice, transfer and community. Nevertheless, these are areas that are sometimes ignored, marginalised or dislocated from the central arguments about teaching and learning thinking and practices in higher education.
>
> (p. 211)

Innovative forms of learning (and teaching), in this interpretation, appear to be largely a mechanism for stimulating thinking and reflection.

Teaching

Interestingly, there appear to have been fewer syntheses conducted into research on higher education teaching than there have been on higher education learning, though, clearly, the syntheses discussed in the preceding section on interdisciplinary and innovative learning addressed both teaching and learning. It should be emphasized once more, therefore, that the distinction between research on teaching and research on learning is a fine one. Most such studies have relevance for both, particularly as these terms have been defined narrowly for the purposes of this chapter.

A number of teaching topics have, however, attracted systematic reviews, comprehensive literature reviews and meta-analyses, notably teaching excellence and the scholarship of teaching and learning.

Teaching excellence

In the UK, the former Higher Education Academy (HEA) has sponsored a series of detailed literature reviews over the last decade or so on the subject of teaching (and learning) excellence in higher education (Gunn and Fisk 2013, Little et al 2007, Strang et al 2016). This particular terminology does not appear to have been picked up in other countries, however, where the focus has been more on student evaluation of teaching (discussed in Chapter 12).

The first of these literature reviews (Little et al 2007) identified a key issue underlying the interest in teaching excellence in higher education:

> [A] recurring critical theme within the literature argues that the current focus on teaching (and to a lesser extent learning) excellence is symptomatic of an ever-present contemporary desire to measure higher education performance by means of systematic criteria and standardised practices, wherein 'form' and 'process' predominate and the 'what' is in the background; arguably it is the 'what' that forms the essence of what is being valued and recognised as distinctive about higher education, and within that, what might constitute an excellent learning experience.
>
> (p. 3)

This suggestion that teaching, and learning, excellence might be a variable quality, such that what is 'excellent' for one might not be so for another (but might still be 'good' or 'good enough'), potentially undermines the whole enterprise.

The latest HEA review (Strang et al 2016), confined to the period since 2012, confirms this view. It notes that 'the lack of robust empirical evidence found by this review must be acknowledged, with the literature dominated by opinion pieces based on secondary, documentary analysis rather than rigorous comparison group studies' (p. 5). The nature of teaching excellence, therefore, remains somewhat unclear, perhaps because the construct itself is not so highly valued by many in academia.

The scholarship of teaching and learning

The scholarship of teaching and learning is a US-based but international movement that emphasizes the importance of university teachers taking a scholarly approach to their work (Boshier and Huang 2008, Boyer 1990, Kreber 2001). It has attracted a good deal of attention over the last three or four decades but appears to have only resulted in one systematic review. In this, Tight (2018a) argues that

> [a]n inherent problem with the scholarship of teaching and learning is that, despite the slippage in interpretation noted, most research remains (true to the original intention) small-scale, short-term and local in orientation. That is acceptable if the intention is simply to engage in individual scholarship – with all of the wheel re-invention that this will necessarily involve – but if the aim is to have a wider impact, some comparison and synthesis of findings is called for, and even, perhaps, coordinated, large-scale studies.
> (p. 72)

The close link between academic (or educational) development (see Chapter 15) – but not the more quantitative educational psychology research – and teaching and learning research is very evident here. The scholarship of teaching and learning is also, of course, practised under other headings, such as pedagogical research.

Other topics

Other research syntheses have been rather more focused and individual (see also the discussion of learning design and interventions in Chapter 8).

In an early study, Luiten, Ames and Ackerson (1980) examine studies of advance organizers – a particular learning strategy that sets out what is to be learnt and how at the beginning of each learning session – and their impact on learning and retention. Their meta-analysis covered 135 studies (around one-third related to higher education), concluding that

> [t]he average advance organizer study shows a small, but facilitative effect on learning and retention. The small effect may well be a function of the short duration of treatment of the typical study (all too often an experiment is concluded within one or two class periods). Moreover, the findings indicate that advance organizers facilitate learning in all content areas examined, albeit broadly defined, and with individuals of all grade and ability levels.
> (p. 217)

Clearly, if perhaps unsurprisingly, then, carefully structured and planned learning has a beneficial impact.

Wagner and Szamoskosi (2012) examined research on the effectiveness of direct academic motivation enhancement interventions through a meta-analysis (n = 17). They concluded that 'multidimensional intervention programs, which target several motivational factors at the same time, are more effective and, thus, more advisable' (p. 97). There are clear links here to the research on self-regulated learning discussed earlier in this chapter.

Balwant (2016) carried out a meta-analysis of the literature on transformational instructor-leadership, an approach to encouraging academic or faculty development, and its relationship to student outcomes. Searches were conducted through Scopus, Web of Knowledge and Google Scholar, with twenty-two relevant studies identified. Balwant found that '[t]ransformational instructor-leadership is specifically positively associated with students' motivation, perceptions of instructor credibility, satisfaction, academic performance, affective learning, and cognitive learning' (p. 38).

Ramis et al (2019) provide a systematic review of theory-based strategies for teaching evidence-based practice (EBP) to undergraduate health students, identifying twenty-eight relevant studies, only five of which were aligned to one or more theoretical frameworks. They concluded that

> [d]espite the requirements for undergraduate students to be capable EBP users after they graduate and the call for EBP education to be specific for the intended audience, the literature identifies limited theory-based evidence directed at undergraduate EBP education with a focus on preparing students to build capability and confidently use evidence in their professional practice. Of the included studies, interventions grounded in theory were found to have a small but positive effect on EBP attitudes. Other common components were identified relating to time needed for learning as well as role modeling.
> (p. 11)

This is a somewhat disappointing result, as it questions both the use of theory to inform teaching and the usefulness of current evidence-based practice teaching approaches.

Finally, Winberg et al (2018) offer a critical literature review of studies of how academics develop pedagogical competence while learning to teach STEM (science, technology, engineering and mathematics) subjects. They identified seventy-seven relevant studies and came to the following, rather concerning, conclusions:

> The key finding of this critical review of the literature on learning to teach the STEM disciplines in higher education is how little focus there was on the STEM disciplines themselves; the majority of studies reviewed did not address the key issue of what makes the STEM disciplines difficult to learn and challenging to teach. We did not, for example, find studies that drew on STEM 'threshold concepts' in academic staff development, although this approach is more common in research studies on STEM student learning. Instead, interventions to improve teaching in the STEM disciplines tended to focus on the practical issues of lesson planning, facilitation, presentation skills, and reflective practice. While these generic aspects of teaching in higher education are important, they are only a part of STEM pedagogical competence. What was missing in the studies was the kinds of professional learning that would enable STEM university teachers to provide 'epistemological access' to STEM knowledge: to its logic, systems, processes and values. This provision should be at the heart of STEM academic development, yet the literature shows how little we know about teaching STEM concepts. The professional development of STEM university teachers has over-emphasised generic forms of teaching practice and neglected discipline-specific teaching practice.
> (p. 11)

This finding highlights the debate between generic and disciplinary approaches to training or developing academics in their teaching roles. Counter to Winberg et al, however, it might be argued that much about STEM teaching is fairly generic in nature and that, if the disciplines are paramount, we can't really talk about STEM disciplines but should focus on each discipline (or sub-discipline) separately.

Methodological approaches

An interesting aspect of research into teaching and learning in higher education is that – unusually for higher education research – it has encouraged methodological development and innovation and that these have also been the subject of systematic review. One particular example, phenomenography, will be considered here. Another, learning analytics, is considered in Chapter 8.

Tight (2016a) offers a systematic review of the development and application of phenomenography to teaching and learning research in higher education (though it has also been applied to researching other levels of education and occasionally outside education altogether). Phenomenography was initially developed in Sweden in the late 1960s/early 1970s and applied to education as well as higher education. It is a technique for identifying and understanding the variations in perceptions of a given phenomenon of interest (such as learning or teaching).

Tight notes that 'phenomenography is closely associated with an interest in higher education practice, particularly the student learning experience, and in seeking to improve this: for example, through the encouragement of deep, rather than surface, learning, and the employment of variations in teaching approaches' (p. 331). It is linked to the research into approaches to learning discussed earlier in this chapter but has yet to enjoy widespread adoption in higher education research.

Conclusions

It is clear that teaching and learning research in higher education is closely linked to both psychology and academic (or educational) development. Many of the systematic reviews and meta-analyses referred to in this chapter are, however, based on a relatively small number of studies, so it is apparent that further research is needed and that the conclusions we may draw now need to be measured or qualified.

- Research into learning approaches, styles and patterns has been useful for thinking about how students learn, but it has yet to have much practical input into how we teach.
- The development of self-regulated learning in students is of critical importance in enhancing learning effectiveness.

- Interdisciplinary learning and teaching, while much heralded, appears to have made little inroad into higher education.
- Teaching excellence does not appear to be a helpful direction for research.
- While the scholarship of teaching and learning and cognate movements have encouraged higher education teachers to be more involved in small-scale research, their wider impact has been limited.
- The debate about generic and/or disciplinary approaches to teaching is ongoing.

Chapter 5
Course design – types of instruction

Introduction

Course design is probably by far the most researched of the eight topic areas I have identified and used to organize this book. It is certainly the area that has been the subject of the greatest number of syntheses within higher education research. Just over half of all of the higher education research syntheses that I have identified – 289 or 56 per cent (see Table 1 in Chapter 3) – relate to this broad topic area. There are roughly equal numbers of meta-analyses (114) and systematic reviews (133) represented, as well as thirty-six substantive literature reviews, and six studies that combined meta-analysis and systematic review.

For the purposes of discussion, these research syntheses have been grouped under six sub-themes, each of which – to keep chapters to a reasonable length – is considered in a separate chapter:

- Types of instruction (Chapter 5, the present chapter)
- Types of learning (Chapter 6)
- Distance, online and e-learning (Chapter 7)
- Curriculum (Chapter 8)
- Assessment (Chapter 9)
- Outcomes (Chapter 10)

Each of these sub-themes has been the subject of a good number of research syntheses (see Table 5 in Chapter 3), in each case more than all of the other seven main themes identified, with the exceptions of the student experience (the subject of Chapter 11) and quality (Chapter 12). There is, though, some variation in popularity, with distance, online and e-learning standing out as the subject of sixty-nine research syntheses, followed by outcomes with sixty-eight and types of instruction with forty-three.

Interestingly, each of the six sub-themes also demonstrates a roughly even split between meta-analyses and systematic reviews, with the sole exception of curriculum, which is dominated by systematic reviews (twenty-seven to only five meta-analyses). The sub-theme of distance, open and online learning has also been subject to more systematic reviews than meta-analyses (thirty-one to twenty-three) and, with fourteen substantive literature reviews also identified, exhibits a preference for qualitative syntheses. Types of instruction and types of learning, however, both show a slight preference for quantitative syntheses.

Other groupings of sub-themes would, of course, have been possible, but these six groups work well enough. There are also, inevitably, overlaps between these groupings, as there are between the main themes. Thus, the distinction between types of instruction and types of learning (the two topics considered in this chapter and the following one) is essentially one of scale, with the latter seen as more over-arching.

The issues considered under the heading of distance, online and e-learning are much the same as those examined elsewhere; it is merely that the technology in use is different and in some ways somewhat more sophisticated. The curriculum theme is, to some extent, a catch-all for issues that did not readily fit under any of the other headings. Assessment and outcomes are also closely related, with the former focusing on how the higher education experienced by students is measured and the latter considering the end result of higher education and its impact.

Turning now to the focus of this chapter, types of instruction (see Table 5 in Chapter 3), a total of forty-three research syntheses have been identified relating to this topic, or 15 per cent of the course design total. Of these, twenty-three were meta-analyses, fifteen were systematic reviews, four were literature reviews and one combined elements of meta-analysis and systematic review.

Some instructional types have attracted two or more systematic reviews or meta-analyses, indicating a substantial body of research and interest. These include peer instruction, game-based learning, audience response systems (ARSs) and flipped classrooms. Others have, to date, been only the subject of a single published meta-analysis or systematic review. We will consider these bodies of research and their syntheses in turn.

Peer instruction, mentoring and tutoring

Peer instruction, mentoring and/or tutoring are overlapping types of activity, where fellow students are engaged in giving each other instruction, support or feedback (see also the discussion of peer assessment in Chapter 9). They are also sometimes referred to as supplemental instruction, though this term has other and/or broader meanings as well (i.e. additional instruction), as supplemental instruction may be provided in a number of ways and not only by peers.

The underlying idea behind peer instruction, mentoring and tutoring is that this improves students' understanding – both for the students giving the instruction and those receiving it: the roles will typically be shared – of what they are studying. Thus, those involved in peer instruction will necessarily have to cast the material they are discussing in their own words and, in doing so, will be more aware of the issues they face in understanding it and what they still do not understand. This should feed through into improvements in student performance. If done efficiently, peer instruction should also reduce pressure on the teaching staff, with the teaching role shared – at least to some extent – with the students.

In a relatively early study, Goldschmid and Goldschmid (1976), a Swiss team, offered fairly comprehensive guidance from their review of the literature and practice:

> A number of peer-teaching models including discussion groups led by undergraduate students, proctoring, student learning groups, the learning cell, and student counseling of students (*parrainage*) have evolved. Several issues and problems may confront the instructor who wants to use undergraduates as teachers: selection of student partner, functions of student teacher, cooperation vs. competition, the structure of the learning situation, preparation of the student teachers, benefits of peer teaching, the role of the professor, financial aspects and instructional facilities. The evidence reviewed suggests that peer teaching, best used in conjunction with other teaching and learning methods, has great potentials for both student 'teacher' and student 'learner', especially if one seeks to enhance active participation and develop skills in cooperation and social interaction.
>
> (p. 9)

What is perhaps most striking about this analysis is the diversity of types of peer teaching already then recognized, strongly suggesting that the practice had arisen on a number of occasions and in different places.

Twenty years later, Topping (1996) reviewed the literature on the effectiveness of peer tutoring, and he also developed a typology of it. He concluded that

> three methods of peer tutoring in further and higher education have already been widely used, have been demonstrated to be effective, and merit wider use in practice – these are Cross-year Small-group Tutoring, the Personalised System of Instruction and Supplemental Instruction. Same-year dyadic reciprocal tutoring has been demonstrated to be effective, but has been little used, and merits much wider deployment. Same-year dyadic fixed-role tutoring and peer assisted writing have shown considerable but not necessarily consistent promise and should be the focus of continuing experimentation and more research of better quality. In three areas there are barely the beginnings of a satisfactory body of evaluation research: dyadic cross-year fixed-role tutoring, same-year group tutoring and peer assisted distance learning.
>
> (p. 339)

As well as encompassing a diverse series of practices and approaches, peer tutoring, suitably supported, has demonstrated its effectiveness in contributing to instruction in higher education.

More recently, Dawson et al (2014) carried out a systematic review of articles published between 2001 and 2010 (n = 29) focusing on peer-assisted study and/or supplemental instruction. Their conclusions were rather more measured than those of Topping:

> Although, at best, we can say that in many instances, SI [supplemental instruction] seemed to have been effective (keeping in mind possible publication bias), it does

provide some indications that SI *worked* on some level for some groups of students. Although there is a marked lack of an evidence base in demonstrating effectiveness in the field of learning support interventions, SI has benefited from at least a degree of empirical research over more than 40 years in many different countries.

(p. 633, emphasis in original)

But perhaps 'some indications' on 'some level' for 'some groups of students' is a reasonable or acceptable result, one that many instructional innovations or interventions would be happy to achieve.

Stigmar (2016) provides a critical literature review of peer-to-peer teaching in higher education, identifying a similar number of relevant studies to Dawson et al: thirty studies from thirteen countries. His conclusions were also mixed:

The main conclusions are that generic skills development and metacognitive training benefit from peer teaching. University teachers need to stimulate students' metacognitive skills and lifelong learning in a knowledge society through peer-led teaching. My review does not suggest that peer teaching result [sic] in greater academic achievement gains ... It remains unclear whether peer teaching stimulate [sic] students' deep level learning. The reason for this uncertainty is that several of the included studies for review are methodologically weak and limited.

(p. 134)

While suggesting that peer teaching was helpful for some purposes, but not so much for others, Stigmar notes, 'University teachers identify and esteem other pedagogical benefits such as improving students': critical thinking, learning autonomy, motivation, collaborative and communicative skills' (p. 124). In other words, the benefits accrue at least as much to the peers doing the teaching – through clarifying their understanding of the topic in hand – as to those in receipt of it.

Balta et al (2017) focus, in their meta-analysis, on the effect of peer instruction on learning gain (see also Chapter 10). Based on an analysis of twenty-nine studies, they find that '[p]eer Instruction has a positive impact on learning compared to traditional teaching methods, and differences can be observed in both informational and cultural variables. It appears to be most effective in collectivist countries and in individualist countries that place a high value on social interaction, compared to those encouraging individual learning' (p. 65).

This is a stronger conclusion than that reached by Stigmar, particularly in terms of learning gain or achievement. It does suggest, though, that peer instruction should not be implemented in isolation or without careful thought and, interestingly, that it might work better in certain countries or systems.

In their literature review (n = 54), Terrion and Leonard (2007) focus on the characteristics of successful student peer mentors: 'The review resulted in a taxonomy of five prerequisites for the student peer mentor, two student peer mentor characteristics that support the career-related function and eight characteristics that support the psychosocial function' (p. 161). The five prerequisites or more general characteristics identified, none of which are particularly surprising, were the ability and willingness to commit time, gender and race (in some contexts), university experience, academic achievement and prior mentoring experience.

Skaniakos and Piirainen (2019), a Finnish team, examined peer group mentoring, carrying out a meta-analysis (and, unusually, also a phenomenography: see the discussion of methodological approaches in Chapter 4) of 'two primary studies of teacher students' and teacher group tutors' conceptions of peer group mentoring' (p. 21). They stress the importance of the individual's participation in the group, professional development with others, and community enabling sharing and development, and argue that 'social activity forms places for learning communities in the form of peer group mentoring. They can form a sociocultural environment, a space for different students to learn, even communities of practice' (p. 29).

If well handled, therefore, peer instruction, mentoring and tutoring can help transform a class of students into a learning community. Even so, it will not work well with all students, some of whom would rather work on their own. The experience of group work and learning which it engenders is, however, one of the key qualities looked for in graduates by employers (see also Chapter 10).

Game-based learning

Game-based learning has been a more recent topic for research than peer instruction, mentoring and teaching and thus has only very recently been the subject of research syntheses. Most of those identified were published during the last few years, with earlier syntheses mostly focusing on school pupils or industrial trainees.

It may be the case that the relatively late permeation into higher education has something to do with games being seen as juvenile and low level and not, therefore, suitable for the serious business of degree-level study and above. However, the use of simulations for learning – which have a relatively long history in health, medicine and cognate subjects (including prior to the development of online learning) – forms part of this topic.

Shin, Park and Kim (2015), a Korean team, offer a meta-analysis (n = 20) of the effectiveness of the use of patient simulation in nursing education. They found 'significant post-intervention improvements in various domains for participants who received simulation education compared to the control groups, with a pooled random-effects standardized mean difference of 0.71, which is a medium-to-large effect size' (p. 176). The potential benefits of using simulations in health education are, of course, many, including allowing practice before real patients are involved.

Carenys and Moya (2016) focus, in their systematic review, on digital game-based learning (DGBL) as applied to accounting and business education. Searching relevant databases for the period from 2003 to 2013, they identified fifty-four relevant studies. They clearly see this area of activity as ripe for major development:

> The engagement stemming from the use of digital games as learning tools, together with the switch to a new student-centred educational model and the arrival of the

> 'Net generation', all demand a transformation in higher education, particularly a reformulation of methodologies and learning processes. In this new approach, digital games are expected to play a key role, while the impact of DGBL is only just beginning to be understood.
>
> (p. 642)

The reference to the 'net generation', however, needs to be taken with a pinch of salt. The assumption that all young people are necessarily 'digitally literate' and expecting higher education to be delivered largely through digital means is fallacious. Most people, young and old, still like at least some face-to-face attention.

The meta-analysis by Clark, Tanner-Smith and Killingsworth (2016) covered the period from 2000 to 2012, identifying '69 unique study samples included in 70 reports from 68 journal articles' (p. 93) that related to K-16 (i.e. undergraduate) students. They found that '[o]verall, results indicated that digital games were associated with a 0.33 standard deviation improvement relative to nongame comparison conditions. Thus, digital games conditions were on average more effective than the nongame instructional conditions included in those comparisons' (p. 108).

This is an impressive finding, though Clark et al go on to caution that 'the design of an intervention is associated with as large an effect as the medium of an intervention' (pp. 109–10). In other words, the digital games have to be well designed and delivered to maximize their impact, an approach that would also be open to those delivering the 'nongame' instructional conditions.

Vlachopoulos and Makri (2017) provide a systematic review (n = 123) of the literature on games and simulations pedagogy in higher education. They conclude that

> [t]his review ... sheds light on behavioural outcomes of using games in instructional design. The emphasis is on the positive effects, namely the development of social and soft skills, emotional skills, the empowerment of collaboration with peers, and the promotion of interaction and feedback ... The current review concludes by highlighting the affective outcomes, and the emphasis is given on motivational and engaging factors that lead to emotional development, satisfaction, self-efficacy and self-assessment ... Despite the significant benefits in learning outcomes highlighted in this paper, the high cost of designing games and simulations is still a significant challenge.
>
> (p. 27)

Subhash and Cudney (2018) present another systematic review (n = 41), coming up with a similar list of benefits:

> The systematic literature review identified several benefits of using gamified learning, such as improved student-engagement, motivation, confidence, attitude, perceived learning, and performance. Improved student attitudes, engagement, and performance were the most significant benefits from using gamification and game-based learning applications. This makes a strong case for the application of gamification and game-based learning in higher education.
>
> (p. 205)

Game-based learning, like many other elements of course design, is, therefore, subject to cost-benefit analysis. The benefits are potentially substantial, though perhaps not for all students, but so are the costs, and the benefits could potentially also be delivered by means other than games-based learning.

Audience response systems

Audience response systems, commonly known as clickers, are electronic devices that allow students in lectures – even, or especially, those with large audiences – to respond to questions, often multiple-choice questions, posed by the lecturer. The lecturer may then pick up on the displayed responses, correct any evident errors in students' thinking and perhaps adapt what they were planning to do in the remainder of their lecture. The introduction of audience response systems has, like many innovations, encouraged evaluative research and latterly synthesis.

Almost from the beginning, these syntheses were generally positive in tone. Thus, Judson and Sawada (2002) reviewed the literature over the preceding thirty-three years. They stress 'the pedagogical practices of the instructor, not the incorporation of the technology, as being key to student comprehension. Electronic response systems are viewed as a tool that holds a promise of facilitating earnest discussion' (p. 167). As with all technological developments, then, what counts is how and how well they are used.

Writing five years later, Caldwell (2007) concluded from their review that

> clickers offer a powerful and flexible tool for teaching. They can be used in a variety of subjects with students of almost any level of academic training. Clickers may occupy either a peripheral or central role during class. They can be incorporated into a standard lecture course to increase interaction between students and instructor or used as part of a more radical change in teaching style toward primarily active learning in class (whether it be peer learning, debate, or other activities).
>
> (p. 19)

Simpson and Oliver (2007) compared the use of audience response systems, or voting systems as they termed them, before 2002 with the period between 2002 and 2006. They argued that

> voting systems are best understood as a tool rather than a teaching approach ... there appears to be consensus that they do not 'cause' good learning; however when used as part of a wider effort to support active engagement with learning there is evidence that they can support increased motivation and attainment, at least in part as a result of their ability to provide rapid feedback on the learning process ... it is generally agreed that these systems represent an opportunity to improve lecturing. The emphasis on engagement and interaction can prompt staff to rethink their conception of teaching.
>
> (p. 203)

With lectures widely recognized as a sub-optimal means of teaching in higher education, associated with loss of attention and student boredom, the availability of systems to stimulate and engage students – used appropriately – has a high likelihood of success.

Kay and LeSage (2009) identified fifty-two articles on audience response systems (ARSs) for analysis in their comprehensive review. They examined the different strategies used:

> Promising ARS general strategies reported included explaining why an ARS is being used, asking practice questions, taking time to develop effective, meaningful questions, developing questions that stimulate class discussion, focussing on higher level as opposed to factual questions, asking only two to five questions per hour, and limiting the number of options in a multiple choice question to four or five. Effective ARS motivational strategies involved using ARSs to increase participation and engagement. Promising ARS assessment strategies included collecting formative feedback and contingency teaching. Finally, with respect to learning strategies, using ARS to increase attention levels, improving the quality of classroom interaction, peer based instruction, and requiring students to read extra materials before an ARS class appeared to work well.
>
> (p. 245)

This is a very useful set of guidelines, though most of them would apply to other forms of intervention as well.

Good (2013) also came to generally positive conclusions from her literature review: 'Active learning techniques in conjunction with clicker technology seemed to positively impact student learning. When using social/peer interactions, there was a positive increase in the generative learning opportunities due to the discussions happening with peers' (p. 30).

Finally, Castillo-Manzano et al (2016) conducted a global meta-analysis of the effect of audience response systems on academic performance. Some fifty-one papers published between 2008 and 2012 were included in the analysis. They came to interesting conclusions:

> Our results provide a positive, although moderated pooled effect of ARS on examination scores that is much greater in experiments performed in non-university contexts than at the university level. Specifically, the categories of university disciplines in which ARS interventions are implemented seem to influence their usefulness for achieving better academic marks, being more effective when either Pure Soft Sciences or Applied Hard Sciences are considered.
>
> (p. 109)

It may be, then, that – beyond giving a general push to students to attend and participate – audience response systems are best suited to particular disciplines or forms of teaching. The repeated mentions in the syntheses referenced to their use together with, or as part of, active and peer learning (see the discussion in an earlier section of this chapter) strategies are also strongly suggestive of the need for a broader-based approach.

Flipped classrooms

The flipped classroom is another recent educational innovation, which involves the work that is done in the conventional classroom – essentially the transmission of information on the subject being studied – being done outside of the classroom in the students' own time instead (through directed reading). Class time is thus left free to focus on dealing with problems in understanding the subject, discussing key issues and working on assessed work.

Bishop and Verleger (2013) offer a relatively early survey of practice and research on this topic. They identified twenty-four relevant studies published up until 2012. However, as they noted that 'of all the studies on the flipped classroom, there is only one that has examined student performance throughout a semester' (p. 12), it was clear then that more research was needed.

Brewer and Movahedazarhouligh (2018) provide a literature review of studies that have explored the effectiveness of flipped learning in higher education. They conclude that '[r]esearch to date indicates that learner outcomes will improve if we assist instructors in higher education to maximise students' learning experiences by using the data on the basis of the outcomes of the implementation of this model to drive those decisions and effectively shift student accountability for learning using flipped methods' (p. 414). They might be said, therefore, to be strong advocates of the method.

Lundin et al's (2018) systematic review was based on 530 references identified using Scopus up until mid-2016. They come to a more measured conclusion than Brewer and Movahedazarhouligh:

> [R]igorous and empirically well-grounded studies currently seem to be rare in the research on flipped classrooms. Very few studies can make generalisable or transferrable knowledge claims and thereby contribute to the development of the field of interest around flipped classrooms. Therefore, it is difficult to identify when, under what circumstances and in what ways the flipped classroom approach might be relevant as a pedagogical choice.
>
> (p. 17)

This is a common problem in judging educational innovations, of course, as the enthusiasm and conviction of the innovators can override the need for careful evaluation. Perhaps more tellingly, those who have tried a flipped classroom approach, and have not found the anticipated improvements in student attitudes and performance, or have found the efforts involved too much are highly unlikely to seek to publish their findings.

A third synthesis, in this case a meta-analysis, by van Alten et al (2019) examined 114 studies published between 2006 and 2016 of flipped classrooms in higher and secondary education (104 of which reported on higher education). They found

> a small positive effect on learning outcomes, but no effect was found on student satisfaction regarding the learning environment. In addition, we found considerable heterogeneity between studies. Moderator analyses showed that students in flipped

classrooms achieve higher learning outcomes when the face-to-face class time was not reduced compared to non-flipped classrooms, or when quizzes were added in the flipped classroom.

(p. 1)

Another meta-analysis, focusing on the learning outcomes of college students, is provided by Shi et al (2019a), a Chinese/American team. Searching Web of Science, the Education Resources Information Center (ERIC) and Elsevier ScienceDirect, they identified thirty-three relevant studies and concluded that

the pedagogical approach was the only significant factor examined that influences the effectiveness of flipped classroom instruction. These results indicate that the flipped classroom instructional model helps college students to improve their cognitive learning ... The flipped classroom was also found to be more effective when instructors integrate individualized active and collaborative pedagogical approaches.

(pp. 1–2)

The latter approaches will, of course, necessitate a good deal of planning and thought on the part of the instructor, so the flipped classroom should not be seen as an easy ride.

Xu et al (2019) offer both a meta-analysis and a systematic review, with a particular focus on the use of the flipped classroom in nursing education in China (n = 22). They reached very positive conclusions: 'The flipped classroom increased the students' skills score compared with the traditional teaching method. Additionally, it improved the cooperative spirit and sense of teamwork, practical ability, enjoyment of the course, expression and communication, the curriculum's effects, interest in participation, ability to think and analyse problems, and resolution and resilience' (p. 67).

Kraut et al (2019) provide a critical review of the medical education literature on the flipped classroom, identifying fifty-four relevant publications. They draw a number of conclusions:

[A] flipped classroom ... is effective for procedural learning ... students in a flipped classroom setting may learn more than students in a traditional classroom setting ... the flipped classroom model is beneficial for learning higher cognition tasks ... learners are more engaged with flipped classroom, but satisfaction depends largely on teacher prep work.

(pp. 530–3)

Lo and Hew (2019) focus on engineering education, providing a meta-analysis of twenty-nine studies of K-12 and higher education classrooms over the ten-year period from 2008 to 2017. Most, twenty-five, of the studies were from the United States and all but one concerned higher education. They conclude that

[c]ompared to the traditional lecture-based approach, our meta-analysis provides quantitative evidence of an overall significant effect in favor of the flipped classroom. The result of our moderator analysis further indicates that providing a review at the start of face-to-face instruction, along with individual and small-group activities during class time, offers the best method for improving student achievement in some engineering

courses. We, therefore, suggest such a combination of in-class activities be used in the future practice of flipped engineering courses. In future research, we recommend student achievement data and the design of flipped classroom activities be thoroughly reported to enhance our understanding of the effects of the flipped classroom and each instructional activity in engineering education.

(p. 539)

Despite such positive findings, however, the efficacy of flipped classrooms is still a matter of some debate.

Other types of instruction

As well as peer instruction, game-based learning, audience response systems and flipped classrooms, systematic reviews and meta-analyses of types of instruction have focused on a diverse range of topics. A substantial number of these, all meta-analyses, were carried out in the 1970s, 1980s and 1990s by two Americans, the Kuliks and their collaborators.

Meta-analyses by the Kuliks

Kulik and his colleagues were prominent relatively early in carrying out meta-analyses in this area. Many of these syntheses considered instructional approaches related to what we now know as distance, online or e-learning (see Chapter 7), but which were based on research carried out in conventional classrooms, which is why they are discussed in this chapter.

Thus, in 1979, Kulik, Kulik and Cohen published separate meta-analyses of Keller's personalized system of instruction (n = 75) and Postlethwait's audio-tutorial approach (n = 48) (1979a, 1979b), in both cases reporting generally positive results.

In the following year, they published a meta-analysis on the effectiveness of computer-based teaching (n = 59), finding 'small but significant contributions' (1980a, p. 525) to both course achievement and student attitudes, alongside substantial reductions in instructor's time. Kulik and Kulik returned to the topic five years later (1985) with a meta-analysis of 101 reports. They concluded:

Findings indicate that computer-based education [CBE] usually has positive effects on college students (CBE raised student examination scores by 0.26 standard deviations in the average study); CBE effects were somewhat lower in unpublished studies than they were in published reports; CBE effects were also somewhat lower in the hard, nonlife sciences than in the social and life sciences and education; CBE produced small but positive changes in student attitudes toward instruction and computers; and CBE also reduced substantially the amount of time needed for instruction.

(p. 1)

Kulik, Kulik and Cohen (1980b) examined instructional technology in general, with a meta-analysis of 312 studies, concluding that

> [t]he studies that we located gave us a basically positive picture of instructional technology. Results of most of the studies of student achievement and student ratings came out in favor of the classes taught with instructional technology ... It would be foolish, however, to pretend that the effects of instructional technology were large ones.
>
> (p. 204)

Kulik, Cohen and Ebeling (1980) published a further meta-analysis focusing on the effectiveness of programmed instruction in higher education (n = 57).

Kulik and Kulik (1980) focused on individualized instruction in general, identifying 213 studies in 209 published reports. They concluded from their meta-analysis that

> [i]ndividualised instruction has a positive effect on student achievement in the studies we located. In 155 of the 213 studies included in this meta-analysis, examination performance in the individualised class was superior to examination performance in the conventional class; 58 studies favoured conventional instruction. Of the 101 studies reporting a significant difference due to teaching method, 85 were in favour of individualisation, and 16 in favour of conventional teaching.
>
> (p. 65)

Cohen, Ebeling and Kulik (1981) provided a meta-analysis of visual-based college teaching (i.e. still projection, film, multimedia, closed circuit television, educational television, use of video for observation or in feedback: n = 74). They found that '[i]n the typical study, students learned slightly more from visual-based instruction than from conventional teaching ... visual-based instruction had no special effect on course completion, student attitudes, or the correlation between aptitude and achievement' (p. 26).

Nine years later, Kulik, Kulik and Bangert-Drowns (1990) carried out another meta-analysis, this time on the effectiveness of mastery learning programmes (n = 108). This built on the earlier synthesis of studies on Keller's personalized system of instruction; though it included some school-based studies, most of the research related to higher education. They concluded that

> [t]he effects appear to be stronger on the weaker students in a class, and they also vary as a function of mastery procedures used, experimental design of studies, and course content. Mastery programs have positive effects on student attitudes towards course content and instruction but may increase student time on instructional tasks. In addition, self-paced mastery programs often reduce the completion rates in college classes.
>
> (p. 265)

Overall, in carrying out a succession of related meta-analyses, the Kuliks and their collaborators were able to demonstrate that a range of instructional innovations – focusing on the individualization or personalization of instruction and the use of technological aids – could have positive effects on the learning experience and results.

Other research syntheses

In addition to the Kuliks, many other researchers have undertaken syntheses of research into other types of instruction in higher education. Their topics have been enormously varied, from note-taking to instructional animation to intelligent tutoring systems to English medium instruction.

Timmerman and Kruepke (2006) followed up the Kuliks' work over twenty years later in a meta-analysis of the effectiveness of computer-assisted instruction (CAI), identifying 118 relevant studies published between 1985 and 2004.

> The results indicate that students who use CAI fare better than their traditional instruction counterparts. Exploration of variables that may moderate effects indicated that (1) CAI social science content was associated with the largest performance gains followed by physical sciences, life sciences, and language/humanities; (2) average effects were larger when CAI was compared to lecture/discussion; (3) CAI performance benefits were greater in studies published from 1985–1994 than 1995–2004; (4) CAI performance gains were greater for undergraduate students; and (5) CAI used multiple times had higher average effects than CAI used once. Analysis of media richness constructs revealed that (1) CAI delivered with an audio channel was associated with the highest performance gains, followed by text, text with graphics, video, and physical apparatus; (2) CAI that provided students with feedback did not yield larger effect sizes than CAI that did not; and (3) course specific CAI had larger effects than generally published CAI.
>
> (p. 90)

Henk and Stahl (1985) carried out a meta-analysis of research into the effectiveness of the rather older technology of note-taking to enhance recall from lectures (n = 21). The '[r]esults indicated that the process of taking notes in itself does little to enhance recall performance (encoding hypothesis), but that permitting students to review their own notes (external storage hypothesis) clearly results in superior recall achievement' (p. 1). There would, though, seem to be little point in taking notes if they were not to be reviewed at some point. Kobayashi (2005) updated this work twenty years later in a meta-analysis of fifty-seven studies, mostly relating to higher education, confirming a positive but modest effect.

More recently, Hoffler and Leutner (2007) carried out a meta-analysis to compare the benefits of instructional animation and static pictures, identifying twenty-six relevant studies (seventeen of which concerned higher education) published between 1973 and 2003 and providing seventy-six comparisons:

> [W]e found a rather substantial overall advantage of animations over static pictures, and this advantage becomes particularly evident under specific combinations of instructionally relevant circumstances. There is evidence that animations are specifically superior to static pictures when the depicted motion in the animation explicitly refers to the topic to be learned. However, when the visualization is intended to play a decorational rather than a representational role, animations are not superior to static pictures.
>
> (pp. 735–6)

This confirms that the use of additional stimuli can have positive effects when they are relevant, but not if they are used just for the sake of it.

In a related study, Adesope and Nesbit (2012) examined the issue of verbal redundancy – from the concurrent presentation of text and speech – in multimedia learning environments, conducting a meta-analysis of fifty-seven studies, mostly focused on postsecondary education. They found that

> outcomes comparing spoken–written and written-only presentations did not differ, but students who learned from spoken–written presentations outperformed those who learned from spoken-only presentations. This effect was dependent on learners' prior knowledge, pacing of presentation, and inclusion of animation or diagrams. Specifically, the advantages of spoken–written presentations over spoken-only presentations were found for low prior knowledge learners, system-paced learning materials, and picture-free materials. In comparison with verbatim, spoken–written presentations, presentations displaying key terms extracted from spoken narrations were associated with better learning outcomes and accounted for much of the advantage of spoken–written over spoken-only presentations.
>
> (p. 250)

Steenbergen-Hu and Cooper (2014) provide a meta-analysis of research (n = 35) into the effectiveness of intelligent tutoring systems (ITS: adaptive, interactive, computer-assisted learning environments). They came to a series of helpful conclusions:

> (a) Overall, ITS had a moderate positive effect on college students' academic learning; (b) ITS were less effective than human tutoring, but they outperformed all other instruction methods and learning activities, including traditional classroom instruction, reading printed text or computerized materials, computer-assisted instruction, laboratory or homework assignments, and no-treatment control; (c) ITS's effectiveness did not significantly differ by different ITS, subject domain, or the manner or degree of their involvement in instruction and learning; and (d) effectiveness in earlier studies appeared to be significantly greater than that in more recent studies.
>
> (p. 331)

Belland et al (2017) carried out a meta-analysis of empirical research (n = 144) on computer-based scaffolding (i.e. support) in STEM (science, technology, engineering and mathematics) education. They reported that the

> [r]esults of our random effect meta-analysis (a) indicate that computer-based scaffolding showed a consistently positive effect on cognitive outcomes across various contexts of use, scaffolding characteristics, and levels of assessment and (b) shed light on many scaffolding debates, including the roles of customization (i.e., fading and adding) and context-specific support. Specifically, scaffolding's influence on cognitive outcomes did not vary on the basis of context-specificity, presence or absence of scaffolding change, and logic by which scaffolding change is implemented. Scaffolding's influence was greatest when measured at the principles level and among adult learners.
>
> (p. 309)

The provision of additional instructional resources, like intelligent tutoring systems or computer-based scaffolding, is likely, therefore, to have a positive effect overall. It will also, however, like games-based learning, come with a cost, so some cost-benefit analysis is needed to justify their usage.

Macaro et al (2018) offer a systematic review of English medium instruction (EMI) in higher education (n = 83), which is – with the acceptance of English as the modern lingua franca – one of the major growth areas of higher education provision outside of the English-speaking countries. They 'conclude that key stakeholders have serious concerns regarding the introduction and implementation of EMI despite sometimes recognising its inevitability. We also conclude that the research evidence to date is insufficient to assert that EMI benefits language learning nor that it is clearly detrimental to content learning' (p. 36). These are rather mixed findings, which must cast some doubt on policies of pursuing English medium instruction largely for financial benefit.

However, Rubio-Alcala et al (2019), carrying out a systematic review focusing on the quality indicators of bilingual, plurilingual and multilingual provision in higher education (n = 65), came to rather different conclusions. While they emphasized the limitations of the research so far carried out, they concluded that 'this type of education benefits students' performance and second language proficiency, with a higher impact on receptive skills … there is general satisfaction of participation with the programs' (p. 191). Bilingual, plurilingual or multilingual provision, where feasible, may, therefore, be preferable to purely English language provision.

Santos, Figueiredo and Vieira (2019) provide an integrative literature review of research into innovative pedagogical practices in higher education, focusing on student-centred learning. They analyse ten articles published between 2012 and 2016, concluding that '[t]he use of new pedagogical practices promotes the involvement of students, improves critical and creative thinking, reduces apathy and contributes to peer-learning' (p. 12). While the sample size is small, this would support the general conclusion that students appreciate it, and benefit, when their instructors try to do things somewhat differently.

Conclusions

- Peer instruction can be of considerable value, both for those students receiving the instruction and those delivering it.
- Games can provide an effective means of instruction, but their costs and benefits need careful and comparative assessment.
- Audience response systems can effectively enhance learning in large classrooms, particularly in certain disciplines.
- The flipped classroom, appropriately planned and supported, can offer a more demanding and engaging learning approach.
- Most reported instructional innovations, carried out carefully and for appropriate reasons, tend to have at least some positive effects.

Chapter 6
Course design – types of learning

Introduction

There is, as was pointed out in the introduction to Chapter 5, something of an overlap between 'types of instruction', the subject of that previous chapter, and 'types of learning', the focus of this one. Some of the topics discussed could undoubtedly have been included under either or both headings, or the chapters could have been combined (but that would have been rather unwieldy). However, the topics discussed in this chapter are, arguably, broader in scope and more all-encompassing approaches to course design than those examined in the previous chapter.

In total, thirty-five relevant research syntheses were identified for this chapter, comprising about 12 per cent of those identified for course design as a whole. They were fairly evenly spread between meta-analyses and systematic reviews, with eighteen of the former and fourteen of the latter, together with three substantive literature reviews.

There are a number of specialist higher education journals that focus on the topics discussed in this chapter: e.g. *Teaching in Higher Education*; *College Teaching*; the *Journal of Problem Based Learning in Higher Education*; and *Higher Education, Skills and Work-Based Learning*.

Some of the topics discussed in this chapter have been the subject of considerable bodies of research over the years, leading to a number of systematic reviews and/or meta-analyses. These include the various forms of group learning, problem-based learning, and the relations between learning and work. Other topics have been less, or only recently, studied, so are represented by a single systematic review or meta-analysis.

Group learning

Group learning has been a staple of education, and particularly higher education, from the beginning. The underlying idea is, of course, that students learn more, and more quickly, when they study alongside and with each other (see also the discussion of peer instruction, mentoring and tutoring in Chapter 5). Viewed from another perspective, of course, it would be unrealistic to educate students on a one-to-one basis, except in certain specialist contexts.

Group learning also mimics the kinds of relationships that students will need to function with in later life, particularly in working contexts (see also the discussion of achievement in Chapter 10). Most employers expect and require their employees to work effectively as part of a team, and this ability is a key skill sought in graduates.

There are, of course, many different forms of group learning, and it is also commonly referred to by cognate terms such as 'collaborative', 'cooperative' or 'team-based learning'. The questions then are, which forms to adopt or develop, what size and make-up of groups to employ, and how to make group learning most effective?

A relatively early meta-analysis of this field of research was completed by Springer, Stanne and Donovan (1999). Their particular focus was on the effectiveness of small group learning for undergraduates in STEM (i.e. science, technology, engineering and mathematics) subjects, though they used the alternative acronym and ordering of SMET. Defining small group learning as 'cooperative or collaborative learning among two to ten students' (p. 27), they searched the literature from 1980 onwards, identifying thirty-nine relevant studies. They concluded that

> [t]he meta-analysis demonstrates that various forms of small-group learning are effective in promoting greater academic achievement, more favorable attitudes toward learning, and increased persistence through SMET courses and programs. The magnitude of the effects reported in this study exceeds most findings in comparable reviews of research on educational innovations and supports more widespread implementation of small-group learning in undergraduate SMET.
> (p. 21)

More recently, Riebe, Gerardi and Whitsed (2016) focused their systematic review on 'the conditions and influences affording or constraining teamwork pedagogy' (p. 619). Analysing fifty-seven articles, they discovered that

> [e]ducators prioritized instruction, curriculum design, team composition, and assessment factors when researching teamwork pedagogy. The interactive effects of educator, student, and institutional factors and their influence on transaction costs were presented as affordances and constraints shaping the uptake of teamwork pedagogy, thereby providing a critical insight for educators engaged with teamwork as part of their course design.
> (p. 640)

The emphasis here is on the efforts necessary, primarily from the instructor and the students, to incorporate worthwhile group learning activities within a course. From an institutional point of view, suitable and flexible learning spaces, possibly including multiple smaller rooms, also have to be available. Using group learning is not, therefore, a resource neutral strategy.

Dearnley et al (2018) focused on the use of team-based learning (TBL) in the particular context of nursing and midwifery education. Their systematic review of articles published between 2011 and 2017 identified sixteen relevant studies. They concluded from them that

> [t]here is a tentative, though growing body of evidence to support TBL as a strategy that can impact on student engagement, student satisfaction, attainment, practice development and transformative teaching and learning. The literature indicates that implementing TBL within the curriculum is not without challenge and requires a sustained and structured approach. Staff and students need to understand the processes involved, and why they should be adhered to, in the pursuit of enhanced student experiences and outcomes for nurses and midwives in Higher Education.
>
> (p. 75)

The investment of time and resource to develop group or team learning should, therefore, bring benefits. The issue is about the balance of costs and benefits.

Zhang and Cui (2018) also focused on nursing education, investigating what they termed collaborative learning (n = 29): 'The strategy of instruction was found useful for improving nursing knowledge and skill performance, improving student clinical competency, as well as promote [sic] student group skills and learning behavior (e.g., class engagement, motivation for learning, self-confidence)' (p. 378).

Collaborative learning was seen as having particular potential, but also greater demands, in inter-professional forms of learning in health care. This is where the range of specialists involved in health care – e.g. doctors, nurses, physiotherapists, social workers – are brought together to work cooperatively on particular patients' long-term care. Such approaches have more general relevance beyond health care in broader social and community work and in the emergency services.

Swanson et al (2019) carried out a meta-analysis to investigate the impact of team-based learning (TBL) on content knowledge: thirty relevant studies were identified, of which seventeen were suitable for meta-analysis. They found that

> [t]he overall mean effect size of 0.55 indicates a moderate positive effect of TBL on content knowledge when compared to non-TBL comparison groups. In addition, group size moderates the magnitude of this effect, with smaller groups associated with better outcomes.
>
> (p. 46)

The latter is an interesting finding, suggesting that groups need to be small enough so that all members can get to know each other, contribute and benefit. This would also make 'freeloading' or 'loafing' (i.e. not participating but still benefitting from the work of the group) less possible.

Cooley, Burns and Cumming (2015) examined the specific role of outdoor adventure education (OAE) in facilitating group work in higher education (n = 10):

> The studies reviewed provided some support in favour of OAE benefitting students' perceived groupwork skills, the functioning of existing student work groups, attitudes and confidence towards groupwork, and the cooperative and social environment within higher education. However, this evidence was limited by methodological weaknesses such as the use of non-validated questionnaires and a variety of problems with study design and analytical methods. Research was also lacking into the long-term impact of OAE on students' groupwork behaviour and their experience of higher education and subsequent employability.
>
> (p. 567)

Outdoor adventure approaches are also extensively applied in other levels of education and in the workplace (e.g. in management training).

From this broader perspective, Poitras (2012) focused specifically on the issue of conflicts within groups, comparing research in university and work settings. His meta-analysis of twenty-eight studies came up with two key findings:

> Firstly, all effect sizes were significant and the association between relationship conflict and satisfaction level was the strongest impact of conflict. Our results suggest that satisfaction, as well as related variables such as stress, intention to quit and commitment, should be included more often in conflict studies. Secondly, research setting was found to be a significant moderator of the association between task conflict and satisfaction level, task conflict and performance level as well as relationship conflict and performance level. Our results suggest that research conducted in a university setting likely underestimated the impact of conflicts on satisfaction and performance levels because subjects have a lower vested interest in conflicts that arise in a university setting than in the workplace.
>
> (p. 128)

Overall, then, while it is clear that the various forms of group learning can have a positive impact on individual students' learning and overall experience, there are downsides. Group learning does not suit all students equally well. Some individuals may 'freeload', particularly in larger groups, and where all aspects of the group's work are left up to its members to manage, high performers' grades may be held down, and there may be conflicts between the group members. As with all forms of learning, careful planning and management is called for.

Problem-based learning

Problem-based learning (PBL) embodies the belief that learning is most interesting and productive when it is based on investigating and attempting to answer real-world problems. Problems may be posed to, and answered by, individual students or, more commonly, groups (see the previous section). In some higher education institutions the entire curricula for particular subjects may be based on this approach.

Problem-based learning has been the subject of a series of meta-analyses, most notably in medical education (e.g. Gao et al 2016, Huang et al 2013, Koh et al 2008, Vernon and Blake 1993, Wang et al 2016), where the approach is most popular. In the earliest of these studies, Vernon and Blake (1993) synthesized the available research from 1970 to 1992, conducting five separate meta-analyses on thirty-five studies from nineteen institutions:

> PBL was found to be significantly superior with respect to students' program evaluations and measures of students' clinical performance. PBL and traditional methods did not differ on miscellaneous tests of factual knowledge and tests of clinical knowledge ... The comparative value of PBL is also supported by data on outcomes that have been studied less frequently, i.e., faculty attitudes, student mood, class attendance, academic process variables, and measures of humanism. In conclusion, the results generally support the superiority of the PBL approach over more traditional methods.
> (p. 550)

Koh et al (2008) carried out a systematic review of thirteen studies, concluding that '[p]roblem-based learning during medical school has positive effects on physician competency after graduation, mainly in social and cognitive dimensions' (p. 34). Huang et al (2013) focused on dental education in China, carrying out a meta-analysis of eleven randomized control trials, finding that 'PBL had a positive effect on gaining higher theoretical and practical scores. However, the pooled result did not show any positive effect on gaining higher pass rates' (p. 377).

Gao et al (2016) focused on paediatric education, also in China, again presenting a meta-analysis of eleven randomized control trials. They concluded that '[t]he PBL group was significantly superior to the Lecture-Based Learning group for the paediatrics theoretical test score, case analysis score and overall student satisfaction, and the differences were statistically significant' (p. 136). Wang et al (2016) present a third Chinese meta-analysis, this time relating to physical diagnostics education and finding that 'PBL in physical diagnostics education in China appeared to be more effective than [sic] traditional teaching method in improving knowledge and skills' (p. 1).

The evidence is, then, perhaps particularly in medical education and in China, that problem-based learning is often a better alternative to more conventional forms of education. Constructing, or re-constructing, the curriculum in a problem-based format will, of course, take some time and effort but should involve no more maintenance than a conventional curriculum when this has been done. There would, however, potentially be additional ongoing costs if group work was involved.

Problem-based learning has also attracted more general research syntheses. In a relatively early example, Albanese and Mitchell (1993) conducted what they termed 'a meta-analysis type review' (p. 52) of the literature published between 1972 and 1992. While they were based in a medical school, their analysis was more general. They concluded that

> [c]ompared with conventional instruction, PBL ... is more nurturing and enjoyable; PBL graduates perform as well, and sometimes better, on clinical examinations and faculty evaluations; and they are more likely to enter family medicine. Further, faculty tend to enjoy teaching using PBL. However, PBL students in a few instances scored lower on basic sciences examinations and viewed themselves as less well prepared in the basic sciences than were their conventionally trained counterparts. PBL graduates tended to engage in backward reasoning rather than the forward reasoning experts engage in, and there appeared to be gaps in their cognitive knowledge base that could affect practice outcomes. The costs of PBL may slow its implementation in schools with class sizes larger than 100.
>
> (p. 52)

Consequently, they cautioned against its widespread adoption until more was known, which the later medical education studies at least partly provided.

Dochy et al (2003), a Belgian/Dutch team, conducted a meta-analysis of forty-three articles to examine the effects of problem-based learning on knowledge and skills and to identify possible moderators of these effects. They found that

> there is a robust positive effect from PBL on the skills of students. This is shown by the vote count, as well as by the combined effect size. Also no single study reported negative effects. A tendency to negative results is discerned when considering the effect of PBL on the knowledge of students. The combined effect size is significantly negative. However, this result is strongly influenced by two studies and the vote count does not reach a significant level. It is concluded that the combined effect size for the effect on knowledge is non-robust. As possible moderators of PBL effects, methodological factors, expertise-level of students, retention period and type of assessment method were investigated. This moderator analysis shows that both for knowledge and skills-related outcomes the expertise-level of the student is associated with the variation in effect sizes. Nevertheless, the results for skills give a consistent positive picture. For knowledge-related outcomes the results suggest that the differences encountered in the first and the second year disappear later on. A last remarkable finding related to the retention period is that students in PBL gained slightly less knowledge, but remember more of the acquired knowledge.
>
> (p. 533)

Whether that last finding is so remarkable is questionable. Knowledge gained through active, investigative learning is likely to be better remembered. On the other hand, the amount of interaction and in-depth exploration required by a problem-based learning curriculum is likely to limit the scope of the curriculum to some extent.

Two years later, Gijbels et al (2005), the same team as Dochy et al (2003), examined the influence of assessment on the effects of problem-based learning through a meta-analysis (n = 40). They concluded that '[i]n general, the effect of PBL differs according to the levels of the knowledge structure being measured. PBL had the most positive effects when the focal constructs being assessed were at the level of understanding the principles that link concepts, the second level of the knowledge structure' (p. 45).

More recently, in their meta-analysis, Liu et al (2019) also focused on the effects of problem-based learning, but in the particular context of pharmacology education (i.e. we are back to medical education). Based on thirty-seven controlled trials:

> The meta-analysis found that PBL had a positive effect on gaining higher theoretical scores assessed through examinations. The results of questionnaires for students' feedback showed that PBL was superior to conventional teaching methods in improving students' outcomes of self-study, learning interest, team spirit, problem solving, analyzing, scope of knowledge, communication, and expression. These results suggest that PBL in pharmacology education is considered superior to traditional lecture-based learning.
>
> (p. 43)

Kim et al (2019), in a more generic study, focused on the use of computer-based scaffolding to support problem-centred instruction for STEM education. Their meta-analysis included studies of all levels of education (n = 145), though about half the sample related to higher education. They concluded that

> computer-based scaffolding leads to positive effects when students are solving problems individually, as well as in pairs, triad, and small groups. Effect sizes were larger when students worked in pairs and individually than when working in triads and small groups, and the effect size was significantly greater when specific guidance for collaboration was not provided in addition to scaffolding, versus when it was. (p. 23)

All in all, then, the results of research syntheses of problem-based learning, in medical education and beyond, are generally positive, suggesting that it is a better approach than more conventional forms of teaching. While less knowledge might be covered in the time available, this knowledge is likely to be more in-depth and more memorable.

Learning and work

Research syntheses have been used to examine related aspects of the link between learning and work in course design. The topics covered include the impact of work placements, education designed to encourage entrepreneurial activity, work-integrated learning and the effect of employment on studying (see also Chapter 10, on outcomes, particularly the section on achievement, where the question of what students take from higher education into the workplace is discussed).

Placements and internships

Placements, internships, practica and cognate terms describe arrangements where students spend a portion of their time away from the university, typically in a relevant work environment. This is standard practice when students are studying professional subjects – e.g. accounting, architecture, engineering, law, medicine, nursing, social work, teaching – designed to prepare them for employment in a specific sector and/or a specific role. The placement may be for an extended period (e.g. one year out of a four-year 'sandwich' degree) or may involve regular shorter periods throughout the degree programme.

As well as preparing students for their future working lives, placements and internships can help them to decide whether this is the sector they wish to work in and – if so – in which role. From the employers' perspective, placements help to ensure a supply of work-ready graduates and may also serve a specific recruitment role.

Velez and Giner (2015) considered the effects of business internships on students, employers and higher education institutions. They identified fifty-seven relevant studies:

> The majority of the qualitative studies (n = 24) indicated positive evaluations of the internship experience. In addition, the quantitative studies (n = 33) provided empirical evidence of the effectiveness of business internships in improving students' chances of employment in a career-oriented job after graduation; enhancing their job and social skills; and assisting them in deciding their career paths. Employers gain the benefit of students' emerging skill sets at highly affordable compensation rates and save on recruitment costs because they can hire prospective workers from among their interns. They also benefit from stronger ties with the academic world. Internship programs are also beneficial to higher education institutions in that colleges and universities can attract potential students, enhance their reputation and visibility, and strengthen bonds of collaboration between the academic world and industry.
>
> (p. 127)

From this assessment it would seem that, overall, business internships were meeting their intended aims.

In an earlier literature review, Ryan, Toohey and Hughes (1996) looked at the purpose, value and structure of the practicum, which fulfils a similar role to the business internship in professional higher education. They found that

> whilst the practicum is widely accepted as a valuable and successful component of professional education, it has a number of shortcomings; and the lack of good quality research into the practicum makes it difficult to draw unequivocal conclusions … [There were] persistent problems … with practicum placements which are poorly structured and poorly supervised, resulting in experiences that may actually undermine learning.
>
> (pp. 355, 370)

This is a more critical conclusion than that arrived at by Velez and Giner, reflecting the difficulties in organizing and overseeing sufficient good quality placements to meet student demand.

Inceoglu et al (2019) carried out a systematic literature review of research on work placements (n = 40), finding that '[p]lacement participation elicits an overall positive (but small) effect on career outcomes: graduates who completed a work placement found employment more quickly. Work placements also changed students' perceptions of self-efficacy, their knowledge, skills, and attitudes' (p. 317).

However, there were criticisms of the quality of the research being synthesized: 'the reviewed studies were overwhelmingly pragmatic rather than theory-driven in their approach, which was closely linked to the observations that methodological approaches were often not sufficiently developed ... Hardly any of the reviewed studies examined the processes by which the placement experience affects career outcomes' (p. 328). Clearly, there is plenty of scope for further research in this area.

Eick, Williamson and Heath (2012) focused on placements in nurse education and, in particular, on their role in student attrition (see also the discussion in Chapter 10). Their search identified eighteen relevant studies published between 1995 and 2011. They concluded that '[a]s for all student attrition, there was no single reason (related to placements) why students chose to leave, however, being a young or male student were major factors, along with being exposed to unpleasant placement experiences, the attitudes of placement staff, and lack of support' (p. 1299).

Lee et al (2019) present a systematic review of research into field placement outcomes for international students (n = 27), who could be expected to find them particularly challenging. They did not come to firm conclusions, however, 'primarily due to the small sample sizes involved, research design limitations with no use of randomisation or comparison groups, and limited follow-up that had not investigated longer term outcomes, such as employment of students post-graduation' (p. 145).

Other learning/work relationships

In addition to work placements and internships, there are a myriad of other learning/work relationships that have been researched, some of which – entrepreneurship education, work-integrated learning and student employment while studying – have been the subject of research syntheses.

Nabi et al (2017) carried out a systematic review of the impact of entrepreneurship education (EE: i.e. education that encouraged students' entrepreneurial thinking and plans), based on 159 articles published between 2004 and 2016. They find the existing research to be not particularly helpful: 'EE impact research still predominantly focuses on short-term and subjective outcome measures and tends to severely underdescribe the actual pedagogies being tested' (p. 277). Much of the research on learning and work, like other topics, has its limitations.

Lasen et al (2018) examined the quality of work-integrated learning (WIL) – a model of practice where learning is embedded in the work experience – assessment design in higher education, identifying twenty relevant intervention studies published between 1990 and 2015. They found that

> high-quality design of assessment was characteristic of the field, albeit with opportunity for promotion of more robust WIL assessment partnerships. Resourcing and professional development need to support research-active WIL academics from all disciplines and their professional partners and students to (a) design and participate in assessment and reflective practices, which promote integration of students' learning, across university and work settings, and achievement of higher-order learning outcomes

and (b) pursue a collaborative research agenda involving robust evaluation research, inclusive of quantitative studies.

(p. 14)

Finally, looking at the relationship between learning and work in a rather different way, Neyt et al (2019) focused on studies published between 1997 and 2017 (n = 50) that had examined the impact of student work on educational outcomes. In other words, their focus was on students who were working while they were studying, which is an increasingly common arrangement as more and more students have to meet rising fees and living costs themselves.

Interestingly, Neyt et al found that '[s]tudent employment seems to have a more adverse effect on educational decisions (continuing studies and enrolment in tertiary education) than on educational performance (test and exam scores)' (p. 896). However, while the decision not to continue study, or not to enrol for further study, might seem 'adverse' from the perspective of the higher education institution(s) involved, it might make perfect and positive sense to the student concerned, particularly if they have gained entry to a potentially remunerative career.

Other types of learning

In addition to group learning, problem-based learning, and the relations between learning and work, higher education researchers have investigated a diverse range of other types of learning, some of which have subsequently been the focus of systematic reviews or meta-analyses. Research into action research/active learning, service learning and learner-centred initiatives has been the subject of more than one synthesis.

Action research and active learning

Gibbs et al (2017) provide a literature review of the use of action research (AR) in higher education, focusing on teaching practice and student engagement. Action research is where research is undertaken, often in collaboration with the research participants, in order to improve practice (i.e. to take action). They concluded that

> [t]he intricacies of the relationship between pedagogic AR in higher education are impacted upon by the disciplines involved and the extent to which they and the professions embrace AR as a valued research method. How AR is used to research pedagogy in higher education is linked to this broader use of AR. Reviewing the current literature suggests that some of its strengths and weaknesses in relation to pedagogy and higher education are mirrored in its use in the broader disciplinary and professional arena.
>
> (p. 14)

The aim of action research in higher education should not be simply to improve teaching or learning practice and techniques, they argue, but 'the transformation of social, cultural, discursive and material conditions under which individual practice takes place' (p. 14).

Freeman et al (2014) focus on the related field of active learning and its effect on student performance in STEM subjects. In active learning, learning is stimulated by pursuing relevant activities (see also the earlier discussion in this chapter of problem-based learning, which some would class as a form of active learning). Their meta-analysis considered 225 studies and came up with positive results:

> [A]verage examination scores improved by about 6% in active learning sections, and ... students in classes with traditional lecturing were 1.5 times more likely to fail than were students in classes with active learning. The results ... support active learning as the preferred, empirically validated teaching practice in regular classrooms.
>
> (p. 8410)

Active learning would appear, therefore, to better engage students; however, like all more innovative types of learning, there are added costs in developing and maintaining relevant curricula.

Service learning

Service learning is a particularly popular approach in the United States, though its availability and usage vary by institution and subject. It involves students spending some of their time unpaid, but usually for course credit, working in the community. While this is typically in the area local to the higher education institution with which they are studying, international forms of service learning have also become popular in recent years.

Novak, Markey and Allen (2007) present a meta-analysis of nine studies that compared courses with and without a service learning – 'a pedagogical model that connects meaningful community service experiences with academic course learning' (p. 150) – component. They came to positive conclusions:

> [C]ommunity service learning improves academic understanding of subject matter, skills learned, and ability to apply knowledge and reframe complex social issues ... service learning consistently provides improvement in these desired outcomes when compared to programs or courses without such service learning opportunities ... the failure to provide students an opportunity to participate in the exercise reduces the level of student improvement.
>
> (p. 153)

Part of the observed improvement, of course, depends upon the relevance of the service learning to what the individual student is studying or where they are seeking to work after graduation.

More recently, Salam et al (2019) have provided a systematic review of studies of service learning (n = 133). They concluded that 'service learning offers reciprocal benefits for all stakeholders, by imparting significant contributions in the overall betterment of local community ... [and] has been widely adopted in several academic disciplines' (p. 17).

As with placements and internships, however, providing service learning opportunities – unless it is left up to the students to organize these themselves – does require some dedicated staffing to put in the work required to initiate links and maintain ongoing relationships with relevant community organizations.

Learner-centred initiatives

The common factor behind the research syntheses considered in this subsection is that they all focus on the close involvement of the student or learner (of course, some of the other approaches discussed in this chapter have this focus as well).

Cornelius-White (2007) carried out a meta-analysis of research into learner-centred teacher-student relationships, arguing that 'positive teacher-student relationships are associated with optimal, holistic learning' (p. 113), a point which most teachers would find hard to disagree with. He synthesized '119 studies from 1948 to 2004 with 1,450 findings and 355,325 students' (p. 113) and concluded that

> [o]verall, learner-centered teacher variables have above-average associations with positive student outcomes ... Positive relationships, nondirectivity, empathy, warmth, and encouraging thinking and learning are the specific teacher variables that are above average compared with other educational innovations. Correlations for participation, critical thinking, satisfaction, math[ematics] achievement, drop-out prevention, self-esteem, verbal achievement, positive motivation, social connection, IQ, grades, reduction in disruptive behaviour, attendance, and perceived achievement are all above average and are presented in decreasing order.
>
> (p. 134)

While these findings may be unsurprising, however, they are hard for teachers to implement consistently on a day-to-day basis (see also the discussion of teaching in Chapter 4).

Mercer-Mapstone et al (2017), an Australian/American/Canadian collaboration, provide a systematic literature review of research into students as partners (SaP), an approach which 're-envisions students and staff as active collaborators in teaching and learning' (p. 1). They stress four themes:

> [T]he importance of reciprocity in partnership; the need to make space in the literature for sharing the (equal) realities of partnership; a focus on partnership activities that are small scale, at the undergraduate level, extracurricular, and focused on teaching and learning enhancement; and the need to move toward inclusive, partnered learning communities in higher education.
>
> (p. 1)

They also emphasize 'that SaP as a theory, an ethos, and a practice is as complex, nuanced, and multifaceted as the educational institutions within which partnerships unfold' (p. 19). Clearly, this is not a strategy to be adopted by the uncommitted.

Levett-Jones, Cant and Lapkin (2019) offer a systematic review of the effectiveness of empathy education (education designed to improve one's ability to recognize others' feelings), in this case specifically for undergraduate nursing students, finding that

[n]ine of 23 empathy education studies in undergraduate nurse education demonstrated practical improvements in empathy. The most effective interventions were immersive and experiential simulations that focused on vulnerable patient groups and provided opportunities for guided reflection. We noted the research designs were limited in terms of levels of evidence and use of subjective measures.

(p. 80)

Empathy is clearly a quality that is sought in nurses but was also one of the factors identified by Cornelius-White (2007) in his analysis of teacher-student relationships in higher education generally.

Other syntheses

Olivares-Donoso and Gonzalez (2019) report on a review of twenty studies on student participation in undergraduate research and research-based courses in science. They found that

in general, both experiences are beneficial. From this finding, we propose that universities should make efforts to design research experiences where students play an active role and are not only following predetermined sets of activities, that a proper balance between research-based courses and undergraduate research should be sought, that both experiences should be explicitly integrated across the curriculum, and that particular features of each institution need to be considered in designing and developing research experiences.

(p. 105)

Those proposals might, however, seem to be a little far-reaching and in need of further supportive research.

Nesbit and Adesope (2006) undertook a meta-analysis of studies that examined student learning using node-link diagrams (also known as concept and knowledge maps), identifying fifty-five studies and sixty-seven effect sizes, most of which were of postsecondary students. They came to positive conclusions, but with some reservations:

The meta-analysis found that, in comparison with activities such as reading text passages, attending lectures, and participating in class discussions, concept mapping activities are more effective for attaining knowledge retention and transfer. Concept mapping was found to benefit learners across a broad range of educational levels, subject areas, and settings. Much of this benefit may be due to greater learner engagement occasioned by concept mapping in comparison with reading and listening, rather than the properties of the concept map as an information medium. There is evidence that concept mapping is slightly more effective than other constructive activities such as writing summaries and outlines. But the small size of this effect raises doubts about its authenticity and pedagogical significance. The advantages of concept mapping were more pronounced in better-designed studies, particularly those that used random assignment of participants to treatment groups.

(p. 434)

These results might be compared with those on the benefits of note-taking (discussed in Chapter 5 in the other syntheses sub-section).

Finally, Chernikova et al (2019), a German research team, offer a meta-analysis of research into facilitating diagnostic competences in medical and teacher education (n = 35). They conclude that

> [d]iagnostic competences are facilitated effectively through problem-solving independent of the learners' knowledge base. Scaffolding types providing high levels of guidance are more effective for less advanced learners, whereas scaffolding types relying on high levels of self-regulation are more effective for advanced learners.
>
> (p. 1)

Here, scaffolding refers to the support given to the learners involved, which may come from the teacher or the students themselves employing self-regulated learning strategies (discussed further in Chapter 4).

Conclusions

- Group learning can have a positive impact on individuals' learning, while developing relevant skills for their working lives.
- Problem-based learning is well established and generally effective, particularly for deep learning and retention.
- The linkages between learning and work are multifaceted and multi-directional, but far from fully researched.
- All of the different kinds of interventions discussed come with costs, chiefly in terms of staff time, so require careful consideration before implementation.

Chapter 7
Course design – distance, online and e-learning

Introduction

Distance, online and e-learning are successive terms or labels, but by no means the only ones, applied to those forms of learning that do not occur in what may be regarded as the conventional or traditional face-to-face format. Instead, learners and their teachers are separated in time and/or space, and various forms of technology have been, and are, used to interface between them.

Indeed, one point to stress here is that there is nothing 'new' about these approaches. Thus, distance education – although the term only came into widespread use in the 1970s, it has already been largely superseded – dates back at least 200 years to the early days of correspondence education. And, if one were minded, one could take the history of these approaches back even further, perhaps 2,000 years to Paul's letters to the early Christian churches, or to similar examples.

It is important not to lose this perspective when discussing the application of modern technological developments to learning, as it is easily overlooked when examining the potential of the latest piece of kit or software. This is particularly so, as the proponents of the latest technology often seem to be looking for learning applications (i.e. sales), rather than starting with learning needs.

Here we should also emphasize that, fundamentally, the issues faced in delivering higher education through distance, online and e-learning are essentially the same as those faced in conventional face-to-face instruction. Hence, the studies and syntheses identified and discussed elsewhere in this book are of relevance to distance, online and e-learning, just as the studies examined in this chapter are of relevance more generally as well. In other words, you can put an 'e' or 'm' in front of 'learning', but it is still learning.

With the continuing expansion in the use of technology to support learning, either on its own or as a supplement to more conventional provision, substantial bodies of research have developed in these areas. These have in turn resulted in a mixed and growing array of systematic reviews and meta-analyses. Indeed, distance, online and e-learning accounted for sixty-nine of the research syntheses identified for this book (see Table 5 in Chapter 3), making up the largest proportion, 24 per cent, of the six sub-topics into which course design has been divided, and 13 per cent of the overall total.

One-third of these research syntheses, twenty-three, were in the form of quantitative meta-analyses. Just under two-thirds were qualitative, with thirty-one systematic reviews and fourteen substantive literature reviews identified. There was also one study (Gegenfurtner and Ebner 2019) which combined elements of meta-analysis and systematic review.

Some specialist academic journals, such as the *International Journal of Educational Technology in Higher Education*, focus on the topics discussed in this chapter. Others, such as the *British Journal of Educational Technology*, *Distance Education* and *Open Learning*, cover other levels or types of education as well.

In this chapter, we will begin by examining generic syntheses of research into distance, online and e-learning, before moving on to consider those that have compared their success or achievement to conventional face-to-face provision. We will then look at systematic reviews and meta-analyses that have considered research on mobile learning, one of the latest topics of interest, and blended and ubiquitous learning, the burgeoning field where learning technology is used to support conventional forms of instruction. Finally, more specialized research syntheses will be considered.

Generic syntheses

Distance, online and e-learning are successive terms that have been coined to refer to what is essentially the same phenomenon: i.e. teaching and learning that does not take place face to face but makes use of technology to enable interaction with learners wherever they are and at whatever time is convenient to them for learning (synchronously or asynchronously). These are not, however, the only terms that have been created or used to refer to this burgeoning but long-lasting phenomenon.

Indeed, one characteristic of this field is the wide variety of competing, succeeding and sometimes confusing terms in use, often in combination. For example, 'internet-based', 'mobile', 'networked', 'ubiquitous' and 'virtual reality-based learning' are all currently in usage, while older terms such as 'computer-assisted instruction', 'correspondence', 'at-a-distance' and 'open learning' have largely been superseded. In addition to remembering that there is little that is really new here, beyond the application of the latest technology to learning, one also needs to be clear about what is being discussed and how it relates to other examples or cases.

Moore et al (1990), writing in the American context, provide a relatively early literature review of research in the field of distance learning, covering all levels of education and with a focus on interactive telecommunications media. They come to measured conclusions:

> [W]e have the means to open educational opportunity to more learners and to improve the quality of education for all, including lifelong, continuing education to the adult

population. We can say with considerable optimism that when the distance education approach is correctly applied, it works well. Now it is time to move on from the period of small scale, uncoordinated and not well designed experimentation, too little coordinated planning of courses, too little cooperation in using delivery systems, too little over-all thinking by policy makers at state and national levels.

(p. 45)

This has the tone of a manifesto, arguing for the general adoption and articulation of the benefits of distance education. Perhaps unsurprisingly, that has yet to happen in the United States, where responsibility for education (including higher education) remains largely the responsibility of the individual states and where there is an extensive private sector of provision.

However, a number of countries, both developed and developing, have established national distance education universities, starting with the Open University in the United Kingdom (where Moore once worked) in 1969. Nevertheless, competition and lack of coordination remains the general rule, with most universities increasingly dabbling in online provision, or at least blended learning, to some extent.

Schlosser and Anderson (1994) produced another literature review of the field four years after Moore et al. They were also positive about the potential of the technology:

Students learning at a distance have the potential to learn just as much and as well as students taught traditionally. The factors that determine learning are the same for distant students as they are for traditional students, including student characteristics such as motivation, intelligence, level of preparation, and instructor variables such as quality of teaching, organization, and structure of the course. In spite of the fact that students perform as well in a distance education environment as in a traditional classroom, and appreciate the flexibility and convenience offered by distance education, students prefer the traditional classroom. Good distance teaching pedagogy is not fundamentally different from good traditional teaching technique.

(p. 28)

Of course, preference for the traditional classroom is not surprising, as this is what the vast majority experience in school. In such circumstances, distance education may seem a second-best alternative, only to be engaged in because face-to-face learning is impractical or impossible. This may be because of work or family commitments or – in countries like Australia, Canada, Russia or the United States – because the nearest higher education institution is simply so far away.

More recently, a number of North American (mostly Canadian-based) meta-analyses have sought to compare the benefits of distance and face-to-face higher education. Thus, Allen et al (2004) compared the effectiveness of distance and traditional education, finding 'little distinction between traditional and distance learning classrooms on the basis of performance' (p. 413). Interestingly, this varied depending upon the subject or context for the study:

For military-related instruction, the distance learning environment lowered performance (but the sample size was very small). For the natural sciences and education courses, the effect was virtually zero. However, for foreign language instruction, the use of distance technology demonstrated a clear superiority for that technology.

(p. 413)

Bernard et al (2004) went further, examining 232 studies published between 1985 and 2002, focusing on student achievement, attitude and retention (studies of the reasons for student success and achievement are considered further in the next section of this chapter). Similarly to Allen et al, they 'found evidence, in an overall sense, that classroom instruction and DE [distance education] are comparable, as have some others. However, the wide variability present in all measures precludes any firm declarations of this sort' (p. 416). They also noted that 'in general, DE research is of low quality, particularly in terms of internal validity (i.e., control for confounds and inequalities). We found a dearth of information in the literature; a more replete literature could have led to stronger conclusions and recommendations for practice and policy-making' (p. 416).

Having established the view that distance education was as good as conventional instruction, follow-up meta-analyses focused on how to deliver distance education most effectively. Lou, Bernard and Abrami (2006) examined studies looking at the effects of synchronous as compared to asynchronous provision (i.e. whether communications between learners and instructors took place at the same or different times):

Analyses of 218 findings from 103 studies were conducted according to how media were used to support DE [distance education] pedagogy. The results indicate that the effect sizes for synchronous instructor-directed DE were consistent and not significantly different from zero; in asynchronous DE, media only supporting independent learning was generally less effective than media supporting collaborative discussion among students, although both subsets were significantly heterogeneous.

(p. 141)

The effectiveness of distance education provision appeared, therefore, to be somewhat compromised when it was asynchronous, but also depended upon whether collaborative learning was involved (see also the discussion of group learning in Chapter 6). This is interesting, as it suggests that distance education is most effective when it closely mimics the conventional classroom experience.

Bernard et al (2009) then examined research on interaction treatments designed to facilitate student-student, student-teacher or student-content interactions in distance education provision:

The major conclusion from this review is that designing ITs [interaction treatments] into DE [distance education] courses, whether to increase interaction with the material to be learned, with the course instructor, or with peers, positively affects student learning. The adjusted average effect of 0.38 represents a moderate and significant advantage for ITs over alternative instructional treatments, including less prominent ITs. We can only speculate on the internal mental processes that these ITs foster, but we believe that an increase in cognitive engagement and meaningfulness may be the result of different amounts and types of interactivity induced through the presence of ITs.

(p. 1264)

In other words, as with face-to-face learning, distance education works better if students are encouraged or required to engage with each other (see also the discussion of peer instruction, mentoring and tutoring in Chapter 5), with their teachers and with the material they are studying.

Zhao et al (2005) carried out a meta-analysis of studies on the effectiveness of distance education, identifying fifty-one relevant articles:

> The results show that although the aggregated data of all available studies show no significant difference in outcomes between distance education and face-to-face education as previous research reviews suggest, there is remarkable difference across the studies. Further examination of the difference reveals a number of factors that led to the differences in outcomes across programs. This study led to some important data-driven suggestions for and about distance education: interaction is key to effective distance education; live human instructors are needed in distance education; the right mixture of human and technology seems most beneficial; distance education may be more appropriate for certain content; some learners may be more able to take advantage of distance education; and distance education seems to get better. The findings highlight an important and often neglected fact about the distance education literature: distance education programs, just like traditional education programs, vary a great deal in its [sic] outcomes. The study also suggests that existing conceptual frameworks for understanding face-to-face education are also applicable and should be applied to investigation efforts of distance education.
>
> (p. 1836)

There is a sense here of a 'coming of age' in distance education research, recognizing that, like face-to-face education, distance education varied in quality and effectiveness, that the reasons for this variation were increasingly understood, and that much could be learned from research on face-to-face education (and vice versa).

Jahng, Krug and Zhang (2007) carried out a meta-analysis of research published between 1995 and 2004 comparing student achievement in online and face-to-face post-secondary education, identifying twenty relevant studies from nineteen articles. Their findings both confirmed and advanced those of Bernard and his collaborators:

> The result of comparing overall weighted mean effect size of student achievement showed no significant difference between the two settings. However, the student achievement comparison revealed an interesting result when the primary studies were categorized by whether the experimental study conducted a pre-test or not. In the pre-tested group of studies, student achievement in ODE [online distance education] was significantly higher than F2FE [face-to-face education] even though there was no difference for prior knowledge between ODE and F2FE. On the other hand, student achievement from the no pre-test group of studies resulted in no significant difference between the two settings.
>
> (p. 1)

In other words, controlling for prior knowledge, there was evidence that online students significantly outperform those studying face to face. It is interesting to speculate on the reasons for this, which may have something to do with the greater amount of support materials provided, as a matter of course, for online students. Jahng, Krug and Zhang, however, focused on the methodological weakness of some of the studies included in their meta-analysis.

Means et al (2009) provide a meta-analysis of evidence-based practices in online learning. Searching the literature published between 1996 and 2008, they identified fifty-one independent effects comparing achievement from online and face-to-face learning:

> *The meta-analysis found that, on average, students in online learning conditions performed better than those receiving face-to-face instruction.* The difference between student outcomes for online and face-to-face classes – measured as the difference between treatment and control means, divided by the pooled standard deviation – was larger in those studies contrasting conditions that blended elements of online and face-to-face instruction with conditions taught entirely face-to-face. Analysts noted that these blended conditions often included additional learning time and instructional elements not received by students in control conditions. This finding suggests that the positive effects associated with blended learning should not be attributed to the media, per se.
>
> (p. ix, emphasis in original)

Four years later, Means et al (2013) published a revised version of this meta-analysis, using fifty effects from forty-five studies. They reiterated their conclusion that 'purely online learning has been equivalent to face-to-face instruction in effectiveness, and blended approaches have been more effective than instruction offered entirely in face-to-face mode' (p. 35). Most recently, Castro and Tumibay (2019), a Philippines pairing, have provided a literature review of studies of the efficacy of online learning courses, coming to generally supportive conclusions.

It might be argued, of course, that blended learning, in combining the benefits of face-to-face and online learning, would be expected to be more effective than either face-to-face or online learning on their own (see also the later discussion in this chapter of blended and ubiquitous learning).

Success and achievement

Several systematic reviews and meta-analyses have focused on the factors affecting success and achievement in distance, online and e-learning (rather than simply comparing it to conventional or face-to-face education, the focus of the previous section). Note that some syntheses of the application of earlier technologies, such as computer-assisted learning and programmed instruction, typically alongside face-to-face education in the classroom, are considered in Chapter 5, in the section on other types of instruction. The general issue of student achievement in higher education is also considered in Chapter 10.

In an early study, Schramm (1962) considered the relative merits of instructional television, using the results from 425 studies of both school and college education. He concluded:

(a) that under some conditions and used in some ways, instructional television can be highly effective and (b) that the pertinent question is no longer whether a teacher can teach effectively on television, but rather how, when, for what subjects, and with what articulation into classroom activities instructional television can most effectively be used.

(p. 165)

Forty years later, Machtmes and Asher (2000), building on the work of Schramm and others, employed meta-analysis to explore the effectiveness of what were then called telecourses (i.e. televised instruction) in higher education. They identified nineteen relevant studies published between 1943 and 1997 and concluded that '[t]here does not appear to be a difference in achievement between distance and traditional learners. Of the ten instructional features that were analyzed, only three had an impact on student achievement. These three features were type of interaction available during a broadcast, type of course, and type of remote site' (p. 42). The merits of distance and traditional learning would seem, therefore, to be relatively stable.

Cheawjindakarn, Suwannatthachote and Theeraroungchaisri (2012), Basak, Wotto and Belanger (2016) and Kebritchi, Lipschuetz and Santiague (2017) each focused on the factors underlying the success or otherwise of online higher education (see also de Laat et al 2006, Kattoua, Al-Lozi and Alrowwad 2016, Tess 2013, Yadav, Tiruwa and Suri 2017).

Cheawjindakarn et al (2012), a Thai team, identified nineteen papers on this topic published between 2000 and 2012. They identified five key critical success factors:

1) institutional management – market research, program framework, operational plan, cost effectiveness, 2) learning environment – course management system, technical infrastructure, access and navigation, 3) instructional design – clarify of objectives, content quality, learning strategies, psychology of learning, learning assessment, 4) services support – training, communication tools, help desk, and 5) course evaluation.

(p. 65)

Significantly, these factors could be applied, with perhaps only some minor changes in terminology, to face-to-face or conventional provision.

Basak et al (2016), a Canadian team, identified thirty-one relevant articles, which they used to construct a framework of critical success factors in the implementation of e-learning in higher education. Their listing was rather more comprehensive, or disaggregated, than that of Cheawjindakarn et al, detailing technological, institutional, pedagogical, management, ethical, evaluation, resources and social interaction factors, many of which were closely related to each other. Once again, however, the same factors could be applied with little change to all types of higher education.

Kebritchi et al (2017), an American team, covered the period 1990 to 2015 and came up with 104 articles that discussed the issues and challenges facing online higher education:

Three major categories of findings were identified: issues related to online learners, instructors, and content development. Learners' issues included learners' expectations, readiness, identity, and participation in online courses. Instructors' issues included changing faculty roles, transitioning from face-to-face to online, time management, and teaching styles. Content issues included the role of instructors in content development, integration of multimedia in content, role of instructional strategies in content development, and considerations for content development.

(p. 4)

This analysis gets much closer to the issues involved in successfully introducing online higher education, drawing attention to the need to re-train instructors used to face-to-face education, and to whether instructors are involved in the development of the material they are responsible for supporting.

Mothibi (2015), a South African researcher, carried out a meta-analysis of the results of fifteen studies published between 2010 and 2013, focusing on the relationship between e-learning and students' academic achievement. She found that the use of information and communication technologies in higher education teaching 'has a significant positive impact on students' educational overall academic achievements' (p. 6). This would again support the view that adding technological resources to the higher education teaching environment is likely to improve student engagement and performance (see also Bond et al 2020).

In another meta-analysis, Merchant et al (2014) examined virtual reality-based instruction (i.e. games (n = 13), simulations (n = 29) and virtual worlds (n = 27)), looking at studies of both K-12 and higher education (see also the discussion of game-based learning in Chapter 5). They found that each of these approaches was effective in improving learning outcomes, but that '[i]n general, game-based learning environments were more effective than virtual worlds or simulations, with overall effect sizes that were roughly twice as large' (p. 36).

Shi et al (2019) focused on technology-enabled active learning environments (TE-ALEs) in their meta-analysis, identifying thirty-one high-quality peer-reviewed journal articles:

Meta-analysis showed that the calculated effect size of TE-ALEs more positively influenced students' cognitive learning than traditional lecture-based environments. Moderator variable analysis suggested that social context, study design, and sample size were significant factors that influence the effectiveness of TE-ALE. TE-ALEs were found more effective when instructors employed individualized learning contexts as well as when bias was reduced in randomized controlled trials. TE-ALEs were also found to be more effective in small courses rather than in large courses.

(pp. 1–2)

DePape, Barnes and Petryschuk (2019), a Canadian team, examined students' experiences with virtual and augmented reality (VR and AR) through a systematic review (n = 23). They gave a measured appraisal of their usefulness:

Our review revealed VR and AR have the ability to engage higher education learners. However, these platforms cannot be used as a one size fits all model. That is, educators have to have a clear sense of how these platforms add but critically, do not replace traditional teaching and learning practices. Thus, there are factors to consider with these platforms as well as with the learners themselves when incorporating this technology at the higher education level.

(p. 42)

In other words, the great majority of students are unlikely to want to learn wholly through virtual or augmented reality means; contact with real people (teachers and other students) is highly desirable.

Garzón and Acevedo (2019) focused on the impact of augmented reality on students' learning gains, carrying out a meta-analysis of sixty-four articles published between 2010 and 2018. They concluded that augmented reality (AR)

> has a medium effect on students' learning gains. We compared AR applications, as a pedagogical resource, with other types of pedagogical resources including multimedia resources, traditional lectures, and traditional pedagogical tools. The results of this comparison indicate that the learning gains are higher when the intervention involves AR resources. Furthermore, there are certain conditions that moderate the effect of AR on the learning gains. The results indicate that the intervention is more effective when carried out in informal settings. Regarding the level of education, *Bachelor or equivalent level* students seem to benefit the most from AR. Likewise, AR systems show a higher impact when used to teach subjects related to *Engineering* and *Arts and Humanities*.
>
> (p. 256)

Radianti et al (2020) provide a systematic review of immersive virtual reality (VR) applications in higher education (n = 38). They also concluded that much more needed to be done before such practices became mainstream throughout higher education:

> The review results show that the interest in immersive VR technologies for educational purposes seems to be quite high, which is indicated by the variety of the research domains that have applied this technology in teaching. The majority of authors treated VR as a promising learning tool for higher education, however, the maturity of the use of VR in higher education is still questionable. Technologies described in most of the reviewed articles remained in an experimental state and were mostly tested in terms of their performance and usability. This article also reveals that very few design-oriented studies constructed their VR applications based on a specific learning theory, which serves as technical development guidance. Moreover, few papers thoroughly describe how VR-based teaching can be adopted in the teaching curriculum. These facts can hinder the rapid adoption of immersive VR technologies in to teaching on a regular basis. We acknowledge that, in some domains such as engineering and computer science, certain VR applications have been used on a regular basis to teach certain skills, especially those that require declarative knowledge and procedural–practical knowledge. However, in most domains, VR is still experimental and its usage is not systematic or based on best practices.
>
> (p. 26)

Taking a rather different tack, Henritius, Löfström and Hannula (2019) undertook a systematic review of research into students' emotions when engaging in virtual learning. They focused on ninety-one articles published between 2002 and 2017 in four selected international journals:

> The review showed that the most common emotion-related concept was 'satisfaction'. The most common context for the articles was a complete non-physical learning environment (e.g. Second Life). Approximately 60% of the articles used quantitative methods. The most common design for studying emotions was an explanatory design. Students' emotions were mainly studied through concepts related to emotion (e.g. 'satisfaction'). Yet only a few of the studies focused on the fluctuation of emotions in the course of events, relying instead on post hoc data that treat students' emotions as traits rather than states.
> (p. 80)

Research into success and achievement in distance, online and e-learning, therefore, embraces much the same themes as research into conventional or traditional learning (see also the discussion of outcomes in Chapter 10).

Mobile learning

Another version or generation of distance, online and e-learning, mobile learning or m-learning (i.e. the use of mobile telephones and devices for learning), has attracted recent research interest and been the subject of several systematic reviews during the last few years. All of the syntheses identified have been completed very recently, i.e. within the last decade or so.

Frohberg, Göth and Schwabe (2009), a Swiss team, provide a critical analysis of 102 mobile learning projects published before the end of 2007. They concluded that

> [M]obile Learning can best provide support for learning in context. There, learners are asked to apply knowledge and not just consume it. Novices are often not ready to do so, thus Mobile Learning should better address more advanced learners first. Content delivery can often be provided by other means; therefore, Mobile Learning should provide instruments to provoke deep reflection, communication and cooperation. With learners participating in pairs or groups, they do not become isolated. Special tools for monitoring and moderation give learners more elbow room, without losing transparency for the teacher and without risking disorientation of learners.
> (p. 323)

This usefully provides a series of guidelines, stressing that mobile learning should be seen as part of the overall learning experience (see also the discussion of blended learning in the next section), should involve group activities (see also the discussion of group learning in Chapter 6) and should make use of learning analytics (discussed in Chapter 8) to monitor activity.

Hung and Zhang (2012), an American team, using text mining techniques, provide what they term a categorical meta-trend analysis of 119 articles on mobile learning (ML) published in the period 2003 to 2008. Their key findings were as follows:

> (a) ML articles increased from 8 in 2003 to 36 in 2008; (b) the most popular domain in current ML is Effectiveness, Evaluation, and Personalized Systems; (c) Taiwan is most prolific in five of the twelve ML clusters; (d) ML research is at the Early Adopters stage; and (e) studies in strategies and framework will likely produce a bigger share of publication in the field of ML.
>
> (p. 1)

The pre-eminence of Taiwanese researchers is interesting: 'with strong and aggressive e-learning initiatives, Taiwan's government has been providing financial, managerial and legislative support to promote e-learning development in recent years ... Taiwan's e-learning initiatives were intended to stimulate the development of IT [information technology] industries' (p. 13).

Hwang and Tsai (2011), two Taiwanese researchers, also focused on trends in mobile and ubiquitous learning research, examining the output of six major technology-based learning journals over the period 2001–10 (n = 154; 59 of which focused on higher education), identifying and charting a rapidly growing field of study. Naismith et al (2004) also offer a literature review of research on mobile learning and technology. They identify six theory-based categories of activity – behaviourist, constructivist, situated, collaborative, informal and lifelong, learning and teaching support – and conclude that

> [m]obile technology can effectively support a wide range of activities for learners of all ages. While implementation examples can be broadly categorised within the main theories and areas of learning relevant to mobile technology, the most successful adopt a blended approach to their use. Mobile technologies provide for each student to have a personal interaction with the technology in an authentic and appropriate context of use. This does not mean, however, that the use of mobile devices is a panacea. Significant technological and administrative challenges are encountered along with a more ill-defined challenge: how can the use of mobile technologies help today's educators to embrace a truly learner-centred approach to learning?
>
> (p. 32)

There are two tensions evident here: first, that mobile technology is being applied to higher education because it exists, and most young people already make a great deal of use of it for other purposes; and, second, that mobile technology is seen as being useful in addition to, or alongside, existing practices.

Unlike the previous studies, Wu et al (2012), another Taiwanese team, carried out what they termed a meta-analysis. While it reports quantitative, as well as qualitative, findings, it might be better described as a combination of meta-analysis and systematic review. They examined 164 articles on mobile learning published between 2003 and 2010. They present

> seven new findings: 1) The research purpose of most mobile learning studies focuses on effectiveness, followed by mobile learning system design. 2) Surveys and experimental

methods were the preferred research methods, regardless of whether the research purpose focused on evaluation or design. 3) Research outcomes in mobile learning studies are significantly positive. 4) Mobile phones and PDAs [personal digital assistants] are the most commonly used devices for mobile learning, but these may be replaced in the future by new emerging technologies. 5) Mobile learning is most prevalent at higher education institutions, followed by elementary schools. 6) Mobile learning most frequently supports students in the professions and applied sciences, followed by the humanities and formal sciences. 7) The most highly cited articles fall into the categories of mobile learning system design and … effectiveness.

(p. 826)

Alrasheedi, Capretz and Raza (2015) collated 'results from 30 studies conducted in 17 countries, where 13 critical success factors were found to strongly impact m-Learning implementation' (p. 257). They concluded that 'although the aspects required for successful take-up are largely in place, they are heavily skewed toward the personal decision type of adoption' (p. 273). In other words, success was largely down to the individual students and staff involved.

Pimmer, Mateescu and Grohbiel (2016) examine thirty-six empirical papers focusing on mobile and ubiquitous learning, coming to positive conclusions about their potential dependent on the kinds of learning approaches being employed:

Instructionist qualities of mobile learning applications in higher education that are based on the presentational and testing capabilities of mobile devices can facilitate distributed and more frequent practice and can activate learners in and across classrooms. Beyond instructionism, the hybridisation of situated, collaborative and constructionist approaches via the use of mobile devices can also create new and unprecedented educational opportunities. This integration can result in situated awareness that connects knowledge from formal learning settings more directly with informal learning practices and, in turn, makes these educational experiences more readily available for later reflection and discussion in the classroom.

(p. 499)

The links made here between formal (i.e. in the classroom) and informal (i.e. when learning is not the primary goal) learning are illuminating, suggesting how the use of mobile learning may form part of a hybrid or blended learning experience.

Krull and Duart's (2017) systematic review identified 233 articles of interest, coming up with 3 key findings:

(a) mobile learning in higher education is a growing field as evidenced by the increasing variety of research topics, methods, and researchers; (b) the most common research topic continues to be about enabling m-learning applications and systems; and (c) mobile phones continue to be the most widely used devices in mobile learning studies, however, more and more studies work across different devices, rather than focusing on specific devices.

(p. 1)

This essentially confirms, but is more focused than, the earlier analysis by Wu et al (2012).

Most recently, Crompton and Burke (2018; see also Fu and Hwang 2018; Stretton, Cochrane and Narayan 2018) carried out a systematic review of published studies of the use of mobile learning in higher education over the period 2010–16 (n = 72):

> Major findings include that the majority of the studies focused on the impact of mobile learning on student achievement. Language instruction was the most often researched subject matter domain. The findings reveal that 74% involved undergraduate students and 54% took place in a formal educational context.
>
> (p. 53)

We may confidently expect this research field, and the number of research syntheses of it undertaken, to grow for the foreseeable future.

Blended and ubiquitous learning

Blended learning may be thought of as a midway stage between distance, open and online learning, on the one hand, and conventional face-to-face learning. It involves the use of forms of technology-enhanced learning, in varying combinations, alongside classroom learning. In contemporary higher education, it can be thought of as endemic, whether deliberately practised and labelled as such, as universities, departments and individual teachers (and students) rely more and more on the increasing number of available online materials and applications (including many, of course, that they have written themselves).

The term 'ubiquitous learning' is also sometimes used to refer to much the same thing, signifying that e-learning and mobile learning are now almost invariably linked up with more conventional forms of learning (ubiquitous learning is also discussed in tandem with mobile learning in the previous section). The (questionable) assumption here is that mobile devices are available to everyone everywhere and that we (or at least the young people who make up the bulk of the student body, though not their instructors) are all 'digitally literate'.

Bernard et al (2014), a prolific Canadian team referred to previously in this chapter, discuss how meta-analysis may be applied to studying blended learning and technology use in higher education. Schmid et al (2009) looked at the effectiveness of using computer technology in conventional higher education classrooms. Their meta-analysis of a representative sample of 231 studies identified

> three additional pieces of evidence suggesting how technology use relates to learning in higher education environments. First, in analyzing the overall effects of technology applications in higher education, we found that technology use appears to have its limits when it comes to affecting learning achievement … Second, we found that technologies supporting cognition, broadly defined, produce significantly better

results than technologies used to present or deliver content ... Third, we found a differentiation between the levels of technology saturation. Contrary to the intuitive expectation that 'more is better', conditions of low and moderate technology saturation led to larger average effects than more highly saturated classroom uses.

(p. 105)

This fits in with what many advocates of blended learning approaches argue; namely that a certain balance between technology use and conventional forms of learning is key, allowing each to support the other.

A follow-up study (Schmid et al 2014; see also Tamim et al 2011) of 1,105 studies published between 1990 and 2010 came to the conclusion that 'learning is best supported when the student is engaged in active, meaningful exercises via technological tools that provide cognitive support' (p. 285). Again, though, this conclusion, with the reference to technological tools omitted, would apply equally well to other forms of learning.

Brown (2016) provides a systematic review of studies on the adoption and use of online tools in face-to-face teaching (n = 58). He identified six 'influences that cut across the literature': 'faculty member's interactions with technology, academic workload, institutional environment, interactions with students, the instructor's attitudes and beliefs about teaching, and opportunities for professional development' (p. 1). In other words, it all depends upon the interest of, time available for, and support provided to individual instructors. A keen individual innovator can get so far, but for substantive and continuing change their department, and preferably their whole institution, has to be committed.

Vo, Zhu and Diep (2017) carried out a meta-analysis of the effect of blended learning on student performance (n = 40, with 51 effect sizes). They confirm

the effect of BL [blended learning] on student performance in a higher education setting. Although being considered as a small effect according to standard criteria (Cohen's d), the weighted mean effect is significant, which supports the perspective that BL can result in better learning outcomes for higher education students. By using disciplines and method of end-of-course evaluation as categorical moderators, we found that the effect of BL on student performance in STEM [science, technology, engineering, mathematics] disciplines is significantly higher than that of non-STEM disciplines. Nevertheless, end-of-course assessment, be it one-moment or multiple-component assessment, does not result in differences in the average mean effect.

(p. 26)

The greater impact on STEM, rather than non-STEM (often acronymed as HASS: humanities, arts and social sciences), is interesting. Vo, Zhu and Diep suggest that the explanation may be that 'STEM disciplines are grounded on well-established theories and thus teaching is more direct ... STEM subjects focus on the application and testing of ideas with linear argumentation (pure disciplines) and development of problem-solving and practical skills (applied disciplines)' (p. 24). This makes it somewhat more straightforward to develop online support materials.

Galvis (2018) provides a literature and good practices review of blended learning studies for those interested in changing their teaching and learning approach. Smith and

Hill (2019) reviewed ninety-seven articles published in fifteen selected journals during the period 2012 to 2017 that focused on blended learning in higher education. They found that

> [t]he research echoes many of the findings in earlier literature reviews on blended learning, namely that blended learning research tends to be practical in nature, small-scale, individually focused, and outcomes orientated. This supports the view that while blended learning has been a feature of higher education for approaching twenty years, it is still developing and is not yet fully embedded and institutionalised in higher education institutions either as an area of practice or a field of research. Its limited presence in the general higher education literature suggests that it remains something of specialised rather than general interest.
>
> (p. 392)

While their assessment seems reasonable, the same point might, again, be made about many developments and innovations in higher education.

Other researchers prefer the term 'ubiquitous learning' to either 'mobile' or 'blended learning', recognizing that the use of technological devices is so widespread throughout society, and thus learning, that it is no longer remarkable. A problem here is that the application of so many innovations has a positive effect on teaching and learning, in part because both students and instructors are enthused by trying something different. The issue then becomes which innovation or innovations, out of all of those possible, have the greatest impacts?

Virtanen et al (2017) offer a scoping literature review of ubiquitous learning environments in higher education. They claim that 'the use of ubiquitous learning environments heralds a new era in higher education. Ubiquitous learning environments enhance context-aware and seamless learning experiences available from any location at any time. They support smooth interaction between authentic and digital learning resources and provide personalized learning opportunities' (p. 1). However, they were only able to identify seven relevant published studies, so to claim 'a new era' may be a little ahead of the curve.

Mutlu-Bayraktara, Cosgun and Altan (2019) focus on the important issue of cognitive load (i.e. the amount of mental activity involved) in what they term multimedia learning environments, providing a systematic review of ninety-four articles published between 2015 and 2019. They found that

> [t]here was a tendency to use subjective methods more often than objective methods to measure cognitive load in investigations. In addition to cognitive load, learning, prior knowledge, and motivation were measured most frequently in these studies. In the reviewed studies, multimedia design, material type, presentation format, and individual differences were the most selected focus of research.
>
> (p. 1)

They then presented a range of recommendations for further research.

Bruguera, Guitert and Romeu (2019) provide a systematic review of research into the use of social media in professional development, which takes place within and beyond higher education. They identified forty-four relevant articles published between 2013 and 2017 and noted that

> numerous empirical studies coincide in indicating that social media can be a useful communication platform and serve as open and rich digital spaces for professionals to exchange information, opinions and ideas. Overcoming geographical, temporal and economic barriers is one of the key points to use them for professional development purposes. In addition, the speed with which social media content is updated is pointed out as also very relevant, though we also found serious concerns about what are referred to as privacy conflicts.
>
> (p. 12)

Other researchers have stuck to older terminologies and/or focused on particular technologies or approaches. Thus, Pinto et al (2012) carried out a systematic literature review of the use of what they referred to as internet and communication technologies in higher education, noting different views on their innovative nature and capacity to disrupt existing practices:

> Research embraces different perspectives, emphasizing that Internet and Communication Technologies use is not potentiating innovation or disruptiveness of more traditional forms of education, while another perspective argues that there is disruptiveness that is becoming ever more powerful, promoting changes in the roles and way teachers and students work. The present review suggests that web 2.0 technologies has [sic] promoted new forms of communication, interaction and sharing between users and content in formal education settings.
>
> (p. 850)

Kirkwood and Price (2014) provide a critical literature review of technology-enhanced learning (TEL) and teaching, terms which they note are loosely and differentially applied, covering the period from 2005 to 2010 (n = 47). They argue that

> [w]hile technology has increasing influence throughout higher education, there is still much to be learned about its effective educational contribution. This review has highlighted variations in both the purpose of TEL interventions and the ways that enhancement has been conceived. Underpinning this is a conflation of two distinct aims:
>
> • changes in the means through which university teaching happens; and
> • changes in how university teachers teach and learners learn.
>
> Many of the studies reviewed concentrated on the means: replicating and supplementing existing teaching. Few considered the second aim, how. The ways in which academics conceptualise teaching and learning with technology have significant and interrelated impacts upon their students' experience of learning. The potential of technology to transform teaching and learning practices does not appear to have achieved substantial uptake, as the majority of studies focused on reproducing or reinforcing existing practices.
>
> (p. 26)

In other words, the emphasis has been on the technology per se and not on how it might best be employed to support teaching and learning in higher education.

Gegenfurtner and Ebner (2019) focus specifically on the use of webinars (web-based seminars) in higher and professional education, carrying out both a systematic review and a meta-analysis. They identified twelve studies containing fifteen separate data sets:

> The findings suggest that webinars were slightly more effective than control conditions (online asynchronous learning management systems and offline face-to-face classroom instruction), but the differences were trivial in size. Differences were moderated by webinar, participant, achievement, and publication characteristics.
>
> (p. 1)

Webinars, therefore, offer a useful alternative format where other forms are not practical.

Lambert (2020) considers whether massive open online courses (MOOCs) – one of the most prominent educational catchphrases of the early twenty-first century – contribute to student equity and social inclusion. She carried out a systematic review of the research literature published between 2014 and 2018. She came to mixed but broadly positive conclusions:

> The literature fell into two main groups: empirical reports on outcomes for students, and those providing policy or practitioner guidance. A globally diverse set of 46 studies and reports were examined, including 24 empirical evaluations of programs reaching over 440,000 disadvantaged learners in both distance and blended learning settings. Most literature claimed an interest in advancing *student equity* (enrolled or tertiary preparation learners) and/or *social inclusion* (community learners) with low-skills, low confidence, and/or low levels of previous education. In contrast to the existing literature, this study found that there was a flourishing of multi-lingual and Languages other than English programs and those addressing regional socio-economic disadvantage. Most cases involved MOOCs and free online resources combined with additional forms of support, including face-to-face study groups.
>
> (p. 1)

There are clearly, therefore, a lot of materials available online to help support disadvantaged students.

Querol-Julian and Camiciottoli (2019) take a slightly different perspective, in presenting a systematic review (n = 61) of studies of the combined impact of online learning technologies and English medium instruction (EMI) in the international higher education classroom:

> Findings showed that most research has focused on the language-related issues of learners, and little attention has been paid to the crucial issue of lecture comprehension, which is mainly caused by the low level of proficiency of students/instructors and domain-specific vocabulary. Moreover, studies have almost exclusively addressed face-to-face settings, indicating a need to expand EMI research to include online lecture settings that are increasingly frequent in international higher education.
>
> (p. 2)

Despite the wealth of research into distance, online and e-learning in higher education that has been carried out, the criticisms remain. There is a lack of cumulation and sophistication, and the same research questions are still being addressed now, in much the same ways, that were first tackled twenty, thirty or forty years ago.

Other syntheses

Several other systematic reviews or meta-analyses have focused on particular aspects of distance, online or e-learning. Many of these parallel the research and research syntheses that have been carried out on conventional or face-to-face forms of higher education. Thus, here are three syntheses focusing on group learning online (see also Chapter 6).

Lou, Abrami and d'Apollonia (2001) carried out a meta-analysis of research into small group and individual learning using technology: '486 independent findings were extracted from 122 studies involving 11,317 learners' (p. 449). They found that

> on average, small group learning had significantly more positive effects than individual learning on student individual achievement (mean ES [effect size] = +0.15), group task performance (mean ES = +0.31), and several process and affective outcomes. However, findings on both individual achievement and group task performance were significantly heterogeneous ... variability in each of the two cognitive outcomes could be accounted for by a few technology, task, grouping, and learner characteristics in the studies.
>
> (p. 449)

Cherney, Fetherston and Johnsen (2018) provide what they term a meta-synthesis, but which I would term a systematic review, of the research literature on online course student collaboration (n = 41). They note that

> [a]lthough the existing literature has provided a number of insights on group formation, roles, interaction, collaboration, and social factors in online student groups, several limitations exist ... current literature presents conflicting results and conceptual definitions, is notably lacking in true empirical data, and is mainly written by, and for, education scholars.
>
> (p. 115)

Thomas and Thorpe (2019) focus on the facilitation of online groups in higher education, comparing that literature with that concerning face-to-face groups. They conclude that '[f]acilitating online groups effectively and using teacher presence to foster social presence places significant demands on teachers' time. Equipping academics and students with the skills to effectively learn online remains a big challenge' (p. 69).

Just as in face-to-face provision, therefore, while the use of group work in higher education can bring significant benefits, it does not necessarily reduce the input required from the instructor.

Conole and Alevizou (2010) produced a literature review of the use of Web 2.0 tools in higher education for the UK's then Higher Education Academy. They concluded that '[w]hile there is sufficient rhetoric about the potential of Web 2.0 technologies for higher education, the evidence of actual and situated practices on the effective use of Web 2.0 in the sector is fragmented' (p. 43).

Some syntheses have examined very specialist research literatures. Novak, Razzouk and Johnson (2012) focused on the use of social annotation tools in particular, finding only sixteen relevant studies and offering a series of recommendations for their application. Zhou and Lam (2019) carried out a systematic review of the literature (n = 36) on the use of metacognitive scaffolding to support students undertaking online information searches.

E-leadership, focusing on the people, roles and skills needed to drive increased use of technology-enhanced learning (TEL), has been the subject of at least two recent reviews (see also the discussion of academic development in Chapter 15). Jameson (2013) noted the limited literature available then focusing on the topic. Five years later, Arnold and Sangra (2018) reviewed the literature published between 2013 and 2017, identifying forty-nine relevant articles. They conclude, somewhat unsurprisingly, that 'at a time when HE [higher education] leaders still need to develop their capacity for strategic thinking with respect to the integration of technology for learning and teaching ... further research into (e-)leadership for TEL in higher education would be welcome' (p. 25).

The related topics of digital literacy, inclusion and competence have also attracted attention. Khalid and Pedersen (2016) focused on studies of digital exclusion (n = 9), relating it closely to social exclusion and accessibility. Spante et al (2018) examined the research on digital competence and literacy (n = 107), focusing on the different definitions and usages of these terms. Both challenged the idea that all contemporary students are digitally literate, experienced in the use of online tools and expecting to apply them in their higher education.

Muljana and Luo (2019) provide a systematic literature review of studies published between 2010 and 2018 that examined online student retention (n = 40). They noted that 'student retention rates are significantly lower than those in the traditional environment' (p. 19), which is not surprising since a relatively high proportion of online students are mature and studying part-time. They concluded that for 'achieving higher retention rates, the recommended tactics signify the employment of early intervention, effective communication, high-quality instructional feedback and strategies, guidance to foster the appropriate behavioral characteristics, and collaboration among stakeholders to support online students' (p. 38). These are, again, much the same strategies recommended for retaining full-time students (see the discussion in Chapter 10).

Gray and Crosta (2019) examined online doctoral supervision, identifying 152 relevant articles through their systematic review. On this basis, they argue that

> good practice in online doctoral supervision resides mainly in nurturing a good and healthy online relationship between the student and the supervisor and this is not an easy task if we consider that this relationship is mediated by the use of technology. Very often the way in which synchronous technology is used by the supervisor and the

digital pedagogies underpinning this technology can determine success or failure in this relationship. The frequency and type of this online communication has a great impact too together with frequent renewal of reciprocal rules and expectations without taking anything for granted.

(pp. 184–5)

While Gray and Crosta place particular emphasis on the use of technology in mediating the student/supervisor relationship, this is also an issue in conventional student supervision. Even where students are studying full-time, and supervised by full-time staff, a good deal of communication takes place by email, text and telephone (see also the discussion of postgraduate study in Chapter 8).

Other syntheses have focused on online learning in particular disciplines. Thus, Trenholm, Peschke and Chinnappan (2019) focused on online undergraduate mathematics instruction, carrying out a systematic review of relevant large-scale studies. They identified five such studies, all American, and concluded, 'Clearly, from multiple perspectives, FO [fully online] mathematics instruction has not been successful in comparison with traditional F2F [face-to-face] mathematics instruction' (p. 1094). This finding, though it is only based on a small number of studies, may, of course, be specific to mathematics.

Barteit et al (2020) evaluated the use of e-learning for medical education in low- and middle-income countries (LMICs), arguing that this might enable more affordable access. Their systematic review identified fifty-two relevant studies published between 2007 and 2017 and found that

> [m]ost e-learning interventions were pilot studies (73%), which mainly employed summative assessments of study participants (83%) and evaluated the e-learning intervention with questionnaires (45%). Study designs, evaluation and assessment methods showed considerable variation, as did the study quality, evaluation periods, outcome and effectiveness measures. Included studies mainly utilized subjective measures and custom-built evaluation frameworks, which resulted in both low comparability and poor validity. The majority of studies self-concluded that they had had an effective e-learning intervention, thus indicating potential benefits of e-learning for LMICs.

(p. 1)

More extensive, controlled and comparative studies would be needed, however, to allow the generalization of these findings.

Joda et al (2019) examined research on augmented and virtual reality (AR and VR) in dental medicine, identifying sixteen studies for their systematic review. They concluded that

> AR/VR-applications are of increasing interest and importance in dental under- and postgraduate education offering interactive learning concepts with 24/7-access and objective evaluation. In maxillofacial surgery, AR/VR-technology is a promising tool for complex procedures and can help to deliver predictable and safe therapy outcomes.

(p. 99)

One can readily appreciate, of course, how augmented and virtual reality applications, like the previous and continuing use of simulations, might be of considerable use in health and medical education.

Conclusions

- Distance, online or e-learning can be as effective as more conventional, face-to-face forms of higher education.
- Similar conclusions have been reached regarding mobile and ubiquitous learning.
- The application of technology-enhanced learning alongside conventional forms of learning has particularly beneficial effects, making use of the best of the different approaches in combination.
- Technology-enhanced learning is particularly effective when used in connection with group work and active forms of learning.
- However, the context for the application of distance, online and e-learning always needs to be born in mind, together with how those involved conceptualize teaching and learning with technology.

Chapter 8
Course design – curriculum

Introduction

This chapter examines the curriculum, a topic which is seldom explicitly considered in higher education research (when compared with school education research, where it has its own journals and research groups). Curriculum covers both the overall organization and design of the educational experience and the more detailed activities involved in or linked to that. It is, therefore, a research topic of critical importance.

Curriculum could also be regarded, in the context of this book, as something of a catch-all term. In effect, it includes all of the topics or issues that did not neatly fit under one of the other five course design sub-themes (covered in Chapters 5, 6, 7, 9 and 10). This may suggest, of course, both why it is important – in higher education as much as in other levels of education – and why it has often been overlooked.

A series of key research areas – including learning design and interventions, the developing area of learning analytics, postgraduate study, sustainability and other topics – may be recognized. Research on these and related issues has a major impact upon course design within higher education across the world. In these areas there have developed substantial bodies of research, resulting in a mixed array of systematic reviews, substantive literature reviews and meta-analyses.

The research for this book identified thirty-seven research syntheses relevant to this chapter or about 13 per cent of the total identified for course design as a whole. The majority of these, twenty-seven, were qualitative systematic reviews, with only five meta-analyses, four substantive literature reviews and one study which had elements of both systematic review and meta-analysis.

The journal *Innovations in Education and Teaching International* focuses on the issues discussed in this chapter, publishing numerous case studies of curricular change. They are also picked up in a variety of other, less specialist, journals.

Learning design and interventions

This section considers a number of research syntheses that focus on learning design or learning interventions in different, even disparate, ways.

Learning design

To start with the most unusual of the studies of learning design, Lloyd and Bahr (2016) provide what they term a meta-synthesis (i.e. a systematic review in the context of the usage adopted in this book) of the articles (n = 149) published in the *Journal of Learning Design* during its first decade, 2005 to 2015, focusing in particular on two recurring 'motifs', blended learning (see Chapter 7) and authentic learning. On these two motifs they argued that

> [w]hile blended learning was clearly understood as a singular entity, its form and implementation had changed over time largely influenced by changes in available technology. Authentic learning was a single idea but not a singular entity. Its form and implementation was a direct consequence of the cognitive and affective demands of the discipline it supported.
>
> (p. 10)

Other syntheses of the output of particular journals are considered in Chapter 3.

A number of syntheses have focused on research into the application of universal design, or universal design for instruction (UDI) to higher education. Universal design began as a movement in the 1950s focused 'on removing physical and environmental barriers that prevent access for individuals with disabilities. In the 1970s, the concept … [focused on the] integration of all people within all environments' (Roberts et al 2011, p. 5). A series of principles for universal design were set out, including equitable use, flexibility in use, simple and intuitive, perceptible information, tolerance for error, low physical effort, size and space for approach and use, community of learners and instructional climate.

Roberts et al provide a systematic review of eight articles on this topic, concluding that

> [a]lthough the authors of the articles reviewed promoted the use of UDI in postsecondary education for educating pre-service teachers, training faculty members, improving web accessibility; and presented the viewpoints of students and service providers as evidence of the effectiveness of UDI use in postsecondary education, there is very little research to support its effectiveness as a means to improve postsecondary student outcomes.
>
> (p. 13)

This, it has to be said, is a rather underwhelming conclusion.

Rao et al (2014) provide what they call a descriptive review of thirteen studies on the application of universal design, five of which were in higher education. They concluded that the findings of the studies supported the use of UD principles by providing evidence of the benefits and positive outcomes for students and educators. However, because the studies used a range of research designs, most of which did not establish causality of effectiveness, the evidence should be interpreted with caution as a set of preliminary positive results based on varied methods of analysis.

(p. 162)

The systematic review by Seok et al (2018) identified seventeen relevant studies focusing on universal design for learning (UDL) at postsecondary level, concluding that 'the analysis revealed that these studies, conducted on the application of UDL principles, showed that this approach was effective; thus, underscoring the benefits of UDL in educating students with and without disabilities at the postsecondary level' (pp. 185–6).

A fourth synthesis, by Schreffler et al (2019), presents a systematic review of the use of universal design for learning in STEM higher education, with a particular focus on meeting the needs of disabled students. Restricting their scope to articles published after 2006, they identified only four relevant studies. Despite the number of syntheses generated, it seems clear, therefore, that rather more research is needed on the application of universal design in higher education.

Learning interventions

Learning interventions, in their broadest sense, are discussed in each of the chapters that deal with course design (i.e. Chapters 5 to 10) in this book. For example, studies that focus on the impact of learning interventions on student achievement are a major component of Chapter 10, where outcomes are discussed. In this subsection, the focus is on research syntheses that did not readily fit into one of the other chapters.

Denson (2009) presents a meta-analysis of studies of the impact of curricular and co-curricular diversity activities in the United States, with particular emphasis on their effect on racial bias in higher education (n = 27). She concludes that

> there is indeed value in implementing diversity-related programs on college campuses. And, institutions that currently have these diversity-related interventions already in place may be reassured to know that these various activities are generally effective in reducing students' racial bias. However, the magnitude of the effectiveness of these interventions depends on certain factors, such as level of institutional support, comprehensiveness of approach, a diverse racial composition, and most important, whether or not intergroup contact is a major component of the intervention.
>
> (p. 825)

The emphasis placed on the importance of intergroup contact is clearly key here; unless one has meaningful contact with the 'other', they will always remain the 'other'. The experience of ethnic minority groups in higher education is considered further in Chapter 11.

Interventions in higher education have been interpreted and researched in a variety of ways. Evans, Muijs and Tomlinson (2015) carried out a systematic review (n = 273) of articles that examined interventions that had a high impact on student engagement.

Tellingly, they found that only thirty-six (13 per cent) of these articles were of high quality. Five elements of good pedagogical practice were identified: the use of real-life examples, the use of experiential approaches, advance access to course materials, ensuring the accessibility of the ideas presented, effective assessment and feedback practice. Of course, none of these practices are either innovative or surprising, but the confirmation of their effectiveness is reassuring.

Sneyers and De Witte (2018) provide a meta-analysis of the impact of three kinds of policy intervention (academic probation, student-faculty mentoring and need-based grants) on student enrolment, retention and graduation (n = 25; see also the discussion in Chapter 10). The findings are positive for these interventions:

> Student-faculty mentoring … seems to have a positive and significant effect on retention (d =.15) and graduation (d =.10) … the average intervention effect of mentoring on retention is equivalent to a 7.5% improvement in retention and a 5% increase in graduation for the intervention groups … Need-based grants also have positive significant effects on enrollment (d =.05), retention (d =.05), and graduation (d =.05). Need-based grants lead to an increase in enrolment, retention, and graduation of 2.5% for the intervention group.
>
> (p. 224)

While these effect sizes are small, Sneyers and De Witte argue that the costs involved in achieving them are also small, so the effort may be worthwhile.

Chan et al (2019) carried out a systematic review of research into academic advising schemes, with particular reference to nursing education, identifying thirty-seven relevant empirical studies. They concluded that

> [i]n general, both advisors and advisees found the scheme to be beneficial and useful. The majority of the reviewed studies focused on the perspective of the advisees, an initial understanding of which could be achieved by reviewing the advisees' views of their advising experience, their preferences, and their perception of the benefits of academic advising and the barriers to accessing it. For both advisors and advisees, the lack of time was a common issue.
>
> (p. 73)

It is, of course, unsurprising that those making use of academic advising schemes would find them useful, nor that constraints on the time available would be a problem.

Santos, Figueiredo and Vieira (2019), a Portuguese team, offer an integrative literature review of research on innovative pedagogical practices in higher education, by which they meant student-centred approaches to teaching. Surprisingly, they only identified ten relevant articles published between 2012 and 2016. Nevertheless, from this relatively small data set they came up with some strong conclusions:

> Four thematic categories have emerged from this review: dissonance between teaching concepts and teaching strategies; mixed approaches with ICTs [information and communication technologies] association; digital simulation and approaches to teaching in large classes. Regarding the students, all the strategies examined in this

review result in: greater motivation and consequent involvement with unit contents and the course; development of critical and reflective thinking; higher level of cognitive skills and, consequently, deep learning. They also improved their ability to communicate and interact with peers, as well as with teachers, despite some difficulties, such as: delays in their contribution to the proposed activities; obstacles in the development of collaborative content; persistent difficulty in being critical and creative ... In some contexts, it was noticeable [that there was] a prevailing dissonance between the teachers' beliefs, concerning teaching, and the pedagogical strategies (collaborative learning and peer evaluation) they claimed to apply.

(p. 17)

That final sentence indicates a key issue with implementing learning interventions in higher education. That is, if the intervention is determined centrally (in an institution, department or course team), all of those involved in delivering it need to be 'onside' if its delivery is to be most effective.

Learning analytics

Learning analytics has become an increasingly popular practice within higher education during the last decade:

Learning Analytics refers to the measurement, collection, analysis and reporting of data about the progress of learners and the contexts in which learning takes place. Using the increased availability of big datasets around learner activity and digital footprints left by student activity in learning environments, learning analytics take us further than data currently available can.

(Sclater, Peasgood and Mullan 2016, p. 4)

This has been made possible, of course, by the prevalence of blended learning approaches (see Chapter 7), where more and more student activity is now taking place online on universities' own learning management systems: e.g. to access learning materials, submit assignments, receive feedback, etc.

Analysing this data through learning analytics enables the presentation of up-to-date and useable information to staff and students in the form of what are called 'dashboards'. These are readily interpretable and often colourful and diagrammatic summaries of students' progress and position, both individually and in comparison with their class groups. In their review, Sclater et al anticipated the increasing use of data analytics in the future 'as a tool for quality assurance and improvement ... boosting retention rates ... assessing and acting upon differential outcomes among the student population ... [and] as an enabler for the development and introduction of adaptive learning – i.e. personalised learning delivered at scale' (p. 5).

Avella et al (2016) provide a systematic review of the use of learning analytics methods in higher education. Using Google Scholar, ERIC, ProQuest and Ebsco Host databases to search for relevant articles, they found '10 focused on issues related to learning analytics (LA) methods, 16 on benefits, and 18 focused on challenges' (p. 15):

> LA uses various methods including visual data analysis techniques, social network analysis, semantic, and educational data mining including prediction, clustering, relationship mining, discovery with models, and separation of data for human judgment to analyze data. The benefits include targeted course offerings, curriculum development, student learning outcomes, behavior and process, personalized learning, improved instructor performance, post-educational employment opportunities, and enhanced research in the field of education. Challenges include issues related to data tracking, collection, evaluation, analysis; lack of connection to learning sciences; optimizing learning environments, and ethical and privacy issues.
>
> (p. 13)

While a great deal is hoped for from the application of learning analytics, it also, as indicated, comes with risks. Underlying these is a problem key to the adoption of all learning technologies in higher education (and elsewhere; see also Chapter 7): i.e. is learning analytics a technology looking for a use, rather than something that is genuinely useful? It is, however, almost too late to pose this question as learning analytics are now so widely applied.

Bodily and Verbert (2017) offer 'a comprehensive literature review of student-facing learning analytics reporting systems that track learning analytics data and report it directly to students' (p. 405), identifying ninety-three relevant publications. They found that

> [t]he most prevalent system characteristics were tracking resource use data, reporting data in visualizations, using data mining to process data, and providing recommendations to students. The least prevalent system characteristics were tracking other sensor data, conducting a needs assessment to identify the needs of the system end-user, asking students if they perceived an achievement change based on their system use, and examining the effect of these systems on student skills (e.g., awareness, meta-cognition, motivation, etc.).
>
> (p. 410)

They called for much more evaluative, large-scale, observational and quasi-experimental research. This would enable a better appreciation of not just how learning analytics were being used, but to what effect, and how they might be better used.

Sonderlund, Hughes and Smith (2018) provide a systematic review of the effects of learning analytics interventions (in this case on student performance) targeting students perceived to be at risk of dropping out or failing their courses. Only eleven relevant studies were found, however, just three of which critically reviewed the effectiveness of the interventions. They identify the key issue here as being 'Once at-risk students have been identified, what is the best way to intervene and help them?' They note that the 'interventions that we have identified center on the idea that alerting students to their risk status, and engaging them on this basis, will change their performance for the better' (p. 20).

Given the lack of research, however, this belief remains unproven; it may be the case that students at risk are the least likely or able to take notice of such interventions. There are also risks associated with incorrectly identifying which students are at risk or not at risk and about the kind of data used in making these identifications.

Gedrimiene et al (2019) focused on the use of learning analytics in vocational education and training (VET). They identified sixty studies for analysis in their review, most of which dealt with higher or work-based education. They argue that 'VET could benefit from applications and methods that allow for tracking and evaluation of student performance in on-the-job training as well as incorporating competencies from various educational settings. However, extant LA implementation literature in educational institutions is scant, focusing on higher education and dominated by private vendors' (p. 11).

Liz-Dominguez et al (2019), a Spanish team, carried out a systematic review of the literature on predictors and early warning systems in higher education. They restricted themselves to articles published since 2012, identifying twenty-five relevant studies, concluding that

> [o]verall, this study highlights the many possibilities that predictive analytics provides in order to boost the learning process. At the same time, it is evident that building a single solution that will work well for many different types of learning environments is a very difficult task. This remains one of the greatest challenges within the learning analytics discipline.
>
> (p. 96)

Aldowah, Al-Samarraiea and Fauzy (2019) provide a review of the use of educational data mining and learning analytics (EDM/LA) in higher education, identifying 402 relevant studies published between 2000 and 2017. They 'find that the application of EDM/LA can provide significant benefits, and therefore urge higher education institutions to adopt them where feasible' (p. 31). While, yet again, more research is clearly needed, the potential benefits could be significant.

Postgraduate study

Some syntheses have focused specifically on research into postgraduate study. In the United States, Kuncel and his collaborators have had a long-standing interest in the use of assessment in the selection of students (Kuncel, Hezlett and Ones 2001, Kuncel et al 2010). In 2001 they

> examined the validity of the Graduate Record Examinations (GRE) and undergraduate grade point average (UGPA) as predictors of graduate school performance. The study included samples from multiple disciplines, considered different criterion measures, and corrected for statistical artifacts. Data from 1,753 independent samples were included in the meta-analysis, yielding 6,589 correlations for 8 different criteria and 82,659 graduate students.
>
> (p. 162)

They found that 'the GRE and UGPA are generalizably valid predictors of graduate grade point average, Ist-year graduate grade point average, comprehensive examination scores, publication citation counts, and faculty ratings. GRE correlations with degree attainment and research productivity were consistently positive' (p. 162).

In 2010, Kuncel et al carried out a meta-analysis of studies which had considered whether admissions tests, in this case the Graduate Record Examination (GRE) in the United States, predicted performance on master's and doctoral programmes. They found nearly 100 studies relating to nearly 10,000 students, providing

> considerable evidence for the validity of the GRE for both master's- and doctoral-level programs. Averaging across the two tests and grade measures, the validity of the GRE varied only .03 between master's (.30) and doctoral (.27) programs. Based on the data currently available, the GRE is a useful decision-making tool for both master's- and doctoral-level programs.
>
> (p. 350)

Two other syntheses focused specifically on research into doctoral study. Jones (2013) examined '995 papers written on issues of doctoral studies through the years 1971 to 2012' (p. 83), with thematic analysis identifying six central themes:

> *Teaching* focuses on ensuring that … there is adequate preparation for doctoral students to become teachers. Discussions on *Doctoral program design* tend to focus on improving and refining the doctoral program to ensure optimum admission, fair assessment, and stronger industry alignment. *Doctoral writing and research* literature addressed … the increased need for, and pressure to, write and publish more … [and] an increase in collaborative designs to increase efficiencies and to widen access to industry and to cross-disciplinary content. The issues on *employment and career* tended to be reactionary discussions focusing on temporal issues of over- or under-supply of doctoral students and their consequent employment in the industry. The *student-supervisor relationship* looked at elements which work to ensure an optimum relationship between the student and their supervisor … *the doctoral student experience* discusses the impact on progress and completion of a student's experience during the PhD program.
>
> (p. 99, emphases in original)

This offers a useful categorization of the key issues encountered in undertaking doctoral study.

Mackie and Bates (2019) examined what they termed the doctoral education environment, which essentially consisted of the fifth and sixth of Jones's themes, in their scoping review. Their particular focus was on the relation between this and students' mental health problems (n = 26). Their analysis identifies a closely interrelated set of factors affecting students' mental health which may not be easily resolvable:

> One thing that is noticeable in this review is that the main stressors captured in it are mostly embedded in and mediated by research ecologies. For example, financial insecurity can lead to excessive teaching workload and this can in turn lead to role conflict. Unsatisfactory supervision can be hard for candidates to negotiate in the face of uncertain career prospects, as supervisory endorsement may be perceived as

necessary for further employment. Lack of transparency in university processes places a burden on inexperienced supervisors who may need to navigate these on behalf of candidates. Such supervisors may themselves be at risk of developing mental health problems. And so on. The fact that these can overlap implies that problems may not be able to be tackled on a one-off basis.

(pp. 575–6)

The doctoral student experience could be said to be the least regulated area of higher education provision, but it seems doubtful that it will remain so as massification spreads to this level, encouraging further research and synthesis.

Sustainability

One area of the curriculum – and of higher education in general – attracting increasing interest in general, research interest, and hence research syntheses, in recent years has been sustainability. This may be presented as a role for the curriculum, a responsibility of higher education institutions (see also the related discussion in Chapter 14) or as an all-encompassing duty.

Figueiro and Raufflet (2015) provide a systematic review of the topic with a focus on management education, identifying sixty-three relevant articles published between 2003 and 2013. They note that

> most articles are descriptive, focusing on specific, unique experiences in a given institution or with a particular teaching method or tool, few situate themselves within the broader philosophy and design of management education ... no stable categories emerge from these articles and very few studies integrate the three levels of educational philosophy – teaching, program design, and learning ... While all articles highlight the need for curriculum change, very few specify how this change could and would be achieved by course design or explicit educational paradigms.
>
> (p. 22)

In short, most of the studies reviewed were accounts of specific innovations or interventions designed to highlight sustainability issues in the management education curriculum.

Wu and Shen (2016) attempt a comprehensive overview of higher education for sustainable development (HESD) – the recognition that higher education has a major role to play in encouraging a sustainable developmental approach – by examining the literature for the 2005–14 decade. Using the EBSCO, ProQuest and ScienceDirect databases and the publisher Emerald's website, 372 relevant articles were identified. They found some interesting trends:

> [R]egarding the developing context of HESD during the DESD [the United Nations' Decade of Education for Sustainable Development], in the first half-decade, most articles

focused on environment protection, environmental science education and environmental engineering education. After this period, researchers highlighted the concept of integration applied to ESD [education for sustainable development], the promotion of citizenship, the importance of ESD in business schools and the assessment of performance in ESD. Regarding the development of teaching and curricula, researchers focused significantly on EE [environmental education] in the fields of engineering and science and the relationship between the environment and sustainability in the period 2005–2010; however, in the second half-decade, researchers promoted the concepts of interdisciplinary integration and emphasized the importance of business ESD.

(p. 646)

This analysis demonstrated clearly how the debate and reaction in higher education had matured over the period examined.

Caniglia et al (2017) focused on transnational collaborations between universities to advance research and education for sustainability. Their systematic review identified 46 articles relating to 147 higher education institutions and concluded that 'it is important to adopt an integrated approach to transnational collaboration … a comprehensive perspective cannot reduce collaboration efforts to purely administrative or technical endeavors. Instead, it needs considering [sic] also cultural, institutional, social, and personal aspects' (p. 772).

The focus of Lozano et al's (2017) literature review was 'on the connection between how courses are delivered (pedagogical approaches) and how they may affect sustainability competences' (p. 1). They offer a framework for further work based on twelve competences and twelve pedagogical approaches, ideas which others interested in developing sustainability in the curriculum could readily pick up on.

Murray's (2018) literature review focuses on the student perspective, examining student-led action for sustainability in higher education, with thirty-eight relevant articles identified. She concluded that

this review has demonstrated an increasing area of activity and scholarship devoted to understanding student-led action for SHE [sustainability in higher education]. While representative of a relatively small sample size, conclusions can nonetheless be drawn from these results to guide future scholarship. Findings demonstrate that the geographical gaps represented by this literature review showcase the need for increased representation across the globe. It is suggested that future research should include multi-site and comparative studies to expand beyond single case study approaches and should produce scholarship that provides tangible takeaways for students and institutions. While these findings demonstrate that students are influencing SHE through multi-stakeholder collaborations, collective action and interdisciplinarity, gaps remain in our understanding of the extent to which students influence institutional change for sustainability, best practices to SHE and the intersections with social justice more broadly. While many gaps remain in our understandings of the extent of student influence on SHE more broadly, many opportunities exist for HEIs [higher education institutions] to benefit from the collective actions of these stakeholders.

(pp. 1105–6)

Hallinger and Chatpinyakoop (2019) offer a bibliometric review of research on higher education for sustainable development (HESD) over the twenty-year period from 1998 to 2018. They identified a substantial number of relevant articles (n = 1,459):

> The review documented a rapidly growing knowledge base of recent vintage, mostly authored by scholars located in developed societies. Four core journals were identified, based on the volume of HESD publications and citation impact. Author co-citation analysis revealed three research clusters that underlie this knowledge base: Managing for Sustainability in Higher Education, HESD Competencies, and Implementation of HESD.
>
> (p. 1)

They offer this as a baseline from which the further development of the research field may be traced in the future.

Weiss and Barth (2019) present a systematic review of the global research landscape of sustainability curricula implementation processes for the period 1990 to 2017, identifying 270 relevant publications. They found that

> [a] steadily growing number of case studies – mainly in North America, Europe and Asia – have been carried out since 1999. This publication trend indicates that sustainability curricula implementation in higher education has gained momentum and that many HEIs [higher education institutions] around the world have initiated attempts to integrate sustainability. Nevertheless, experiences from many countries and regions (e.g. Africa, Latin America and the Caribbean) are underrepresented. A similar pattern can be seen via citation analysis, in which a 'Western' influence is apparent. The citation network analysis leaves unanswered the question of how cases learn from one another as the results reveal that 'non-Western' countries, in particular, are not well interlinked.
>
> (p. 18)

This is partly, of course, but not wholly, the result of searching for English language publications only. It does remain the case, however, that the higher education experience of developing countries (the Global South) is significantly under-represented in the higher education research literature and not just on sustainability initiatives but generally (see the overall analysis of the research syntheses identified for this book in Chapter 3).

Reading and writing

Reading and writing are fundamental to the higher education experience, and have been quite extensively researched, but not by those who would identify themselves as higher education researchers. Relatively few relevant research syntheses have been identified.

Baker et al (2019) provide a scoping study (n = 32) of research into academic reading, arguing that '[t]here has been a significant silence in the literature around what constitutes reading in higher education, the sociocultural complexities of reader engagement with text, and contemporary understandings of situated experiences regarding reading practices in the disciplines, especially for traditionally under-represented student groups' (p. 142). They conclude that

> [t]his study highlights the necessity for further research that approaches students' reading practices from an equity/social justice perspective. There is a clear relationship between schooling, students' higher-education literacy practices, and success, for all that success is often viewed through a normative pass/fail lens, and this is particularly the case for non-traditional students. In this high-stakes context, the extent to which non-traditional students can access disciplinary knowledge through reading becomes especially important.
>
> (p. 153)

Rey (2012) examines research on the seductive detail effect (i.e. the presentation of interesting but irrelevant information that distracts from learning), through a meta-analysis of thirty-nine experimental effects reported in the literature. The results

> support the existence of a seductive detail effect in terms of retention (small to medium effect size) and transfer performance (medium effect size) … this meta-analysis and other empirical studies support the assumption that different variables, such as the presence of a time limit in the learning or test phase, the kinds of seductive details, CL [cognitive load], and the learning domain, can moderate the seductive detail effect.
>
> (p. 233)

Taking a rather different perspective, Hilton (2019) synthesizes the research on the use of open educational resources (OER) published between 2015 and 2018 (n = 29). He finds that 'students achieve the same or better learning outcomes when using OER while saving significant amounts of money. The results also indicate that the majority of faculty and students who have used OER had a positive experience and would do so again' (p. 1).

Strobl et al (2019) provide a review of research into the technologies used to support academic writing, covering both higher and secondary education. They note that, while the field has developed significantly, support remains patchy. They identified

> 44 tools across 26 quantitative and qualitative features related to writing processes, pedagogical approaches, feedback modalities and technological specifications. The results uncover an imbalance of available tools with regard to supported languages, genres, and pedagogical focus. While a considerable number of tools support argumentative essay writing in English, other academic writing genres (e.g., research articles) and other languages are under-represented. With regard to the pedagogical focus, automated support for revising on the micro-level targeting factual knowledge (e.g., grammar, spelling, word frequencies) is well represented, whereas tools that support the development of writing strategies and encourage self-monitoring to improve macrolevel text quality (e.g., argumentative structure, rhetorical moves) are infrequent.
>
> (p. 33)

Clearly, then, there remains plenty of scope for the development of tools to support students' writing.

Other topics

A number of syntheses have examined research into other specific aspects of the curriculum. They are somewhat of a mixed bag.

Medeiros, Ramalho and Falcao (2018) present a systematic review of research into teaching and learning introductory programming in higher education (n = 89): '[T]he most frequently cited issues were problem-solving abilities and mathematical knowledge … the major issues cited were related to motivation and engagement, problem-solving, and the syntax of programming languages … the need for appropriate methods and tools for teaching programming at the introductory level were the most cited issue [for teachers]' (p. 11).

Fernandez et al (2019) also focused on computing, but at the other end of the scale, namely supercomputer usage. Through an analysis of thirty-four relevant articles, they summarize the most relevant factors in improving training, and the factors that improve results, while offering an analysis of the limitations found in improving the performance of learners and possible solutions for these limitations.

Tight (2014d) provided a systematic review of the literature on threshold concepts in higher education: these are disciplinary concepts which students frequently find it difficult to understand, but which it is essential for them to understand if they are to progress further in the discipline. He concluded that:

> [t]he success of threshold concepts as a theory may … be judged in terms of how well it performs in comparison to, or in combination with … other frameworks. The difficulty, of course, lies in assessing its performance. But simply identifying, and agreeing upon, more and more threshold concepts in more and more disciplines and sub-disciplines will not, in itself, be enough.
>
> (p. 263)

Bolden and Petrov (2008) carried out a literature review of employer engagement with higher education, with a focus on work-based learning for those in employment in the UK (see also the discussion of learning and work in Chapter 6 and of outcomes in Chapter 10). The most telling of their conclusions was the following:

> The expansion of employer engagement in HE [higher education] places new expectations on the role of HE in society and challenges the perception of universities as a primary source of knowledge. In particular, the need to collaborate with employers and other organisations in the design, delivery and assessment of learning may erode traditional academic autonomy and the impartiality of HE. Increasingly HEIs [higher education institutions] may find themselves moving from being the principal providers of HE to assuming a quality assurance, coordination and accreditation role. As the pressures on universities to excel in different aspects of teaching, learning and research expand further strategic differentiation between institutions is likely and may lead to fragmentation of the sector.
>
> (p. 6)

This kind of argument has been doing the rounds for some time, however, and most employers still seem happy to leave most of the educational work at this level to higher education institutions.

Roy et al (2019) provide a systematic review of the outcomes of short-term international student mobility programmes (n = 75). They consider cultural, personal, employment and career outcomes and boundary conditions (i.e. factors affecting the amount of participation) and

> draw five main observations that underpin a future research agenda. First, although many studies have investigated the cultural and personal outcomes of student mobility, comparatively few have investigated the employment and career outcomes resulting from participation in international student mobility … Second, few prior studies draw on theory to explain how international short-term mobility programs influence cultural, personal, and employment/career outcomes … Third, very few studies have investigated the outcomes of student mobility outside Europe and North America … Fourth, practically none of the studies in our review have deliberately sought to study the negative outcomes of short-term mobility programs … Finally, weak study designs are typically employed in previous research examining the outcomes of international short-term student mobility.
> (pp. 1638–9)

Finally, Reyes et al (2019), an American team, offer both a meta-analysis and a critical review of research into the evaluation of leadership development programmes for students (n = 73). They conclude that

> [o]ur results suggest that LD [leadership development] programs in higher education work in the studies examined – both learning and transfer increased as a result of these LD programs. However, the samples identified within our meta-analysis also pointed to a concern that appears to be common within this area of literature—endogeneity bias … In practice, it appears that LD programs that are being used in education have been following guidelines from scientific research (e.g., the spacing principle, using multiple delivery methods), but there is still room for improvement (e.g., providing feedback, measuring outcomes using a triangulation approach to measurement). Other design, delivery, and implementation elements need further research specific to student leadership development.
> (p. 13)

The characteristic role of the research synthesis in identifying aspects or areas of a topic that need further research is once again demonstrated here.

Conclusions

- Curricular interventions typically have a positive impact, but this may be largely a 'Hawthorne effect': i.e. the participants respond positively to the increased attention associated with changes in practice.

- The potential dissonance between teachers' pedagogic beliefs and their practice, particularly where this is effected by top-down initiatives, needs careful consideration.
- The usefulness of learning analytics for students and teachers has yet to be definitively demonstrated.
- Doctoral education, as an expanding area of provision, merits further investigation. Master's level provision continues to be under-researched.
- Sustainability in the curriculum promises to be a major research theme for the foreseeable future.

Chapter 9
Course design – assessment

Introduction

This chapter discusses syntheses of higher education research relating to the theme of assessment. As with most of the other areas of course design considered in Chapters 5, 6, 7, 8 and 10, these syntheses comprise a reasonably balanced mix of meta-analyses and systematic reviews. The research for this book identified a total of thirty-seven relevant research syntheses for discussion in this chapter or 13 per cent of the total identified for course design. These comprised fourteen meta-analyses, eighteen systematic reviews and five substantive literature reviews.

There is one specialist higher education journal which focuses on the topics discussed in this chapter, *Assessment and Evaluation in Higher Education*, plus a range of more generic ones which also publish assessment-related research.

Research into assessment in higher education concerns the vital questions of how well students are performing in their studies and how their performance can be explained in terms of other factors (e.g. previous education and achievement, socio-economic background, motivation and commitment). It also addresses the underlying or fundamental questions of how best to assess students and how to report back to them on their performance in an effort to improve it.

Syntheses of research on assessment in higher education have focused on formative and summative forms of assessment, on the roles of peers, self and teachers in assessment, and on feedback. Two more recent interests have been what is termed authentic assessment and, in a reflection of contemporary concerns in a massified, and increasingly online, higher education market, the extent to which students cheat and how this might be countered. Each of these fields of research will be considered in turn.

Assessment may be categorized in a number of different ways. For example, in terms of whether it takes place at the end of the course (summative assessment), to measure how well a student has learnt from the course as a whole, or during the course (formative assessment), with the intention of informing the students and their teachers of their progress and how this might be improved. In practice, of course, both approaches might be adopted. Formative and summative assessments are the focus of the first section of this chapter.

Another way of classifying assessment is in terms of who is doing the assessment. Teacher assessment may be regarded as the normal or standard practice, though students may be assessed by teachers who did not teach them. Peer assessment, when each student is assessed by one or more of their fellow students, is also increasingly popular, and self-assessment, when the student judges their own work, may be encouraged as well, particularly when the aim is to develop students' awareness of their abilities. As with formative and summative assessment, teacher, peer and self-assessment may also be practised together in the same course. Peer, self and teacher assessment are the subject of the second section of this chapter.

There are, of course, other possible ways of categorizing assessment. One further obvious way would be in terms of whether the assessment is of an individual student or of the work of a group of students (see the discussion of group learning in Chapter 6). Or the focus could be on the nature of the assessment being carried out: e.g. examinations, essays, reports or assignments, oral presentations. While these approaches have all been subject to research, they don't yet, however, appear to have been the subject of research syntheses.

Formative and summative assessments

Formative and summative assessments differ in terms of both the timing (respectively during the course or at the end of the course) and intention (improvement of the student's performance for the former, judgement of the student's performance in the latter).

Turning first to summative assessment, Sasanguie et al (2011) provide a systematic review of research on the advantages and disadvantages of keeping the teaching and assessment functions distinct (e.g. by having colleagues assess one's students or by using an external examiner system), which would arguably be fairer and less liable to bias. They carried out what they term a formal literature review, using the PsycINFO, Web of Science and ERIC databases, identifying eighteen relevant articles. They concluded:

> The present review clearly shows that there is a striking diversity with respect to the relationship between different roles of lecturers. Practices differ, terminology differs, and last but not least, arguments for and against any position differ. Furthermore, the review illustrates that, in the absence of empirical evidence, the discussion about coupling or segregating teacher roles remains a highly speculative endeavor.
> (p. 908)

In other words, more research is clearly needed into this topic.

Turning to formative assessment, Black and Wiliam (1998) provide a substantial literature review (n ~ 250), building on the work of Crooks (1988) and Natriello (1987), and covering school as well as college classrooms. They note that 'studies show firm evidence that innovations designed to strengthen the frequent feedback that students receive about their learning yield substantial learning gains' (p. 7). They link the growth of formative assessment to a paradigm change in thinking about educational practice.

Gauntlett (2007) carried out a follow-up literature review on the same topic for the then Centre for Excellence in Teaching and Learning in the UK focused on Mental Health and Social Work. He identified forty-six more recent and relevant articles and recommended continued research and further synthesis.

Gikandi, Morrow and Davis (2011) produced an integrative narrative review of the literature on formative assessment in online and blended higher education (see also Chapter 7), identifying eighteen relevant studies. They concluded that

> online formative assessment has a potential to engage both teachers and learners in meaningful educational experiences. It offers a pedagogical strategy that forms a foundation for shifting the assessment culture in ways that support diverse learning needs and foster equitable education. In particular, it offers online learners opportunities for enhanced interactivity and formative feedback, which in turn engage them with valuable learning experiences including active, contextual, interactive, collaborative, multidimensional, reflective and self regulated aspects of meaningful learning. In these ways, online formative assessment can support higher education to meet the needs of 21st century learners.
>
> (p. 2347)

Formative assessment, linked with appropriate feedback mechanisms (see the discussion of feedback in a later section in this chapter), is now viewed as standard 'good practice' in developed systems of higher education. The key issues regarding it are not pedagogic but economic: how to deliver it effectively in a mass higher education system without significantly increasing either staff workloads or student fees. The discussion in the next section suggests some possible directions to take, further embedding students in their own learning and that of their colleagues.

Peer, self and teacher assessment

An alternative way of thinking about assessment is in terms of who the assessors are and what their relationship to the assessed is. The research on summative and formative assessment just referred to adopts the conventional perspective; that the person being assessed is the student and that the person doing the assessment is either their teacher (usually) or another teacher/examiner.

Research, however, has also explored the more novel or innovative occasions where the assessor is either the student themselves (i.e. self-assessment) or one or more of their peers (i.e. their fellow students or peers – peer assessment: see also the discussion of peer instruction, mentoring and tutoring in Chapter 5).

It is common, of course – both in practice and in research – to combine self-assessment with peer assessment and/or teacher assessment. It is also common for peer assessment to be reciprocal, with pairs of students assessing each other's work, or all the students in a group assessing all of the other group members. More recently, however, with the advent of online submission and assessment of students' work, and particularly where peers are expected to grade the work as well as provide comments, it is now more usual for the process to be anonymized and for assessors to be randomly allocated.

Interestingly, research syntheses of these topics appear to be chiefly in the form of meta-analysis, probably because assessment is so often numerical. A key concern has been to compare self, peer and teacher assessment scores, on the assumption that the teacher's score is the correct one or is at least the most accurate.

In a relatively early study, Harris and Schaubroeck (1988) carried out a meta-analysis to compare peer, self and teacher (or supervisor) ratings, identifying 'a total of 36 independent self-supervisor correlations, 23 independent peer-supervisor correlations, and 11 independent self-peer correlations' (p. 49). They found

> a relatively high correlation between peer and supervisor ratings (p = .62) but only a moderate correlation between self-supervisor (p = .35) and self-peer ratings (p = .36). While rating format (dimensional versus global) and rating scale (trait versus behavioral) had little impact as moderators, job type (managerial/professional versus blue-collar/service) did seem to moderate self-peer and self-supervisor ratings.
>
> (p. 43)

Ten years later, Topping (1998) reviewed the research literature on peer assessment in higher education, identifying 109 relevant articles, of which 67 included useful numerical data. He concluded that

> peer assessment is of adequate reliability and validity in a wide variety of applications. Peer assessment of writing and peer assessment using marks, grades, and tests have shown positive formative effects on student achievement and attitudes. These effects are as good as or better than the effects of teacher assessment. Evidence for such effects from other types of peer assessment (of presentation skills, group work or projects, and professional skills) is, as yet, more limited. Computer-assisted peer assessment is an emerging growth area.
>
> (p. 249)

Falchikov and Goldfinch (2000) also looked at studies that compared peer and teacher marks (n = 48). They concluded that

> [p]eer assessments were found to resemble more closely teacher assessments when global judgements based on well understood criteria are used rather than when marking involves assessing several individual dimensions. Similarly, peer assessments better resemble faculty assessments when academic products and processes, rather than professional practice, are being rated. Studies with high design quality appear to be associated with more valid peer assessments than those which have poor experimental design. Hypotheses concerning the greater validity of peer assessments in advanced rather than beginner courses and in science and engineering rather than in other discipline areas were not supported. In addition, multiple ratings were not found to be better than ratings by singletons.
>
> (p. 287)

More recently, Li et al (2016) similarly undertook a meta-analysis of studies comparing peer and teacher ratings, focusing on those published since 1999, which yielded 269 comparisons from 69 studies. They noted that

> [t]he estimated average Pearson correlation between peer and teacher ratings is found to be .63, which is moderately strong. This correlation is significantly higher when: (a) the peer assessment is paper-based rather than computer-assisted; (b) the subject area is not medical/clinical; (c) the course is graduate level rather than undergraduate or K-12; (d) individual work instead of group work is assessed; (e) the assessors and assessees are matched at random; (f) the peer assessment is voluntary instead of compulsory; (g) the peer assessment is non-anonymous; (h) peer raters provide both scores and qualitative comments instead of only scores; and (i) peer raters are involved in developing the rating criteria.
>
> (p. 245)

Some syntheses have focused on the use of peer review in second language learning contexts. Thus, Chen (2016) offers an analysis of twenty studies of computer-mediated peer feedback, concluding that

> the findings suggested that in the technology mode of peer feedback, students appear to give more suggestions ... that different compositions of groups generate different types of interactions ... by giving sufficient peer-feedback training, purpose explanation and combining two modes of peer feedback, the students will benefit the most from the activities.
>
> (p. 386)

Building on Chen's study, Chang (2016) reviewed 103 relevant articles published between 1990 and 2015, noting that most studies focused on Chinese or Taiwanese students and that there was a need for research on other nationalities.

These studies seem to be consistently confirming, therefore, that peer assessment can be a useful supplement or even alternative to teacher assessment, particularly where the student peers are well prepared, trained and guided in the process. As the discussion of peer instruction, mentoring and tutoring in Chapter 5 indicated, peer assessment also brings educational benefits to those doing the assessment. For example, they develop a better understanding of what they are learning and of the standards they are performing at.

It has to be acknowledged, of course, that the idea of the teacher as some kind of 'objective' gold standard in marking must be questioned. Teachers also vary in their assessments, whether different teachers of the same piece of work or the same teacher assessing the same piece of work at different times or in different circumstances. Comparing peer assessment scores with those produced by the teacher is, therefore, at best an inexact comparison.

Self-assessment has been researched in much the same way as peer assessment. Falchikov and Boud (1989; see also Boud and Falchikov 1989) carried out a meta-analysis of studies that compared self and teacher assessments, examining fifty-seven studies containing ninety-six comparisons. They found that

> [f]actors that seem to be important with regard to the closeness of correspondence between self- and teacher marks were found to include the following: the quality of design of the study (with better designed studies having closer correspondence between student and teacher than poorly designed ones); the level of the course of which the assessment was a part (with students in advanced courses appearing to be more accurate assessors than those in introductory courses); and the broad area of study (with studies within the area of science appearing to produce more accurate self-assessment generally than did those from other areas of study)
>
> (p. 395)

Kuncel, Crede and Thomas (2005), however, in an American study, come to a more cautious conclusion:

> Results based on a pairwise sample of 60,926 subjects indicate that self-reported grades are less construct valid than many scholars believe. Furthermore, self-reported grade validity was strongly moderated by actual levels of school performance and cognitive ability. These findings suggest that self-reported grades should be used with caution.
>
> (p. 63)

In a recent study, Panadero, Jonsson and Botella (2017) use meta-analysis to explore the relationships between self-assessment, self-regulated learning (discussed in Chapter 4) and self-efficacy (i.e. one's belief in one's own abilities) (n = 19). They found that 'self-assessment interventions have a positive influence on students' SRL [self-regulated learning] strategies and self-efficacy' (p. 96).

Most recently, Andrade (2019) offers a critical review of the literature on self-assessment published between 2013 and 2018, identifying seventy-six relevant articles. She concludes that 'the evidence presented in this review strongly suggests that self-assessment is most beneficial, in terms of both achievement and self-regulated learning, when it is used formatively and supported by training. What is not yet clear is why and how self-assessment works' (p. 10).

It would seem, therefore, that both peer assessment and self-assessment have positive and increasing roles to play in contemporary higher education practice.

Feedback

As some of the studies that have been quoted make clear, assessment need not be solely about providing a grade. More detailed written (or oral) comments and suggestions are also needed – particularly in formative assessment – if any improvement is to be hoped for. This broader aspect of assessment is commonly referred to as feedback and has been attracting increasing research attention, and hence research syntheses, in recent years.

Van der Kleij, Adie and Cumming (2019) offer what they call a meta-review (i.e. a systematic review) of the student role in feedback, synthesizing sixty-eight relevant studies published since 1969. This provides an interesting perspective:

Four student role categories were established: no student role (transmission model); limited student role (information processing model); some student role (communication model); and substantial student role (dialogic model). While reviews have evolved towards the student-centred perspective, this is not a linear progression over time and critical ideas about the student role in feedback have been overlooked or only partially or simplistically adopted.

(p. 303)

In an early meta-analysis, Bangert-Drowns et al (1991) review fifty-eight effect sizes from forty reports, finding mixed results (see also Kluger and DeNisi (1996) for an extensive historical review of feedback studies in all sectors):

[O]ne is struck by the counterintuitive finding ... that feedback does not always increase achievement and, in fact, is sometimes associated with decrements in achievement. A full third of the 58 findings were negative; four of these were significantly negative. Effect sizes ranged, however, from very low to very high in magnitude.

(p. 232)

However, a more nuanced analysis demonstrated that the effect of feedback depended upon the type of feedback and how it was given, with learners suitably prepared to receive and act upon the feedback:

[A] fairly coherent picture emerges of the operation of intentional mediated feedback to improve the retrieval of specific information. When students are informed of the correct answer after responding with relatively little prompting to questions on relatively complex presentations, their ability to accurately retrieve information later is greatly improved. In less optimal conditions, however, feedback's importance diminishes. More specifically, feedback is most effective under conditions that encourage learners' mindful reception.

(p. 233)

Like most things in education, therefore, feedback needs to be done well and carefully, with appropriate training and practice, if it is to have the intended effect.

Azevedo and Bernard (1995) focused on the effects of feedback in computer-based instruction: i.e. where the computer, based on pre-determined scripts, provides the feedback in response to students' answers (see also Chapter 7). Their meta-analysis of twenty-two studies found strong and positive results:

The importance of feedback as a critical component of instruction and learning is exemplified by the magnitude and direction of the mean effect size involving studies with immediate posttest administration. The unweighted mean effect size of .80 indicates that achievement outcomes were greater for the feedback group than the control group. This large effect size was interpreted as computer-presented feedback raising achievement scores by four-fifths of a standard deviation.

(p. 121)

Shute (2008) reviews the research on formative feedback, identifying 141 relevant publications. She concludes that 'formative feedback should address the accuracy of a learner's response to a problem or task and may touch on particular errors and misconceptions, the latter representing more specific or elaborated types of feedback. Formative feedback should also permit the comparison of actual performance with some established standard of performance' (p. 175). She offers extensive guidelines for the provision of formative feedback to different kinds of students.

Evans (2013), in a widely cited article, offers a systematic review of research into assessment feedback in higher education from 2000 to 2012, identifying 460 relevant articles. She

> highlights the multiplicity of students' and lecturers' responses to the assessment feedback process and the value of bringing together a number of theoretical frameworks to assist our understanding of assessment feedback. Integration of cognitivist and constructivist approaches to feedback in terms of the requirements of the task, subject, and context is vital to move the assessment feedback research agenda forward. By doing this, a more comprehensive examination of both transitory responses to feedback (short- or long-lived depending on the context) and those more stable feedback responses of individuals, across contexts, relating to personal histories of feedback situations, values, beliefs, goals, and concerns will be achieved.
> (pp. 106–7)

Evans here highlights the complexity and variability of the feedback process, with students responding in different ways to feedback and having their preferences of feedback approach.

Li and De Luca (2014) review thirty-seven relevant empirical studies of feedback published between 2000 and 2011, mostly from the UK and Australia. The overriding impression they give, like Evans, is of variety:

> These studies have explored undergraduate students' wide-ranging perspectives on the effectiveness and utility of assessment feedback, the divergent styles of assessment feedback of lecturers and tutors in various disciplines, teachers' divergent interpretations of assessment criteria and confusion about the dual roles of assessment feedback, and the divergences between teachers' beliefs and practices.
> (p. 378)

While some divergence is to be expected and welcomed – feedback practices in theoretical physics, for example, may differ from those in criminology – some minimal shared appreciation of the possibilities among higher education teachers would be helpful.

Other syntheses have been focused on particular kinds of feedback. Thus, Huisman et al (2019) provide a meta-analysis of research on the impact of formative peer feedback on students' academic writing in particular (n = 24).

> Engagement in peer feedback resulted in larger writing improvements compared to (no-feedback) controls and compared to self-assessment. Peer feedback and teacher feedback resulted in similar writing improvements. The nature of the peer feedback significantly moderated the impact that peer feedback had on students' writing

improvement, whereas only a theoretically plausible, though non-significant moderating pattern was found for the number of peers that students engaged with.

(p. 1)

Fukkink, Trienekens and Kramer (2011) carried out a meta-analysis of the use of video feedback, with a particular focus on those training to be professionals (e.g. doctors, teachers). They found that

> the video feedback method has a statistically significant effect on the interaction skills of professionals in a range of contact professions. The aggregate effect, calculated on the basis of 217 experimental comparisons from 33 experimental studies involving a total of 1,058 people, was 0.40 standard deviation (SE = 0.07). The effects of training were greater for programs working with a standard observation form of target skills that were central to the program. Results were more positive for outcome measures that measured positive skills rather than negative ones.

(p. 45)

Mahoney, Macfarlane and Ajjawi (2019), seemingly unaware of Fukkink et al's study, provide a qualitative synthesis (i.e. systematic review) of video feedback in higher education. They identified thirty-seven studies using what they term talking head, screencast or combination screencast approaches. They concluded that

> [w]hile the research considered in this review has found that the medium of video feedback has a generally high level of acceptability to students and markers, it has not yet been established whether the format improves students' learning and performance and, if so, how this impact compares with other feedback formats. Video feedback also continues to perpetuate a monologic, 'information transmission' approach to feedback, albeit in a novel guise that gives the suggestion of dialogue.

(p. 173)

Reddy and Andrade (2010) provided a critical review of the developing literature on the use of assessment rubrics (i.e. written guidance, usually in tabular form, on the grading of assessments) to enhance feedback in higher education. They noted that

> [s]tudies of rubrics in higher education have been undertaken in a wide range of disciplines and for multiple purposes, including increasing student achievement, improving instruction and evaluating programmes. While, student perceptions of rubrics are generally positive and some authors report positive responses to rubric use by instructors, others noted a tendency for instructors to resist using them. Two studies suggested that rubric use was associated with improved academic performance, while one did not. The potential of rubrics to identify the need for improvements in courses and programmes has been demonstrated. Studies of the validity of rubrics have shown that clarity and appropriateness of language is a central concern. Studies of rater reliability tend to show that rubrics can lead to a relatively common interpretation of student performance. Suggestions for future research include the use of more rigorous research methods, more attention to validity and reliability, a closer focus on learning and research on rubric use in diverse educational contexts.

(p. 435)

Students may also be encouraged and trained to use rubrics for self and peer assessment (see the previous section) and even involved in their construction.

More recently, Cockett and Jackson (2018) produced an integrative literature review of the use of rubrics, identifying fifteen relevant studies. They concluded:

> It is clear from the literature that there are some advantages to be gained by using rubrics to enhance feedback to students. Increased student skills in self-assessment, self-regulation and ability to understand and clarity of assessment criteria are all important gains that can be delivered. However rubrics cannot be seen as a panacea for all of the concerns that are raised by students about the quality, usefulness and consistency of assessment feedback.
>
> (p. 12)

What is also clear, though, is that the movement is towards increasing transparency in the assessment process.

Previous and current assessment

A significant body of research has examined the relationship between previous assessment (e.g. school leaving grades) and higher education assessment results. This has led in turn to a number of research syntheses.

Schuler, Funk and Baron-Boldt (1990) carried out a meta-analysis on the predictive validity of school grades, identifying 63 German studies containing 102 separate samples. They note that

> [t]he meta-analysis of German studies on the predictive validity of school grades yields coefficients as high as in recent meta-analysis of the most valid diagnostic instruments (cognitive tests) predicting success at university and in vocational training. The higher comparative values from American studies on prediction of academic success can be explained by the greater similarity between school and university education in the USA compared to in the FRG [Federal Republic of Germany]. However, in the area of vocational training success prediction German school final grades are of higher validity than the American ones. Using a similar argument, this may be due to the fact that the German vocational training system with its dual structure contains parallels to the school system whereas this sort of uniform education system is totally missing in America.
>
> (p. 102)

In the United States, Kuncel, Kochevar and Ones (2014; see also the discussion of postgraduate study in Chapter 8) produced a meta-analysis of the predictive power of letters of recommendation in admissions decisions. They found that '[o]verall, letters of recommendation, in their current form, are generally positively but weakly correlated with multiple aspects of performance in post-secondary education. However, letters do appear to provide incremental information about degree attainment, a difficult and heavily motivationally determined outcome' (p. 101).

Cheating

On the downside, there has also been growing interest in recent years in student cheating or plagiarism, with the increasing availability of material online seen as a particular issue or temptation. In an early review, Whitley (1998) examined 107 studies published between 1970 and 1996:

> The studies found cheating to be more common in the 1969–75 and 1986–96 time periods than between 1976 and 1985. Among the strongest correlates of cheating were having moderate expectations of success, having cheated in the past, studying under poor conditions, holding positive attitudes toward cheating, perceiving that social norms support cheating, and anticipating a large reward for success.
>
> (p. 235)

All of this sounds fairly believable, even understandable, if not excusable.

Newton (2018) offers a contemporary systematic review of the research literature on commercial contract cheating; that is, the proliferation of individuals and organizations offering to complete students' assignments, or even attend examinations on their behalf, for an agreed price. The conclusions are somewhat depressing:

> Seventy-one samples were identified from 65 studies, going back to 1978. These included 54,514 participants. Contract cheating was self-reported by a historic average of 3.52% of students. The data indicate that contract cheating is increasing; in samples from 2014 to present the percentage of students admitting to paying someone else to undertake their work was 15.7%, potentially representing 31 million students around the world.
>
> (p. 1)

It would seem, therefore, that all higher education institutions and employees need to be much more aware of the likelihood that some of their students are cheating, how to identify this and what they might be able to do about it.

Other topics

Other research syntheses have focused on detailed practical questions concerning assessment in higher education. Thus, Bangert-Drowns, Kulik and Kulik (1991) carried out a meta-analysis of findings on the impact of the frequency of classroom testing:

> The meta-analysis showed that students who took at least one test during a 15-week term scored about one half of a standard deviation higher on criterion examinations than did students who took no tests. Better criterion performance was associated with more frequent testing, but the amount of improvement in achievement diminished as the number of tests increased.
>
> (p. 89)

This suggests both that regular testing can play a formative role in preparing students for the final examination and that there is an optimum number (which might, of course, vary between students) of such tests before students start to lose interest.

Brady, Devitt and Kiersey (2019) provide a systematic literature review of academic staff attitudes on the use of technology for assessment (see also Chapter 7), analysing sixty-five articles published between 2012 and 2017. Their analysis indicated that it was relatively early in the adoption cycle to come to any definitive conclusions:

> This study shows that TfA [technology for assessment] is still at an early stage of adoption with limited pedagogical underpinnings or theoretical frameworks. Critically even though discussion of academic staff efficiencies was dominant, there was a lack of quantification in terms of design, set-up and ongoing maintenance, time and resource costs or gains. Despite a sense that institutional supports could be critical, there was limited insight into the type or scale of resources and institutional structures that could best support and drive adoption.
>
> (p. 15)

Crooks (1988) reviews the extensive literature on classroom assessment, at both higher and other levels of education, coming to the overall conclusion that 'classroom evaluation has powerful direct and indirect impacts, which may be positive or negative, and thus deserves very thoughtful planning and implementation' (p. 438). Gregg and Nelson (2012) carried out a meta-analysis on studies (n = 9) of the effectiveness of extra time as a test accommodation for adolescents with learning disabilities transitioning to higher education but came to no clear conclusions.

In recent years there has been increased interest in the provision of what has been called authentic assessment, that is, assessment that replicates the kind of practices that would occur in the workplace (see also the discussion of learning and work in Chapter 6). There has been one research synthesis to date of which I am aware. Villarroel et al (2017) carried out a systematic review of the literature on this topic from the period 1988 to 2015 (n = 112). They note that

> [t]he literature identifies multiple benefits to students (and to employers) from the use of authentic assessment. However, devising authentic assessment, particularly in systems with strong traditions of 'testing', is not easy as we lack a robust concept on which to base guidance for assessment design and operation. This article has attempted to contribute to the debate by clarifying three key dimensions of authentic assessment. These dimensions provide guidance for teachers seeking more authentic assessment, including assessment-related teaching practices which develop 'authentic' capabilities for employment. The breadth of the dimensions and their reflection in the proposed four step model encourages the integration of discipline-specific skills and knowledge with application in the workplace, but also, importantly, with the generic capacity to evaluate and improve performance. They also highlight the complexity of learning for authentic practice, and the potential of assessment to create a richer learning environment and build capability for higher order and lifelong learning.
>
> (p. 11)

There is clearly a lot of potential here, but more work and research needs to be done in order to come up with workable approaches.

Conclusions

- The provision of formative assessment is of critical importance if student performance is to improve during study.
- Self and peer assessment can be as accurate and useful as teacher assessment.
- Feedback can have a powerful effect on student achievement if it is carefully given, varied and students are aware of its importance.
- Higher education institutions face a major task in dealing with student cheating.

Chapter 10
Course design – outcomes

Introduction

This chapter discusses syntheses of higher education research relating to its outcomes. A total of sixty-eight research syntheses were identified for discussion in this chapter (see Table 5 in Chapter 3), together comprising 24 per cent, the second largest proportion, of the total for course design. As with most of the other areas of course design considered in Chapters 5 to 9, these syntheses comprise a reasonably balanced mix of meta-analyses and systematic reviews. Thus, there are thirty-one meta-analyses and twenty-eight systematic reviews, together with six substantive literature reviews and, unusually, three studies which combine meta-analysis and systematic review.

There are a number of specialist higher education journals that focus on the topics discussed in this chapter, including the *Journal of College Student Development* and the *Journal of College Student Retention*. Many other more generic journals also publish relevant articles.

Research into higher education outcomes is concerned with both the immediate and longer term consequences of participation in higher education, though it is usually the former that is focused on. What do students leave higher education with, in terms of generic skills and competencies as well as disciplinary knowledge? How well prepared are they for their future work, professional or broader life roles? These are clearly key questions for higher education.

Outcomes are the end stage (at least temporarily – students may, and increasingly do, return for further study) of the higher education process, an expression of what the student has achieved and what they have to offer. They may be set out in qualitative or quantitative terms, either generically or with reference to specific elements.

Clearly, it is important to all parties and stakeholders (e.g. students themselves, universities, actual and potential employers, the government, the general public) to understand and appreciate what the outcomes of higher education are, both in general and for particular disciplines and individual students. Hence there is a strong interest in this topic, which has been reflected in research and then in the number of published meta-analyses, literature reviews and systematic reviews.

One characteristic of this literature, and others, is the use of different terms to mean much the same thing. Thus, there are discussions of achievement, capabilities, key or generic skills and/or competencies, and of learning gain, value added and/or employability, all of which relate to, somewhat overlapping, aspects of this topic.

Of the systematic reviews and meta-analyses identified for, and discussed in, this chapter, many have concerned themselves with achievement and other generic outcomes from higher education (see Fraser et al 1987). Of those others which have looked at more specific outcomes, studies of the critical thinking abilities produced through higher education – seen by many as the quintessential academic skill – have attracted particular attention. Other outcomes have also been the subject of research, including professional identity, information literacy and oral presentation.

In addition, a number of research syntheses have concerned themselves with the transfer of students between higher education institutions and with their persistence and retention.

Achievement during higher education

The question of what students achieve during their higher education is clearly fundamental. After all, if they achieved nothing or next to nothing their participation would be irrelevant, a waste of time and other resources. On the contrary, having invested a great deal of their time, and also these days a considerable amount of their money, in their higher education, students wish to benefit from the experience as much as possible.

Their achievement may be measured in a variety of ways (see the previous chapter) and may consist of a range of both generic and specific skills and knowledges. Research syntheses regarding these skills and knowledges are considered in the latter part of the chapter. In this section and the next one we will review syntheses that have focused on research into what affects student achievement.

This section has been divided, for convenience, into six subsections. These consider generic studies of the factors affecting student achievement in higher education and then focus more specifically on the impact of student characteristics and behaviour, psychological attributes, study skills and other factors. First, however, we will briefly review and pay tribute to one of the key texts that has been produced on this topic, the three editions of *How College Affects Students* (Mayhew et al 2016, Pascarella and Terenzini 1991, 2005).

How college affects students

The first edition of this book (Pascarella and Terenzini 1991) was subtitled 'findings and insights from twenty years of research'. It builds upon an earlier book by Feldman and Newcomb (1969) and on other work (e.g. Astin 1977, Bowen 1977) in synthesizing twenty years of empirical research. The focus is on American research and writing, with over 2,600 studies produced since 1967 considered (the book is 894 pages in length!).

Pascarella and Terenzini describe their analytical approach as 'narrative explanatory synthesis' (1991, p. 10), with some supplementary use of meta-analysis. They located their studies through the use of abstracting documents and databases, selected conference proceedings and colleagues. The book is organized in terms of the impact of higher education on learning and cognitive development, personal growth and change, socio-economic attainment and quality of life. Their general conclusion is that

> our synthesis of the evidence indicates that the college years are a time of student change on a broad front. A number of the shifts we observed appear to be fairly substantial in magnitude. Indeed, the changes that occur during college from freshman to senior year are generally the largest 'effects' we noted in our synthesis. It is the breadth of change and development, however, that is perhaps the most striking characteristic of the evidence. Students not only make statistically significant gains in factual knowledge and in a range of general cognitive and intellectual skills; they also change on a broad array of value, attitudinal, psycho-social, and moral dimensions. There is some modest tendency for changes in intellectual skills to be larger in magnitude than changes in other areas, but the evidence is quite consistent in indicating that the changes coincident with the college years extend substantially beyond cognitive growth.
> (p. 557)

The second edition (Pascarella and Terenzini 2005) focuses on the research completed and published since 1990 – in the words of the book's sub-title, 'a third decade of research'. The approach and structure of the book (827 pages!) remain broadly the same, and their conclusion re-emphasizes that of the first edition: 'Although the evidence from the 1990s on change during college is nowhere near as extensive as the evidence uncovered in our 1991 review, there is little that would lead us to revise our earlier conclusion that maturation during the undergraduate years is holistic in nature and embraces multiple facets of individual change' (p. 572).

The latest edition (Mayhew et al 2016), sub-titled '21st century evidence that higher education works', has seven co-authors, including Pascarella and Terenzini, and runs to just 764 pages. The focus is on 1,848 peer-reviewed articles, with conference papers and theses excluded. Search engines such as Google Scholar, ERIC and PsycINFO were used for the first time, along with hand searches of key American journals. The authors identify 'some large changes during college, especially for improvements in critical thinking skills, moral reasoning, and intellectual and social self-confidence' (p. 524). However, they qualify their findings in the following fashion:

> [I]t is important to note that the single strongest predictor of a student's outcomes at the end of college is that student's characteristics on the same construct when entering college. Therefore, while college can (and often does) profoundly shape learning, growth, and development, the precollege environment has a substantial impact on the attributes of college graduates.
> (p. 572)

Anyone interested in student achievement during, and after, higher education – particularly in the United States, but elsewhere as well – would do well to consult these three research syntheses.

Generic studies

Generic studies of student achievement during higher education attempt to provide an overview of the impact of the higher education experience. They do so, however, in somewhat different ways.

Hattie, Biggs and Purdie (1996; see also Hattie 2009) provide a meta-analysis of the effects of learning skills interventions on student learning, examining fifty-one studies (just under half of the sample were higher education students): 'Such interventions typically focused on task-related skills, self-management of learning, or affective components such as motivation and self-concept' (p. 99). They concluded that

> most intervention does work most of the time. After all, the effect size over all studies was 0.45; and a very respectable 0.57 for performance. Even when we allow for the very clear success of mnemonic-type programs [those offering simple guides to help memory], this figure becomes 0.53 on transformational, or higher-cognitive-order, performance. This is as good as any figure reported for teaching methods elsewhere. When classified according to level of structural complexity, single-component interventions concentrating on near transfer of a specific task-related skill were more effective than multiple-component interventions. Relational interventions, which aimed to change a range of metacognitive behaviors in context, were also systematically effective in near transfer situations; far transfer of skills was less likely to have occurred.
> (pp. 128–9)

This is not, of course, a surprising conclusion, for two main reasons. First, students are usually aware that a learning skill intervention is underway and tend to respond positively to such attempts to improve their learning. Second, and relatedly, very few negative findings are reported in the research literature; in other words, where a learning intervention does not appear to work, those responsible do not go out of their way to publicize this.

Dochy, Segers and Buehl (1999) examined the research on the relations between prior knowledge, assessment and outcomes (n = 183). They concluded that

> [w]hile prior knowledge generally had positive effects on students' performance, the effects varied by assessment method. More specifically, prior knowledge was more likely to have negative or no effects on performance when flawed assessment measures were used. However, in some studies, flawed methods yielded informative results. Thus, in educational research the implications of assessment measures must be considered when examining the effects of prior knowledge.
> (p. 145)

Again, it is unsurprising that prior knowledge – which would be related with success in prior assessment – is related to student performance, since, as Mayhew et al (2016, quoted in the previous section) make clear, the strongest predictor of student performance is their prior performance.

Schneider and Preckel (2017) undertook a systematic review of meta-analyses concerning achievement in higher education. They 'included 38 meta-analyses investigating 105 correlates of achievement, based on 3,330 effect sizes from almost 2 million students' (p. 565). On the basis of this substantive analysis, they find that

> [i]nstructional methods and the way they are implemented on the microlevel are substantially associated with achievement in higher education. This emphasizes the importance of teacher training in higher education. Among the different approaches to teaching, social interaction has the highest frequency of high positive effect sizes. Lectures, small-group learning, and project-based learning all have positive associations with achievement provided they balance teacher-centered with student-centered instructional elements. As yet, instruction and communication technology has comparably weak effect sizes, which did not increase over the past decades. High-achieving students in higher education are characterized by qualities that, in part, are affected by prior school education, for example, prior achievement, self-efficacy, intelligence, and the goal-directed use of learning strategies … The effect sizes of the meta-analyses included in this systematic review indicate that such an evidence-based approach has great potential for increasing achievement in higher education.
>
> (p. 596)

This largely confirms the findings and arguments of Hattie, Biggs and Purdie (1996) and Dochy, Segers and Buehl (1999), just quoted. Learning interventions effect student performance and achievement, particularly when they emphasize student-centred approaches. However, the advantages of better prior schooling and achievement remain. There is also an issue, of course, of the costs associated with any learning intervention.

Most recently, Saa et al (2019), an international team from the United Arab Emirates and Vietnam, undertook a systematic review of studies using predictive data mining techniques to identify the factors affecting student performance in higher education. They critically reviewed thirty-six research articles published in the period between 2009 and 2018. They found that 'the most common and widely used factors for predicting students' performance in higher education are students' previous grades and class performance, students' e-Learning activity, students' demographics, and students' social information' (p. 14).

Student characteristics and behaviour

A series of studies have explored the relationships between various student characteristics or behaviours and their achievement.

Crede, Roch and Kieszczynka (2010) carried out a meta-analysis to explore the relationships between class attendance, grades and student characteristics. Following extensive online searches:

> The final database for the relationship of class attendance with academic outcomes consisted of 99 correlations from 90 independent samples representing data from a total of 28,034 students. In addition, the database also included 83 correlations for the relationship between attendance and other student characteristics, representing data from 33 independent samples and 11,110 students. The data set contained articles

and dissertations covering 82 years, from 1927 to 2009, and consisted of 52 published articles and 16 unpublished dissertations or papers.

(p. 278)

They came to a strong conclusion:

> Class attendance appears to be a better predictor of college grades than any other known predictor of college grades – including SAT [scholastic aptitude test] scores, HSGPA [high school grade point average], studying skills, and the amount of time spent studying. Indeed, the relationship is so strong as to suggest that dramatic improvements in average grades (and failure rates) could be achieved by efforts to increase class attendance rates among college students.
>
> (pp. 288–9)

Blimling (1989) provides a meta-analysis of the research on the relationship between college residence and academic performance published from 1966 to 1987 (n = 21). His findings were mixed:

> To rely solely on the results of the 21 studies in which residence hall students were compared with students living at home might lead one to conclude that residence hall students perform better academically than do students living at home, and that living in a residence hall influences this superior performance positively. A closer examination of the studies, however, suggests that the latter assertion is inaccurate. When only studies that controlled for differences in past academic performance were used, the reviewed research does not show that living in a conventional residence hall significantly influences academic performance over living at home.
>
> (p. 559)

Further research and synthesis in this area seem overdue, given the developments over the last thirty years and the greater variety of accommodation options now available to students.

Sackett et al (2009) examined studies on the role of socio-economic status (SES) in explaining the relation between admissions tests and subsequent academic performance. Data from forty-one colleges and universities were supplemented by a meta-analysis of sixty-six studies and a re-analysis of available longitudinal data sets:

> Our analyses of multiple large data sources produced consistent findings. First, SES was indeed related to admissions test scores. In broad, unrestricted populations, this correlation was quite substantial (e.g., $r = .42$ among the population of SAT [Scholastic Aptitude Test] takers). Second, scores on admissions tests were indeed predictive of academic performance, as indexed by grades. Observed correlations in samples of admitted students averaged about $r = .35$ for admissions tests ... Third, the test – grade relationship was not an artifact of common influences of SES on both test scores and grades ... Fourth, the SES – grade relationship was consistent with a model of a mediating mechanism in which SES influences test scores, which are subsequently predictive of grades. SES had a near-zero relationship with grades other than through this SES – test – grade chain of relationships.
>
> (p. 17)

Despite all of the recent and continuing efforts to widen participation in higher education, and better engage under-represented groups, those from higher class backgrounds – who will, of course, often have gone to better schools and have a higher prior achievement – still, therefore, appear to have a significant advantage.

On a more mundane level, Kim and Seo (2015), a Korean team, carried out a meta-analysis of studies looking at the relationship between procrastination and student performance. They identified 33 relevant studies involving 38,529 students. While they concluded, unsurprisingly, that 'procrastination was negatively correlated with academic performance', they also noted that 'this relationship was influenced by the choice of measures or indicators' (p. 26).

Psychological attributes

A considerable amount of research, and subsequent research syntheses, has explored the relationship between students' psychological characteristics and their higher education achievement.

Richardson, Abraham and Bond (2012) provide a meta-analysis of research into the psychological correlates of students' academic performance (expressed as grade point average (GPA)). The psychological correlates were ordered into five groups: personality traits, motivational factors, self-regulatory learning strategies, students' approaches to learning and psychosocial contextual influences. The PsycINFO and Web of Knowledge databases were searched between 1997 and 2010, identifying 217 relevant articles, from which 54 data sets were randomly selected for analysis. Their

> results confirmed ... conclusions that effort regulation and academic self-efficacy are important correlates of tertiary GPA. In addition, the data show that cognitions specific to academic performance (i.e., performance self-efficacy and grade goal) were the strongest correlates of GPA. The data thus emphasize the importance of goal setting and task-specific self-efficacy.
>
> (p. 374)

Honicke and Broadbent (2016) also focused on academic self-efficacy and performance. For their systematic review, they searched the literature published between 2003 and 2015 and found fifty-nine relevant articles. They concluded that

> [i]n addition to confirming the important role of high levels of ASE [academic self-efficacy] in influencing increased levels of academic performance, the current review brings to light additional variables that act to moderate or mediate this relationship ... Further research is required that specifically investigates academic performance and variables that significantly correlate with ASE such as goal orientation subtypes and cognitive factors like effort regulation ... longitudinal studies that focus on interventions designed to manipulate and improve ASE and performance are required in order to establish causality and understand temporal patterns among these variables.
>
> (p. 81)

Trapmann et al (2007), a German team, provide a meta-analysis of the relationship between the five-factor model (FFM: the five factors are agreeableness, conscientiousness, emotional stability/neuroticism, extraversion and openness) of personality and academic performance (n = 58). The '[r]esults show that the influence of personality traits on academic achievement depends on the success criterion. While Neuroticism is related to academic satisfaction, Conscientiousness correlates with grades. Extraversion, Openness to Experience, and Agreeableness have no significant impact on academic success' (p. 132).

Poropat (2009) carried out a similar synthesis two years later. While he considered all levels of education, most of the eighty studies analysed related to higher education. He concluded that

> personality is definitely associated with academic performance ... the results of this research have ... established a firm basis for viewing personality as an important component of students' willingness to perform. And, just as with work performance, Conscientiousness has the strongest association with academic performance of all the FFM dimensions; its association with academic performance rivaled that of intelligence ... Yet the complications highlighted by the moderator analyses indicate that the relationship between personality and academic performance must be understood as a complex phenomenon in its own right.
>
> (p. 334)

Unsurprisingly, then, but reassuringly, both self-efficacy (i.e. the student's view of their ability) and effort or conscientiousness are closely linked to student performance and achievement.

An earlier meta-analysis by Bourhis and Allen (1992) examined the impact of communication apprehension (CA: i.e. fears about communication, whether related to public speaking or simply conversing with others) on achievement, identifying twenty-three articles of relevance containing thirty experiments, mostly on college students. They found that '[a] small but stable relationship exists between CA and cognitive performance ... as CA increases cognitive performance decreases' (p. 73).

Study skills

Study skills are, of course, an obvious factor impacting upon student achievement in higher education, and hence another target for research and synthesis. There is a close relationship here to the psychological attributes discussed in the previous section.

Robbins et al (2004) focused on the relationship between psychosocial and study skill factors and college outcomes (n = 109), examining the data on both performance and persistence. They also found 'relationships between retention and academic goals, academic self-efficacy, and academic-related skills. The best predictors for GPA were academic self-efficacy and achievement motivation' (p. 261).

Robbins et al (2009) built on this study in re-examining the mediating role that psychosocial factors play between college interventions and college outcomes, using integrated meta-analytic path analysis. They 'highlight the importance of both academic skill and self-management-based interventions; they also note the salience of motivational and emotional control mediators across both performance and retention outcomes' (p. 1163). In other words, a mix of skills/ability and motivation/self-efficacy appears key to better performance and achievement.

Crede and Kuncel (2008) carried out a meta-analysis to investigate 'the construct validity and predictive validity of 10 study skill constructs for college students' (p. 425), assembling a large database:

> The database for the relationships between SHSAs [study habits, skills and attitudes] and academic performance consisted of 961 correlations from 344 independent samples representing 72,431 college students. In addition, 424 correlations between SHSA predictors and cognitive ability tests and 80 correlations between SHSAs and personality tests were also coded.
> (p. 432)

They concluded that study skills were the 'third pillar' – alongside prior academic performance and admissions test scores – supporting academic performance:

> We have shown that study skills, study habits, study attitudes, and study motivation exhibit relationships with academic performance that are approximately as strong as the relationship between academic performance and the two most frequently used predictors of academic performance: prior academic performance and scores on admissions tests. This finding, together with the relative independence of SHSA constructs from both prior academic performance and admissions test scores, suggests that study skills, study habits, study attitudes, and study motivation play a critical and central role in determining students' academic performance.
> (p. 444)

Other factors

A number of other factors have been explored for their impact upon student achievement.

Larwin, Gorman and Larwin (2013) examined the impact of testing aids (i.e. student produced crib sheets) and open-book examinations on student performance. Their meta-analysis identified fifteen relevant studies with thirty effect sizes and concluded that

> the 'low-tech' inclusion of testing aids into the postsecondary classroom can have a positive impact on student achievement in terms of exam performance ... Unlike open-textbook testing, the use of student prepared testing aids may enable and encourage students to prepare for examinations with higher levels of engagement.
> (pp. 440–1)

Schwinger et al (2014) used meta-analysis to explore the relationship between academic self-handicapping (a strategy for regulating the threat to self-esteem) and performance, identifying thirty-six studies with forty-nine effect sizes, mainly but not wholly in higher education. They concluded 'that educational interventions to enhance academic achievement should additionally focus on preventing self-handicapping' (p. 744). In other words, students need to be encouraged not just to do their best but to make sure they have done all they can even if this involves some risks.

Sisk et al (2018) employed meta-analyses to explore whether growth mindsets (beliefs that attributes are malleable with effort) were important for academic achievement. Only weak effect sizes were found, though the authors argued that 'students with low socioeconomic status or who are academically at risk might benefit from mind-set interventions' (p. 549).

Higher education and subsequent achievement

Other researchers have focused on the relationship, or lack of it, between achievement in higher education and subsequently at work. After all, one of the main functions of higher education is widely accepted to be the preparation of students for their working lives, either in a specific profession which their degree is directly related to (e.g. accounting, civil engineering, medicine, teaching) or more generally.

Cohen (1984) carried out a meta-analysis of 108 studies of the relationship between college grades and various criteria of adult achievement. He found that

> [t]he average correlation between grade average and a composite success criterion was .18, a small effect. Correlations between grade average and eight other criteria of adult achievement were also small, ranging from .09 to .20 ... The results of this meta-analysis may be somewhat discouraging to those who place a great deal of importance on the predictive value of grades.
>
> (p. 281)

In the same year, Samson et al (1984) published what they termed a 'quantitative synthesis' of 35 studies containing 209 correlations of the relationship between academic and occupational performance. While they found a significant relationship, it was so small that 'academic grades or test scores [were] nearly useless in predicting occupational effectiveness and satisfaction' (p. 318).

Bretz (1989) provided another meta-analysis, building on an earlier literature review by Hoyt (1965), identifying fifty relevant publications containing sixty-two measurements that had been published between 1917 and 1983. He confirmed Cohen's analysis, finding that 'college GPA [grade point average] is generally a poor predictor of adult work-related achievement' (p. 17).

There do not appear to have been any more recently published research syntheses. The general conclusion seems to be, however, that achievement in higher education is only a poor guide to subsequent achievement. This should probably not be an undue cause for concern, however, as higher education only lasts for a few years, while one's subsequent career and life should last for decades, allowing plenty of time for further development and other influences.

Other generic studies

Higher education is not, of course, solely about the attainment of a particular qualification or grade. It is supposed to provide other general benefits as well, and these have, naturally, also been the subject of research and synthesis. The focus has been variously on what has been termed value added, employability, graduate skills, academic capabilities, generic competencies or learning gains. Clearly, though a little confusing, all of these terms are closely related.

Grosemans, Coertjens and Kyndt (2017) carried out a systematic review of the research in this area that focused on the role of learning and fit in the transition to work process, identifying forty-five relevant studies. They noted the relative lack of research into employers' perspectives, and the different, if overlapping, perspectives held by the stakeholders involved:

> Results indicate that most emphasis is put on theoretical knowledge, communication, problem-solving and learning skills. Although the perception on what has to be learned differs for employers, educators, and graduates, each group valued generic competencies most.
>
> (p. 67)

Higher education researchers based in the UK and Australia tend now to think of the transition to work in terms of graduate employability. Artess, Hooley and Mellors-Bourne (2017; for an Australian review see Small, Shacklock and Marchant 2018) carried out a review of the literature published on this topic in the period 2012 to 2016 (n = 187) for the UK Higher Education Academy. They usefully identified a series of strategies that universities and colleges could, and did, take to enhance their students' employability:

> embedding employability in the curriculum and ensuring that students are able to make a connection between employability outcomes and their discipline; providing a range of co-curricular and extra-curricular opportunities for students to enhance their employability; building links with the labour market and encouraging students to do the same. The literature finds value in a wide range of connections between HEPs [higher education providers] and employers. In particular, there is evidence of the impact of providing students with real connections to employers and actual experience of the labour market; supporting students to increase their confidence, self-belief and self-efficacy through their studies; encouraging reflection and increasing students' capacity to articulate and communicate their learning to employers; encouraging student mobility and fostering a global perspective; using institutional career guidance services as organising and co-ordinating structures for HEPs' employability strategies. However, in order to achieve this, the role of the services needs to be broadly conceived.
>
> (p. 7)

This raises an issue which is common to many university and college support services (see also the discussion in Chapter 11), namely whether provision is best provided generically and centrally by the institution concerned or whether it is important to take a specific disciplinary approach. Of course, the response to this issue may vary depending upon the discipline, with professional disciplines such as accounting, education, engineering, medicine and nursing having much clearer and specific links to particular employers.

The flipside of employability is, of course, under-employment (i.e. where graduates are employed in jobs that do not require or need graduate qualifications), and this has also been the focus of research and systematic review. Scurry and Blenkinsopp (2011) looked, in particular, at the different ways in which graduate under-employment was defined and articulated in the research literature:

> [U]nderpinning many of these issues is the enormous challenge of defining what today should be understood as appropriate employment for graduates, a challenge that is linked to the differing expectations of such employment held by a range of stakeholders including students, graduates, employers, and governments. There is a need for future research on the area of graduate underemployment that explores the unfolding and dynamic nature of the phenomenon, in particular the ways in which underemployed graduates make sense of their situation over time. We suggest that an important basis for developing our theoretical understanding of graduate underemployment is to draw upon relevant theoretical frameworks from career studies – specifically those on the objective-subjective duality of career, career indecision, and career success.
>
> (p. 655)

Kim and Lalancette (2013) talk of the value added by higher education, in the context of a report for the Organization for Economic Cooperation and Development (OECD) relating to the international Assessment of Higher Education Learning Outcomes (AHELO) project. Their literature review discussed a variety of approaches to the measurement of value added, concluding that

> value-added measurement can provide policy makers and prospective students with evidence of student learning in educational institutions for external accountability purposes. It can also be used internally by institutions to inform discussions on ways to improve general education programmes or the general intellectual skills of their students. The results of value-added measurement can help institutions identify their own strengths and weaknesses in their service provisions and learn more about achieving learning outcomes by benchmarking against other institutions admitting students of similar entering academic ability.
>
> (p. 36)

In their systematic review, Calonge and Shah (2016) use the terms 'employability' and 'graduate skills', rather than 'value added', focusing on the potential of MOOCs (massive, open, online courses) to develop and enhance these. They find 'evidence that corporations have and are exploring bridging the skills gap, in partnership with MOOC platforms and universities. In many instances, corporations are specifically exploring how MOOCs could be offered at scale as interactive continuing professional development (CPD) opportunities to their employees or as refresher courses to their often technology-savvy and geographically-dispersed workforce, using a quick and cost-effective "learn-certify-deploy" pattern' (p. 82). MOOCs are single courses rather than full degree programmes, so their potential is naturally somewhat more limited, but more immediate in impact.

Osmani et al (2019) also examined research into graduates' employability skills, with a particular focus on differences between what employers wanted and what graduates offered in the fields of accounting and finance (A&F) and information and communication technology (ICT) in the UK. Their systematic literature review identified sixty-one relevant articles. Perhaps unsurprisingly

> [t]his study portrays clear evidences of a mismatch of priorities between academic literature and actual practitioners in terms of graduate attributes ... Such mismatches exist because of the nature of the suppliers (universities) and demand (employers). The focus should be on how employability is instilled rather than what skills are taught. Furthermore, the variation shown here between A&F and ICT is another evidence of how different sectors are looking for different skills. This confirms recent reports regarding the inconsistency of the demand leading to inability of universities to satisfy 'all' employers following the current employability curriculum.
>
> (p. 430)

Of course, the supposed mismatch between what universities produce and what employers want or need is one of the longest standing debates, going back at least as far as the nineteenth century when universities were first being founded in numbers. University provision varies, and each employer has their own needs and preferences, so, unless universities work on a one-to-one basis with employers, which is obviously impractical in most cases, it is hard to see anything like complete satisfaction being achieved.

Braithwaite and Corr (2016) provide a meta-analysis of studies, mainly experimental, that have sought to analyse the development of academic capabilities, which they link to employability, noting that '[o]ne longer term outcome of such enhanced academic capabilities may be seen in employability, the success of which requires bundles of cognitive, affective and interpersonal capabilities that develop over life' (p. 169).

A related concern has to do with how these academic capabilities, or whatever term is preferred, are developed in higher education. One continuing debate here concerns whether the development of such capabilities should be embedded in the curriculum (i.e. in every course across the university) or taught separately from the disciplines. Chan et al (2017) examined the literature on the development of generic competencies in the higher education curriculum (n = 56), concluding that

> teaching pedagogy, curriculum and students' experience and learning strategy are currently not aligned to ensure the adoption of a systematic approach to developing generic competencies ... disciplinary differences alone may not be sufficient to explain the many variations of understandings of generic competencies. Developing a common understanding of generic competencies is therefore essential for building a conceptual base on which a generic competencies agenda can be built.
>
> (p. 7)

This sounds reasonable. If we do not have a reasonably common understanding of what generic competences higher education develops, it is very difficult to develop policy and practice in this area.

Rogaten et al (2019) offer a systematic review of affective, behavioural and cognitive learning gains in higher education:

> 52 studies (n = 41,009) were coded into affective, behavioural and/or cognitive learning gains. The review found a rich but diverse variety of adopted methodologies and approaches to 'measure' affective, behavioural and cognitive (ABC) learning gains. Nonetheless, there is a lack of consistency in the ways in which learning gains are currently measured and reported. These inconsistencies and limitations hamper effective comparisons of learning gains and teaching excellence. We recommend a greater emphasis on longitudinal measurement of learning gains using validated approaches.
> (p. 321)

There is clearly a considerable but rich diversity of approaches to considering and measuring higher education outcomes and their impacts, as well as a varied terminology. An obvious direction for the development of future research is, therefore, to try and bring these competing approaches closer together.

Specific outcomes

Syntheses have also been produced of research into many more specific higher education outcomes. While the most popular has clearly been critical thinking, syntheses of research on professional development and other specific skills will also be considered here.

Critical thinking

Among the studies of more specific outcomes of higher education, particular attention has been paid to critical thinking. This is partly because critical thinking is assumed to be both endemic to, and a core quality of, higher education. Research has, therefore, set out to demonstrate or question the validity of this assumption. There have been a number of both meta-analyses and systematic reviews of the relevant research, focusing on quantitative and qualitative findings, respectively.

In a relatively early meta-analysis, Gellin (2003) synthesizes the research literature on the development of critical thinking skills in higher education published in the 1991–2000 period (n = 8). He found that 'on average, undergraduate students involved in a variety of activities [such as employment, hobbies or sport] outside the classroom experienced a .14 effect gain in critical thinking compared to students who were not involved' (p. 752).

Abrami et al (2008) focused on instructional interventions that impacted upon critical skills (CT) development. They found 117 studies based on 20,698 participants, which yielded 161 effects with an average effect size of 0.341 and a standard deviation of 0.610. The distribution was highly heterogeneous … These findings make it clear that improvement in students' CT skills and dispositions cannot be a matter of implicit expectation. As important as the development of CT skills is considered to be, educators must take steps to make CT objectives explicit in courses and also to include them in both preservice and in-service training and faculty development.

(p. 1102)

This does, of course, raise the question of whether and how critical thinking can be taught. More recently, Abrami et al (2015) undertook another meta-analysis designed to address this question. They focused on strategies for teaching students to think critically, including '341 effects sizes drawn from quasi- or true-experimental studies that used standardized measures of CT as outcome variables' (p. 275). They concluded that

there are a number of promising teaching strategies for helping students develop CT skills and dispositions. Specifically, there are strong indications that dialogue, authentic instruction, and mentorship are effective techniques for the promotion of this goal. These techniques appear to be particularly effective when combined.

(p. 305)

Tackling the same question, Niu, Behar-Horenstein and Garvan (2013; see also Behar-Horenstein and Niu 2011) identified thirty-one relevant studies published in the period 1994–2009. They concluded that 'in general, critical thinking teaching interventions are effective and lead to an improvement in students' critical thinking skills … However, we must also recognize that the magnitude of the average effect of critical thinking teaching in college is small' (p. 126). They recommend, therefore, more research into which interventions are the most effective.

In a more recent meta-analysis, Huber and Kuncel (2016; n = 71) come to the more positive conclusion that 'both critical thinking skills and dispositions improve substantially over a normal college experience' (p. 431): i.e. without making any special provision for developing them. This led them to 'argue against investing additional time and resources in teaching domain-general critical thinking' (p. 460), but without dismissing its possible usefulness within disciplinary teaching.

This finding should, though, reassure many of those working in higher education, suggesting that the experience of higher education should be sufficient to develop critical thinking abilities without any specific intervention.

Complementing these meta-analyses is a recent systematic review by Tiruneh, Verburgh and Elen (2014; n = 33):

The findings revealed that effectiveness of CT [critical thinking] instruction is influenced by conditions in the instructional environment comprising the instructional variables (teaching strategies and CT instructional approaches), and to some extent by student-related variables (year level and prior academic performance). Moreover, the type of CT measures adopted (standardized vs. non-standardized) appear to influence evaluation of the effectiveness of CT interventions. The findings overall indicated that there is a shift towards embedding CT instruction within academic disciplines, but failed to support effectiveness of particular instructional strategies in fostering acquisition and transfer of CT skills.

(p. 1)

However, the last few years have seen a veritable outpouring of syntheses of research into the development of critical thinking in higher education. Four of these formed part of a journal special issue, in which Ahern et al (2019) focused on engineering education, Lorencová et al (2019) on teacher education, Payan-Carreira et al (2019) on higher education for the health professions, and Puig et al (2019) on the professions in general.

Ahern et al argued that 'it is difficult to identify the most effective instructional strategies for CT through a review of published studies, given the relatively low number of studies in existence' (p. 824), but concluded that '[t]here is a need for a more cohesive approach to CT in engineering programmes, where skills are taught across the programme and where there are links and relationships formed across modules and stages' (p. 824).

Lorencová et al (2019) provide an analysis of thirty-nine published articles, concluding that 'the personal (i.e. students' learning style and motivation), methodological (i.e. methods, tools, duration, feedback), and contextual (i.e. classroom climate, supportive initiatives) features of the intervention are important for effective CT instruction and the improvement of student teachers' CT skills and dispositions' (p. 844).

For their study, Payan-Carreira et al (2019) considered twenty-eight studies, arguing that

> learning strategies that actively engage students in learning, along with longer interventions, might be preferred than traditional lectures to enhance CrT/CR/CJ [critical thinking/clinical reasoning/clinical judgement] skills and dispositions. However, the limited number of studies comparing different active strategies, along with the lack of a solid theoretical background and characterization of the intervention design, the variability of the sampled population, and the type of assessment instruments, impairs the comparison of the effectiveness of the described learning activities.
>
> (p. 840)

Puig et al (2019) focused on twenty-seven studies, noting that

> a large majority of the papers focused on teaching CT skills rather than dispositions. Although humanities and interdisciplinary studies do not make them explicit, it seems that analysis and evaluation are the most frequently addressed CT skills in STEM [science, technology, engineering, mathematics], Social Sciences and Biomedical Science studies ... Another finding is that most of the interventions carried out in all of the fields used an immersion approach, and the infusion approach was the second most common approach ... This points to a tendency of ... encouraging the embedding of CT within specific subject-domains as a way ... of helping students to become critical thinkers, rather than teaching CT as a separate subject ... it is apparent that improvements in the students' CT are more likely to occur when the teaching of said

skills is explicit rather than implicit ... The combination of more than one teaching strategy is frequent, above all in Social Sciences.

(p. 867)

In another recent systematic review, Soufi and See (2019) considered whether the explicit teaching of critical thinking improved critical thinking skills in English language learners in higher education. Considering thirty-six relevant studies, they found that 'only explicit instruction in general critical thinking skills was found to have the best evidence of effectiveness. However, because most of the studies were small-scale and/or methodologically flawed, the evidence is not strong enough to be conclusive. Evidence for the other approaches was even weaker' (p. 140).

Some doubt remains, therefore, about the 'best' way of encouraging the development of critical thinking skills in higher education. The advocates of explicit and implicit approaches, and of generic and disciplinary strategies, or of no particular strategy beyond what already exists, each has some evidence to support their argument.

Professional development

Professional development is a common concern of those higher education programmes designed largely to prepare students for particular professions: e.g. accounting, engineering, law, medicine, nursing, social work or teaching.

Trede, Macklin and Bridges (2012) reviewed the literature on the role of higher education in professional identity development, finding twenty relevant articles. They found the literature to be undeveloped and concluded that '[t]here is a need for upfront and focused discussions on what professional identity development means, and what its conceptualization means for educating and developing future professionals' (p. 382).

A few years later, Barbarà-i-Molinero, Cascón-Pereira and Hernández-Lara (2017) examined the literature on the same topic, focusing on fourteen articles. They also found the literature to be underdeveloped and mostly focused on single disciplines and a few of the factors involved.

Other research syntheses have focused on professional development in some of those specific disciplines. Dunst et al (2019) examined research on the pre-service professional preparation of teachers: their 'metasynthesis included 118 meta-analyses and 12 surveys of more than three million study participants' (p. 1). The

> findings clearly indicated that active university student and beginning teacher involvement in mastering the use of instructional practices and both knowledge and skill acquisition by far stood out as the most important preservice teacher preparation practices. These included extended student teaching experiences, simulated instructional practices and microteaching, faculty coaching and mentoring, clinical supervision, different types of cooperative learning practices, and course-based active student learning methods.

(p. 1)

Hayeslip (1989) reports on a meta-analysis (n = 5) of studies into the relationship between higher education and police performance. He concluded that

> [i]t has been shown in this study that by cumulating across studies we can find consistent agreement that education and police performance are moderately related. This contradicts the conclusions of a number of narrative reviews of the literature on the effects of education on police. Such a conclusion is based on tentative findings, however, due to the limited number of studies included in the analysis.
>
> (p. 57)

This is an area, therefore, in which more research is needed, both focusing on professional development in particular disciplines and, in a comparative fashion, across a range of disciplines.

Other specific skills

Research on a varied range of specific skills developed by higher education has been subject to synthesis, including information literacy, oral presentation, entrepreneurship, reflection, student-to-student connectedness and empathy. These syntheses will mostly be reported briefly, as they do not necessarily come to definitive conclusions.

Weightman et al (2017) provide a systematic review, and also a smaller meta-analysis, of information literacy programmes in higher education, contrasting the effects of face-to-face, online and blended formats (see also Chapter 7). In all, thirty-three studies were identified that had been published between 1995 and 2016. The results were consistent in finding no significant benefit of, or preference for, a particular mode of presentation:

> A large majority of studies (27 of 33; 82%) found no statistically significant difference between formats in skills outcomes for students. Of 13 studies that could be included in a meta-analysis, the standardized mean difference between skill test results for face-to-face versus online formats was -0.01 (95% confidence interval -0.28 to 0.26). Of ten studies comparing blended to single delivery format, seven (70%) found no statistically significant difference between formats, and the remaining studies had mixed outcomes. From the limited evidence available across all studies, there is a potential dichotomy between outcomes measured via skill test and assignment (course work) which is worthy of further investigation. The thematic analysis of student views found no preference in relation to format on a range of measures in 14 of 19 studies (74%). The remainder identified that students perceived advantages and disadvantages for each format but had no overall preference.
>
> (p. 21)

Van Ginkel et al (2015) carried out a systematic review with the aim of identifying design principles for the development of oral presentation competence, identifying fifty-two relevant articles published in the previous twenty years. Seven design principles – dealing with learning objectives, learning activities and assessment strategy – were identified from this analysis.

Mattingly et al (2019) examined the literature relating to entrepreneurship in pharmacy education and practice through a systematic review (n = 27). They found that no consensus for entrepreneurship in pharmacy practice or education currently exists. In order to improve instructional design and assessment for pharmacy entrepreneurship education, a core set of KSAs [knowledge, skills and attitudes] for a pharmacist entrepreneur construct must be identified. The most commonly cited KSAs in related literature that are not already part of the Accreditation Council for Pharmacy Education standards include risk-taking, strategic planning, marketing, competitiveness, and social responsibility. These may serve as a starting point for enhancing pharmacy curricula to embrace pharmacist entrepreneurship.

(p. 273)

Van Beveren et al (2018) conducted a systematic review of the purposes of reflection in higher education in the social and behavioural sciences (focusing on social work, psychology and teacher education; n = 42). They found a considerable variety in usage of the term:

Our review clearly illustrates the complexity and openness of reflection as an educational concept both at a conceptual and an empirical level within the disciplines of teacher education, social work and psychology. Different practices and forms of thinking are considered reflective and the teaching of reflection is attributed a broad diversity of educational values and purposes. Based on our findings, we argue for an explicit articulation of the value-bases and theoretical traditions underpinnings one's (research on) practices of teaching reflection as this opens the debate on the conceptual meaning of reflection, its claims on what constitutes 'true knowledge' and 'good practice' in social sciences as well as its possible empowering or disempowering effects when implemented in educational contexts.

(p. 7)

Reflection, like critical thinking (discussed earlier in this chapter), is seen in many disciplines, particularly the social sciences and the professions, as an essential quality to develop in students. It clearly merits further critical research and synthesis.

MacLeod et al (2019) carried out a systematic review of student-to-student connectedness – by which they mean students relating to and studying with each other – in higher education, identifying twenty-four relevant articles. They noted that

it has become apparent that student-to-student connectedness positively influences students' well-being and academic success in face-to-face environments. Student-to-student connectedness has been observed as positively related to an array of beneficial student learning outcomes and has been shown to support learning amidst imperfect instructional conditions.

(p. 19)

The expansion of this research into technology-mediated learning environments was anticipated.

Spatoula, Panagopoulou and Montgomery (2019) offer a meta-analysis of changes in empathy during undergraduate medical education – something which would be expected or at least hoped for – based on twelve identified studies. Their analysis 'indicated significant evidence that self-ratings of empathy changed across the years of medical education. However, we need to be cautious because this effect was only significant when empathy was assessed using the JSPE [Jefferson's Scale for Physician Empathy]' (p. 895).

Institutional transfer, persistence and retention

The issues surrounding institutional transfer of students and persistence have long been of particular concern in the United States, given the distinction between two-year (community colleges) and four-year (universities) institutions. Students have to transfer between institutions if – like many students from non-traditional backgrounds – they commence their studies in the former and wish to complete a full degree in the latter.

Murdock (1987) offers an early meta-analysis of research on the relationship between financial aid and student persistence, based on thirty-one American studies. She came to the following conclusions:

> Financial aid does promote student persistence and thus achieves, at least to some degree, a major goal of federal and many state student financial aid programs ... Financial aid has a stronger effect on the persistence of two-year students than four-year students ... Financial aid appears to have a stronger effect on the persistence of private institution students than on public institution students ... Financial aid has a stronger effect on persistence during the latter years of college than on the freshman year, particularly in terms of graduation probability.
>
> (pp. 91–3)

Diaz (1992) provides a meta-analysis of studies on the effects of transfer from community college to university on students' academic performance, identifying sixty-two relevant studies:

> The studies showed that although community college transfer students in 79% of the studies experienced transfer shock, the majority of the magnitude of GPA [grade point average] change was one half of a grade point or less. Of the studies that showed that community college transfer students experienced transfer shock, 67% reported that students recover from transfer shock, usually within the first year after transfer. Significantly, 34% of these studies showed community college transfer students recovered completely from transfer shock, 34% showed nearly complete recovery, and 32% showed partial recovery.
>
> (p. 279)

Schudde and Brown (2019) applied both systematic review and meta-analysis techniques to considering the diversionary effects of community college entrance in the United States. From 245 possible studies over the period from 1970 to 2017, they used 50 studies with 140 effect sizes. They concluded that

> [m]any community college entrants face financial and geographic constraints that make community college their most feasible pathway to a baccalaureate. However, our findings support a theory of diversionary effects. Compared with entering a baccalaureate-granting institution, entering a community college substantially lowers a student's probability of earning a bachelor's degree.
>
> (p. 264)

Earlier, Burley (1994b) carried out a meta-analysis of studies researching the effects of developmental studies (i.e. academic support) programmes in American community colleges (n = 10). He noted that 'reported studies indicate improved retention rates. It would seem that those programs with strong learning theoretical bases work better than those programs that are watered-down versions of regular college classes' (p. 16). In the same year, Burley (1994a) published another meta-analysis (n = 27), in this case focused on studies of the persistence of students on developmental studies programmes. This found 'no practically significant difference between the students in developmental programs and similar students in control groups' (p. 21).

Goradia and Bugarcic (2019) focused on the tools used to identify first-year at-risk students in health science courses (see also the discussion of learning analytics in Chapter 8). A 'mixed methods' systematic review identified thirteen relevant studies 'highlighting the significance of multiple factors in identifying at-risk students, including collecting information on personal characteristics, study strategies, social support, academic performance, GPA [grade point average] scores, and financial constraints' (p. 4).

In a related study, Aljohani (2016) offers a comparative international review of research into the factors that assist in or inhibit student retention, a key issue for higher education institutions. He finds, unsurprisingly, that 'the central factors were the quality of students' institutional experiences and their level of integration into the academic and social systems of their academic institutions. These factors relate to students' experiences with the administrative system of their academic institution, including the admission, registration and disciplinary rules and policies and the availability and quality of student services and facilities' (p. 40).

Taylor, Lalovic and Thompson (2019) provide a much more focused systematic review of the factors affecting the retention of Aboriginal and Torres Strait Islander health students in the Australian higher education system. Agrusti, Bonavolontà and Mezzini (2019) offer a systematic review of the use of educational data mining techniques in dropout prevention (see also the discussion of learning analytics in Chapter 8). They focus on seventy-three studies, identifying '6 data mining classification techniques, 53 data mining algorithms and 14 data mining tools' (p. 161).

What seems curious is the lack of recent general syntheses of studies of student retention in higher education (but see Tight forthcoming – b). This is an area that has been extensively researched and seen some early theoretical development (e.g. Spady 1970, Tinto 1975, 1993). It may be due, at least in part, to a decline in research using the somewhat negative term 'student retention', and its gradual replacement by the more positive term 'student engagement', though that is also an area in need of research synthesis.

Conclusions

- Student achievement may be predicted by an extensive range of factors, most notably prior achievement, but the relationship is far from perfect.
- More work needs to be done to bring together the different approaches taken to considering and measuring higher education outcomes.
- There is extensive debate over the generic skills that higher education is expected to develop and how it should do this.
- There is no major link between achievement in higher education and subsequent achievement in work and life.
- There are a number of proven strategies for developing critical thinking skills in students, but these may be developed through students' experience of higher education as well.

Chapter 11
The student experience

Introduction

Of the eight topic or thematic areas into which this book has been organized, the student experience is the second most popular for research syntheses after course design, accounting for sixty-seven, or 13 per cent, of those identified for this book (see Table 1 in Chapter 3). This is hardly surprising, of course, since the nature and quality of the student experience – here broadly conceived to cover the totality of students' experiences, educational and non-educational, while they are studying – is one of the most important factors in ensuring an effective higher education system.

While most (51) of the syntheses of research into the student experience in higher education that have been published have been in the form of systematic reviews, there have also been a number of meta-analyses completed (11). In addition, two substantive literature reviews have also been included, together with three studies which combined meta-analysis and systematic review.

There are several specialist higher education journals that focus on the topics discussed in this chapter. They include the *Journal of Diversity in Higher Education*, the *Journal of International Students* and the *Journal of Postsecondary Education and Disability*. Others take a more organizational perspective, including the *College Student Affairs Journal*, the *Journal of Student Affairs Research and Practice* and the *Journal of Higher Education Outreach and Engagement*.

In this chapter the discussion has been organized in terms of four main foci for student experience research: into types of students, levels of study, support services and other issues. The discussion of syntheses of research into types of students has been broken down into four main areas: students of particular ethnicities and/or nationalities, students with particular characteristics, students with disabilities, the diversity experience.

Types of students

Systematic reviews and meta-analyses of the experience of different types of students, or of students with particular characteristics, take a number of different forms. Here they have been organized into four main groups. First, there are syntheses focusing on the experience of students of particular ethnicities and/or nationalities. Second, there are those focusing on students with particular characteristics, such as sex, sexual orientation, socio-economic background and recent history. Third, there are studies of students with particular disabilities. Fourth and finally – turning the lens around – there are studies of the impact of all of this increasing diversity on the student experience.

It should be stressed that this organization is a pragmatic one, based on the way in which the research literature is organized, and should not be seen as an attempt to define students by particular characteristics. Ethnicity and nationality, for example, are not the same thing and we need to be careful not to assume or imply that they are. On the other hand, many students choose not to declare their disabilities or sexual orientation, and socio-economic background remains an area of contention. These analyses must, therefore, remain partial.

Students of particular ethnicities and/or nationalities

Interest in research into the experience of students from particular ethnic backgrounds is, unsurprisingly, particularly strong in the United States – partly because this was the first higher education system to move towards mass participation and partly because it contained large ethnic minority groups. The initial focus was on African-American or black students, who were often served by specific institutions, and has more recently moved on to include Hispanic (i.e. from Spanish-speaking backgrounds), native American and other ethnic groups.

Researchers based in other countries have yet to catch up with this interest, though the experience of students from ethnic minority groups is now often considered as part of a widening participation agenda. In an increasingly international higher education market, the experience of students of particular nationalities studying in other countries has also become of interest. Such students may face analogous issues to those faced by home or native students from ethnic minorities, but also others specific to them (notably cultural and linguistic). Immigrant students are a further category sharing a mixture of the characteristics of international and ethnic minority students.

Rovai, Gallien and Wighting (2005) provide a synthesis of the literature on African-American academic performance in higher education, referred to as the minority achievement gap. Their interest is in the causes of this gap and what can be done to ameliorate it:

> This article identifies a number of factors that contribute to the minority achievement gap. These include the transmission of knowledge by schools in cultural codes, mismatches between teaching styles and African American learning style preferences,

weak institutional support for minority students, a fragile racial climate on predominantly White campuses, racial stereotyping, peer influences, low expectations, and weak study habits. Additionally, a number of research-based interventions are described that can mitigate the challenges many African Americans encounter on college campuses. These include student enrollment in pre-college Upward Bound programs and, once in college, participation in learning activities such as tutoring services and study groups; faculty use of immediate communication behaviors; use of a pedagogy that 'filters curriculum content and teaching strategies through [students'] cultural frames of reference to make the content more personally meaningful and easier to master' (Gay 2000, p. 24); presentation of instruction that facilitates students using choices and engaging in the learning process as they work from their strengths; and energizing the campus social environment.

(p. 367)

These are, of course, strategies which would likely work effectively with other student groups as well and, indeed, with students as a whole. They might also be applied effectively to bring the diverse student body somewhat closer together.

Nowadays, the quickest growing ethnic group in the United States is those from Hispanic backgrounds (Latinos) who, in addition to facing many of the same issues that African-Americans do as students, also typically have the problem of studying in their second language. Flink (2018) argues that

understanding the cultural, linguistic, and socioeconomic challenges that Latinos face when participating in higher education is necessary when considering pedagogical, institutional, emotional, and social needs. Examining the specific characteristics, challenges, and obstacles of Latino immigrants, and Latino ELLs [English language learners], allows for a more informed understanding of how future research and institutional policies may be shaped.

(p. 411)

Much the same issues are also faced by most of the increasing number of international students now studying abroad in the higher education systems of the United States, the UK, Australia, France, Germany and elsewhere.

Qianqian (2018) reports the results of a systematic review of the experience of Chinese international students in the American higher education system. Using the ProQuest Sociology, Education Research Complete, ERIC and Google Scholar databases, Qianqian identified twenty-one recent relevant published studies focusing on three main issues: language barriers, acculturation and social networking. She came to some fairly critical conclusions regarding the usefulness of the research to date:

Firstly, while the vast majority of the studies reviewed identified some kind of challenges Chinese international students experience in their overseas academic experiences, few studies conducted in-depth analysis of the relationship between such challenges and race; instead, culture was unfairly blamed for all these negative experiences. This has betrayed a colorblind racism ideology, which denies the unique challenges Chinese international students face as a racially minoritized group in American society, and undermines the possibility to better understand and support them by addressing those challenges from their root causes ... Secondly, given the many distinctions between international student and immigrant populations, an international student-oriented theoretical framework should be developed and adopted by future research on Chinese international students, so as to replace the currently dominant frameworks targeting immigrants. Last but not least, considering ... that Chinese international students represent a heterogeneous group, future research could be conducted to compare the experiences of Chinese international students from different regions (i.e., Hong Kong, Mainland China, and Taiwan) or with different educational backgrounds.

(p. 1193)

Zhai, Gao and Wang (2019) provide a systematic review of research into Chinese students' reasons for choosing to study in Australia, currently the third most popular destination for international students, and their reasons for returning to China afterwards. They selected sixty-eight articles for analysis and 'developed four themes influencing Chinese students' choice of Australia, including academic requirement and attainment, employment and future career prospects, host country environment, and social connections and three themes for returning: emotional needs, culture and integration in Australia, and career opportunities in China' (p. 1). Clearly, the decision to study abroad, and then to return (or not) home, involves a complex series of considerations.

Sharif (2019) carried out a systematic review of twenty studies looking at the relations between acculturation (the processes by which people from another culture become accustomed to the new culture they have entered), on the one hand, and creativity and innovation, on the other. This suggested that there were many potential benefits from the involvement of students from different cultural backgrounds in higher education, if they could be persuaded to adopt a more bicultural approach:

[T]he acculturation strategy of biculturalism has been found to be linked to greater individual creativity and innovation. These findings signify that cultural identification influences students' ability to not only generate new ideas, but also to implement those ideas into tangible products or services to solve problems and benefit lives. Students strongly identifying with two or more cultures as in the case of biculturalism are able to reach new insights through combinations of diverse ideas from their various cultural frameworks ... This bridging of disparate knowledge that has been hitherto unconnected results in the development of new and original concepts and understandings.

(pp. 49–50)

Progress in this direction will also, of course, depend crucially on how well the host nation and institution are able to adapt to this approach.

Wekullo (2019) focused on international student engagement in her systematic review, identifying forty-eight relevant articles published between 2007 and 2018. She found that

[t]he ways students became engaged and the areas attracting them varied depending on the student's background, major, race/ethnicity, and type of institution. Even so, the literature was inconsistent with regards to the areas in which international students were

> most engaged. Whereas some studies showed that international undergraduate students were more involved in activities that led to high levels of learning (i.e., interacting with other students and faculty) and personal development (i.e., technology), others showed that students were less engaged in academic activities. The literature provided evidence that international students had uneven experiences relating to social and academic topics, as well as networks and perceived discrimination. These experiences varied depending on factors such as region, length of stay in the host country, competence level, academic program, and quality of interpersonal relationships with members of their organization and community.
> (p. 332)

The uneven experience of international students will also vary in terms of the presence of other international students on the course or in their institution, and whether and how their teachers recognize and make use of the varied student experiences present.

Safipour, Wenneberg and Hadziabdic (2017) examined the student experience in the international higher education classroom. They restricted their systematic review to qualitative articles published in the period 2010–15, using the ERIC, PsycINFO, Science Direct and Google Scholar databases, ending up with twenty-nine articles for analysis. They identified three main sets of issues: '1) Language barriers and its [*sic*] challenges, 2) Impact of transferring to a new academic culture, and 3) Stereotypes and negative attitudes' (p. 807). These issues will, of course, be familiar to any academic who has had significant dealings with international students.

Khan et al (2015) adopted a similar strategy, focusing solely on international medical graduates (IMGs – i.e. medical students who remain in the host country after graduation to work), but still identified fifty-nine relevant published studies. Their focus was on the UK, where IMGs make up over one-third of the medical workforce. Khan et al concluded that

> IMGs migrate to foreign countries in pursuit of better medical education, desire for better income, general security and improved prospects for the family, but in doing so, they are confronted with psychosocial problems, cultural differences, hurdles in career progression and passing exams. IMGs lack awareness of the ethical, legal and cultural system and also lack knowledge of professional standards and guidance prior to registration. The overall pass rate for IMGs in Royal College exams has been consistently low and more so in PACES [practical assessment of clinical examination skills], GP [general practitioner] and psychiatry exams. There is a serious need to take significant steps to improve IMG's employability and productivity in the UK that would be beneficial to the NHS [National Health Service], UK patients and the concerned doctors.
> (p. 756)

Clearly, there is a mutual dependency here, with international graduates wishing to benefit from the enhanced career opportunities available in the host country and employers being reliant on recruiting significant numbers of them in order to keep their businesses going.

With higher education an increasingly international activity, and the student body in most Western countries increasingly diverse, we may expect research and research syntheses in these areas to become more prevalent in the future.

Students with particular characteristics

Internationally, the two student characteristics most frequently researched for their impact upon the student experience have been gender and social class. With higher education historically focusing on white men from well-to-do backgrounds, there has been a natural research interest in the experience of women and working-class students, alongside those from ethnic minorities. These research interests have led, in their turn, to syntheses through systematic reviews, substantive literature reviews and meta-analyses.

Recent systematic reviews of the experience of women students have focused in particular on the case of mature women, arguably a doubly disadvantaged group. Adu-Yeboah (2015) focused on studies published in the 2004–13 period, hand-searching twenty-six relevant journals and searching the British Education Index, the Australian Education Index and ERIC for other studies, identifying eight studies for data extraction. While regretting the small number of completed studies, and their focus on the experience of mature women students in highly developed countries, she noted that

> a key finding of this review is that support from friends, tutors and administrators is crucial in mature women's progression and successful completion of HE [higher education]. Overall, HE-based support does not emerge as an important source of support, and in some cases, students even lack knowledge about them [sic].
>
> (p. 156)

Lin (2016) carried out a more extensive review of studies on the same topic, focusing on the lengthier period 1970–2015 and consulting the Educational Resources Information Center (ERIC), ProQuest Education Journals, PsycINFO and PsycARTICLES databases, though her study was confined to the American literature and experience. She came to similar conclusions to Adu-Yeboah: '[T]he commitments of multiple roles, lower level of self-confidence, and insufficient family and social support for female adult students would generate higher level of stress, anxiety, and others [sic] than their male peers as well as traditional counterparts' (p. 122).

In a relatively early study, Kasworm (1990) examined research on the experience of older students, both women and men, in general. She provides what she terms 'a qualitative meta-analysis methodology' (p. 346) – i.e. what I would term a systematic review – of research into adult undergraduates in American higher education. Searching ERIC, Higher Education Abstracts and Psychological Abstracts, as well as specific journals, for the period 1940–86, she identified ninety-six documents for content analysis:

> Five major domains of reality were identified from this review of past research on adult undergraduate students in traditional higher education. Each of these domains of reality were described as an image, a perceptual framework which was descriptively and inferentially expressed in the studies of that category. The domains included:
>
> - Image of Implied Deficiency,
> - Image of Student Entry and Adaptation,
> - Image of Description and Characterization,

- Image of Psychosocial Development, and
- Image of Equity and Outcome.

(p. 348)

After exploring the accumulated research on each of the domains or images, Kasworm concludes that

[t]hese five domains have identified a variety of issues for researchers regarding the key assumptions and past practices in the study of adult undergraduates. The future development of quality theory and research is dependent upon a stream of research activity placed within a coherent theoretical base. We, as members of the research community, need to create these frameworks and research agendas concerning adult undergraduates in higher education. This agenda should address the theoretical understanding of the adult's relationship to an undergraduate experience as well as key questions about the adult student as learner, adult student as worker/homemaker, and adult student as family/community leader. It should bring organizational and ecological perspectives to the understanding of undergraduate structures and processes in relation to the adult student's involvement.

(p. 367)

This rather extensive list of issues for future researchers has only, however, been partially addressed so far.

Nichols and Stahl (2019) employ the theoretical framework provided by intersectionality – which explores how 'systems of inequity, including sexism, racism and class bias, intersect to produce complex relations of power and (dis)advantage' (p. 1255) – in their systematic review of fifty articles:

This corpus of studies, in developing rich descriptions and thoughtful multilayered analysis of higher education as experienced intersectionally, clearly demonstrates that an instrumental approach to diversity (as measured by performance metrics) can never be sufficient. As a knowledge project, intersectionality advocates a distinctly non-traditional epistemology for generating complex bodies of knowledge, and an expressly political project – promoting social justice and the transformation of the institutional order for historically and multiply marginalised and faculty [sic]. The effective use of intersectionality as a theoretical framework in higher education research calls for an examination of the social identities that participants bring to, and form within, systems of inequality in all their forms, and the relationships between the two.

(p. 1265)

Intersectionality explicitly recognizes that the great majority of students, and people in general, are disadvantaged in some way and that many are multiply disadvantaged.

Rubin (2012) provides a meta-analysis of the relation between students' social class and their integration in the higher education experience. Using PsycINFO, ERIC and Scopus, he searched for relevant publications up until 2011, identifying thirty-five relevant studies. He concluded that

> [t]he present meta-analysis provides the clearest evidence to date that working-class students tend to be less integrated than middle-class students in higher education institutions. This social class difference is relatively pervasive, generalizing across students' gender and year of study as well as across different measures of social class. A key finding is that type of social integration measure moderates the size of the social class-social integration relation ... suggesting that multidimensional measures of social integration are more sensitive to social class differences.
>
> (pp. 31–2)

The multidimensionality of integration – and of the underlying discrimination – is again recognized, as it is with intersectionality.

Nikula (2018) offers what she terms a meta-method analysis (and which I would term a systematic review) of thirty-one studies reporting on socio-economic inequalities in Finland and New Zealand – two developed nations which would widely be regarded as fairly advanced in such matters – stressing the underlying problem of socio-economic status being defined in different ways. She highlights 'the variety that is present in studies examining socioeconomic inequalities in higher education' (p. 2316) and notes the consequent difficulties of comparing findings, both within and between countries.

Ives and Castillo-Montoya (2020) take a different approach to the widening participation agenda in focusing on studies of students who are the first in their family (or the first generation) to enter and experience higher education. They analysed fifty-nine studies in their systematic review, finding that

> researchers employed limited types of instruments and procedures to study first-generation college students and relied heavily on a few seminal frameworks theorized from dominant students. Despite the contributions of the existing scholarship ... the majority of the literature we reviewed was imbued with normative assumptions, which contributes to an assimilationist culture within higher education. We highlighted, however, an alternative view of first-generation college students as learners whose lived experiences, when connected to academic content, can contribute to their academic learning, advancement of disciplines, self-growth, and community development. We refer to this view as an interconnected and multi-directional approach to learning.
>
> (p. 30)

Heaslip et al (2017) provide an integrative literature review of research into attempts to widen participation in nursing education, specifically in the UK, identifying fourteen relevant studies published between 2013 and 2016. They concluded that '[w]hilst widening participation is a key issue for both nurse education and the wider profession there is a lack of conceptualisation and focus regarding mechanisms to both encourage and support a wider diversity of entrant' (p. 66).

Systematic reviews have also been carried out into research focusing on the student experience of smaller student groups. Thus, focusing on sexuality, Duran (2018) has synthesized studies of the experience of queer students of colour, while Hafford-Letchfield et al (2017) focused on transgender students. Working in the American context, Duran found sixty-eight relevant articles, concluding that 'considerable strides have been made in bringing awareness to this previously invisible demographic on university campuses. At the same time, higher education scholars and practitioners would benefit from additional research seeking to comprehend this population' (p. 8). Hafford-Letchfield et al identified twenty relevant studies internationally, though most were American, concluding in a similar vein:

> Post-compulsory education has much to learn about transgender and gender non-conforming issues, particularly from students themselves. As most studies come from the USA, internationally, there are relatively few empirical studies that examine the experiences of transgender and gender non-conforming students. The research reviewed here captured the complex, provocative nature of gender-nonconforming identities and specifically recognized ways that education can improve their experiences. It confirms that students prefer to live beyond a binary frame of reference.
>
> (p. 11)

Bradbury-Jones et al (2019) took a more focused approach to research into the experience of students who identify as lesbian, gay, bisexual, trans and/or queer (LGBTQ), addressing their experience of professional practice placements (which are discussed more generally in Chapter 6). A total of twenty-two relevant articles were identified, from which three primary themes emerged:

> Environment: which relates to the way that homophobic and transphobic discrimination is experienced in professional practice. Influence: the importance of faculty on the environment as both a positive and negative force. Interventions: how students support LGBTQ people who use their services and how educators intervene with students who identify as LGBTQ.
>
> (p. 1)

Aside from sexuality, other systematic reviews have considered research on the experience of student armed service members and veterans (Barry, Whiteman and Wadsworth 2014), students from refugee backgrounds (Mangan and Winter 2017), undocumented students (Bjorklund 2018) and students who had been in foster care (Johnson 2019). In an American study, Barry et al (2014) searched ERIC, PsycINFO, Sociological Abstracts, MEDLINE, CINAHL and ProQuest databases, identifying thirteen relevant empirical investigations. They found that

> [c]ompared to civilian peers, SSM/V [student service members/veterans] exhibit disproportionately higher rates of health risk behaviors and psychological symptoms, and personal and educational adjustment difficulties (i.e., inability to connect with peers and faculty on campus). Combat-related trauma is a contributing factor to these differences. The current evidence-base is scant, lacking nationally representative and/or longitudinal data to inform policies and programs for SSM/V.
>
> (p. 30)

In an international study, Manghan and Winter (2017) searched four databases to find only eight relevant studies, from which they identified an 'overarching theme of invalidation'

(p. 486) relating to students from refugee backgrounds. Pursuing a closely related topic, undocumented students, in the American context, Bjorklund (2018) identified many more relevant studies – eighty-one – and concluded that

> undocumented students confront significant financial barriers, shoulder unique psychological and social burdens tied to their legal status, and lack access to forms of social capital that facilitate postsecondary success. At the same time, they bring a host of assets to college campuses – including civic engagement and resilience – that are underutilized.
>
> (p. 631)

Johnson (2019) focuses on studies of the experience of students who were formerly in foster care, described as 'one of the most underserved student populations in higher education' (p. 1). A systematic review identified forty-six relevant studies, identifying factors associated with student success while noting that this student group continued to lag behind in terms of achievement.

Clearly, as the student body becomes larger and more diverse, more research attention will need to be devoted to understanding – and improving – the experience of disparate groups of students.

Students with disabilities

Other syntheses of research into particular types of students, or students with particular characteristics, have examined students with disabilities, who make up a growing minority of the student population.

Garrison-Wade and Lehmann (2009) compared the results of five published meta-analyses with their own research to build a framework for understanding the transition of students with disabilities to community college in the United States. Kutscher and Tuckwiller's (2018) focus was on studies of the persistence of students with disabilities in higher education. They found twenty-six relevant studies, though not all were of the highest quality, concluding that 'we know very little about the characteristics and contexts that support their persistence in postsecondary education' (p. 18).

Kimball and Thoma (2019) provide what they call an 'ecological' synthesis of the literature on the experience of disabled students published in seven leading journals between 2011 and 2018 (n = 85). This allows them to identify key questions for research and practise at different levels, from the individual, through microsystem, mesosystem, exosystem and macrosystem to the chronosystem (which concerns the changing broader society).

The experience of autistic students in particular has been the subject of a number of systematic reviews. Toor, Hanley and Hebron (2016) searched ERIC, PsycINFO, MEDLINE, Embase and CINAHL Plus, identifying twelve relevant studies focusing on students with autism seeking to enter higher education. From these studies they identified six superordinate themes: the involvement of professionals, academic factors, environmental factors, social factors, well-being, communication and understanding. They also discussed the facilitators, obstacles and needs of students that pervaded these themes along with the implications for counsellors and psychologists working in schools.

Nuske et al (2019) searched Medline, CINAHL, ProQuest, PsycINFO, Scopus and Informit, with, like Toor et al, a focus on the transition of autistic students to higher education, identifying eleven published articles:

> Findings showed that individuals with ASD [autism spectrum disorder] experience challenges associated with: core and associated characteristics of ASD, self-disclosure and awareness, and mental health and wellbeing. Family members reported significant challenges associated with systemic policies, which impacted on their ability to support their family member with ASD. It is highlighted that an individual and flexible approach to transition support, and increased academic and professional staff awareness and understanding of ASD, are critical to the transition experience of students with ASD in higher education.
>
> (p. 1)

Kuder and Accardo (2018) focused on research into programmes and services designed to support autistic students. They identified eight relevant studies: 'three that examined the effects of cognitive-behavioral interventions, three that reported the results of methods to enhance social communication skills, one study of a transition to college program, and one evaluation of a variety of widely used accommodations' (p. 722).

Anderson et al (2019) identified twenty-four relevant empirical studies of interventions for postsecondary students with autism, concluding that

> there were insufficient experimental studies for any intervention to be classified as evidence based. Many studies, however (including the 17 pre-experimental studies that were uninterpretable with respect to causation), demonstrated feasibility and social validity for a range of interventions, including mentoring, transition programs, CBT [cognitive behavioral therapy], academic skills, and social skill development, suggesting they may have promise and warrant further investigation.
>
> (p. 1556)

Much, therefore, remains to be researched on this topic.

Corby, Cousins and Slevin (2012) focused on the experience of adults with intellectual disabilities in general, while Hartrey, Denieffe and Wells (2017) considered students with mental health difficulties, and Pino and Mortari (2014) examined research on dyslexic students. Hartrey et al (2017) identified nineteen papers of relevance, arguing on this basis that

> students with mental health difficulties face barriers arising from symptomology, fear of disclosure due to stigma, lack of mental health literacy (on their part and also on the part of academic staff) and discriminatory obstacles in the way that accommodations are organised for them compared to other groups of students with disabilities. The reviewed literature highlights the need to examine ways to support progression of students with mental health difficulties beyond traditional methods of reasonable accommodations and adjustments. Whilst academic accommodations are perceived to have great value by students, there is a need to take a broader view of participation to examine and understand how these students experience inclusiveness on campus outside of the examination process.
>
> (pp. 42–3)

Pino and Mortari (2014) came up with very similar findings from a synthesis of fifteen studies of students with dyslexia, identifying 'five cross-study thematic areas: student coping strategies, being identified as dyslexic, interaction with academic staff, accessibility and accommodations, and using assistive technologies and information and communication technologies' (p. 346).

Similar issues are, of course, often faced in a more general sense by students who do not have disabilities, are not aware that they have disabilities or choose not to declare them; so it may be argued that changing higher education to help those with declared disabilities can only benefit the whole student body.

The diversity experience

Taking a different perspective, Bowman (2010, 2011) has undertaken meta-analyses of the college diversity experience in the United States: i.e. is it beneficial for all students to participate in more diverse classrooms? He first (2010) examined the relationship between diversity experience and cognitive development. He searched ERIC, PsycINFO and Dissertation Abstracts Online, identifying a final sample for the meta-analysis consisting of '58 separate effects from 17 studies with a total of 77,029 undergraduate students' (p. 12). His findings were very positive, with

> strong evidence that several types of diversity experiences – interpersonal interactions with racial and nonracial diversity, diversity coursework, and diversity workshops – are positively related to cognitive development. Indeed, interactions with racial diversity are more strongly linked with cognitive growth than are interactions with nonracial diversity, which suggests the particular educational importance of fostering a racially diverse student body. These positive effects are apparent not only for cognitive tendencies but also for basic cognitive skills, such as critical thinking and problem solving.
>
> (p. 22)

Bowman's second meta-analysis (2011) examined the relation between diversity experience and civic engagement. The 'final sample for the meta-analysis consisted of 180 separate effect sizes from 27 works with a total of 175,950 undergraduate students' (p. 38). Again, the conclusions were positive:

> [A] significant, positive relationship is observed regardless of the types of diversity experience, the type of civic outcome, and the measurement of civic growth. This consistency implies that even the most rigorous, conservative study will generally find a positive effect of college diversity interactions on civic outcomes.
>
> (p. 49)

Taking a rather different perspective, Ogunyemi et al (2019), an American team, consider the effect of microaggressions – 'brief, low-intensity events that convey negative messages toward marginalized groups' (p. 1) – in the learning environment. A systematic review of articles published between 1998 and 2018 identified forty relevant studies. Their findings are depressing:

Microaggressions were prevalent and 'invisible' in colleges with minority students seemingly worn down by ongoing strategies used to confront the inherent associated stresses. Difficult racial dialogues were characterized by intense emotions in both professors and students that interfered with successful learning experiences. Coping strategies that correlated positively with microaggression and psychological stress included disengagement, cultural mistrust, stigma for seeking psychological help, alcohol use, and intolerance of uncertainty. Factors tending to ameliorate microaggression and psychological stress included engagement, dispositional forgiveness, help-seeking attitudes, self-efficacy in coping with daily hassles, and social connectedness. Political activism was helpful in Latinx [Hispanic], but exacerbated microaggression related stress in African American students.

(p. 1)

There is clearly some way to go yet before a welcoming and inclusive higher education environment is available to all who wish to benefit from it. Higher education clearly benefits from being diverse, but not everybody yet recognizes this.

Levels of study

There have been rather fewer syntheses of research on the student experience at different levels of study than undergraduate (e.g. postgraduate taught or research students: see also the discussion of postgraduate study in Chapter 8) than there have been on types of students. Most research syntheses focusing on types of students have either examined studies of the student body as a whole or concentrated on undergraduates, who make up the great majority of that total.

Some studies have, however, combined these two perspectives, as in Hutchings et al's (2019) systematic review of the determinants of attraction, retention and completion for aboriginal and Torres Strait islander higher degree research students in Australia. Unsurprisingly, only a relatively small number of relevant publications (12) were identified, leading the authors to recommend increased work and research in this area.

Other systematic reviews have focused on the research student experience (somewhat curiously, I have not found any research syntheses focusing on the rather larger number of master's students). Leonard et al (2006) provide a literature review on the impact of working context and support on the postgraduate research student learning experience. Starting from 1,135 references, they focused on 120 studies relating to the UK research student experience. While their aim was to make recommendations to the body funding the research, the Higher Education Academy, their conclusion was constrained:

One of the main outcomes of this study has been the identification of the general paucity and sometimes inadequacy of the existing literature on the working context and support for postgraduate research students in the UK. It is difficult to formulate implications for policy and practice on the basis of what is available.

(p. 43)

Thune (2009) had a more specific focus, examining research on the experience of research students who were working at the university/industry interface (see also the discussion of learning and work in Chapter 6). She noted that

> [t]he studies reviewed here emphasize that doctoral students involved in collaborative arrangements with industry have a markedly different researcher training experience than non-collaborative students. The physical surroundings in which they work, the supervision they receive, the research projects they work on and the norms of conduct they are exposed to are much more heterogeneous than what non-collaborating students are exposed to. But at the same time, the students' assessments of the PhD experience are fairly similar, and the research productivity (number of publications and presentations) of the students is not very different either.
> (p. 645)

There is clearly considerable scope for more research, and more research syntheses, examining the postgraduate student experience.

Support services

Given the importance attached to ensuring the quality of the student experience, it is not surprising that considerable attention has been devoted by universities and colleges to the effective provision of services to support this experience. That has inevitably attracted research to evaluate the support services, and thence systematic reviews and meta-analyses to summarize and synthesize the results of that research.

One focus for such research has been the provision of support designed to retain students who might otherwise withdraw or drop out, with clear financial and reputational consequences for the institution concerned (see also the discussion of institutional transfer, persistence and retention in Chapter 10). In an early meta-analysis, Kulik et al (1983) synthesized the findings from sixty evaluations of college programmes for high-risk and disadvantaged students in the United States. They concluded that

> [s]pecial programs devised for high-risk college students have had basically positive effects on these students. This generalization holds true when the effects of these programs are measured by changes in GPA [grade point average] and when effects are measured by changes in persistence in college. The generalization also holds true for different types of programs for the high-risk college student: reading and study skills courses, guidance sessions, and comprehensive support services. These programs raised student GPAs by .25 to .4 standard deviations. The special programs also raised persistence rates from 52 to 60 percent remaining in college.
> (pp. 407–8)

Relatedly, Herbaut and Geven (2019) – also from an American perspective (though a few non-US studies are included) – provide a contemporary systematic review of the literature (n = 75) on outreach and financial aid. They find that

[o]utreach interventions targeted at students in high school or recent graduates seem to be a relatively cost-effective tool to address inequalities in access to higher education, as long as the interventions go beyond providing general information about higher education. Substantial improvements have been identified when disadvantaged students were offered personalized counseling activities or simplification of application tasks, especially when counselors actively reach out to targeted students to ensure their participation ... Financial aid is more expensive, and the evidence on its effectiveness for disadvantaged students varies largely depending on the type of aid ... It is possible that enrollment as a response to aid follows a threshold effect and that need-based aid is only effective when it covers a significant part of unmet financial need ... It also seems that an early commitment of aid, while students are still in high school, leads to a much larger impact on higher education access.

(pp. 32–3)

In addition to recruiting as many suitable students as possible, and keeping as many of them as possible content and on-course, one of the other key support services which higher education institutions seek to apply, and are judged on their successfulness in, concerns the transition from higher education to subsequent employment, especially for full-time undergraduate students (see the discussion of outcomes in Chapter 10).

The other major aspect of support services which have been the subject of research syntheses has been those studies which have examined services targeted at students with physical or mental health issues (see also the previous section on types of students). Lombardi et al (2018) provide a systematic review of instruments used in disability assessment, for either or both students and employees.

A number of analyses, both meta-analyses and systematic reviews, have focused in particular on students' mental health. Conley, Durlak and Kirsch (2015) carried out a meta-analysis of the effectiveness of university mental health prevention programmes for higher education students, based on 103 published studies. They concluded that 'when comparisons on specific outcomes were possible, skill-training programs including supervised practice were significantly more effective than the other two groups of programs in reducing symptoms of depression, anxiety, stress, and general psychological distress, and in improving social-emotional skills, self-perceptions, and academic behaviors and performance' (p. 487).

Conley et al (2017) followed this study up with a further meta-analysis of studies (n = 79) of 'the effectiveness of indicated prevention programs for higher education students at risk for subsequent mental health difficulties based on their current subclinical levels of various presenting problems, such as depression, anxiety, or interpersonal difficulties' (p. 129), with generally promising findings.

Winzer et al (2018) carried out both a meta-analysis and a systematic review into studies as to whether mental health interventions with students had sustainable results. Searching MEDLINE, PsycINFO, ERIC and Scopus for relevant randomized control trials published between 1995 and 2015, twenty-six relevant studies were identified. They found that '[t]he evidence suggests long-term effect sustainability for mental ill health preventive interventions, especially for interventions to reduce the symptoms of depression and symptoms of anxiety. Interventions to promote positive mental health offer promising, but shorter-lasting effects' (p. 2).

Spencer et al (2017) focused in particular on occupational therapy interventions for mentally ill students. Their systematic review of just seven articles found support for 'the use of supported education programs consisting of goal setting, skill development, and cognitive training, as well as student-directed planning' (p. 1).

Research syntheses have also examined other, perhaps less obvious, aspects of higher education support services. For example, Flores and Hartlaub (1998) provide a meta-analysis of studies focusing on what can be done to reduce the incidence of rape on campus. They found '18 studies of which 11 were ultimately used to extract 15 effect sizes' (p. 439).

> The results indicate that intervention programs can effectively reduce rape-myth acceptance. This is encouraging considering the severity of the problem and the relative ease of administering most of the interventions. The major moderating variable of interest was the type of intervention employed. Studies among these categories failed to differ from each other. This result implies that no particular modality is superior to any other. Similarly, we found no direct relationship between the length and effectiveness of an intervention.
> (p. 443)

Whiting et al (2019) provide a systematic review of studies of behavioural interventions designed to increase condom use among college students in the United States (n = 7).

> Four of the interventions were developed using the three constructs of the information, motivation, and behavioral skills model, and all four found significant increases in condom use or condom use intentions. Additionally, interventions that included modules to increase self-efficacy for condom use, taught participants where to get condoms and how to negotiate condom use with partners, or elicited positive associations (feels) toward condoms saw increased condom use or intention to use condoms.
> (p. 877)

Ashford et al (2018) focus on college recovery programmes, identifying ten relevant studies published between 2000 and 2017, finding that 'collegiate recovery programs and communities have implemented strategies that effectively support students in recovery' (p. 411).

In other words, interventions in each of these disparate areas seem to work, at least to some extent.

Other issues

Along with types of students, levels of study and support services, many other aspects of the student experience have been the subject of research, leading in a number of cases to systematic reviews or meta-analyses. The issues researched may be generic to all students or specific to particular groups.

To start with the generic, van Rooij et al (2018) examined the first-year undergraduate experience, in particular what determined success (see also Chapter 10). They focused on the Dutch-speaking systems of the Netherlands and Flanders (part of Belgium), identifying thirty-nine relevant articles. They concluded, unsurprisingly, that 'ability factors, prior education characteristics, learning environment characteristics and behavioural engagement indicators were most successful in explaining success' (p. 36).

Diamond et al (2014) undertook an extensive review of research on the provision of information about higher education to students for the UK higher education funding bodies. They argued that

> [u]ltimately, decision-making that concerns HE [higher education] involves less rational consideration than might be first assumed. Factors other than those that can be accounted for in terms of money and time, such as emotional responses, play a significant part in determining the outcome of choices facing prospective students, whether they influence the decision consciously or not. Research suggests that affective factors are not only amongst the strongest influencers of decisions but also contribute to the satisfaction that results from that choice.
>
> (p. 6)

There are, of course, factors other than money, time and emotional response involved in student decision-making, including most notably the reputation of the institutions, departments and courses under consideration. This concerns not just what students and their parents, friends and teachers think about the different higher education options open to them, but also increasingly how these are rated in national and international ranking systems.

It is surprising, therefore, that while a great deal of quantitative data is available on national and international ranking systems, and these have been the subject of much discussion and critical assessment, there does not yet seem to have been a research synthesis carried out (but see the discussion of the research/teaching nexus in Chapter 16).

One issue which has lent itself to meta-analysis, particularly in the American context – which is unsurprising, given the early establishment there of a mass higher education system, with a variety of public and private institutional providers – is the question of student price response.

Heller (1997), building on the earlier work of Leslie and Brinkman (1987, 1988), summarized the general findings of the research at that time: 'As the price of college goes up, the probability of enrolment tends to go down' (p. 649), which sounds pretty much what you would expect. He also noted, however, that there were variations in this relationship related to tuition fees, available financial aid, income group, race and sector.

Gallet (2007) provides a more recent meta-analysis of sixty relevant studies on this topic, which he uses to

> help explain some of the variation in elasticity estimates across the literature. For example, for both tuition and income elasticities, short-run estimates are more inelastic than long-run estimates. Also, quantity demanded is less responsive to tuition and income in the U.S. than other countries; and, particularly noticeable in the case of the

tuition elasticity, how quantity and price are measured, coupled with the estimation method, are important determinants of the tuition elasticity.

(p. 7)

Other systematic reviews on the student experience tend to focus on more specific issues, which could be seen as issues needing attention, often for particular groups of students. Thus, in a relatively early treatment of what is now an important contemporary concept, Owen (2002) provides a review of the research literature on wellness, as it impacts both students and staff, concentrating mainly on its definition and measurement.

Sharp, Sharp and Young (2018) focus on the interesting, but easily overlooked or avoided, topic of student boredom, and how this impacts on student engagement and achievement. Based on an examination of 287 identified items, they argue that

> the academic boredom observed among undergraduate students at university is an achievement-related emotion worthy of serious consideration ... the study of academic boredom as part of a greater emotional dynamic and integrated network of other causal factors associated with student engagement and achievement is only now beginning to attract the attention it deserves.
>
> (p. 26)

This does not imply, of course, that academic boredom needs to be avoided at all costs – it is, after all, an inevitable consequence of engaging in academic activity – more that it needs to be recognized and minimized as much as possible.

The increasing use of information and communication technologies (ICT) in higher education has attracted a good deal of attention (see also Chapter 7), and some researchers have examined this in terms of its impact on the student experience. Thus, Khalid and Pedersen (2016) present a systematic review of research concerning digital exclusion and the digital divide in higher education. From their analysis they identify three key sets of factors:

> [S]ocial exclusion (i.e., low income, ICT-avoidance as the norm, lack of motivation and commitment, and physical or mental disability), digital exclusion (i.e., lack of hardware devices and Internet services) and accessibility (which include the division between rural and urban areas, as well as disparities in ICT literacy and information literacy). These factors are multi-tiered and overlapping. Studies on the digital divide, digital exclusion, and barriers to ICT adoption in higher education deal with similar factors, but these are experienced differently in different contexts. While generalizing these factors into categories enables a better understanding of the nature of digital exclusion, solving and circumventing them remains complex due [to] their dependency on the particular context of a higher education institution.
>
> (p. 614)

This research is significant because it effectively punctures the assumption that all young people today are digitally literate and expecting their higher education to be at least partly delivered and supported online.

Rinn and Plucker (2019) provide a systematic review of studies of the experience of high-ability college students in the context of 'honors programs' (i.e. more advanced undergraduate courses) in the United States (n = 52):

From the studies presented in this analysis, one might conclude that honors programming is beneficial to high-ability undergraduates across a variety of academic, educational, social, and emotional outcomes. Indeed, every paper we included in this analysis indicated honors programming was associated with positive outcomes. Although we do not disagree that honors programming has beneficial outcomes, we caution the readers to note the importance of precollege variables in interpreting findings related to honors programs. High-ability students who are eligible for honors program participation still must largely self-select into honors programs (after qualification), so the students who choose to participate are likely already high achievers, have positive academic self-perceptions, and are motivated for success.

(p. 208)

Somewhat perversely, therefore, higher education may not always respond as it might to students with high ability.

The downside of the student experience

In addition to those already discussed, there are a number of research syntheses that have examined research on less salubrious or satisfying aspects of the student experience.

Watts et al (2017) focus on a downside of the increasing use of information and communication technologies (ICT) in higher education, namely cyberbullying. Following exhaustive searches, fifty-four relevant documents were identified: 'Articles were used to define cyberbullying, build a historical base of cyberbullying among adolescents, examine factors involved in cyberbullying, describe effects of cyberbullying, and examine this trend among college students' (p. 268). Watts et al concluded that 'cyberbullying continues to be a disturbing trend not only among adolescents but also undergraduate students' (p. 272). There is an issue here, though, of who has the responsibility for dealing with student cyberbullying, particularly if it does not take place on the university's own ICT systems.

In another disturbing analysis, Nazmi et al (2018) present a systematic review of research into food insecurity among college students in the United States, identifying eight relevant studies. Their analysis 'showed that food insecurity among students at US higher education institutions was at least three times higher than observed in nationally representative households ... suggesting that food insecurity may impact one in two students' (p. 8).

Research syntheses have also focused on drug usage and interventions designed to control it. Organ et al (2018) report on

a systematic review of the implementation and reporting of user-centred design (UCD) practices in the development of illicit substance use behavioural interventions in the higher education context (n=7). Our review revealed limited consideration of end user experience and minimal engagement with UCD practices. We argue that these studies do not give sufficient consideration to factors that would have a significant influence [on] their effectiveness and sustainability in normal use conditions.

(p. 1)

Fedina, Holmes and Backes (2018) provide a systematic review of studies on the prevalence of sexual assault on campus. Focusing on the United States, and searching for research published between 2000 and 2015, they identified thirty-four relevant articles:

> Findings suggest that unwanted sexual contact appears to be most prevalent on college campuses, including sexual coercion, followed by incapacitated rape, and completed or attempted forcible rape. Additionally, several studies measured broad constructs of sexual assault that typically include combined forms of college-based sexual victimization (i.e., forcible completed or attempted rape, unwanted sexual contact, and/or sexual coercion).
>
> (p. 76)

Bogen et al (2019) report on research into supporting students in responding to disclosure of sexual violence. Their

> review analysed the websites of 60 members of the Association of American Universities (AAU) to examine how online resources educated students, faculty, family members and residential advisors on appropriately responding to disclosure of sexual violence. University websites often included information on positive and negative social reactions to disclosure. Websites infrequently included scripts of what to say/not to say to a survivor or provided information on vicarious traumatisation. As information on how to support a survivor was not consistently located on a single webpage, work is needed to consolidate information to insure that information on how to support survivors is easily accessed.
>
> (p. 31)

Frajerman et al (2019) provide a systematic review and meta-analysis of research on burnout in medical students before residency, identifying twenty-four relevant studies published between 2010 and 2017. Worryingly, they found that '[n]early one student out of two suffers from burnout' (p. 41), with little evidence of interventions designed to counter this.

In a broadly related way, Eka and Chambers (2019) offer a systematic literature (n = 32) of incivility in nursing education, a supposedly caring profession. They conclude that

> [i]ncivility has been identified as a factual problem in nursing education though perceived differently. Incivility includes a variety of disturbing behavioural acts such as disrespect and undermining others, academic dishonesty, and bullying. Incivility also impacts negatively either physically or psychologically. It is important that nurse educators take action to promote civility in nursing education.
>
> (p. 53)

Also focusing on bullying, Fnais et al (2014) carried out both a meta-analysis and a systematic review of studies on harassment in medical education. They identified fifty-nine relevant studies, of which fifty-one were included in a meta-analysis, which

> demonstrated that 59.4% of medical trainees had experienced at least one form of harassment or discrimination during their training (95% confidence interval [CI]: 52.0%–66.7%). Verbal harassment was the most commonly cited form of harassment

(prevalence: 63.0%; 95% CI: 54.8%–71.2%). Consultants were the most commonly cited source of harassment and discrimination, followed by patients or patients' families (34.4% and 21.9%, respectively).

(p. 817)

Clearly, there is much in the higher education experience that can go wrong and/or which needs continuing vigilance to keep under control.

Conclusions

- The increasing diversity of the student body demands an increasingly diverse student experience.
- Many groups of students are under-researched. There is particular scope for more research into postgraduate students, especially those studying at master's level.
- There are numerous examples of interventions that have been shown to support particular groups of students, while also contributing to the overall student experience.
- Most higher education support services offer valuable assistance to students.

Chapter 12
Quality

Introduction

Quality has been a growing concern in higher education as provision has expanded, with key stakeholders and funders (government, employers, students, staff, institutions) wishing to be assured that the money being invested in higher education was being well spent. There have been two main prongs to this concern, and hence follow-up research and research synthesis.

First, there has been concern with quality at the more individual, experiential level – coming from students and institutions – leading to a focus on the evaluation of courses and their teachers. How well do individual teachers teach, and how good are the courses they deliver?

Second, there has been concern directed at the institutional level, but also involving their component departments and programmes, leading to a focus on what they were doing in terms of quality assessment, assurance and management. What systems and practices do institutions have in place to check and improve the quality of their provision?

Systematic reviews and meta-analyses of research into the quality of higher education are quite well developed and balanced overall. As Table 1 in Chapter 3 showed, forty eight in total have been identified for this book, 9 per cent of the total. They are reasonably equally split between quantitative and qualitative syntheses, with twenty-two meta-analyses, nineteen systematic reviews and seven substantive literature reviews included. However, when the theme of quality is broken down into topics, there does not appear to be as clear a balance.

There is a specialist higher education journal, *Quality in Higher Education*, that focuses on this topic. A number of other more generic journals, focusing on quality or higher education in general, also regularly publish articles on the topic.

Student evaluation of teaching has been the major focus for syntheses of research into quality in higher education for the last four or five decades. These studies are almost all meta-analyses, as numerical data are widely available from regular surveys for such research. This has been particularly the case (at least historically) in North America, where the practice of getting students to rate their teachers at the end of each course is of long standing. Other syntheses, some meta-analyses and some systematic reviews, have examined closely related issues such as student satisfaction.

A further area for research synthesis has been into the overlapping areas of quality assessment, quality assurance and quality management. These have been increasingly applied to higher education and higher education research – having originated in manufacturing industry – during the last three decades. These studies, by contrast to studies of student evaluations, have tended to be systematic reviews. Some have focused on specific approaches to assessing and implementing quality in higher education, such as total quality management and multi-stage evaluation.

Student evaluation of teaching

At the core of research into quality in higher education are considerations of the student's perspective, with the student seen as the chief, if by no means only, stakeholder in or of higher education. Such research has been encouraged over the last few decades by the massification of higher education worldwide, the increasing proportion of its costs being paid for by students and their families, and the resulting view of the student as being the principal 'customer' of higher education.

Student evaluations of teaching (SETs) have been in use for many years, particularly in well-developed mass higher education systems such as that of the United States (Kulik 2001). Originally pen-and-paper exercises, these have now transferred mostly to online evaluations hosted on institutional websites. Among the issues driving research in this area are the validity and reliability of SETs, particularly when they are used in decisions over staff recruitment, payment and promotion; how to encourage students to complete their evaluations, and to do so as fully and honestly as possible; and what factors (i.e. other than the quality of the higher education received, assuming that could be 'objectively' measured) affect the ratings that students provide.

Since SETs are typically numerical in nature, with students invited to rate aspects of their teachers and courses on a Likert-type scale (e.g. from 1 (excellent) to 5 (poor)), the research syntheses in this area are primarily meta-analyses. Qualitative evaluations of teaching are also possible, of course, and may be more informative. The standard or teacher course evaluation surveys may, for example, have space for students to write in detailed comments, or students may be asked to participate in focus group discussions as well. There have, therefore, been a number of systematic reviews completed as well in more recent years.

Early North American studies

An early review, having the characteristics of a meta-analysis but not using that terminology, was carried out by Costin, Greenough and Menges (1971), focusing on the issues of the reliability, validity and usefulness of SETs. It came to overwhelmingly positive conclusions:

> A review of empirical studies indicates that students' ratings can provide reliable and valid information on the quality of courses and instruction. Such information can be of use to academic departments in constructing normative data for the evaluation of teaching and may aid the individual instructor in improving his [sic] teaching.
>
> (p. 530)

Later studies, however, began to unpick these conclusions.

The earliest published analysis of research into student evaluations of teaching – that was explicitly termed a meta-analysis – of which I am aware is by Feldman, one of the key contributors to such research, and dates to 1976. It analyses North American (i.e. American and Canadian) studies dating back as far as 1934 (Starrack 1934) – thirty four using the student as the unit of analysis and eleven using the class – that assess whether SETs are related to students' anticipated or actual grades. Feldman concludes that

> [f]rom existing research in which the individual student is the unit of analysis, the general conclusion is that students' grades in a class are positively related to their evaluation of the course and the teacher. Considering only studies using correlational techniques of analysis, and for which data have been pooled across two or more classes, most of the correlation coefficients fall within a range encompassed by the mid 0.10s at one end and just below 0.30 at the other … Further, and of greater significance, there is evidence that pooling data across classes may mask the fact that grades are more strongly associated with evaluation in some classes, while only weakly or not at all associated in other classes (and possibly even negatively related in still others).
>
> (p. 99)

These findings, of course, raise the possibility of bias in the evaluation process, a spectre which also underlies, from the opposite perspective, the more contemporary debates about inflation in the grades given by teachers to students (largely, it is cynically said, to encourage the students to inflate their own evaluations).

Feldman returned to the topic of SETs a number of times over the following decades (e.g. Feldman 1977, 1978, 1979, 1983, 1984, 1986), focusing successively on the consistency of student ratings, and the effect of course context and characteristics (class size, course level, electivity (i.e. whether the course was compulsory or optional), subject matter, time of day), the circumstances in which the SET was completed (anonymity, use made of SET, presence of teacher), teachers' seniority and experience, the impact of class size (a weak inverse association), and teachers' personalities (weak associations became stronger where perceived personalities were considered) on student ratings. In addition to concerns about potential biases in student ratings, these studies also raised the, perhaps entangled, issue of the validity of SET results, and the broader question of whether SETs could be interpreted as 'objective' measures or were really largely subjective.

Cohen (1980, 1981) was another early meta-analyst on this topic. In his first paper (1980) he analysed twenty-two studies to confirm that SETs had a positive impact on teaching quality, with SET ratings improving from mid-semester to end-of-semester evaluations (a finding confirmed by Menges and Brinko 1986). In the second paper

(1981) he followed up Feldman's initial interest in the relationship between SETs and student grades, analysing forty-one relevant studies. He found that

> [t]he average correlation between an overall instructor rating and student achievement was .43; the average correlation between an overall course rating and student achievement was .47 ... The results of the meta-analysis provide strong support for the validity of student ratings as measures of teaching effectiveness.
>
> (p. 281)

However, Feldman (1989) carried out an extended re-analysis of the studies examined by Cohen, arguing that the effect sizes were not as large as suggested.

Another keen and relatively early meta-analyst in this area has been Abrami, along with a variety of colleagues (including Cohen). They again (Abrami, Leventhal and Perry 1982) focused on the relationship between SET and instructors' personalities, re-examining twelve previous studies of the 'Dr Fox' effect or educational seduction. They concluded: 'Overall, we found that instructor expressiveness had a substantial impact on student ratings but a small impact on student achievement. In contrast, lecture content had a substantial impact on student achievement but a small impact on student ratings' (p. 446). If so, students were basing their SET ratings on characteristics of their instructors other than their teaching.

A later analysis (Abrami, Cohen and d'Apollonia 1988) focused squarely on the validity of SETs, re-examining six previous meta-analyses, some of which had supported their validity while others questioned it. Abrami et al concluded that

> meta-analysis implementation problems were substantially responsible. Specifically, we found the reviews shared five common inclusion criteria but varied on seven criteria. No review included all relevant studies; the average comprehensiveness index was only .58. Only one reviewer coded study features, but the three significant predictors explained only 31% of the variance in effect magnitudes, and the coded characteristics were far fewer than experts described. Furthermore, we found only 47% agreement among the reviews in the individual study outcomes reported. Finally, the reviews differed in whether and how variability in study outcomes was analyzed and in the conclusions reached about outcome homogeneity.
>
> (pp. 173–4)

They ended their article with a series of recommendations for the future conduct of meta-analyses in this area.

In a substantial overview of existing studies published at about the same time, Marsh (1987; cf. Costin, Greenough and Menges 1971) comes to more positive, but also measured, conclusions:

> Research described in this article demonstrates that student ratings are clearly multidimensional, quite reliable, reasonably valid, relatively uncontaminated by many variables often seen as sources of potential bias, and are seen to be useful by students, faculty, and administrators. However, the same findings also demonstrate that student ratings may have some halo effect, have at least some unreliability, have only modest

agreement with some criteria of effective teaching, are probably affected by some potential sources of bias, and are viewed with some skepticism by faculty as a basis for personnel decisions ... Despite the generally supportive research findings, student ratings should be used cautiously, and there should be other forms of systematic input about teaching effectiveness, particularly when they are used for tenure/promotion decisions.

(p. 369)

Characteristically, however, these warnings from the research literature were largely ignored by those, principally university administrators and academic managers, who wished to have a simple and seemingly intelligible quantitative measure which they could use in judging the quality of teaching (and its reward).

L'Hommedieu, Menges and Brinko (1990) provide a 'review and statistical integration of the quantitative research on the feedback college teachers get from student ratings' (p. 232), focusing on the literature published since Cohen's (1980) synthesis (n = 28). Despite problems with methodology and interpretation, they find that '[t]he literature reveals a persistently positive, albeit small, effect from written feedback alone and a considerably increased effect when written feedback is augmented with personal consultation' (p. 240). The latter studies involved direct consultation with students as well as their completion of a form.

Cashin (1995) offers a similarly measured, but generally positive, summary (in essence a systematic review, though it is not identified as such) of the research to date at that time:

There are probably more studies of student ratings than of all of the other data used to evaluate college teaching combined. Although one can find individual studies that support almost any conclusion, for a number of variables there are enough studies to discern trends. In general, student ratings tend to be statistically reliable, valid, and relatively free from bias or the need for control; probably more so than any other data used for evaluation. Nevertheless, student ratings are only one source of data about teaching and must be used in combination with multiple sources of data if one wishes to make a judgment about all of the components of college teaching. Further, student ratings are data that must be interpreted. We should not confuse a source of data with the evaluators who use student rating data – in combination with other kinds of data – to make their judgments about an instructor's teaching effectiveness.

(p. 7)

The cautions that student ratings are only one source of opinion and that they need to be interpreted carefully are doubtless well meant but frequently overlooked in practice.

Wachtel (1998) also offers a review of the literature on SET. While similarly being generally supportive of the research completed to date, he identified a series of avenues down which this might be expanded in future:

Although the use of student ratings of instruction is well-entrenched in North American universities, there are still some useful areas for further research. A few background characteristics have not yet been sufficiently investigated as to whether there is a significant effect on student ratings, e.g. class meeting time, minority

> status and physical appearance of the instructor. Also, it is felt that the effect, if any, of the average age of the students on ratings could be studied, provided that other characteristics such as course level, class size and prior student interest can be controlled for ... educators in individual disciplines may wish to study further the question of whether or not course characteristics would be likely to affect student ratings in the manner in which existing research has predicted, or in a different manner, or not at all, in courses in their own subject area. Further studies of whether or not students are inclined to take written rating forms seriously (whether or not they are formally instructed to do so) would be worthwhile. Perhaps it might also be worthwhile to do further surveys of faculty to determine how often and what types of changes they make in their instruction based on the results of student ratings. Finally, it might be interesting to examine whether the effect of certain background characteristics on student ratings may change depending on whether the course is taught at a highly research-oriented university, or a four-year institution which is more teaching-oriented, or a two-year institution such as a community college.
>
> (p. 205)

This is a fairly comprehensive series of suggestions. Given the generally declining rate of completion of SETs, the question of how seriously those students that do complete them take the exercise is particularly apt, as is the further issue of how representative they might be of the student body as a whole.

Later international studies

More recent meta-analyses have updated and extended these findings, while expanding their geographical purview beyond North America. Thus, Penny and Coe (2004), in the UK context, noting the tension between the teaching improvement and performance measurement functions of SETs, provide an exploratory meta-analysis of the role of consultative feedback with the teachers involved. They identified

> eight consultation strategies that appear to be important for the most effective consultative feedback. It is important to note that although the evidence for these may not be very strong, it represents the best available knowledge to date to guide practice and policy. The eight strategies are as follows: 1. Active involvement of teachers in the learning process; 2. Use of multiple sources of information; 3. Interaction with peers; 4. Sufficient time for dialogue and interaction; 5. Use of teacher self-ratings; 6. Use of high-quality feedback information; 7. Examination of conception of teaching; and 8. Setting of improvement goals.
>
> (p. 245)

Taking these strategies on board seriously would, of course, make the SET process much more time-consuming as well as, hopefully, more effective.

Clayson (2009) returns to the question of whether SETs are related to student learning. He presents a meta-analysis of seventeen articles containing forty-two studies that were published between 1953 and 2007 and concludes that

[o]bjective measures of learning are unrelated to the SET. However, the students' satisfaction with, or perception of, learning is related to the evaluations they give. This explanation suggests that the validity of the relationship between learning and SET is situational and that the associations, and the validities of those associations, depend on a number of factors.

(pp. 26–7)

One may question, of course, whether a truly 'objective' measure of learning exists, but Clayson was referring to 'more objective' measures, such as are possible in disciplines making extensive use of quantitative methods. The related, and perhaps conflated, issue of student satisfaction is discussed in the next section.

In an American study, Wright and Jenkins-Guarnieri (2012) review nine meta-analyses covering 173 studies of SETs and align themselves with Marsh (1987) in concluding that 'SETs appear to be valid, have practical use that is largely free from gender bias and are most effective when implemented with consultation strategies' (p. 683). Through the latter comment, they also show their awareness of Penny and Coe's (2004) work.

Benton and Cashin (2012) provide an update of Cashin's (1995) summary of the literature. Indeed, they repeat the previously quoted conclusion but add the following rider: 'This paper summarizes the general conclusions from the research on student ratings. Whether these conclusions hold true for all contexts is an empirical question. If an institution has reason to believe that these conclusions do not apply, key players should gather local data to address the issue' (p. 13).

From an Australian perspective, Alderman, Towers and Bannah (2012) offer some support for this conclusion. They provide what they call a 'focused literature review and environmental scan' of student feedback systems, finding that 'while student feedback is valued and used by all Australian universities, survey practices are idiosyncratic and in the majority of cases, questionnaires lack validity and reliability; data are used inadequately or inappropriately; and they offer limited potential for cross-sector benchmarking' (p. 261). Their aim was improvement: the 'development of a solid, ethical and well-researched foundation upon which QUT [Queensland University of Technology, their own university] can engage in system organisational change with respect to student evaluation' (p. 274).

Spooren, Brockx and Mortelmans (2013), a Belgian team, using a meta-validity framework developed by Onwuegbuzie et al (2009), offer a review of research published since 2000, focusing on the recurring question of the validity of SETs. They find that

SET remains a current yet delicate topic in higher education, as well as in education research. Many stakeholders are not convinced of the usefulness and validity of SET for both formative and summative purposes. Research on SET has thus far failed to provide clear answers to several critical questions concerning the validity of SET.

(p. 598)

Significantly, when referring to stakeholders, their overriding concern was with the teachers being evaluated. Other, less involved, stakeholders – namely the ones that make the decisions about teachers' employment and conditions – still found SET useful.

Uttl et al (2017) reviewed previous meta-analyses, notably those referred to by Clayson, Cohen and Feldman, and then carried out their own of fifty-one articles containing ninety-seven multi-section studies. Their findings were damning:

> In conclusion, two key findings emerged: (1) the findings reported in previous meta-analyses are an artifact of poor meta-analytic methods, and (2) students do not learn more from professors with higher SETs. The reported correlations between SET ratings and learning are completely consistent with randomly generating correlations … applying publication selection bias. Despite more than 75 years of sustained effort, there is presently no evidence supporting the widespread belief that students learn more from professors who receive higher SET ratings.
>
> (p. 40)

If SETs do not relate to students' learning, as this would suggest, then we need to ask (again) what exactly it is that they are measuring and whether there is any point in continuing their use.

Other researchers have focused on particular disciplines, notably medical education. Schiekirka and Raupach (2015) offer a systematic review of relevant studies published up until 2013: twenty-five studies, twenty-three of which were quantitative and two qualitative, were identified.

> Student ratings of courses in undergraduate medical education reflect student satisfaction with various facets of teaching. This systematic review identified a number of factors impacting on overall course ratings. Depending on the underlying construct of high-quality teaching, these factors might act as confounders, thus threatening the validity of evaluation results. Influencing factors were related to student characteristics, exposure to teaching, satisfaction with examinations and the evaluation procedure itself. Due to the heterogeneity and methodological limitations of included studies, no firm conclusions can be drawn from this review.
>
> (pp. 7–8)

Nicolaou and Atkinson (2019) provide another systematic review of SET research related to medical education, identifying twenty-one relevant studies. Their concern was with what affected the quality of the SET response and how to improve this. They concluded with the following recommendations:

> According to the evidence found in this review an optimum course evaluation is a compulsory course evaluation that takes place both early (before or at the start) and late (end or after) in the course, using a low number (≤10) of closed and open-ended questions delivered via a paper-based mode of delivery (although a blended mode may be also used). It is essential that medical students are educated about course evaluations early in the course and especially understand the crucial role they play in the curriculum and their learning.
>
> (p. 100)

Of course, others than students may be involved in the evaluation of teaching, with fellow teachers offering a significant input. Thomas et al (2014) – a Malaysian-based team – provide a systematic review, undertaking a content mapping of twenty-seven relevant studies on peer review of teaching (PRT; i.e. teachers reviewing each other) in higher education in Western countries. They offer five main conclusions:

> First, the findings demonstrate that PRT is an effective strategy to kick-start transformational reforms within an institution by encouraging faculty members to observe and reflect on teaching performance in addition to identifying areas of improvement with the aid of their colleagues. Second, there is a thin boundary between consensus and conformity in conducting PRT. Although faculty members need to be in agreement on teaching criteria that constitute effective teaching, there is also a danger of conforming to nationally accepted standards of teaching for the sake of gaining the necessary teaching competency. Third, it is possible for higher education institutions to implement peer collaborative reviews across disciplines and cultures ... Fourth ... the PRT process has potential to ease the anxiety and anger among faculty members who are developing teaching portfolios by making the evaluation process a collaborative effort ... Fifth, faculty members need to be trained in time management practices to fit in additional PRT roles.
>
> (p. 153)

This is clearly a much more developmental and supportive approach than that applied in most SETs, though it relies on the existence and largely shared values of a community of higher education teachers.

Student satisfaction and other factors

Another, and more contemporary, approach to evaluating the quality of the student experience is to consider what makes students satisfied – or increases their existing levels of satisfaction – with their higher education experience overall. Gibson (2010) provides a review of studies, focusing in particular on business student satisfaction. He makes a key distinction between the impact on student satisfaction of academic and non-academic variables:

> It is evident that the attributes of the academic program itself are most important to students' overall satisfaction. These attributes include the quality of teaching and the curriculum as well as the achievement of students' learning and career goals. The availability and quality of facilities and services, such as advising and IT [information technology] support, are also somewhat important although there are mixed conclusions about the importance of the physical aspects of service provisioning. The responsiveness of both academic and services personnel, however, is important. Non-academic variables, such as the degree of 'student centeredness' and the degree of social integration experienced by the student, can be particularly important in larger institutions. The non-academic variables often appear to be the cause of dissatisfaction, i.e., positive perceptions are not as important to overall satisfaction as positive

perceptions of academic variables, but negative perceptions may result in dissatisfaction with the overall academic experience.

(p. 257)

Oliveira Santini et al (2017), in a Brazil-based study, carried out a meta-analysis on the same topic, identifying 83 relevant studies internationally containing 469 observations over the period 1986–2016. They identified six antecedent dimensions (perceived value of educational services, resources provided to the student, service quality perception, marketing orientation, identity of the higher education institution, university environment) and one consequent dimension related to satisfaction. They argue that

> the results demonstrate that satisfaction and consequent behavior are significantly influenced by the educational context. The analysis and understanding of these relationships is extremely important for the long-term performance of higher education institutions.
>
> (p. 11)

There is a clear link here to institutional management, and particularly to the marketing function, discussed in Chapter 14.

In addition to examining the satisfaction of students in particular disciplinary areas (as Gibson (2010) did for business students, and Nicolaou and Atkinson (2019) did for medical students), it is also interesting to look at students studying by different modes. In an American study, Allen, Bourhis and Mabry (2002) carried out a meta-analysis to compare the satisfaction of students studying at-a-distance with those in conventional face-to-face settings (see also Chapter 7): twenty-four relevant studies were identified. They found only a slight student preference for the conventional format:

> To the degree that student satisfaction plays a major role in the assessment or evaluation of instructional effectiveness, distance learning represents a format that students evaluate comparably to other potential formats for a course. The objections to distance education should not be based on the issues related to student satisfaction; students find distance learning as satisfactory as traditional classroom learning formats.
>
> (p. 93)

Of course, the quality of the student experience consists of more than either student evaluations or student satisfaction. Tan, Muskat and Zehrer (2016) provide a systematic review of the literature, identifying

> five prevailing research streams: 1) exploration of learning experience; 2) exploration of student experience; 3) gender differences in assessment of higher education experience; 4) improvement in quality of student experience, 5) student satisfaction with higher education experience.
>
> (p. 2)

They note that the 'literature currently portrays the quality of student experience as a student-centric idea with the underpinning aim of improving the quality of higher education for students' (p. 20). In the medium to longer term, however, it may make more sense to concentrate on improving the overall quality of the student experience (see Chapter 11), rather than responding in the short term to evaluation or satisfaction scores with the aim of improving institutional, departmental, course or staff metrics.

Quality assessment, assurance and management

Taking a much broader focus, a number of systematic reviews (but no meta-analyses) have synthesized the research on quality assessment, quality assurance and/or quality management in higher education. One of the key issues here is, of course, the differences and/or overlaps between these closely related terms or perspectives and what they imply about the relationships between managers and academics. Another is how useful or applicable practices devised in industry are to higher education, a complex activity with multiple purposes and outputs.

In an extensive analysis of the American research literature on quality in higher education available over thirty years ago, Tan (1986) concluded that, while much useful research had been done,

> four critical issues remain yet to be resolved. First, no one is certain what reputational studies are measuring – reputation or quality? … The use of objective variables in the assessment of quality … has met with limited success. The main problem has been the assumption by many researchers that faculty research productivity is the major indicator of quality … Third, no one is certain what the definition of quality should be … Finally, even though most studies have been successful at identifying a variety of correlates of quality, none has adequately examined the relationship between quality and the educational development of students.
>
> (pp. 259–60)

In short, much more needed to be done to produce credible results that might then lead to the production of consistent improvements in quality in higher education, with all that this might entail. The association of institutional or departmental quality with the research productivity of their academic staff is still an issue today and underlies much of the debate over the use of international ranking systems (see also the discussion of the research/teaching nexus in Chapter 16).

Writing over thirty years after Tan, Prakhash (2018) reviewed 308 articles on quality in higher education institutions published between 1999 and 2017. He concluded that

> the literature on quality in the HEI [higher education institution] context shows that the literature is dominated by the quality constructs of student learning, engagement, SQ [service quality] and satisfaction, followed by TQM [total quality management], quality assurance, benchmarking and accountability. The findings reveal that the student perspective is gaining

central attention and HEIs are striving to meet students' expectations by operationalising various levers of quality ... The expectations of stakeholders such as students, parents, teachers and employers influence each other and in turn generate demand for various facets of quality ... Parents view quality as related to current investment and future employment. Students view quality as related to the educational process and future employability. Teachers perceive quality as related to the whole education value chain, while employers view quality as primarily related to the student's fitness for the intended work.

(p. 741)

Clearly, the meanings of quality have diversified and grown substantially over the last few decades, making this a complex area for research.

Quality assurance

Harvey and Williams (2010a, 2010b), in two editorials summarizing the output of the journal *Quality in Higher Education* over its first fifteen years – some 320 articles all told – concluded that, while quality assurance in higher education had become a global phenomenon, there was little evidence that externally mandated quality assurance initiatives were having the desired effects within higher education institutions. They also argued that, while quality assurance initiatives had made the workings of higher education institutions clearer to those outside, academics remained largely indifferent to them, except to the extent that they were forced to engage.

In a relatively early study, Wilger (1997) provides a literature review of quality assurance in higher education, examining practice as much as research and noting its prominence in Australia, Hong Kong, Sweden and the UK. Chun (2002) reviews the American research literature on the assessment of higher education quality, noting that it is based on four methods of data collection: (1) actuarial data (i.e. entry qualifications, staff/student ratios, graduation rates); (2) ratings of institutional quality; (3) student surveys; and (4) direct measures of student learning. He notes that the fourth method, while the most obvious focus, is the least used approach, hampered by doubts about what should (or could) actually be measured (cf. the discussion of student evaluation of teaching earlier in this chapter).

More recently, Steinhardt et al (2017) carried out a systematic review, using Scopus, of 1,610 articles published in 399 journals in the 1996–2013 period that focused on the quality assurance of teaching and learning in higher education. Using co-citation analysis they were able to identify four loosely coupled topics on which research concentrated: assessment, quality, quality management and student evaluation of teaching. Within these four clusters

two distinct strands of research on the quality assurance of teaching and learning became evident and emphasized an antagonistic tension in the research. First, the management strand in the Quality-Management-Cluster and Student-Evaluation-of-Teaching-Cluster comprises all aspects of quality assurance. This management strand is in tension with the education strand of research prevalent in the Assessment-Cluster and Quality-Cluster.

(pp. 233–4)

The distinction between quality assurance and quality management is, therefore, by no means clear, with the latter showing a tendency to colonize the former.

Quality management

This management/education tension might be argued as being at the heart of many debates and developments in contemporary higher education. The perhaps more hard-edged industry-derived approaches involved in quality management have attracted at least as much attention as quality assurance.

Owlia and Aspinwall (1997) provide a relatively early review of the application of the set of strategies known as total quality management (TQM) in higher education. This involved both a Delphi-type survey of knowledgeable academics and the examination of case studies of practice in the United States and the UK, as well as a literature review. They note that '[w]hile TQM as a successful managerial strategy is generally accepted in commercial organizations, its role in the public sector, especially in higher education, is still controversial' (p. 540), but conclude that 'there appears to be no apparent reason for rejecting the applicability of TQM as a "general philosophy". If there are problems with its introduction in this environment, their roots should be sought in the system itself rather than in the philosophy' (p. 541).

This would seem, however, to be approaching the issue from an overtly managerial perspective, one where the views of the managed (i.e. the academics) do not count for a great deal. Academics are not known for endorsing general philosophies, except when they are so general – e.g. academic freedom – as to be extremely difficult to enforce, which would also neatly explain the system problems suggested by Owlia and Aspinwall.

Cruickshank (2003) also reviews the literature on the application of total quality management in higher education, with a particular focus on Australia, the UK and the United States, arguing – like Owlia and Aspinwall – that it has not kept pace with developments in industry. She concludes that

> [i]f the application of Total Quality Management in the higher education industry is to be successful, two fundamental areas will need to be addressed. First, assessing the culture of higher education institutions and introducing changes in attitudes, values and beliefs will be paramount ... most faculty members have never worked in a TQM environment ... Second, academic members will need to recognize their institution as a system, and view the institution as a system of interrelated parts.
>
> (pp. 1164–5)

Note, again, the problems with system – most academics have much closer links to their discipline or sub-discipline, which they will likely remain in throughout their career, than to the institution they happen to be working in at a particular point in that career – and also culture identified.

Grant, Mergen and Widrich (2004) offer a comparative analysis of quality management in US and international universities, identifying eighteen articles, nine US and nine international. Focusing on three aspects of quality management – quality-of-design, quality-of-conformance and quality-of-performance – they found some interesting differences:

First, Quality-of-Design and Quality-of-Conformance are heavily used by both US and international universities. Second, as a common theme, Quality-of-Performance is by far the weakest area. Eight out of the 18 articles addressed Quality-of-Performance, two of which are US institutions. Third, five of the 18 institutions used a formal quality management model as the basis for implementing quality … only one was from the US, the other four were international.

(pp. 434–5)

They stress the need, therefore, to improve measurement of quality-of-performance.

From the UK, Becket and Brookes (2008) also review quality management practices in higher education institutions, posing the question 'what quality are we actually enhancing'? Rather like Grant, Merger and Widrich, they identify divided efforts:

[W]ith earlier approaches adapted from industrial models focusing on the quality of administrative and service functions. In contrast, critics of industrial models have undertaken efforts to focus on the quality of the core products of HE [higher education], teaching and learning. Given current environmental trends, the priority now must be to achieve greater harmonisation between the two approaches in HE quality management practices. Rather than disregard the benefits of TQM, there appears to be a need to find another approach that puts teaching and learning at the core but does not neglect the efficiency and effectiveness of administrative and service functions.

(p. 47)

Clearly, the tensions over the application of total quality management identified earlier by Owlia & Aspinwall and Cruickshank still remained.

More recently, using Scopus, Manatos, Sarrico and Rosa (2017), a Portuguese team, identify 127 journal articles of interest on quality management research in higher education. They came to mixed but generally positive conclusions:

Despite the high number of conceptual articles which appear in our review, there is an obvious trend towards a more empirically based debate, especially after the early 2000s … Specifically, such questions revolve around the role of QM [quality management] systems in improving HEIs [higher education institutions], which relate these QM systems to the broader management context of institutions. Nevertheless, it is interesting to observe that the most cited articles are theoretical. The literature also seems to be concerned with the development of QM frameworks in a holistic way, combining different aspects of quality, ultimately reflecting a high level of integration for the dimensions analysed … However, the 'total' integration of QM in HEIs does not yet seem to be a reality. It appears that the QM field is still often treated as a separated field, run by a separate department within HEIs, and is not yet an integrated part of the organisation.

(pp. 170–1)

Tari and Dick (2016), a Spanish/British partnership, adopt much the same approach, though they did not restrict themselves to the quality management (QM) of teaching and learning alone, extending this to cover the research and administrative functions of higher education institutions as well. They used the ScienceDirect, ABI/Inform and Emerald databases, identifying 188 articles for detailed analysis. They concluded that

> [t]he most common topics (representing 76 per cent of articles) are 'QM implementation', 'Models, techniques and tools', and 'QM dimensions'. These results are consistent with the most popular topics found in the industry QM literature with one exception. The effects of QM on organisational performance have not been examined in any depth in HEIs compared to its prominence in the general QM literature. The most important QM dimensions for HEI management are people management, information and analysis, process management, stakeholder focus, planning, leadership, design, and supplier management ... There was no consensus on which QM models best suit HEIs.
>
> (p. 287)

Yet again, therefore, the evidence is that quality management approaches are not being applied wholeheartedly in higher education institutions. This conclusion is supported by a Sri Lankan researcher, Imbulgoda (2019), focusing on the Asia Pacific area and the issue of compliance with quality assurance: twenty-two relevant articles were identified.

Other approaches

Systematic reviews of research into quality in higher education have also examined other, more specific, approaches to quality management or assurance. For example, Cudney et al (2018) offer a systematic review of the application of lean and six sigma approaches, popular managerial strategies, identifying both improvements realized and challenges:

> Student learning was improved by introducing industry projects, which enabled a better understanding of quality improvement activities, improved student productivity and retention, and increased student awareness of industry expectations upon graduation. Teaching was enhanced by creating feedback systems, cost-effective and quality-intensive collaborative learning programmes, and course delivery systems. Administrative processes such as library self-issue, admission, course and curriculum approval, and billing, among other processes, were also improved. The studies in this systematic review also point out several challenges associated with these implementations. These challenges include lack of awareness of Lean and Six Sigma methodologies, failure of institutions in identifying and targeting customers, inability to cope with process changes, lack of interest and commitment from the stakeholders, and difficulty in understanding the methodologies and adapting them to the educational context.
>
> (pp. 11–2)

Laurett and Mendes (2019) provide a systematic review (n = 25) of the application of the European Foundation for Quality Management's (EFQM) excellence model in higher education institutions. They also identify a mixture of potential benefits and barriers:

> [T]he use of the EFQM excellence model can lead to several potential benefits: opportunity to apply for the EFQM Excellence Award, higher customer focus, effective and aim-oriented inner communication, identification of strengths and areas for improvement, costs savings, increased knowledge about quality-related issues, higher staff involvement and commitment in service improvement, development of a common improvement approach, improvement of service quality, a sustained and objective decision making, and a cultural shift. Moreover, the results of the review point to several potential barriers to a sustained implementation of EFQM-based quality improvement systems, and provide significant insights for HEIs [higher education institutions] managers wishing to develop and implement successful systems, concerning critical success factors which have to be carefully considered: a strong intrinsic motivation and commitment of top management, employees' effective commitment and collaboration, staff's training and development, adequate communication and information systems, follow-up processes and an external supportive environment.
>
> (p. 277)

It seems clear, therefore, that, whatever approach to quality assurance and/or management is adopted, those involved in the delivery of higher education need to be involved in and committed to its implementation.

Conclusions

- Student evaluations of teaching (SETs) are effected by a multitude of factors and should not, therefore, be simply interpreted as a clear and unbiased indicator of a teacher's abilities.
- While quality assessment, assurance and management are now endemic throughout higher education, the research suggests that their impact is limited because academics remain to be persuaded about their applicability.
- There is a tension in quality research between assessing what is easy to measure and what should be measured.

Chapter 13
System policy

Introduction

Despite being a widely researched aspect of higher education (Tight 2003, 2012a, 2019a: see Table 2 in Chapter 3) – indeed, something on which virtually everyone connected to higher education has an opinion – system policy research has been the subject of relatively few systematic reviews and hardly any meta-analyses. Only twenty research syntheses, or around 4 per cent of the total, have been identified for discussion in this chapter. Of these, nine were systematic reviews, nine literature reviews and just two meta-analyses (see Table 1 in Chapter 3).

It is interesting to briefly speculate on why this might be the case. Is it that system policy is essentially an ephemeral and moving field, so that, by the time today's policy has been researched and critiqued, it is already out of date and a new policy is in place? In these circumstances, it might seem pointless to attempt to synthesize research on outmoded or changing policies.

However, much the same might be said about, for example, course design or the student experience. These are also constantly in flux, particularly with the rapid contemporary development of information and communication technologies. An alternative view, therefore, and one that underlies and recognizes the systematic reviews and meta-analyses of higher education system policy that have been carried out, is that policies, while continually shifting and changing, contain enough common elements to be worthy of research synthesis.

There must, therefore, be some other explanation or explanations for the relative lack of syntheses of system policy research. Could it be that those who carry out system policy research are not inclined towards, or interested in, synthesizing that research? This also seems unlikely, as there are plenty of substantial books (though often edited) that focus on system policy.

Indeed, the edited volume that summarizes and compares the state of research (and practice) on a particular policy issue in different countries across the globe is a staple of the system policy literature (e.g. Goedegebuure et al 1994, King, Marginson and Naidoo 2011). While these might offer useful summaries of research and thinking on the issue in question, they are not, however, research syntheses of the kind considered in this book.

The particular lack of meta-analyses of system policy also begs some explanation. There is, after all, no real lack of quantitative data on higher education systems, much of it in the form of national statistics. It may, though, simply be that meta-analyses of this data are effectively supplanted by international comparative studies of the kind produced each year by institutions like the Organisation for Economic Cooperation and Development (OECD 2018) and the United Nations Educational, Scientific and Cultural Organization (UNESCO) Institute for Statistics.

There are a number of specialist higher education journals that focus on the topics discussed in this chapter, including *Higher Education Policy*, the *Journal of Higher Education Policy and Management*, and *Policy Reviews in Higher Education*.

The syntheses of system policy research that have been carried out and published have been divided in this chapter into three main types on the basis of their level:

- Studies focusing on international policy developments, or comparing policy developments in a number of different countries;
- Studies examining policy developments in a single country (of which there are relatively few, though this is the focus that has attracted most higher education policy research); and
- Studies considering particular themes of relevance across higher education systems worldwide.

We will consider each of these in turn.

International and comparative studies

International and comparative studies are a popular genre in higher education research. It is natural to seek to compare policy developments in closely connected countries, such as within the European Union (or Europe as a whole) or in the Asia Pacific area. There are also trends which are global in scope and impact upon higher education policy worldwide. These are prolific topics for research, so it is somewhat surprising that there have been relatively few systematic reviews and meta-analyses carried out of the research into these topics.

But there have been some. Those considered in this section focus on globalization, internationalization and massification; transnational higher education; and the Bologna Process.

Globalization, internationalization and massification

Dodds (2008) addressed how we conceptualize globalization, one of the most powerful trends identified in the contemporary world. To do this, she examined all of the articles published in nine higher education and education journals in the year 2005, focusing on those which included substantial references to globalization (n = 41). From these, she identified a number of different conceptions of globalization – as global flows and pressures, as trends such as marketization, as ideology – and considered its relationship to internationalization.

She also noted the varied consequences of globalization identified: a concentration of linguistic and economic power, greater competition between higher education institutions, those institutions being increasingly involved in maintaining and developing national economic advantage, changes in the nature of information and access to it, and the role of higher education institutions themselves in promoting globalization (something which she argued has been overlooked).

Dodds concluded that

> [g]lobalisation remains a contested concept, within studies of higher education as in many other fields. Rather than it being taken to refer unambiguously to global flows, pressures, or trends, its meaning continues to depend on the particular perspective adopted by contemporary researchers. The same conflict is apparent concerning the impacts which are attributed to globalisation, and with regard to the appropriate response to globalisation amongst academics and HEIs [higher education institutions] more generally. Perhaps the only apparent point of consensus amongst contemporary researchers is the claim that globalisation affects HEIs, rather than HEIs themselves being implicated in its promotion … however, this position underplays the often important role of HEIs in encouraging cross-border flows and pressures, and global trends such as marketisation.
>
> (pp. 514–5)

In a broader systematic review of research into globalization and internationalization in higher education, Tight (forthcoming – a) builds on Dodds's analysis, coming to a rather different kind of conclusion:

> [I]t seems curious … that higher education research is arguably less globalized and/or internationalized than the systems and institutions it studies … In moving our thinking about globalization and internationalization in higher education forward, therefore, whether as higher education researchers, policy makers or practitioners, we ourselves need to think and act more globally and internationally.

The tendency for higher education researchers to focus chiefly or solely on their own higher education system – even when participating in comparative international studies – may, of course, also help to explain the relative lack of systematic reviews and meta-analyses of this topic.

Also recently, Permitasari et al (2019), an Indonesian team, have provided a further systematic review of research into internationalization (n = 21), linking it to the notion of sustainability (which is also discussed, in different contexts, in Chapters 8 and 14). They identified a series of popular issues under discussion in this literature: 'the potential of digital manufacturing; use of classes and virtual laboratories; analysis of human resources factors relating to opportunities and competencies; innovation and organizational change in the face of global challenges; and the use of technology-based learning and education systems as learning media' (p. 91). Their analysis is largely positive, seeing internationalization as offering opportunities to the developing world.

Tight (2019b) has also completed a systematic review of research into the related issues of mass higher education and massification. This concerns the tendency of all higher education systems, both in developed and developing nations, to aim to offer provision for as many students – who wish to enrol and are capable of benefitting from the provision – as possible, such that higher education provision expands to its maximum.

This review concluded that 'the elite/mass/universal typology may finally have outlived its usefulness, and that there is a pressing need to re-consider what higher education means in the post-massification era' (p. 93). Universal, or near-universal, participation in higher education cannot offer the same experience to all as the social elite that formerly participated in higher education experienced in the recent past. It may, though, be the case that many of the current social elite continue to have something like that former elite experience, but in elite universities and colleges within the mass higher education system.

Transnational higher education

At the international level, the issues posed by what has been termed transnational higher education – i.e. higher education provided in a country by institutions that are foreign to, or not based in, that country – have become the subject of increasing research.

Kosmutzky and Putty (2016) provide a systematic review of research into transnational, offshore, cross-border and borderless higher education, terms which sound like synonyms but conceal subtle differences of emphasis. Using the International Database of Research on International Education, they identified 1,921 items published up until 2014 for analysis. Their

> network analysis of literature abstracts reveals that the quantitatively dominant terms – cross-border higher education and transnational higher education – are embedded in two quite different semantic networks and illuminate two different perspectives on the global 'mobility' of institutions, programs, and people. On one hand, the term cross-border is concerned with the traversing of existing borders, and is tied to global educational trade and its related policies on provision, regulation, or governance (including quality assurance), thus bringing into relief the national/local dimension; on the other hand, the term transnational points to the transcendence of various social, cultural, and geographic boundaries, and relates to a semantic cluster that address aspects of learning and teaching practices, as well as culture and cultural differences, whereby the 'global' element is more likely to get highlighted as a diffusing process. Thus, the fuzziness of boundaries, real or otherwise, would seem to be a function of the activity or process involved.
>
> (p. 21)

In terms of the globalization/internationalization distinction, therefore, while cross-border has closer affinities to internationalization, transnational links more closely to globalization. Both of the former terms seem softer and more old-fashioned, while the latter pair, by comparison, are harder and more contemporary.

Caniglia et al (2017) take a more focused approach in examining transnational collaboration between institutions of higher education for sustainability (see also the discussion of this topic in Chapter 8, in the context of the curriculum, and Chapter 14, in the context of institutional management). They found 46 articles examining the collaborations between 147 universities, from which they identify success factors for transnational collaboration, including 'combining local and global considerations; making effective use of digital technologies; capitalizing on cultural and national differences; and making the best of available resources' (p. 764). With the exception of the mention of national differences, these factors sound fairly generic to any form of institutional collaboration.

Escriva-Beltran, Munoz-de-Prat and Villo (2018) examine the literature on international branch campuses (IBCs) – of which there were 249 in 33 countries at the beginning of 2017 – from 1960 to 2017 (n = 173). They identify 'nine different thematic research areas in which academics have shown interest: institutional reasons to establish an IBC, models of IBC, student issues, academic staff issues, sustainability, English as a lingua franca, parallelism with a subsidiary of a multinational corporation, and educational and business hubs' (p. 7).

We may expect transnational higher education to be a growth area for the foreseeable future, as more and more countries and institutions get involved, with a consequent impact on research and research syntheses.

The Bologna Process

The Bologna Process – designed to standardize higher education structures and practices within the European Union (EU) – has been arguably one of the most influential international policies of the last few decades, and not just in higher education or education but in general. This influence may readily be demonstrated by the way it has been taken up by countries outside the European Union and far away from Europe.

Wihlborg and Teelken (2014) conduct what they term a longitudinal literature review of research into the Bologna Process, involving ninety-one studies published over the period 2004 to 2013. They note that '[t]he implementation of the Bologna Process (BP) did not go as smoothly as the Bologna Follow-Up evaluations suggest, and the consequences of the BP for the various European higher education systems and universities are much more diverse than represented in these various studies'. They also state that '[r]elatively few research and policy documents taking a more critical stance are currently available' (p. 1084). Perhaps this should not be so surprising, however, as a great deal was riding on the success of the Bologna Process, and most of those writing research and policy documents would have received funding from the EU.

Heinz and Maasen (2019) offer a partial corrective to this analysis, in providing a systematic review of the literature on the role of the social sciences – which they argue has been overlooked – in the creation of the European Higher Education Area (EHEA), the principal outcome of the Bologna Process. They focused on the period from 1999 to 2018, identifying 251 relevant peer-reviewed articles, as well as speeches, reports and books. They conclude that

> [w]hile the social sciences, in their heterogeneity, have all been shown to co-produce the EHEA, they differ in their visibility. While the interdisciplinary fields such as empirical and higher education research are particularly highly visible, as they are often explicitly invited to evaluate, report, and make recommendations for improvements, the classical social sciences are less visible or even invisible, as they are often more interested in broader methodological and theoretical aspects concerning the EHEA. Both perspectives come with downsides: interdisciplinary fields produce reports that are often limited by their statistical methodology and focus on numbers and comparable results. In particular, they seem to be blind vis-à-vis more complex processes, misunderstandings, and re-interpretations of the Bologna objectives taking place below the surface of structural changes. By contrast, classical social sciences follow qualitative methods. Typically, they are more concerned with differences that are crucial for adapting the general ideas of the EHEA to specific national conditions. From this angle, differing velocities, national path-dependencies, and particularities of infrastructures are revealed as important elements in (re-)shaping the Bologna reforms. However, if these results are acknowledged at all, they must be 'translated' … When this happens, however, these studies, too, co-produce the EHEA, even if uninvitedly.
>
> (pp. 10–1)

This is one of the few research syntheses of which I am aware that has drawn attention to the role of higher education and other researchers in influencing, albeit at a remove and in 'translated' or even 'trivialised' form, higher education policy.

National studies

As noted, while most studies of higher education system policy tend to focus on policy at the national level, there are few syntheses available of such research. Thus, only two examples are discussed in this section.

Harman (2005) interestingly takes as his focus the impact of internationalization, discussed in the previous section, but at national level, in this case in Australia. He notes that much of the research has been on the experiences of, and support provided to, international students in Australia (see also Chapter 11), with relatively little on the internationalization of Australian curricula, students and staff. In other words – and this is common in research in other developed countries – the national system has been taken for granted, with the focus on the adaptation to it of those coming to the country to study.

Harman also draws a conclusion of broader relevance:

> Scholars from many different perspectives and disciplines have been involved in the research effort, but their interests have diverged to a marked extent so that work on any particular theme and topic usually has come from a limited group of scholars with shared interests. For instance, most of the work on internationalization of the curriculum and particular teaching efforts has come mainly from academics in such fields as accounting and business studies, management and computer science, and

from specialists in university teaching and learning centres, while discussions of the globalization and the overall impact of internationalization has drawn interest mainly from scholars in comparative education and sociology. Unfortunately, in many cases the various groups of scholars have gone about their research efforts largely in isolation from other scholars with different interests in internationalization.

(p. 133)

This conclusion holds for higher education research (and other fields) as a whole, where researchers tend to confine themselves to specialist silos, delimited by topic, approach, methodology, theoretical perspective and/or nation (Shahjahan and Kezar 2013, Tight 2014b). It also neatly illustrates the need for research syntheses.

Taking a rather different approach, Ithnin et al (2018) provide a meta-analysis – one of the few such quantitative syntheses so far produced in system policy research – of futures studies (nine articles and four reports) that have considered Malaysian higher education (MHE). They conclude that 'the meta-analysis has ascertained that scenario planning and futures studies interventions in the MHE setting have been instrumental in providing a probable framework for the ministry and universities, in realigning and fine-tuning their images of the future towards a holistic university model' (p. 16). Their methodological approach might be usefully adapted to and applied in other national settings.

Thematic studies

Most syntheses of system policy research at the national level focus on particular themes rather than on the overall direction of policy. Sometimes these themes are approached in a seemingly generic fashion, with no national context specified, but it is clear from the discussion that there is an underlying national context. Many of these syntheses focus on research into policies concerning what are often termed 'non-traditional students', i.e. those whose participation has transformed higher education into mass higher education (see also the discussion of the student experience in Chapter 11).

Non-traditional students

Bennion, Scesa and Williams (2011) offer a literature review of research into part-time undergraduate study in the UK and comparable systems (n = 22):

> Overall, the literature review established that there are substantial and wide-ranging benefits from studying part-time. However, these benefits differ according to the focus of the studies undertaken (for example, subject of study, level of study, institution), as well as according to self-reported reasons for studying. For some individuals, employment and labour market issues dominate both in their motivations for studying and in the benefits they received. For others, issues such as identity, friendships and leisure were more important.
>
> (p. 159)

Those studying part-time are typically in employment, usually full-time employment, so part-time study may be their only option.

Wirihana et al (2017) provide an integrative literature review of studies of higher education in 'regional' Australia – that is, away from the big cities of Sydney, Melbourne, Brisbane, Perth and Adelaide, where most of the population and provision is – with a particular focus on nursing education. They conclude that

> [t]here are benefits to having regional university campuses but significant challenges are experienced by academics and students on these satellite campuses. Regional satellite campus students and academics have different experiences to their metropolitan counterparts and therefore the local context needs to be considered.
> (p. 317)

This echoes the point made earlier about the mass higher education experience being qualitatively different from the former (and to some extent continuing) elite higher education experience.

Widening participation research has been a particular focus of synthesizing studies. Gorard et al (2006) reviewed widening participation research, primarily in the UK, for the former Higher Education Funding Council for England (HEFCE), noting that

> [a] large body of research since the 1950s has found that the determinants of participation, and non-participation, are long-term. There is a clear pattern of typical learning 'trajectories' which are both shaped by, and constrain, learning experiences. Thus, the key social determinants predicating lifelong participation in learning involve time, place, gender, family, and initial schooling. Such findings emphasise the importance of reviewing evidence on participation through the 'lifecourse' of each individual, and compromises the analytic utility of the 'barriers' metaphor.
> (p. 5)

The barriers metaphor referred to has been a popular means for explaining non-participation in higher education: i.e. in terms of the various constraints (e.g. social background, schooling, finance) that have to be overcome in order to participate successfully. Gorard et al prefer to talk in terms of determinants and the life course, seeing widening participation in a longitudinal context.

The review by Gorard et al was followed up seven years later by Moore, Sanders and Higham (2013) in a report for HEFCE and OFFA (the then Office for Fair Access). They provide a thematic literature review of this research in the UK on key target groups for widening participation – people from lower socio-economic groups, mature students, part-time learners, learners from ethnic minority groups, vocational and work-based learners, disabled learners, and care leavers – groups which do, of course, overlap to a considerable extent. They then offer recommendations for developing practice in the areas of outreach and progression; information, advice and guidance; retention and student success (see also the discussion in Chapter 10); impact of financial support; flexible provision; progress to postgraduate study; employers; employability and economic growth.

Younger et al (2018), another UK-based team, carried out a systematic review of research into the effectiveness of widening participation interventions. Their review targeted existing systematic reviews (n = 4) and experimental studies (n = 12), most of which were conducted in the United States, coming to rather disappointing conclusions:

> [T]his systematic review found no robust evaluations of UK-based interventions. It found some evidence of the effectiveness of black box WP [widening participation] programmes (those with multiple elements in a single programme) and financial incentives, but these interventions were almost all developed for the US context and tested in that setting. The limitations of many of the studies in this review, such as potential biases in matched comparison groups, would also be likely to apply to studies designed in the UK.
>
> (p. 29)

In another unusual study, Webb et al (2017) carry out what they term a conceptual meta-analysis – but which in our terms is more of a systematic review, though the methodological approach is not made explicit – of the use of Bourdieu's theory in widening participation research. They argue for less 'pick and mix' approaches and more detailed and careful applications. Bourdieu (the same is the case with other social theorists, such as Foucault and Derrida) is frequently referred to in passing in higher education research in an effort to provide theoretical framing and credibility.

Other studies

Somewhat paralleling the work on widening participation, Brennan, Durazzi and Tanguy (2013) offer a literature review of research into the wider benefits of higher education (n ~ 50; see also Chapter 10). They note that

> [w]hile much of the literature focuses on the significance of gaining a higher education qualification for progression in the labour market and for the resultant effects on lifestyle and aspirations, there is also a significant body of literature which provides evidence of significant differences between higher education graduates and other members of society on a range of other dimensions. The most frequently cited ones appear to be citizenship, civic engagement, crime, health and general well-being.
>
> (p. 8)

In other words, higher education may be good for you in a whole variety of ways.

In one of the few genuine meta-analyses carried out on research into system policy, Huang, van den Brink and Groot (2009), a Dutch team, examine the effect of education (including higher education) on social capital. They synthesize 154 evaluations on social trust and 286 on social participation from 65 studies:

> The meta-analysis provides support for the existence of a relative effect of education on social participation, and of a reciprocity mechanism between the dimensions of social capital. The analysis also suggests that the erosion of social participation during the past decades has coincided with a decrease of the marginal return to education on social capital.
>
> (p. 454)

There is clearly a complex, and largely mutually beneficial, relationship between higher education and society which is being explored through these research syntheses.

Finally, Viegas et al (2016), a Brazilian team, explore critical aspects of sustainability in higher education through a literature review of the existing research (see also the discussion of the systematic review by Permitasari et al (2019) of this topic in the context of internationalization earlier in this chapter). They identified eighty-five relevant analyses published in the period 2000–15. They suggest that their 'analysis provides a means of benchmarking existing practice for Sustainability in Higher Education, and can be used as the basis for building capacity in a systematic way' (p. 260).

Conclusions

- The related trends of globalization, internationalization and massification are changing the nature of higher education and the behaviour of higher education institutions.
- Transnational higher education will be the focus of more research and research syntheses in the foreseeable future.
- More critical assessments of the implementation of the Bologna Process in Europe and beyond are needed.
- Syntheses of the large bodies of research and commentary on national system policy are also called for.

Chapter 14
Institutional management

Introduction

With the growth in the number, size and complexity of higher education institutions, institutional management has become an important area for higher education practice and thus for research. It has moved from being something undertaken, often on a part-time basis for a limited period of time by senior academics, with little or no training or support, to a professional operation employing lots of specialist non-academics and a burgeoning number of essentially former academics on a new career track.

Consequently, a growing number of research syntheses of the outputs of this research have been carried out: twenty-six in total were identified in Table 1 in Chapter 3, which means that this topic only accounts for about 5 per cent of the total number of syntheses identified in this book. Interestingly, the great majority of these syntheses, twenty-two, have been systematic reviews, with only two meta-analyses identified, suggesting that quantitative research – or at least published quantitative research (much internal, and presumably sensitive, institutional research does exist) – on this topic is limited. In addition, two substantive literature reviews were identified.

There are a number of specialist higher education journals which focus on the issues discussed in this chapter. They include the *Journal of Higher Education Policy and Management*, the *Journal of Marketing for Higher Education* and *Planning for Higher Education*.

The discussion in this chapter has been organized in terms of the level of management at which the research and the syntheses have been targeted: macro, meso or micro. Broadly speaking, the macro level is interpreted as being concerned with the outwardly facing institution, the meso level with the practical operation of the institution, and the micro level with details of management. It is recognized, of course, that these distinctions are not hard and fast and that there are inevitably overlaps, but this has proved to be a useful and practical way for organizing the chapter.

Interestingly, the macro/meso/micro distinction, as well as being the subject of research, has also been a focus of at least one systematic review (n = 42), examining the use of agent-based modelling and simulation (ABMS): 'a "bottom-up" modelling paradigm in which system-level behaviour (macro) is modelled through the behaviour of individual local-level agent interactions (micro)' (Gu and Blackmore 2015, p. 883). This review found that 'ABMS has been used to model the university system, university collaboration, academic activities, application and enrolment, and student performance' (p. 894), as well as in teaching.

Macro-level issues

In its outwardly facing role, institutional management in higher education has multiple responsibilities, and these are increasing in number year by year. In many cases universities and colleges have set up dedicated staff, teams or offices to focus on each of these roles, promoting and monitoring relevant activities. Universities and colleges are now typically one of the major employers – if not the major employer – in the towns and cities in which they are located.

Several of these institutional responsibilities or roles have been the subject of systematic reviews or meta-analyses during the last decade. These include so-called third mission activities (i.e. alongside the other two core 'missions' of teaching and research), sustainable development, academic drift, funding, and economies of scale and scope.

Third mission activities

Peer and Penker (2016), based in Austria, carried out what they termed a meta-analysis (though, in the usage of this book, it has more of the characteristics of a systematic review) of the role of higher education institutions in regional development – part of what is now termed their third mission – looking at both the English and German language literatures (n = 102). They noted differences in the types of knowledge involved and the changing research priorities over the period examined and identified:

> [T]wo main challenges for decision makers and practitioners who want to improve the interplay of HEIs [higher education institutions] and their surrounding region. The first is to deal with those areas, where scientific knowledge is still uncertain such as the role of HEIs for the establishment of cooperation and network structures, the impact of HEIs in supporting the regional economy with highly qualified graduates, impacts on the migration behavior of highly qualified graduates, the potential of HEIs to raise the regional innovation ability, and the 'new' roles for HEIs in and for the region (e.g., 'entrepreneurial', 'engaged', 'sustainable' university). The second challenge refers to the characteristics of the knowledge gained: many research outcomes and results are context-specific. As a result, HEI-region relations seem to be unique, being shaped by the specific internal structural characteristics of the region and the overriding cultural and political framework conditions as well as by the size, research focus, and study

programs offered by the HEI itself. This context-specificity is mirrored by the case study approach as the prevailing research design applied in past research.

(p. 245)

There is need, therefore, for broader-based and comparative research on this topic. Just as regions differ in their characteristics, so do higher education institutions. For some, their regional contribution may consist largely of establishing a local business or science park, to spin off innovations from research into start-up companies, or engage in joint enterprises with established businesses.

Third mission activities need not, however, be wholly economic in their focus: there may also be an important social or community element. This might include, for example, involvement in local adult education provision, running arts and sports centres, and the establishment of satellite campuses (to widen participation: see also the discussion in Chapter 13) throughout the region.

Thus, Jorge and Pena (2017) reviewed the literature on the social responsibility of higher education institutions:

> [T]he institutional context highlights the social dimension of universities and their important role in society as an educator of future leaders and policy makers. This suggests that there is a need to integrate social responsibility principles into their teaching and research activities as well as into their management and community engagement activities.
>
> (p. 303)

Jorge and Pena focused on the period 2000–15 and on publications in fifteen specialist academic journals (n = 314). They found that 'in spite of the changes carried out in the university sector which have emphasised the social dimension of universities, there is still a long way to go on the subject of USR [university social responsibility]' (p. 315). This links neatly, of course, to the subject of sustainability.

Sustainability

Sustainability is, arguably, also in the area of the third mission: thus, the 'sustainable' university is identified by Peer and Penker (2016) as one of the optional roles to play in the region. This issue clearly impacts as well, however, on the teaching and research roles of the university (see also the discussion of sustainability in the context of the curriculum in Chapter 8). There have been at least two recent systematic reviews on the role of higher education institutions in sustainability.

Ceulemans, Molderez and van Liederkerke (2015) focus on research into sustainability reporting, the process through which higher education institutions (and others) 'transparently communicate their values, actions and performance towards sustainable development to various stakeholders' (p. 127). They conclude that

> the topic of SR [sustainability reporting] has been approached in a rather fragmented way in the HESD [higher education for sustainable development] literature, while the scientific field would benefit from more in-depth studies, preferably supplemented

by empirical evidence ... The most important topic for further research ... is ... the potential for organizational learning and change.

(p. 138)

Findler et al (2019), an Austrian/Swedish partnership, adopt a different perspective, in focusing on research concerning the impact of higher education institutions on sustainable development. They examined relevant publications for the 2005–17 period (n = 113). Though their focus is somewhat different from that of Ceulemans et al, they come to very similar conclusions:

> [M]ore research with a holistic perspective that considers the impacts of all core elements would be a fruitful addition to the many in-depth case studies available. This would allow for a comprehensive understanding of the impacts of HEIs [higher education institutions] on SD [sustainable development].
>
> (p. 32)

We clearly have a lot further to go in understanding both the impact of higher education institutions on sustainability and their role in promoting it.

Other macro-level issues

Other macro-level systematic reviews have examined a range of other key issues impacting upon institutional management.

Tight (2015c) reviewed studies of academic drift, the tendency for institutions of higher education to aspire to, and/or work towards, higher status. For example, university colleges seek to become fully fledged universities, while established universities wish to be regarded as 'world-class'. Tight noted that

> academic drift was not a wholly original idea when it was first put forward [in the UK] in the early 1970s. American higher education researchers had previously written about the vertical or upward extension of institutions, just as they have more recently written about mission creep or drift. More generally, there were a number of precursor theories in existence – including institutional isomorphism, the social division of labour and convergence theory – which expressed much the same ideas as academic drift, but not necessarily in the context of higher education.
>
> (p. 95)

In other words, the way we think about higher education institutions, and how this then impacts upon policy and practice, owes a lot, consciously or subconsciously, to other thinkers in other places in other disciplines. This is true, of course, to a greater or lesser extent, of our thinking on most topics, within higher education and beyond.

Uslu et al (2019) provide what they term a meta-synthesis (i.e. a systematic review) of research on the entrepreneurial university. They identified twenty-five relevant articles from the top ten higher education journals in the SCImago rankings. Their content analysis of these articles found that 'both for universities and academics, entrepreneurship is overwhelmingly characterised by the commercialisation of scholarly activities that enrich institutional income revenue as well as academics' personal income' (p. 285). As with the third mission, discussed earlier in this chapter, social and community forms of entrepreneurship do not get so much attention.

Zhang, Kang and Barnes (2016), a China/New Zealand team, carried out a systematic review of higher education institution funding in developed countries, focusing on articles in twenty-nine higher education journals over the period 2006–15 (n = 178). They concluded that

> [t]his systematic literature review has revealed key patterns, theories, and issues in higher education funding in the past few decades. The key patterns include funding reduction and tuition fee increases, privatization and corporatization of higher education institutions, performance-based funding, and funding for internationalization. The theories that are specifically influential to higher education funding include new institutional economics, resource dependence theory and political economy. The issues that are subject to further debate are: higher education as a public good or a private good, academic capitalism, educational equity, and the role of econometrics.
>
> (p. 539)

Indeed, these issues are at the heart of most contemporary debates on higher education in developed countries, both within academia and across society as a whole. The way in which higher education institutions are funded has a major impact upon their character and operation.

One meta-analysis – in this case a meta-regression analysis – has been identified that considered a macro-level issue in institutional management. Zhang and Worthington (2018), an Australian pairing, focused on economies of scale and scope. Economies of scale have to do with how large (higher education) institutions should be to secure the lowest possible unit costs, while economies of scope relate to whether joint production (e.g. in the higher education context, of undergraduate and postgraduate students) produces cost savings. This is a topic where multiple measurements in different institutions and systems have been carried out over the years.

Zhang and Worthington identified forty-two studies that had been reported during the period 1981–2013 from Australia, the United States, the UK, Italy and China. The findings were not clear cut, however, and the authors concluded that

> functional form and allowances for managerial efficiency have a significant impact on the estimated scale economies. In contrast, for scope economies, the key discriminating factors appear to be when the analysis was conducted, the diversity of the sample, and the national level of economic development.
>
> (p. 156)

In general, therefore, it is difficult to say what size and make-up of higher education institution is the most economically efficient, but, at a specific level, it is possible to identify institutions which are more or less efficient (this issue is discussed further in the next section).

Meso-level issues

Most syntheses of research into institutional management in higher education concern the meso level, that is the general issues faced in the day-to-day operation of institutions. All of those identified here are systematic reviews, though one (Lechtchinskaia, Uffen and Breitner 2011) was mistakenly, in my view, labelled as a meta-analysis.

The topics reviewed include information and knowledge management, leadership, institutional efficiency and other specific managerial functions.

Information and knowledge management

A number of studies have examined research on universities' adoption and usage of information and knowledge management systems. Thus, Lechtchinskaia, Uffen and Breitner (2011) considered the critical success factors for the successful adoption of integrated information systems, identifying twenty-one relevant articles and 'stakeholder participation, business process reengineering and communication' as the key factors (p. 1).

They concluded that '[t]he unique constellation of characteristics of HEIs [higher education institutions], namely fragmented organizational and technical structures, distributed authority and low process-orientation reveal the need for a different project management approach in comparison to ERP [enterprise resource planning] implementation in private companies' (p. 8). This would not, of course, be a surprising conclusion for most of those who work in higher education.

Pinho, Franco and Mendes (2018) review the importance of web portals in supporting information management in higher education institutions (n = 126). They identified four key topics in this literature: '(1) Software used in web portals, (2) Internal and external benefits of using web portals, (3) Acceptance of technology and (4) Information management and storage' (p. 87), and stressed the need for more research.

Another Portuguese team, Carvalho, Pereira and Rocha (2019), focused on research into maturity models (i.e. guides and references) for information systems: 'These models provide information for organizations in order to address the problems they face in a structured way, providing a reference point to assess their capabilities and a roadmap for improvement' (p. 3).

They conclude that 'none of the identified models has sufficiently focused on the capability of IS [information system] support's complex, diversified, interoperable and dynamic organizational processes in the HEI [higher education institution] sector. From this perspective, it is necessary to design a new model to fill the gap' (p. 12). This, again, supports the view that higher education institutions are a very particular kind of institution, in need of special or bespoke attention.

Qasem et al (2019), a Malaysian team, examine cloud computing adoption in higher education institutions (n = 206). Their systematic review produced a taxonomy of the research they were analysing: reviews/surveys, research studies on cloud computing (CC) adoption, development attempts and broad framework proposals. They noted that

'CC technology leads to change in the way of work of teachers, educators, and HEIs [higher education institutions]' (p. 63738), but that more research was needed.

Secundo et al (2019), an Italian team, carried out a structured literature review of research into knowledge management (KM) in entrepreneurial universities, which is clearly a critical function or role. They identified 150 relevant articles:

> Findings show that literature on KM models and tools in the entrepreneurial university is fragmented and dominated by unrelated research. Content analysis shows heterogeneous literature, but four major research streams emerge: knowledge transfer in university–industry collaboration; knowledge creation in entrepreneurship education; KM processes for university spin-offs; entrepreneurial university to support knowledge-based regional development. The results show a failure to address the implications of findings for policy makers, which risks making KM in entrepreneurial universities research irrelevant.
>
> (p. 1)

Zawacki-Richter et al (2019) provide a systematic review of research on the use of artificial intelligence applications in higher education, identifying 146 relevant studies published between 2007 and 2018. They identify four main areas of application: profiling and prediction, assessment and evaluation, adaptive systems and personalization, and intelligent tutoring systems. They stress

> the almost lack of critical reflection of challenges and risks of AIEd [artificial intelligence in education], the weak connection to theoretical pedagogical perspectives, and the need for further exploration of ethical and educational approaches in the application of AIEd in higher education.
>
> (p. 1)

Knowledge management would appear, therefore, to be another role on which higher education institutions, particularly entrepreneurial ones, need to get a grip.

Leadership

Leadership is a key issue in the institutional management of universities and colleges. Higher education institutions are somewhat unusual in distributing this function throughout their levels of operation, such that most academic employees lead on something, whether it is a particular course or module, or student recruitment or staff development in the department concerned.

Bryman (2007) reviewed the literature on effective departmental leadership from 1985 to 2005 published in the United States, the UK and Australia, finding twenty relevant articles. From these he identified thirteen key leadership behaviours:

- clear sense of direction/strategic vision
- preparing departmental arrangements to facilitate the direction set
- being considerate
- treating academic staff fairly and with integrity

- being trustworthy and having personal integrity
- allowing the opportunity to participate in key decisions/encouraging open communication
- communicating well about the direction the department is going
- acting as a role model/having credibility
- creating a positive/collegial work atmosphere in the department
- advancing the department's cause with respect to constituencies internal and external to the university
- providing feedback on performance
- providing resources for and adjusting workloads to stimulate scholarship and research
- making academic appointments that enhance department's reputation

He concluded that

> [t]hese 13 aspects comprise many aspects of leader behaviour that can be found in the leadership literature more generally, such as the emphases on vision, integrity, consideration and sense of direction. However, there are also aspects of department chair leadership that are more strikingly connected to the specific milieu of higher education.
> (p. 706)

Following on from Bryman, Dopson et al (2018), a British/Australian team, focus on the related topic of leadership development in higher education. They identified thirty-two relevant articles published up until the time of their study (2018), with their analysis suggesting, somewhat disappointedly, that

> [H]igher-Education-based LD [leadership development] programmes are absorbing substantial time, attention and resources so they should be better investigated than at present. Our search suggested the current literature base is small-scale and fragmented. Notably, there are few published, large-scale, empirically informed studies which explore the practices, content and (more ambitiously) the long-term impact of the many LD programmes in Higher Education. Moreover, the studies reviewed were often localised, weakly theorised and disengaged from wider or recent sectoral developments. We now suggest candidate research projects exploring LD programmes in UK Higher Education in greater depth, mindful that in the long term they should lead to more international research.
> (p. 13)

The conclusion that, while higher education institutions run or support leadership development programmes, they do not know how well they are working is concerning.

Taking a broader perspective still, Tight (2014a) reviews the discussion of collegiality and managerialism in the higher education literature, concluding, among other things, that these qualities are not as juxtaposed as commonly imagined. Like most dichotomies, the distinction is also simplistic and idealistic, with collegiality being portrayed as the way things used to be done and managerialism as the unnecessary imposition of a fad from business. It is possible, however, to show collegiality as an academic manager.

This may be illustrated further in a relatively early, but extensive, American review (Schmidtlein and Milton 1990), contrasting how planning is practised in higher education institutions with what the planning literature advocates:

> This review … reveals a lack of both consistent theoretical frameworks and clear empirical evidence to support an uncritical acceptance of existing formal planning approaches. Current conceptions of organizational behavior, particularly in colleges and universities, stress their loosely coupled, decentralized character. Decision making is characterized as incremental and political with considerable value placed on professional autonomy. In contrast, most available planning approaches are rooted in 'rational' and bureaucratic conceptions of decision making and organizational structure.
>
> (p. 32)

Yet again, therefore, the argument is made that higher education institutions tend to operate rather differently from many other, particularly private sector business, institutions.

Institutional efficiency

Rhaiem (2017) addresses the question of academic research efficiency (see also Chapter 16), undertaking a systematic review of the literature published between 1990 and 2012, identifying 102 directly relevant articles. They provide an integrative conceptual framework to summarize and organize their findings:

> This framework regroups, in meaningful categories, inputs and outputs identified through the data extraction grid used as part of the systematic review, as well as the underlying determinants that have a dominant effect on the explanation of efficiency levels of DMUs [decision-making units] that were identified through the vote counting procedure. It is structured in two blocks. The upper block represents the production process of research linking inputs to outputs … the inputs are grouped into six rubrics (human capital, physical capital, research funds, operating budget, cumulative stock of knowledge, and agglomeration effects). Likewise, overall, we distinguished seven outputs (refereed articles, books, book chapters, refereed conferences, professional publications, other deliverables, and quality indicators). The bottom block of the conceptual framework presents eleven major rubrics that regroup the explanatory variables of efficiency variations among DMUs identified in our systematic literature, and confirmed as having dominant effects, by the vote counting method: funding structure, seniority and composition of staff, gender effect, research fields, institutional factors, social capital, size, and effort to protect intellectual property.
>
> (pp. 603–4)

Rhaiem presents these findings as 'a framework which brings together a set of outputs and inputs related to academic research efficiency, and the individual, organizational, and contextual factors driving or hampering it' (p. 581), which could then be applied by institutional managers.

Gralka (2018), taking a more general stance than Rhaiem, examines what the literature has to say about the efficiency of higher education institutions as a whole, with a particular focus on the application of one particular multivariate technique, stochastic frontier analysis. Gralka identifies and assesses sixty-three studies published over the 1998–2017 period, confirming

> the general perception that an increasing number of studies are evaluating the efficiency of HE [higher education] institutions. Most studies are written by natives [i.e. researchers working in higher education], using panel data provided by the respective statistical office to assess public universities. However, the utilized samples, in particular, the number of evaluated institutions and the evaluated timeframe, vary greatly between studies. Surprisingly, few authors compare efficiency across countries. Since suitable datasets are gradually emerging, we expect cross-country evaluations to become more frequent in the future.
> (p. 42)

Also focusing on efficiency studies, Villano and Tran (2019) provide a meta-regression analysis of 109 data envelopment analysis studies of higher education. They come to more positive conclusions regarding the development of the technology than Gralka:

> The methodological improvements of these studies include multi-level performance assessment to serve the increasing demands of both educational leaders and policy-makers in within-country and cross-country perspectives, conducting comparative analysis of different types of ownership and various study groups, incorporating the quality indicators into the efficiency assessment process, and using different techniques to validate the results taking into account statistical inference applying the bootstrap method.
> (p. 13)

In terms of overall empirical findings, Villano and Tran highlight some interesting results:

> [T]he meta-fractional regression models of the upper middle-income nations have lower scores than the high-income nations at the 5% level of significance. Although low income nations seem to have lower efficiency scores than high-income nations, these relationships are not statistically significant at the 5% significance level. In addition, the number of variables, analysis at departmental level, and the panel data are key factors affecting the efficiency results in the surveyed publications.
> (p. 13)

These findings should help institutional managers seeking to improve the efficiency of their institutions.

Specific managerial functions

Other systematic reviews have concentrated on particular managerial functions of higher education institutions. Hemsley-Brown and Oplatka (2006) review the literature on higher education marketing. In all, sixty-three articles published in the 1992–2004 period were identified, with fifteen empirical 'supply side' papers selected for detailed review. They found that the potential benefits of applying marketing theories and concepts that have been effective in the business world are gradually being recognised by researchers in the field of HE [higher education] marketing. However, the literature on HE marketing is incoherent, even inchoate, and lacks theoretical models that reflect upon the particular context of HE and the nature of their services.

(p. 316)

Lafuente-Ruiz-de-Sabando, Zorrilla and Forcada (2018) look at the closely related issues of higher education institutions' image and reputation, identifying seventy articles for review published in forty different journals. They argue that

[t]he gaps identified highlight the need to improve knowledge about the way perceptions (image and reputation) of university institutions are shaped, pinpointing the dimensions or essential aspects that influence their formation and determining whether their degree of influence differs when considering the perspectives of different stakeholders or individuals from different geographical areas.

(p. 8)

There is a clear and recurring theme throughout these research syntheses concerning the overall inadequacy of the research carried out to date and the need for more focused and larger-scale work to supplement this.

Micro-level issues

Syntheses of higher education research focusing on the micro-level of institutional management are relatively uncommon. Just two examples, both systematic reviews, have been identified.

Jackson and Kile (2004), an American team, examine the literature on how the work of higher education administrators influences student outcomes. They searched the ERIC database from 1991 to 2001, eventually identifying seventy-eight relevant studies. While few of these studies directly addressed the issue of interest, the authors argued that 'a nascent nexus emerged between the work of administrators and student outcomes' (p. 298). Hence, they concluded:

As the studies examined confirm, researchers exploring administrative work in higher education should consider the implications of their work for student outcomes. The reverse is also true; researchers examining issues of student success should consider developing implications for the work of administrators in higher education.

(p. 299)

Vrielink et al (2017) provide a systematic review of research into the theory and practice of timetabling in higher education. They identified continuing dissonance between timetabling research and the software solutions offered:

> [T]here still exists a gap between academia and industry. While academia tend to develop intelligent and profound methods to solve timetabling problems, industry appears to develop and design an easy to use interactive tool that aims to meet the needs of teaching and administration staff. Once industry has a productive timetabling application, they stop implementing the latest research on timetabling in their software.
>
> (p. 13)

These two contrasting syntheses offer something of a flavour of the very specific and specialized issues encountered at the micro-level of institutional management.

Conclusions

- Research into the third mission of higher education (i.e. community and economic engagement) remains underdeveloped.
- The context for institutional management in higher education has altered radically with massification and funding changes.
- Collegiality and managerialism coexist within higher education institutions.
- Higher education institutions are rather different from other types of, particularly private sector, institutions and need specialist or bespoke approaches.

Chapter 15
Academic work

Introduction

Interestingly, and uniquely for the eight thematic areas of higher education research used in this book, none of the syntheses identified for this chapter are meta-analyses. Of the total of twenty-six research syntheses identified, twenty-three were systematic reviews and three literature reviews. Together, these make up around 5 per cent of all of the research syntheses identified for this book.

There are two specialist higher education journals that focus on one of the main topics discussed in this chapter: the *International Journal for Academic Development* and the *Journal of Faculty Development*, their titles reflecting the different terminologies in use on the two sides of the Atlantic.

The lack of meta-analyses of research into academic work begs some explanation. It might, most obviously, be related to a relative lack of quantitative studies in this area. However, there has been a succession of international surveys of the experience of academic work (Tight 2010), which provide a great deal of quantitative data. In many countries, statistics are also collected each year on the numbers of academics and their characteristics (e.g. sex, age, discipline, research and/or teaching focus, qualifications, full-time or part-time status).

This kind of quantitative data could be said to lend itself to descriptive and comparative statistical analysis. Researchers do not seem to have done much of the experimental or modelling work that would have produced the effect sizes that could, with repeated studies, have formed the basis for meta-analyses. But the scope for this kind of research – focusing, perhaps, on different kinds of academics, their motivations and their achievements – clearly exists.

The syntheses of research into academic work that have been identified tend to focus on either academic development (i.e. how academics are inducted into and trained in their work roles) or aspects of academic work practices and experiences. We will consider studies on each of these in turn.

Academic development

Research on academic development, and hence syntheses of such research, tends to be relatively recent in nature, as its importance has only been widely recognized in the last few decades. When higher education was a relatively small-scale activity, the need to induct and train academics, primarily to teach, was little recognized; disciplinary expertise was the characteristic sought.

However, with the development of mass systems of higher education, and their associated costs, concerns with quality and value for money have mushroomed (see also Chapter 12), leading to an increasing focus on the initial and continuing development of academic staff. Most established institutions of higher education now have an office and dedicated staff focusing on academic development.

'Academic development' is the term most commonly used for this activity in the UK, while faculty development is preferred in North America. Educational development and instructional development are also in widespread use, or the centre concerned with this activity might be labelled 'teaching and learning' or something similar. Whatever terminology is in use, the concern is with ensuring that all, and particularly new, academic staff have a good grounding, especially in teaching and learning methods (see also Chapter 4).

Some academic development centres go beyond the immediate concern with teaching and learning. Their remit might also, for example, cover basic administrative and managerial duties, such as the maintenance of appropriate records, as well as support for research, including the publication process and grant getting.

The earliest synthesis that I have identified, predictably carried out in the American context, is by Levinson-Rose and Menges (1981). They identified five categories of study: of grants for faculty projects, workshops and seminars, feedback from student ratings, practice-based feedback, and concept-based training. Seventy-one reports and ninety-seven analyses were reported, but meta-analysis was rejected as an approach because the sample was so disparate. While most of the analyses reported were positive, the authors raised doubts about the quality of some of the studies:

> Most comparisons (78%) support the intervention being studied, although the support rate in only those studies in which we have high confidence is considerably lower (62%). More exploratory qualitative studies as well as more rigorous experimental investigations, perhaps involving cross-campus collaboration, are needed.
>
> (p. 403)

Their conclusion then was that 'research on improving college teaching is not a well-defined field. For most studies, the basis in theory is strained and for some it is nonexistent. Work on major conceptual issues remains [to be done]' (p. 418). In another early and substantive literature review in the North American context, Allen (1988) considers the meaning of what he terms faculty development by looking at need, models, activities, organizational principles, participation, benefits and impact, and evaluation.

Amundsen et al (2005), a Canadian team, carried out what they termed an in-depth review of the literature, though it has the characteristics of a systematic review, over the period 1994–2004. They saw themselves as updating previous literature reviews (Emerson and Mosteller 2000, Levinson-Rose and Menges 1981, Weimer and Lenze 1991), but also took an international perspective. They characterized the articles identified as being focused on skills, methods, process or discipline.

Later, Amundsen and Wilson (2012) carried out a conceptual review, identifying six (rather than just four) foci of practice in the literature – skill, method, reflection, disciplinary, institutional, and action research or inquiry – arguing that this offers a more useful approach than one focusing overwhelmingly on impact. They identified 137 relevant articles for their study. They conclude, however, that they 'did not find much evidence of practice systematically building on other published reports of practice' (p. 113), a feature which is fairly common in newly emerging fields like academic development.

In their international systematic review, Stes et al (2010), a Belgian team, renew the focus on the impact of academic development, identifying thirty-six items for analysis. They took care to spread their net as widely as possible, not restricting themselves solely to journal articles:

> Our literature search for studies of the impact of instructional development in higher education was not limited to published sources. In this way we tried to overcome a biased representation. Of the studies that met the inclusion criteria, 9 were unpublished; 4 were conference papers, and 5 research reports. The other 27 studies were published as journal articles. It is surprising that 30 out of the 36 studies in our synthesis were American; only 3 were European, 1 Asian, and 1 Australian.
>
> (p. 47)

Stes et al concluded that

> more attention should be given to studies researching behavioral outcomes, thereby drawing not only on self-reports of participants, but also measuring actual changes in performance. Attempts to capture the effects at an institutional or student level would be very worthwhile as well. Much insight could be gained from well-designed studies with a pretest, a quasi-experimental character and/or using a mixed-method approach. The long-term effects of instructional development remain a terrain for future study too.
>
> (p. 48)

Clearly, the reservations about the quality of some of the research reported, which had been expressed in the earliest syntheses, still remained.

Sugrue et al (2017), a European team, review over 100 papers published between 1995–2015, noting the

> increasing awareness of the extent to which AD [academic development] as a field has asserted its way onto the HE [higher education] landscape during the past 20 years in particular. This achievement, in a relatively short space of time, creates particular consequences. In a rather undulating and uneven landscape, a concerted effort to

create an international discourse on AD may also serve to hide or deny considerable differences, particularly given increased diversity in the HE field.

(p. 11)

Academic development clearly has some way to go yet to establish itself, in part because of the scepticism about it shared by many academics.

Particular activities, parts of the world or groups

Other systematic reviews on this topic have focused on particular academic development activities, parts of the world or academic groups. Thus, Kornhaber et al (2016) examined the research on academic writing retreats (n = 11), a topic also of relevance for students, particularly research students. They found that

> [t]he five key elements of writing retreats conducive to increasing publication output were protected time and space; community of practice; development of academic writing competence; intra-personal benefits and organisational investment. Participants involved achieved greater publication outputs, particularly when provided [with] ongoing support.
>
> (p. 1210)

Academic writing retreats appear to be particularly useful for academics at the beginning of their publication career and for those who find it difficult to identify dedicated time and space.

The systematic review by Gast, Schildkamp and van der Veen (2017), a Dutch team, examined team-based professional development interventions (n = 18). They identify a series of factors at the individual, team and organizational levels that impact upon the success of such interventions:

> [T]eam-based professional development interventions can be successful in fostering teacher learning in higher education ... a university may want to give special attention to influential factors at the individual teacher level, team level, and organizational level when trying to implement a professional development intervention that involves teachers collaborating in a team. For example, the university must create an environment that enhances teacher learning and positively influences the teachers' attitudes. To do so, universities would, for example, need to provide extra time for teachers to spend on the team intervention if extra workload is created by participating in a team. It is also very important to reward teachers for their team achievements, by taking their successes into account during promotion and in the tenure process.
>
> (p. 762)

Such team-based interventions could be particularly useful for course or programme teams at specific points in their life cycle: e.g. when first established, after a major overhaul, in preparation for, or after, quality assessment.

Wimpenny, Beelen and King (2019) focused on academic development designed to support the internationalization of the curriculum, though their qualitative research synthesis only identified five relevant studies. This led them to conclude that

> [i]f universities are to achieve their aim of delivering internationalization to all their students instead of only the mobile 'cultural elite' or those studying in international programmes, many more than the 'champions' of internationalization must be involved. This in turn requires a systemic approach to the integration of international perspectives in socially-just pedagogy. Only then will the benefits of internationalization reach all students.
>
> (p. 12)

Systematic reviews of research into academic development that focus on particular parts of the world include those by Luzeckyj and Badger (2010), which concentrates on Australia, and Phuong, Duong and McLean (2015), whose remit is South-East Asia. Luzeckyj and Badger stress that

> [t]he variety of courses and programs embrace numerous theoretical frameworks and pedagogical practices. The differences between them include a range of sometimes contradictory or conflicting outcomes which make it difficult to compare programs and determine their effectiveness. Evaluation of programs to determine whether the student learning experience is improved as a result of staff participating in them is therefore complex.
>
> (p. 15)

Phuong, Duong and McLean identified thirty-four articles of relevance in their review, mainly stemming from Vietnam, Singapore and Malaysia. Interestingly, they found that

> self-directed learning activities played a more important role in FD [faculty development], compared with formal FD and organizational development. In other words, FD in this region is more of an individual faculty's effort than planned organization wide and becomes personal rather than organizational interventions. As a result, FD activities, with limited support from organizations and/or institutional support centers, focus primarily on improving faculty's teaching-related skills: information and communication technology (ICT) and pedagogy.
>
> (p. 114)

Systematic reviews that have focused on research into particular academic groups have included studies of teacher educators (Phuong, Cole and Zarestky 2018) and those engaged in work-based higher education (Wallin, Nokelainen and Mikkonen 2019). In their review (n = 22), Phuong, Cole and Zaretsky came to somewhat different conclusions on the balance of faculty development (FD) activities to Phuong, Duong and Maclean (2015):

> North American universities provide the most empirical evidence about FD activities, focusing on technology integration in teaching and pedagogical skill improvement. Formal programs, such as serial workshops and developmental relationship, were reported with high frequency, compared to self-directed learning and organizational development activities. Empirical research was heavily based on self-reported, qualitative data and emphasized individual-level outcomes. There is a lack of information regarding the impact of FD activities for teacher educators on subsequent student learning or the downstream effect on school systems. Similarly, institutional involvement in FD remains largely unexplored.
>
> (p. 373)

The lack of evidence on the impact of the developmental activities is a concern but is not untypical for training in general, where the time and resources are rarely available to evaluate what participants do with their new understandings once the training event is over.

The integrative literature review carried out by Wallin, Nokelainen and Mikkonen (2019), a Finnish team, found nineteen relevant studies. On this basis, they identified five central elements of expert learning in work-based higher education (see also the discussion of learning and work in Chapter 6): '(1) knowledge transformation and integration, (2) problem solving, (3) reflection, (4) learning from errors and (5) boundary crossing' (p. 367). They concluded that

> [c]onsistent with earlier research, this review confirms that expertise is developed through transforming and integrating theoretical, practical and self-regulative knowledge. Results suggest that (1) learners should be supported but also allowed to self-manage their learning in order to build agency and self-regulative skills, (2) continuous problem solving with ill-defined, nonroutine problems should be encouraged along with challenges that trigger learning, (3) learners' personal transformation processes and change of identity should be supported, and (4) expertise development should be viewed as an ongoing, context-dependent and individualised process.
>
> (p. 359)

In this context, academic development is portrayed as very much a support function, with most of the developmental work driven by the individual academic's interests.

Academic work practices and experiences

Systematic reviews of research into academic work, other than those examining academic development, have focused on varied, indeed disparate, aspects of practice and/or experience. For present purposes they have been organized into three groups: generic studies which examine academics as a single group, studies of academics with particular characteristics and other more focused syntheses.

Generic studies

Thus, at a fairly generic level, reviews have considered whether academics working in particular disciplines, sub-disciplines or groups may be considered as academic tribes and territories (Tight 2015b) or as communities of practice (Tight 2015a). Both of these theoretical perspectives have proved popular with higher education researchers, with the former stressing differences between groups of academics and the areas they occupy, teach about and research, while the latter emphasizes how groups of academics, of varied levels of experience, can work together on particular projects. In the case of communities of practice, Tight concludes that 'while, like all theoretical frameworks, communities of practice has strengths and weaknesses, it remains useful for thinking about academics, students, their disciplines and how they work together' (p. 111).

Adler and Lalonde (2019), a Canadian pair, looked at the issue of academic identity in the light of encroaching new public management. They identified nineteen relevant qualitative empirical studies:

> The results ... indicate that, paradoxically, academics contribute to the perpetuation of managerialism through protection strategies and institutional maintenance work while acknowledging their painful effects on their identity. Despite the control and monitoring measures put in place by university administrations, academics have assumed a pragmatic approach to identity by using the prevailing spaces of autonomy and engaging in constant self-questioning. Those involved could make better use of these free spaces by adopting projective agency, that is by expanding the areas of support, collaboration and creativity that, by their own admission, make up the academic profession.
>
> (p. 1)

Other reviews have focused on particular academic roles, such as teaching (see also Chapter 4) and research (see also Chapter 16). Thus, Lankveld et al (2017) examined research on the development of academic's teacher identity, synthesizing the findings of fifty-nine studies published between 2005 and 2015. They concluded that

> [u]niversity teachers develop a teacher identity after a few years of being a teacher. This teacher identity is built on other identities, including those of a professional, academic, researcher, or intellectual. We identified several factors that strengthen or constrain the development of teacher identity. Contact with students and staff development programmes were experienced as strengthening teacher identity, whereas the wider context of higher education was generally experienced as having a constraining effect. Additionally, the role of the direct work environment was experienced as either strengthening or constraining, depending on whether or not teaching was valued in the department.
>
> (p. 333)

These findings demonstrate how research, practice and experience effectively join up; the development of an academic teacher identity is helped by academic development (see the previous section of this chapter), but constrained by the emphases apparent within the particular academic workplace.

Academics with particular characteristics

Cama, Jorge and Pena (2016) carried out a review of studies of gender differences in the academic work experience. They focused on fourteen specialist higher education journals (i.e. not journals focusing on gender issues) published during the period 2000 to 2013, identifying seventy-four articles of relevance:

> [T]wo main trends and patterns are identified over the period from 2000 to 2013. First, although the number of articles is quite low in comparison with other topics, the increase in the publication of high quality articles on gender issues in the specialist journals

> that focus on higher education is striking. This could represent an evidence here of the increasing maturity of the field worldwide ... Second, four main themes have been investigated in the research on gender differences between faculty members of universities: faculty tenure and promotion; women in university management teams; policies aimed at promoting gender equity and gender earnings gap between faculty members.
>
> (p. 67)

These are not, of course, new issues, but the implication is that they are gradually being tackled.

Corneille et al (2019) also review the literature on women academics, but in this case women of colour (WOC), particularly in the American context. Their research aligns with that focused on students with particular characteristics, which is also strong in the United States (see Chapter 11). Corneille et al carried out what they called a qualitative meta-analysis (i.e. a systematic review in the terms used in this book) of articles published between 2001 and 2017.

They found forty-two relevant articles: '12 articles describe challenges related to teaching and service; 11 articles discuss challenges related to tenure and promotion; and 19 articles focused on mentoring' (p. 330). Corneille et al conclude that 'recommendations to promote systemic change for WOC faculty in institutions must embrace intersectionality and transformational approaches' (p. 340). In other words, a good deal remains to be done to ensure equality of treatment of women of colour academics in the United States.

In their review, Farkas et al (2019) focus on studies of the mentorship of women working in academic medicine (n = 20). Their findings were generally positive:

> The majority of the programs were designed for junior faculty and used the dyad model of mentoring (i.e., one mentor/one mentee). Frequently cited objectives of these programs were to improve scholarship, promotion, and retention of female faculty. Program evaluations were primarily survey-based, with participant-reported satisfaction being the most frequent measured outcome. Most results showed very high satisfaction. Gender concordance between mentor and mentee did not impact satisfaction. Eight articles reported objective outcomes, including publications, retention, and promotion, and each of these demonstrated an improvement after program implementation.
>
> (p. 1322)

Of course, as these reviews suggest, the experience of academic work – like other kinds of work – is not always or overwhelmingly positive, so there is research, and syntheses of that research, into some of the downsides. For example, Howell and Hoyt (2007), in an American study, review research into the job satisfaction of part-time faculty, the numbers of which (and the proportion of the workforce they account for) are increasing in many countries.

Other syntheses

Other research syntheses, examining academics as a whole rather than academics with particular characteristics, lend support to this view of academe as a sector where work experiences are not always positive.

Thus, Henning et al (2017), a New Zealand team, offer a systematic review of studies of workplace harassment in academia. They identify fifty-one relevant articles published in the period 1994 to 2013, finding that '[t]he published evidence, mainly from North America, suggests that workplace harassment is prevalent in higher education, such as gender harassment, workplace bullying, and mobbing' (p. 521). The identification of mobbing, or group bullying, is particularly concerning.

Cahill et al (2019) offer a meta-ethnography (i.e. a systematic review) of the transition to retirement experiences of academics. A search for the period 2000 to 2016 identified twenty relevant articles:

> Five themes were identified: (a) continuing to work in retirement, (b) the impact of the retirement transition on the academics' identity, (c) changing relationships through the retirement transition, (d) experiencing aging processes, and (e) planning for retirement. For most, retirement is characterized by continuing to work in aspects of their role, maintaining associated relationships, with gradual disengagement from academic activities. For another smaller group, the retirement pathway is experienced as an event, with complete detachment from academic activities.
>
> (p. 177)

As both of these syntheses suggest, academic work has close parallels with other kinds of work, but also particular nuances all of its own.

Gander, Girardi and Paull (2019) focus in their systematic review on an under-researched sector of academic work, namely professional staff, those non-academic staff with 'roles in governance, registry, student services, and so on' (p. 598) who are crucial in supporting the functioning of higher education institutions. Gander, Girardi and Paull identify twenty-three relevant articles, allowing them to identify the 'enablers and barriers that influence career development and progression' (p. 597) of professional staff in higher education. This is an area in which more research – and thus synthesis – can be expected in the future.

Conclusions

- Academic or faculty development has expanded to become a significant aspect of academic work over the last few decades.
- Disciplinary differences remain fundamental to an understanding of academic work.
- The experience of academic work remains gendered.
- More research is needed into the experiences of professional and non-academic staff.

Chapter 16
Knowledge and research

Introduction

Knowledge and research are arguably one of the most fundamental topic areas in higher education research. This area includes not only research into the research function of higher education, but that concerned with what research leads to, the accumulated knowledge that underpins and drives higher education. While this may sound somewhat introverted or circular, these are key topics for research if we are to fully understand higher education.

Perhaps unsurprisingly, however, knowledge and research are under-researched compared to other areas of higher education, notably, of course, course design. Perhaps higher education researchers are reluctant to trespass on other researchers' time and space, or researchers themselves are loath to spend precious research time in explaining their work to outsiders.

It is understandable, therefore, that research in these areas has been the subject of relatively few systematic reviews and meta-analyses. Indeed, the bibliographic searches carried out for this book identified only fifteen relevant research syntheses, about 3 per cent of the total discussed in the book. They comprised an almost equally balanced mix of the quantitative and qualitative: eight meta-analyses and seven systematic reviews. While they are relatively few in number, they do include some of the most influential or impactful syntheses of higher education research.

There are a couple of specialist higher education journals that focus on topics discussed in this chapter: *Research Evaluation* and the *Journal of Scholarly Publishing*.

The chapter starts by considering the systematic reviews and meta-analyses that have been carried out of research into the research/teaching nexus and their impact. It then looks at overviews of studies of the peer review process and of particular areas of research within higher education research.

The research/teaching nexus

Meta-analyses of studies of the relationship between the research and teaching functions of higher education go back, relatively speaking, a long way. One of the most influential and most criticized, by Hattie and Marsh, was published over twenty years ago in 1996 (see also Marsh and Hattie 2002). Having reviewed a range of models suggesting a positive, negative or nil relationship between research and teaching, they focused on fifty-eight (predominantly American) studies that had been published between 1949 and 1992, and that contained ratings of teaching (typically student evaluations: see the discussion of these in Chapter 12) and research (typically number of publications), and their correlation.

Hattie and Marsh found that

> [t]he overall relationship between quality of teaching and research was slightly positive. On the basis of 498 correlations from the 58 studies, the weighted average was .06.
>
> (p. 525)

Realizing that this finding would not be popular, as a belief in the complementarity of research and teaching was – and is – widespread within higher education, they then explored whether one or more intervening or moderating variables might explain this poor relationship. The variables considered included the type of university, domain of study, type of teaching and research productivity, domain of teaching, and time spent on research and teaching. This detailed examination did not, however, modify their overall conclusion:

> We must conclude that the common belief that research and teaching are inextricably entwined is an enduring myth. At best, research and teaching are very loosely coupled.
>
> (p. 529)

They finished the article by suggesting that '[p]erhaps the most profitable research direction is to inquire why the belief of complementarity exists' (p. 533).

Hattie and Marsh's meta-analysis of the research/teaching relationship or nexus was neither the first nor the last. It built upon an earlier meta-analysis by Feldman (1987), a prolific meta-analyst, and incorporated the twenty-nine studies he had analysed, adding a further twenty-nine. Feldman had also reported 'a very small positive association' (p. 227) and sought out mediating factors:

> Pedagogical practices and dispositions of faculty members, as well as certain course or class characteristics (size of class, electivity of course), were examined as potential mediating factors. Potential common causes investigated were academic rank and age of faculty members, their general ability, their personality characteristics, and the amount of time or effort they spend on research activities. The association between research productivity and teaching effectiveness was explored further by considering whether its size and direction varies by career stage of faculty members, their academic discipline, and the type of college or university in which they teach.
>
> (ibid)

He failed, however, to find much in the way of explanation, suggesting that the two activities (research and teaching) were essentially separate or that – at the level of the individual academic – the relationship was so varied as to average out at next to nothing.

More recently, Braxton (1996) took a slightly different approach to assessing whether the relationship was null, conflictual or complementary by using a 'vote counting' method for analysing the twenty-nine studies examined by Feldman and one other study, making thirty in all (it is curious that this was published at the same time as Hattie and Marsh, who doubled Feldman's twenty-nine studies to fifty-eight, though Braxton's is not a full-length article). On this basis, Braxton concluded that

> [f]irst, research does not interfere with teaching effectiveness. This conclusion is particularly salient in research universities in which the Null perspective receives strong confirmation, Moreover, the Conflict perspective has empirical support in only one of thirty studies. Second, a systematic relationship between teaching and research role performance does not exist across different types of colleges and universities. This conclusion stems from the modest support provided both the Null and the Complementarity perspectives.
>
> (p. 8)

This would support the argument that the relationship between research and teaching was highly varied, at both the individual academic and organizational levels.

Systematic reviews – as opposed to meta-analyses – of research into the research/teaching nexus have only been carried out in the last decade or so. The earliest of which I am aware is by Verburgh, Elen and Lindblom-Ylanne (2007) and effectively picked up where the American meta-analyses had left off. Their systematic review identified 116 relevant articles, from across the world as well as the United States, published between 1990 and 2005. Rather than focusing on the results – quantitative or qualitative – of the studies, they looked instead at how the studies had been carried out:

> The studies discussed here have similar research questions; they all concern the presence of a relationship between teaching and research. However, a closer look at the studies reveals that the variables investigated, their measurement as well as the investigated population differ significantly. Given the complexity of the issue, a certain amount of variability is to be expected. However, the analysis reveals an absence of commonality. A solid research framework for investigating the teaching-research nexus seems to be missing ... This review clearly shows that different studies measure different aspects on different populations.
>
> (p. 461)

Their conclusion, therefore, is that more comparable and carefully carried-out research studies into the topic are needed. While this wish has not yet been realized, more recent systematic reviews have added to the debate. Thus, Tight (2016b), echoing Verburgh, Elen and Lindblom-Ylanne, concluded that

> [t]he research/teaching nexus is used in such varied ways, is differently approached in policy and practice, and in different systems, cannot be definitively and clearly shown to exist (or not to exist), and is often poorly articulated or understood.
>
> (p. 304)

He also argued 'that, at some level, there are linkages between research and teaching, if not perhaps as intertwined and immediate as implied by the term research/teaching nexus' (p. 305). Some individual academics may be fortunate enough to have closely linked teaching and research responsibilities, but they are most likely a small minority of the total at any one time.

If, then, the research/teaching nexus is of concern, we need to do what we can to nourish it, even as governments and many other funders of higher education seek to (further) separate the two roles. A similar conclusion was also reached by Burke-Smalley et al (2017) in a systematic review of studies of what they call the research-teaching gap (rather than nexus) in the management discipline. They went so far as to argue that 'the ability to successfully integrate research and teaching is the essence of what it means to excel as a university professor' (p. 510). This might, then, be a role for academic development (discussed in the previous chapter).

The peer review process

The peer review process is endemic to higher education. It is increasingly used in course design, where students are asked or required to review drafts of each other's work (see Chapter 6), as well as in assessing the work of academics – most commonly of articles submitted to academic journals or grant bids submitted to funding bodies – which is the focus here. Three relevant meta-analyses have been identified, all involving some of the same researchers.

Bornmann, Mutz and Daniel (2010), a German/Swiss team, present a meta-analysis of studies of the journal peer review process, focusing on the inter-rater reliability of reviewers. They identify seventy reliability coefficients from forty-eight studies, examining the assessment of 19,443 manuscripts. They found that the inter-rater reliability was low: i.e. journal reviewers seldom agreed with each other. Meta-regression analyses found that neither discipline nor the method of blinding (i.e. anonymizing) manuscripts impacted on this result.

Bornmann, Mutz and Daniel (2007) have also examined gender differences in the grant review process, where bias against women applicants has long been argued. Their meta-analysis of twenty-one studies found

> evidence of robust gender differences in grant award procedures. Even though the estimates of the gender effect vary substantially from study to study, the model estimation shows that all in all, among grant applicants men have statistically significant greater odds of receiving grants than women by about 7%.
>
> (p. 226)

This meta-analysis was then re-examined by Marsh et al (2009: i.e. the original team was then joined by two other, UK-based, researchers), who used a multi-level rather than a traditional approach to meta-analysis. This time, they concluded that there was no significant difference in grant proposal evaluation linked to gender.

Areas of research in higher education research

A number of systematic reviews have focused on particular areas or aspects of research (as opposed to the generic reviews of higher education research discussed in Chapter 3). Five are identified and discussed here.

Kosmutzky and Krucken (2014) focused on international comparative higher education research published in leading international journals, combining a bibliometric approach with a quantitative content analysis. They identified 4,095 articles from the Web of Science over the period 1992–2012 for analysis and found, somewhat surprisingly, that international comparative research (see also Chapter 13) had not expanded relatively over the period. North America, Western Europe and the Asia Pacific region remained the areas most studied, while 'many blind spots exist in parts of the former Soviet Union and in sub-Saharan Africa' (p. 469). They concluded that

> [f]irst, higher education research is highly diverse due to its interdisciplinary and applied, or even mode-2, character of research … Second, international comparative research is genuinely more complex in its nature than nationally based research – it has multifaceted national angles, which make specifically complex research objects.
>
> (pp. 469–70)

Schmidt and Gunther (2016) examine the state of public sector accounting research in higher education, identifying 236 relevant articles published in eighty-three journals between 1980 and 2014. They found a 'highly fragmented body of research' (p. 235), dominated by authors from Anglo-American countries. They concluded that

> research so far seems to have been influenced by the special needs of the local institutional setting; for example, the large private HE [higher education] sector in the US raises the issue of financial vs. public accounting and reporting issues; reforms in accountability/governance of the HE sectors of the UK, Australia and New Zealand have resulted in analysis of their impacts; moderate changes in Nordic countries and Continental Europe with reforms just initiated are giving rise to an as yet underexploited research field.
>
> (p. 261)

Miragaia and Soares (2017) were concerned with sport management research in higher education and examine ninety-eight relevant articles identified over the period 1979–2014. They note the importance of particular journals in developing the field of study and make suggestions for its further development. Many of the same issues, therefore, are encountered in syntheses of very specific areas of higher education research as in more generic studies.

Piggott et al (2019), working in the same disciplinary area as Miragaia and Soares, consider whether interdisciplinary research is being conducted within sports science. Their systematic review identified thirty-six relevant studies: 'Twenty-five studies were categorised as interdisciplinary, with 11 categorised as multidisciplinary' (p. 267), and concluded that 'the field of sports science is beginning to undertake integrated research that combines multiple sub-disciplines' (p. 284). In this context, one might, of course, question the status of sports science as a discipline itself.

Shelley and Schuh (2001) examine the relationship between higher education journal quality, readability and selectivity, focusing on seventeen American higher education journals. Their meta-analysis used established readability indexes to analyse randomly selected portions of text from the beginning, middle and end of articles. They concluded that

> [t]he quality of writing and readability did not vary as a function of selectivity; journals that are more selective about the work they publish tend to feature more complex forms of writing; and general-interest journals are significantly more selective than those with a mandate to publish work in a specialized field.
>
> (p. 11)

Readability remains an issue in higher education research, as it does throughout the social sciences. It is particularly important for general-interest journals, which publish research on all aspects of higher education. If an author writing on a particular specialism seeks to attract a wider readership, therefore, they need to carefully explain (or remove) all specialist terms and present their analysis in an accessible form.

Conclusions

- The relationship between the research and teaching roles of higher education is complex and poorly articulated.
- The peer review process cannot be considered as wholly reliable.
- Different areas of higher education research are developing distinctive foci.
- Higher education researchers need to work on improving the readability of their publications.

Part three
Conclusion

Chapter 17
Conclusion

Introduction

The exploratory systematic review of syntheses of higher education research that has been presented in this book confirms the growing maturity of the field. Not only has a great deal of relevant research been carried out – albeit, on most occasions, on a relatively small scale – but the volume has been so great that other researchers have subjected it to systematic review, substantive literature review or meta-analysis in order to summarize and/or synthesize the findings. This has then provided the impetus for the research undertaken to produce this book.

We should not, however, fall into the trap of assuming that the reverse position also holds; namely, that the relative absence of systematic reviews, substantive literature reviews or meta-analyses indicates a relative lack of research on a given topic or issue. There may be a substantial volume of research – as, for example, in the case of system policy (see Chapter 13) – but the researchers involved have not felt the need, may have been unaware of the possibilities or may have not felt methodologically competent to carry out a synthesizing study.

For current and future researchers – as well as managers and policymakers wishing to make use of the fruits of higher education research – it makes sense to start any particular research project by examining existing research syntheses of their topics of interest. This should both guard against unnecessary wheel reinvention and help to show where further research could most usefully be directed. This book should greatly assist in this respect.

This chapter offers three further reflections on existing syntheses of higher education research. First, it provides a brief summary – distilled from the preceding chapters – of what we know, and by implication what we don't know, about higher education. Second, it highlights and discusses some of the methodological reservations that have been raised about research syntheses, particularly as applied to higher education research. Third, and finally, it sketches out some future priorities for higher education research.

What we know (and don't know)

The research syntheses examined in this book may be grouped into three main kinds. First, there are those which come to generally positive conclusions, confirming or supporting the usefulness of a particular strategy or approach: I will categorize these as 'what we know'. Second, there are those which suggest that we don't, or don't yet, really know enough about a particular topic to come to firm conclusions: these I will categorize as 'what we don't know'. Third, there are areas which have to date either been under-researched or under-synthesized: these are topics which might be prioritized for future research.

I will identify and discuss the first two of these categories in the remainder of this section and return to the third category in the final section of this chapter. Rather than focus on particular initiatives or examples, the discussion will be kept as generic as possible.

What we know

As has already been suggested, there is a great deal that we already know with some confidence from higher education research.

We know about the importance of developing self-regulated learning and critical thinking in students. We know of the key role that group learning plays alongside individual learning, and that this can be supported through peer instruction and assessment.

We know that formative assessment and feedback can greatly support student development and achievement. This requires, however, careful pre-planning and delivery, not just within individual courses but across complete programmes, if it is to be most effective.

We know that technology can help the learning process, both at the simple level (as in the use of audience response systems in lectures) and as the mainstay for instruction, as in distance and e-learning. We also know that this can work better when it is balanced with face-to-face contact, as in blended learning, and when individual activity is supported by group work.

In general, we know that most instructional or curricular innovations can produce positive results, at least in the short term (there is little research that considers anything beyond the short term). This knowledge has to be balanced, however, by an assessment of the costs of such innovations, mostly in terms of staff and student time, but also – as where technology is involved – in terms of equipment, materials and development costs.

What we don't know

There is also, though, a good deal that we do not know about higher education. Sometimes, this is despite a substantial amount of research having been carried out, but with inconclusive results: this is the focus of the present subsection. Alternatively, our not knowing may be due to a relative paucity of research on the topic in question: that is the focus of the final section of this chapter.

Thus, we do not know whether there is a clear relationship between the research and teaching functions of higher education, or what form(s) of quality assurance and/or management would best suit higher education. Neither do we fully appreciate the relationship between higher education and work, though this is partly because this is mediated through the varied disciplines and professions, a topic area that needs more research.

We also do not know how to effectively get students to evaluate the teaching and other provision that they receive, as current practices are not reliable. Nor do we know whether the burgeoning field of learning analytics will provide useful information, both to help students to achieve more and to help institutions to improve their engagement.

While we know that approaches to learning and teaching vary, between students, teachers and courses, we do not know how to manipulate these practices effectively. Nor do we know how best to incorporate the variety of generic or key skills into higher education which stakeholders would like to see developed in students.

Interestingly, while the list of what we know focused very much on what has been termed pedagogical research – dealing with issues of course design and teaching and learning – the list of what we don't know has been more general, covering all areas of higher education research. This is very likely due to the relative popularity of research on different themes and topics (see Table 1 in Chapter 3).

Methodological reservations

Reflecting on the experience of writing this book, and re-reading it before sending off the final draft to the publishers, I was struck by three common refrains. Two of these were frequently identified by the authors of the research syntheses examined: that the quality of the research they were synthesizing was often questionable, and that more research was needed. The third refrain was my own, that the results of many of the syntheses reported were unsurprising.

The first of these points is addressed further in the present section, while the second (as well as being the siren call of researchers in all disciplines across the ages) underlies other sections of this chapter. The third point, about many results being unsurprising, is not meant as a criticism. Indeed, it could be taken as a strength, in that many of the findings of higher education research confirm what you might expect. Perhaps, however, what is surprising deserves more emphasis, which would include many of the topics on which there has been substantial research, but leading to inconclusive results.

The quality of the underlying research on which the syntheses examined have been based has been criticized for a variety of reasons, as has the quality of some of the research syntheses themselves.

To take the criticisms made of the underlying research on which the syntheses are based first, the most common has probably been to do with the design of the research. Most studies, because of the nature of higher education, did not take an experimental approach. In most of the qualitative studies that contributed to the systematic reviews, and even in some of the quantitative studies that underlay the meta-analyses, there was a lack of a comparative or control group.

Compounding these issues was the tendency, given that the great majority of higher education research is small scale in nature, to focus on the short term only. Thus, the longer-term impact of most interventions was largely ignored. Added to this was a lack of engagement with theory, to explain and contextualize what was being reported, which might have helped overcome the short-termism.

A further area of criticism of higher education research as a whole is its underlying positivity. As remarked earlier in this book, it is scarcely in the interests of higher education researchers – or of their employing institutions – to publish accounts of their interventions that didn't work. Hence, the vast majority of the small-scale higher education research that makes it through to publication reports on successful initiatives. This positivity then necessarily feeds into the syntheses of such research studies.

Criticisms of the quality of the research syntheses themselves have most often focused on issues of definition and of selection and inclusion of studies. In the days before online search engines, such problems were more understandable, but there is little excuse currently if relevant studies have been omitted. It is also relatively easy for other researchers, perhaps using or following up on a particular research synthesis, to check up on this.

A related criticism concerns when a research synthesis is based on a small number of studies. While one would not wish to set an arbitrary limit on the minimum number of studies needed, research syntheses that are based on a handful of studies do suggest that perhaps the research field should be allowed to mature a bit more before it is synthesized.

Homogeneity is also quite frequently brought up as a concern. Where the studies upon which a research synthesis is based are more heterogeneous – in terms of their foci, design or reportage, for example – it makes it that much more difficult to interpret the results.

Syntheses of higher education research, while offering us much, do, therefore, need to be carefully evaluated and treated with caution.

Future priorities

Future priorities for research synthesis inevitably lag behind those for research.

It is easy to understand and appreciate the centrality of the pedagogical research themes to higher education research overall. These have been the focus of the majority of the chapters in the book (Chapters 4 to 11), those dealing with teaching and learning, course design and the student experience. Together, as Table 1 in Chapter 3 showed, these accounted for the great majority, 74 per cent, of the research syntheses identified and discussed in this book.

Without discounting the need for more research on certain aspects of these themes, there is, relatively speaking, a need for more research, and in particular more systematic research, on the other main themes identified. This is most notably the case for system policy – a topic on which a substantial amount of research has been carried out, but where it remains largely unsystematized – and for knowledge and research.

Thus, one priority for future research should be on the ways in which the disciplinary (and sub-disciplinary) structure of higher education institutions impacts upon all of their activities. This would enable a greater understanding of what works, and how well it works, in different departments or schools. The unresolved issues around interdisciplinarity also require more research and synthesis.

Arguably, the experience of being an academic merits as much research attention relatively as the student experience currently receives. This would include, for example, its gendered and raced nature; how teaching, research and other roles are accommodated or combined; and the tensions between management and delivery. The increasing numbers of professional and non-academic staff working in higher education also need more research.

Finally, higher education institutions themselves, in all their variety, deserve more critical and external research attention. This could address, for example, how (and how well) they are responding to the increasing demands placed upon them to tackle globalization, sustainability and the third mission.

In some of these areas, the research needed for synthesis probably already exists, while in others synthesis will need to wait on further research.

References

Abrami, P, Bernard, R, Borokhovski, E, Waddington, D, Wade, A, and Persson, T (2015) Strategies for Teaching Students to Think Critically: A Meta-Analysis. *Review of Educational Research*, 85, 2, pp. 275–314.

Abrami, P, Bernard, R, Borokhovski, E, Wade, A, Surkes, M, Tamim, R, and Zhang, D (2008) Instructional Interventions Affecting Critical Thinking Skills and Dispositions: A Stage 1 Meta-Analysis. *Review of Educational Research*, 78, 4, pp. 1102–34.

Abrami, P, Cohen, P, and d'Apollonia, S (1988) Implementation Problems in Meta-Analysis. *Review of Educational Research*, 58, 2, pp. 151–79.

Abrami, P, Leventhal, L, and Perry, R (1982) Educational Seduction. *Review of Educational Research*, 52, 3, pp. 446–64.

Adesope, O, and Nesbit, J (2012) Verbal Redundancy in Multimedia Learning Environments: A Meta-Analysis. *Journal of Educational Psychology*, 104, 1, pp. 250–63.

Adler, C, and Lalonde, C (2019) Identity, Agency and Institutional Work in Higher Education: A Qualitative Meta-Synthesis. *Qualitative Research in Organizations and Management*, DOI: 10.1108/QROM-11-2018-1696.

Adu-Yeboah, C (2015) Mature Women Students' Experiences of Social and Academic Support in Higher Education: A Systematic Review. *Journal of Education and Training*, 2, 2, pp. 145–62.

Agrusti, F, Bonavolontà, G, and Mezzini, M (2019) University Dropout Prediction through Educational Data Mining Techniques: A Systematic Review. *Journal of e-Learning and Knowledge Society*, 15, 3, pp. 161–82.

Ahern, A, Dominguez, C, McNally, C, O'Sullivan, J, and Pedrosa, D (2019) A Literature Review of Critical Thinking in Engineering Education. *Studies in Higher Education*, 44, 5, pp. 816–28.

Albanese, M, and Mitchell, S (1993) Problem-Based Learning: A Review of Literature on Its Outcomes and Implementation Issues. *Academic Medicine*, 68, 1, pp. 52–81.

Alderman, L, Towers, S, and Bannah, S (2012) Student Feedback Systems in Higher Education: A Focused Literature Review and Environmental Scan. *Quality in Higher Education*, 18, 3, pp. 261–80.

Aldowah, H, Al-Samarraiea, H, and Fauzy, W (2019) Educational Data Mining and Learning Analytics for 21st Century Higher Education: A Review and Synthesis. *Telematics and Informatics*, 37, pp. 13–49.

Aljohani, O (2016) A Review of the Contemporary International Literature on Student Retention in Higher Education. *International Journal of Education and Literacy Studies*, 4, 1, pp. 40–52.

Allen, M, Bourhis, N, and Mabry, E (2002) Comparing Student Satisfaction with Distance Education to Traditional Classrooms in Higher Education: A Meta-Analysis. *American Journal of Distance Education*, 16, 2, pp. 83–97.

Allen, M, Mabry, E, Mattrey, M, Bourhis, J, Titsworth, S, and Burrell, N (2004) Evaluating the Effectiveness of Distance Learning: A Comparison Using Meta-Analysis. *Journal of Communication*, 3, September, pp. 402–20.

Allen, P (1988) Faculty Development in Higher Education: A Literature Review, https://digitalcommons.georgefox.edu/soe_faculty/65.

Alrasheedi, M, Capretz, L, and Raza, A (2015) A Systematic Review of the Critical Factors for Success of Mobile Learning in Higher Education (University Students' Perspective). *Journal of Educational Computing Research*, 52, 2, pp. 257–76.

Amundsen, C, and Wilson, M (2012) Are We Asking the Right Questions? A Conceptual Review of the Educational Development Literature in Higher Education. *Review of Educational Research*, 82, 1, pp. 90–126.

Amundsen, C, Abrami, P, McAlpine, L, Weston, C, Krbavac, M, Mundy, A, and Wilson, M (2005) The What and Why of Faculty Development in Higher Education: An In-Depth Review of the Literature. Paper given at Annual Conference of the American Educational Research Association, Montreal.

Anderson, A, Stephenson, J, Carter, M, and Carlon, S (2019) A Systematic Literature Review of Empirical Research on Postsecondary Students with Autism Spectrum Disorder. *Journal of Autism and Developmental Disorders*, 49, pp. 1531–58.

Andrade, H (2019) A Critical Review of Research on Student Self-Assessment. *Frontiers in Education*, 4, p. 87, DOI: 10.3389/feduc.2019.00087.

Arksey, H, and O'Malley, L (2005) Scoping Studies: Towards a Methodological Framework. *International Journal of Social Research Methodology*, 8, 1, pp. 19–32.

Armstrong, R, Hall, B, Doyle, J, and Waters, E (2011) Cochrane Update: 'Scoping the Scope' of a Cochrane Review. *Journal of Public Health*, 33, 1, pp. 147–50.

Arnold, D, and Sangra, A (2018) Dawn or Dusk of the 5th Age of Research in Educational Technology: A Literature Review on (e-)Leadership for Technology-Enhanced Learning in Higher Education (2013–2017). *International Journal of Educational Technology in Higher Education*, 15, 24, p. 29.

Artess, J, Hooley, T, and Mellors-Bourne, R (2017) *Employability: A Review of the Literature 2012 to 2016*. York, Higher Education Academy.

Ashford, R, Brown, A, Eisenhart, E, Thompson-Heller, A, and Curtis, B (2018) What We Know about Students in Recovery: Meta-Synthesis of Collegiate Recovery Programs, 2000–2017. *Addiction Research and Theory*, 26, 5, pp. 405–13.

Asikainen, H, and Gijbels, D (2017) Do Students Develop towards More Deep Approaches to Learning during Studies? A Systematic Review on the Development of Students' Deep and Surface Approaches to Learning in Higher Education. *Educational Psychology Review*, 29, pp. 205–34.

Astin, A (1977) *Four Critical Years: Effects of College on Beliefs, Attitudes and Knowledge*. San Francisco, Jossey-Bass.

Avella, J, Kebritchi, M, Nunn, S, and Kanai, T (2016) Learning Analytics Methods, Benefits and Challenges in Higher Education: A Systematic Literature Review. *Online Learning*, 20, 2, pp. 13–29.

References

Azevedo, R, and Bernard, R (1995) A Meta-Analysis of the Effects of Feedback in Computer-Based Instruction. *Journal of Educational Computing Research*, 13, 2, pp. 111–27.

Bajada, C, Kandlbinder, P, and Trayler, R (2019) A General Framework for Cultivating Innovations in Higher Education Curriculum. *Higher Education Research and Development*, 38, 3, pp. 465–78.

Baker, S, Bangeni, B, Burke, R, and Hunma, A (2019) The Invisibility of Academic Reading as Social Practice and Its Implications for Equity in Higher Education: A Scoping Study. *Higher Education Research and Development*, 38, 1, pp. 142–56.

Balta, N, Michinov, N, Balyimez, S, and Ayaz, M (2017) A Meta-Analysis of the Effect of Peer Instruction on Learning Gain: Identification of Informational and Cultural Moderators. *International Journal of Educational Research*, 86, pp. 66–77.

Balwant, P (2016) Transformational Instructor-Leadership in Higher Education Teaching: A Meta-Analytic Review and Research Agenda. *Journal of Leadership Studies*, 9, 4, pp. 20–42.

Bangert-Drowns, R, Kulik, J, and Kulik, C-L (1991) Effects of Frequent Classroom Testing. *Journal of Educational Research*, 85, 2, pp. 89–99.

Bangert-Drowns, R, Kulik, C-L, Kulik, J, and Morgan, M (1991) The Instructional Effect of Feedback in Test-Like Events. *Review of Educational Research*, 61, 2, pp. 213–38.

Barbarà-i-Molinero, A, Cascón-Pereira, R, and Hernández-Lara, A (2017) Professional Identity Development in Higher Education: Influencing Factors. *International Journal of Educational Management*, 31, 2, pp. 189–203.

Barry, A, Whiteman, S, and Wadsworth, S (2014) Student Service Members/Veterans in Higher Education: A Systematic Review. *Journal of Student Affairs Research and Practice*, 51, 1, pp. 30–42.

Barteit, S, Guzek, D, Jahn, A, Barnighausen, D, Jorge, M, and Neuhann, F (2020) Evaluation of E-Learning for Medical Education in Low and Middle-Income Countries: A Systematic Review. *Computers and Education*, 145, 103726, 18pp.

Basak, S, Wotto, M, and Belanger, P (2016) A Framework on the Critical Success Factors of E-Learning Implementation in Higher Education: A Review of the Literature. *International Journal of Social, Behavioral, Educational, Economic, Business and Industrial Engineering*, 10, 7, pp. 2409–14.

Bearman, M, Smith, C, Carbone, A, Slade, S, Baik, C, Hughes-Warrington, M, and Neumann, D (2012) Systematic Review Methodology in Higher Education. *Higher Education Research and Development*, 31, 5, pp. 625–40.

Becket, N, and Brookes, M (2008) Quality Management Practice in Higher Education: What Quality Are We Actually Enhancing? *Journal of Hospitality, Leisure, Sport and Tourism Education*, 7, 1, pp. 40–54.

Behar-Horenstein, L, and Niu, L (2011) Teaching Critical Thinking Skills in Higher Education: A Review of the Literature. *Journal of College Teaching and Learning*, 8, 2, pp. 25–42.

Belland, B, Walker, A, Kim, N, and Lefler, M (2017) Synthesizing Results from Empirical Research on Computer-Based Scaffolding in STEM Education: A Meta-Analysis. *Review of Educational Research*, 87, 2, pp. 309–44.

Bennion, A, Scesa, A, and Williams, R (2011) The Benefits of Part-Time Undergraduate Study and UK Higher Education Policy: A Literature Review. *Higher Education Quarterly*, 65, 2, pp. 145–63.

Benton, S, and Cashin, W (2012) *Student Ratings of Teaching: A Summary of Research and Literature*. Manhattan, KS, The Idea Center.

Beretvas, N (2010) Meta-Analysis. In Hancock, G, and Mueller, R (eds) *The Reviewer's Guide to Quantitative Methods in the Social Sciences*. New York, Routledge, pp. 255–63.

Bernard, R, Borokhovski, E, Schmid, R, Tamim, R, and Abrami, P (2014) A Meta-Analysis of Blended Learning and Technology Use in Higher Education: From the General to the Applied. *Journal of Computing in Higher Education*, 26, pp. 87–122.

Bernard, R, Abrami, P, Borokhovski, E, Wade, A, Tamim, R, Surkes, M, and Bethel, E (2009) A Meta-Analysis of Three Types of Interaction Treatments in Distance Education. *Review of Educational Research*, 79, 3, pp. 1243–89.

Bernard, R, Abrami, P, Lou, Y, Borokhovski, E, Wade, A, Wozney, L, Wallet, P, Fiset, M, and Huang, B (2004) How Does Distance Education Compare with Classroom Instruction? A Meta-Analysis of the Empirical Literature. *Review of Educational Research*, 74, 3, pp. 379–439.

Bishop, J, and Verleger, M (2013) The Flipped Classroom: A Survey of the Research. American Society for Engineering Education Annual Conference and Exposition.

Bjorklund, P (2018) Undocumented Students in Higher Education: A Review of the Literature, 2001 to 2016. *Review of Educational Research*, 88, 5, pp. 631–70.

Black, P, and Wiliam, D (1998) Assessment and Classroom Learning. *Assessment in Education: Principles, Policy and Practice*, 5, 1, pp. 7–74.

Blair, A (2015) Similar or Different? A Comparative Analysis of Higher Education Research in Political Science and International Relations between the United States of America and the United Kingdom. *Journal of Political Science Education*, 11, 2, pp. 174–89.

Blimling, G (1989) A Meta-Analysis of the Influence of College Residence Halls on Academic Performance. *Journal of College Student Development*, 40, 5, pp. 551–61.

Bodily, R, and Verbert, K (2017) Review of Research on Student-Facing Learning Analytics Dashboards and Educational Recommender Systems. *IEEE Transactions on Learning Technologies*, 10, 4, pp. 405–18.

Bogen, K, Leach, N, Lopez, R, and Orchowski, L (2019) Supporting Students in Responding to Disclosure of Sexual Violence: A Systematic Review of Online University Resources. *Journal of Sexual Aggression*, 25, 1, pp. 31–48.

Bolden, R, and Petrov, G (2008) *Employer Engagement with Higher Education: A Literature Review*. Exeter, University of Exeter.

Bond, M, Buntins, K, Bedenlier, S, Zawacki-Richter, O, and Kerres, M (2020) Mapping Research in Student Engagement and Educational Technology in Higher Education: A Systematic Evidence Map. *International Journal of Educational Technology in Higher Education*, 17, 2, p. 30.

Borenstein, M, Hedges, L, Higgins, J, and Rothstein, H (2009) *Introduction to Meta-Analysis*. Chichester, Wiley.

Bornmann, L, Mutz, R, and Daniel, H-D (2007) Gender Differences in Grant Peer Review: A Meta-Analysis. *Journal of Informetrics*, 1, 3, pp. 226–38.

Bornmann, L, Mutz, R, and Daniel, H-D (2010) A Reliability-Generalization Study of Journal Peer Reviews: A Multilevel Meta-Analysis of Inter-Rater Reliability and Its Determinants. *PLoS ONE*, 5, 12, p. e14331.

Boshier, R, and Huang, Y (2008) In the House of Scholarship of Teaching and Learning (SoTL), Teaching Lives Upstairs and Learning in the Basement. *Teaching in Higher Education*, 13, 6, pp. 645–56.

Boud, D, and Falchikov, N (1989) Quantitative Studies of Student Self-Assessment in Higher Education: A Critical Analysis of Findings. *Higher Education*, 18, pp. 529–49.

Bourhis, J, and Allen, M (1992) Meta-Analysis of the Relationship between Communication Apprehension and Cognitive Performance. *Communication Education*, 41, pp. 68–76.

Bowen, H (1977) *Investment in Learning: The Individual and Social Value of American Higher Education*. San Francisco, CA, Jossey-Bass.

Bowman, N (2010) College Diversity Experiences and Cognitive Development: A Meta-Analysis. *Review of Educational Research*, 80, 1, pp. 4–33.

Bowman, N (2011) Promoting Participation in a Diverse Democracy: A Meta-Analysis of College Diversity Experiences and Civic Engagement. *Review of Educational Research*, 81, 1, pp. 29–68.

Bowman, N (2012) Effect Sizes and Statistical Methods for Meta-Analyses in Higher Education. *Research in Higher Education*, 53, pp. 375–82.

Boyer, E (1990) *Scholarship Reconsidered: Priorities of the Professoriate*. Princeton, NJ: Carnegie Foundation for the Advancement of Teaching.

Bradbury-Jones, C, Breckenridge, J, Clark, M, Herber, O, Jones, C, and Taylor, J (2019a) Advancing the Science of Literature Reviewing in Social Research: The Focused Mapping Review and Synthesis. *International Journal of Social Research Methodology*, 22, 5, pp. 451–62.

Bradbury-Jones, C, Molloy, E, Clark, M, and Ward, N (2019b) Gender, Sexual Diversity and Professional Practice Learning: Findings from a Systematic Search and Review. *Studies in Higher Education*, DOI: 10.1080/03075079.2018.1564264.

Brady, M, Devitt, A, and Kiersey, R (2019) Academic Staff Perspectives on Technology for Assessment in Higher Education: A Systematic Literature Review. *British Journal of Educational Technology*, DOI: 10.1111/bjet.12742.

Braithwaite, R, and Corr, P (2016) Hans Eysenck, Education and the Experimental Approach: A Meta-Analysis of Academic Capabilities in University Students. *Personality and Individual Differences*, 103, pp. 163–71.

Braxton, J (1996) Contrasting Perspectives on the Relationship between Teaching and Research. *New Directions in Institutional Research*, 90, pp. 5–14.

Brennan, J, Durazzi, N, and Tanguy, S (2013) *Things We Know and Don't Know about the Wider Benefits of Higher Education: A Review of the Recent Literature*. BIS Research Paper, URN BIS/13/1244. London, UK, Department for Business, Innovation and Skills.

Bretz, R (1989) College Grade Point Average as a Predictor of Adult Success: A Meta-Analytic Review and Some Additional Evidence. *Public Personnel Management*, 18, 1, pp. 11–22.

Brewer, C, and Movahedazarhouligh, S (2018) Successful Stories and Conflicts: A Literature Review on the Effectiveness of Flipped Learning in Higher Education. *Journal of Computer Assisted Learning*, 34, pp. 409–16.

Broadbent, J, and Poon, W (2015) Self-Regulated Learning Strategies and Academic Achievement in Online Higher Education Learning Environments: A Systematic Review. *Internet and Higher Education*, 27, pp. 1–13.

Brown, M (2016) Blended Instructional Practice: A Review of the Empirical Literature on Instructors' Adoption and Use of Online Tools in Face-to-Face Teaching. *Internet and Higher Education*, 31, p. 1010.

Bruguera, C, Guitert, M, and Romeu, T (2019) Social Media and Professional Development: A Systematic Review. *Research in Learning Technology*, 27, p. 18.

Bruijn-Smolders, M de, Timmers, C, Gawke, J, Schoonman, W, and Born, M (2016) Effective Self-regulatory Processes in Higher Education: Research Findings and Future Directions. A Systematic Review. *Studies in Higher Education*, 41, 1, pp. 139–58.

Bryman, A (2007) Effective Leadership in Higher Education: A Literature Review. *Studies in Higher Education*, 32, 6, pp. 693–710.

Budd, J (1990) Higher Education Literature: Characteristics of Citation Patterns. *Journal of Higher Education*, 61, 1, pp. 84–97.

Budd, J, and Magnusson, L (2010) Higher Education Literature Revisited: Citation Patterns Examined. *Research in Higher Education*, 51, pp. 294–304.

Bunn, F, Trivedi, D, Alderson, P, Hamilton, L, Martin, A, Pinkney, E, and Iliffe, S (2015) The Impact of Cochrane Reviews: A Mixed-Methods Evaluation of Outputs from Cochrane Review Groups Supported by the National Institute for Health Research. *Health Technology Assessment*, 19, 28, p. 128.

Burke-Smalley, L, Rau, B, Neely, A, and Evans, W (2017) Factors Perpetuating the Research-Teaching Gap in Management: A Review and Propositions. *International Journal of Management Education*, 15, pp. 501–12.

Burley, H (1994a) *Persistence: A Meta-Analysis of College Developmental Studies Programs*. Paper presented at the Annual Forum of the Association for Institutional Research.

Burley, H (1994b) *A Meta-Analysis of the Effects of Developmental Studies Programs on College Student Achievement, Attitude and Persistence*. Paper presented at the annual meeting of the American Educational Research Association.

Cahill, M, Pettigrew, J, Robinson, K, and Galvin, R (2019) The Transition to Retirement Experiences of Academics in Higher Education: A Meta-Ethnography. *The Gerontologist*, 59, 3, pp. e177–e195.

Caldwell, J (2007) Clickers in the Large Classroom: Current Research and Best-Practice Tips. *CBE-Life Sciences Education*, 6, pp. 9–20.

Calma, A, and Davies, M (2015) *Studies in Higher Education* 1976–2013: A Retrospective Using Citation Network Analysis. *Studies in Higher Education*, 40, 1, pp. 4–21.

Calma, A, and Davies, M (2017) Geographies of Influence: A Citation Network Analysis of Higher Education 1972–2014. *Higher Education*, 110, pp. 1579–99.

Calonge, D, and Shah, M (2016) MOOCs, Graduate Skills Gaps and Employability: A Qualitative Systematic Review of the Literature. *International Review of Research in Open and Distributed Learning*, 17, 5, pp. 67–90.

Cama, M, Jorge, M, and Pena, F (2016) Gender Differences between Faculty Members in Higher Education: A Literature Review of Selected Higher Education Journals. *Educational Research Review*, 18, pp. 58–69.

Caniglia, G, Luederitz, C, Gross, M, Muhr, M, John, B, Keeler, L, von Wehrden, H, Laubichler, M, Wiek, A, and Lang, D (2017) Transnational Collaboration for Sustainability in Higher Education: Lessons from a Systematic Review. *Journal of Cleaner Production*, 168, pp. 764–79.

Carenys, J, and Moya, S (2016) Digital Game-Based Learning in Accounting and Business Education. *Accounting Education*, 25, 6, pp. 598–651.

Carvalho, J, Pereira, R, and Rocha, A (2019) A Systematic Literature Review on Maturity Models for Information Systems in Higher Education Institutions. *Innovations in Education and Teaching International*, DOI: 10.1080/14703297.2019.1648219.

Cashin, W (1995) *Student Ratings of Teaching: The Research Revisited*. IDEA Paper No. 32. Kansas State University, KS, Center for Faculty Evaluation and Development in Higher Education.

Castillo-Manzano, J, Castro-Nuno, M, Lopez-Valpuesta, L, Sanz-Diaz, M, and Yniguez, R (2016) Measuring the Effect of ARS on Academic Performance: A Global Meta-Analysis. *Computers and Education*, 96, pp. 109–21.

Castro, M, and Tumibay, G (2019) A Literature Review: Efficacy of Online Learning Courses for Higher Education Institution Using Meta-Analysis. *Education and Information Technologies*, https://doi.org/10.1007/s10639-019-10027-z.

Ceulemans, K, Molderez, I, and Liederkerke, L van (2015) Sustainability Reporting in Higher Education: A Comprehensive Review of the Literature and Paths for Further Research. *Journal of Cleaner Production*, 106, pp. 127–43.

Chan, K-Y, Fong, T-Y, Luk, Y-Y, and Ho, R (2017) A Review of Literature on Challenges in the Development and Implementation of Generic Competencies in Higher Education Curriculum. *International Journal of Educational Development*, 57, pp. 1–10.

Chang, Y-H (2016) Two Decades of Research in L2 Peer Review. *Journal of Writing Research*, 8, 1, pp. 81–117.

Chan, C-Y, Chan, H-Y, Chow, H-C, Choy, S-N, Ng, K-Y, Wong, K-Y, and Yu, P-K (2019) Academic Advising in Undergraduate Education: A Systematic Review. *Nurse Education Today*, 75, pp. 58–74.

Cheawjindakarn, B, Suwannatthachote, P, and Theeraroungchaisri, A (2012) Critical Success Factors for Online Distance Learning in Higher Education. *Creative Education*, 21, 3, Supplement, pp. 61–6.

Chen, T (2016) Technology-Supported Peer Feedback in ESL/EFL Writing Classes: A Research Synthesis. *Computer Assisted Language Learning*, 29, 2, pp. 365–97.

Chen, S-Y, and Hu, L-F (2012) Higher Education Research as a Field in China: Its Formation and Current Landscape. *Higher Education Research and Development*, 31, 5, pp. 655–66.

Cherney, M, Fetherston, M, and Johnsen, L (2018) Online Course Student Collaboration Literature: A Review and Critique. *Small Group Research*, 49, 1, pp. 98–128.

Chernikova, O, Heitzmann, N, Fink, M, Timothy, V, Seidel, T, and Fischer, F (2019) Facilitating Diagnostic Competences in Higher Education: A Meta-Analysis in Medical and Teacher Education. *Educational Psychology Review*, https://doi.org/10.1007/s10648-019-09492-2.

Chun, M (2002) Looking Where the Light Is Better: A Review of the Literature on Assessing Higher Education Quality. *peerReview*, winter/spring, pp. 16–25.

Clark, D, Tanner-Smith, E, and Killingsworth, S (2016) Digital Games, Design and Learning: A Systematic Review and Meta-Analysis. *Review of Educational Research*, 86, 1, pp. 79–122.

Clayson, D (2009) Student Evaluations of Teaching: Are They Related to What Students Learn? A Meta-Analysis and Review of the Literature. *Journal of Marketing Education*, 31, 1, pp. 16–30.

Cockett, A, and Jackson, C (2018) The Use of Assessment Rubrics to Enhance Feedback in Higher Education: An Integrative Literature Review. *Nurse Education Today*, 69, pp. 8–13.

Coffield, F, Moseley, D, Hall, E, and Ecclestone, K (2004) *Learning Styles and Pedagogy in Post-16 Learning: A Systematic and Critical Review*. London, Learning and Skills Research Centre.

Cohen, P (1980) Effectiveness of Student Rating Feedback for Improving College Instruction: A Meta-Analysis of Findings. *Research in Higher Education*, 13, 4, pp. 321–41.

Cohen, P (1981) Student Ratings of Instruction and Student Achievements: A Meta-Analysis of Multi-Section Validity Studies. *Review of Educational Research*, 51, 3, pp. 281–309.

Cohen, P (1984) College Grades and Adult Achievement: A Research Synthesis. *Research in Higher Education*, 20, 3, pp. 281–93.

Cohen, P, Ebeling, B, and Kulik, J (1981) A Meta-Analysis of Outcome Studies of Visual-Based Instruction. *Educational Communication and Technology Journal*, 29, 1, pp. 26–36.

Colicchia, C, Creazza, A, and Strozzi, F (2017) Citation Network Analysis for Supporting Continuous Improvement in Higher Education. *Studies in Higher Education*, DOI: 10.1080/03075079.2016.1276550.

Conley, C, Durlak, J, and Kirsch, A (2015) A Meta-Analysis of University Mental Health Prevention Programs for Higher Education Students. *Prevention Science*, 16, pp. 487–507.

Conley, C, Shapiro, J, Kirsch, A, and Durlak, J (2017) A Meta-Analysis of Indicated Mental Health Prevention Programs for At-Risk Higher Education Students. *Journal of Counseling Psychology*, 64, 2, pp. 121–40.

Conole, G, and Alevizou, P (2010) *A Literature Review of the Use of Web 2.0 Tools in Higher Education*. Milton Keynes, the Open University.

Cooley, S, Burns, V, and Cumming, J (2015) The Role of Outdoor Adventure Education in Facilitating Groupwork in Higher Education. *Higher Education*, 69, pp. 567–82.

Cooper, H (2010) *Research Synthesis and Meta-Analysis: A Step-by-Step Approach*. Thousand Oaks, CA, Sage, fourth edition.

Corby, D, Cousins, W, and Slevin, E (2012) Inclusion of Adults with Intellectual Disabilities in Post-Secondary and Higher Education: A Review of the Literature. In P Jones, J Storan and J Braham (eds) *Lifelong Learning Community Development*. Stevenage, UK, Berfort Information Press, pp. 69–86.

Corneille, M, Lee, A, Allen, S, Cannady, J, and Guess, A (2019) Barriers to the Advancement of Women of Color Faculty in STEM: The Need for Promoting Equity Using an Intersectional Framework. *Equality, Diversity and Inclusion*, 38, 3, pp. 328–48.

Cornelius-White, J (2007) Learner-Centered Teacher-Student Relationships Are Effective: A Meta-Analysis. *Review of Educational Research*, 77, 1, pp. 113–43.

Costin, F, Greenough, W, and Menges, R (1971) Student Ratings of College Teaching: Reliability, Validity and Usefulness. *Review of Educational Research*, 14, 5, pp. 511–35.

Crede, M, and Kuncel, N (2008) Study Habits, Skills and Attitudes: The Third Pillar Supporting Collegiate Academic Performance. *Perspectives on Psychological Science*, 3, 6, pp. 425–53.

Crede, M, Roch, S, and Kieszczynka, U (2010) Class Attendance in College: A Meta-Analytic Review of the Relationship of Class Attendance with Grades and Student Characteristics. *Review of Educational Research*, 80, 2, pp. 272–95.

Crompton, H, and Burke, D (2018) The Use of Mobile Learning in Higher Education: A Systematic Review. *Computers and Education*, 123, pp. 53–64.

Crooks, T (1988) The Impact of Classroom Evaluation Practices on Students. *Review of Educational Research*, 58, 4, pp. 438–81.

Cruickshank, M (2003) Total Quality Management in the Higher Education Sector: A Literature Review from an International and Australian Perspective. *Total Quality Management and Business Excellence*, 14, 10, pp. 1159–67.

Cudney, E, Venuthurumilli, S, Materla, T, and Antony, J (2018) Systematic Reviews of Lean and Six Sigma Approaches in Higher Education. *Total Quality Management and Business Excellence*, DOI: 10.1080/14783363.2017.1422977.

Dawson, P, and Dawson, S (2016) Sharing Successes and Hiding Failures: 'Reporting Bias' in Learning and Teaching Research. *Studies in Higher Education*, DOI: 10.1080/03075079.2016.1258052.

Dawson, P, Meer, J van der, Skalicky, J, and Cowley, K (2014) On the Effectiveness of Supplemental Instruction: A Systematic Review of Supplemental Instruction and Peer-Assisted Study Sessions Literature between 2001 and 2010. *Review of Educational Research*, 84, 4, pp. 609–39.

Dearnley, C, Rhodes, C, Roberts, P, Williams, P, and Prenton, S (2018) Team Based Learning in Nursing and Midwifery Higher Education: A Systematic Review of the Evidence for Change. *Nurse Education Today*, 60, pp. 75–83.

Denson, N (2009) Do Curricular and Cocurricular Diversity Activists Influence Racial Bias? A Meta-Analysis. *Review of Educational Research*, 79, 2, pp. 805–38.

Denson, N, and Seltzer, M (2011) Meta-Analysis in Higher Education: An Illustrative Example Using Hierarchical Linear Modeling. *Research in Higher Education*, 52, pp. 215–44.

DePape, A-M, Barnes, M, and Petryschuk, J (2019) Students' Experiences in Higher Education with Virtual and Augmented Reality: A Qualitative Systematic Review. *Innovative Practice in Higher Education*, 3, 3, pp. 22–57.

Diamond, A, Roberts, J, Vorley, T, Burkin, G, Evans, J, Sheen, J, and Nathwani, T (2014) *UK Review of the Provision of Information about Higher Education: Advisory Study and Literature Review*. Leicester, CFE Research.

Diaz, P (1992) Effects of Transfer on Academic Performance of Community College Students at the Four-Year Institution. *Community/Junior College Quarterly*, 16, pp. 279–91.

Dobson, I (2009) The Journal of Higher Education Policy and Management: An Output Analysis. *Journal of Higher Education Policy and Management*, 31, 1, pp. 3–15.

Dochy, F, Segers, M, and Buehl, M (1999) The Relation between Assessment Practices and Outcomes of Studies: The Case of Research on Prior Knowledge. *Review of Educational Research*, 69, 2, pp. 145–86.

Dochy, F, Segers, M, Van den Bossche, P, and Gijbels, D (2003) Effects of Problem-Based Learning: A Meta-Analysis. *Learning and Instruction*, 13, pp. 533–68.

Dodds, A (2008) How Does Globalisation Interact with Higher Education? The Continuing Lack of Consensus. *Comparative Education*, 44, 4, pp. 505–17.

Donaldson, J, and Townsend, B (2007) Higher Education Journals' Discourse about Adult Undergraduate Students. *Journal of Higher Education*, 78, 1, pp. 27–50.

Dopson, S, Ferlie, E, McGivern, G, Fischer, M, Mitra, M, Ledger, J, and Behrens, S (2018) Leadership Development in Higher Education: A Literature Review and Implications for Programme Redesign. *Higher Education Quarterly*, DOI: 10.1111/hequ.12194.

Dunst, C, Hamby, D, Howse, R, Wilkie, H, and Hannas, K (2019) Metasynthesis of Preservice Professional Preparation and Teacher Education Research Studies. *Education Sciences*, 9, 50, DOI: 10.3390/educsci9010050.

Duran, A (2018) Queer and of Color: A Systematic Literature Review on Queer Students of Color in Higher Education Scholarship. *Journal of Diversity in Higher Education*, http://dx.doi.org/10.1037/dhe0000084.

Eick, S, Williamson, G, and Heath, V (2012) A Systematic Review of Placement-Related Attrition in Nurse Education. *International Journal of Nursing Studies*, 49, pp. 1299–309.

Eka, N, and Chambers, D (2019) Incivility in Nursing Education: A Systematic Literature Review. *Nurse Education in Practice*, 39, pp. 45–54.

Emerson, J, and Mosteller, F (2000) Development Programs for College Faculty: Preparing for the Twenty-First Century. *Educational Media and Technology Yearbook*, 25, pp. 26–42.

Escriva-Beltran, M, Munoz-de-Prat, J, and Villo, C (2018) Insights into International Branch Campuses: Mapping Trends through a Systematic Review. *Journal of Business Research*, https://doi.org/10.1016/j.jbusres.2018.12.049.

Evans, C (2013) Making Sense of Assessment Feedback in Higher Education. *Review of Educational Research*, 83, 1, pp. 70–120.

Evans, C, Muijs, D, and Tomlinson, M (2015) *Engaged Student Learning: High-Impact Strategies to Enhance Student Achievement*. York, Higher Education Academy.

Falchikov, N, and Boud, D (1989) Student Self-Assessment in Higher Education: A Meta-Analysis. *Review of Educational Research*, 59, 4, pp. 395–430.

Falchikov, N, and Goldfinch, J (2000) Student Peer Assessment in Higher Education: A Meta-Analysis Comparing Peer and Teacher Marks. *Review of Educational Research*, 70, 3, pp. 287–322.

Farkas, A, Bonifacino, E, Turner, R, Tilstra, S, and Corbelli, J (2019) Mentorship of Women in Academic Medicine: A Systematic Review. *Journal of General Internal Medicine*, 37, 4, pp. 1322–9.

Fedina, L, Holmes, J, and Backes, B (2018) Campus Sexual Assault: A Systematic Review of Prevalence Research from 2000 to 2015. *Trauma, Violence and Abuse*, 19, 1, pp. 76–93.

Feldman, K (1976) Grades and College Students' Evaluations of Their Courses and Teachers. *Research in Higher Education*, 4, 1, pp. 69–111.

Feldman, K (1977) Consistency and Variability among College Students in Rating Their Teachers and Courses: A Review and Analysis. *Research in Higher Education*, 6, pp. 223–74.

Feldman, K (1978) Course Characteristics and College Students' Ratings of Their Teachers: What We Know and What We Don't. *Research in Higher Education*, 9, pp. 199–242.

Feldman, K (1979) The Significance of Circumstances for College Students' Ratings of Their Teachers and Courses. *Research in Higher Education*, 10, 2, pp. 149–72.

Feldman, K (1983) Seniority and Experience of College Teachers as Related to Evaluations They Receive from Students. *Research in Higher Education*, 18, 1, pp. 3–124.

Feldman, K (1984) Class Size and College Students' Evaluations of Teachers and Courses: A Closer Look. *Research in Higher Education*, 21, 1, pp. 45–116.

Feldman, K (1986) The Perceived Instructional Effectiveness of College Teachers as Related to Their Personality and Attitudinal Characteristics: A Review and Synthesis. *Research in Higher Education*, 24, 2, pp. 139–213.

Feldman, K (1987) Research Productivity and Scholarly Accomplishment of College Teachers as Related to Their Instructional Effectiveness: A Review and Exploration. *Research in Higher Education*, 26, 3, pp. 227–98.

Feldman, K (1989) The Association between Student Ratings of Specific Instructional Dimensions and Student Achievement: Refining and Extending the Synthesis of Data from Multisection Validity Studies. *Research in Higher Education*, 30, 6, pp. 583–645.

Feldman, K, and Newcomb, T (1969) *The Impact of College upon Students*. San Francisco, CA, Jossey-Bass.

Fernandez, A, Fernandez, C, Miguel-Davila, A, Conde, M, and Matellan, V (2019) Supercomputers to Improve the Performance in Higher Education: A Review of the Literature. *Computers and Education*, 128, pp. 353–64.

Figueiro, P, and Raufflet, E (2015) Sustainability in Higher Education: A Systematic Review with Focus on Management Education. *Journal of Cleaner Production*, 106, pp. 22–33.

Findler, F, Schonherr, N, Lozano, R, Reider, D, and Martinuzzi, A (2019) The Impacts of Higher Education Institutions on Sustainable Development: A Review and Conceptualization. *International Journal of Sustainability in Higher Education*, 20, 1, pp. 23–38.

Fitz-Gibbon, C (1985) The Implications of Meta-Analysis for Educational Research. *British Educational Research Journal*, 11, 1, pp. 45–9.

Flink, P (2018) Latinos and Higher Education: A Literature Review. *Journal of Hispanic Higher Education*, 17, 4, pp. 402–14.

Flores, S, and Hartlaub, M (1998) Reducing Rape-Myth Acceptance in Male College Students: A Meta-Analysis of Intervention Studies. *Journal of College Student Development*, 39, 5, pp. 438–48.

Fnais, N, Soobiah, C, Chen, M, Lillie, E, Perrier, L, Tashkhandi, E, Strauss, S, Mamdani, M, Al-Omran, M, and Tricco, A (2014) Harassment and Discrimination in Medical Training: A Systematic Review and Meta-Analysis. *Academic Medicine*, 89, pp. 817–27.

Forsberg, E, and Geschwind, L (2016) The Academic Home of Higher Education Research: The Case of Doctoral Theses in Sweden. In J Huisman and M Tight (eds) *Theory and Method in Higher Education Research*, 2. Bingley, Emerald, pp. 69–93.

Frajerman, A, Morvan, Y, Krebs, M-O, Gorwood, P, and Chaumette, B (2019) Burnout in Medical Students before Residency: A Systematic Review and Meta-Analysis. *European Psychiatry*, 55, pp. 36–42.

Fraser, B, Walberg, H, Welch, W, and Hattie, J (1987) Syntheses of Educational Productivity Research. *International Journal of Educational Research*, 11, pp. 145–252.

Freeman, S, Eddy, S, McDonough, M, Smith, M, Okoroafer, N, and Jordt, H (2014) Active Learning Increases Student Performance in Science, Engineering and Mathematics. *Proceedings of the National Academy of Sciences of the United States of America*, 111, 23, pp. 8410–15.

Frohberg, D, Göth, C, and Schwabe, G (2009) Mobile Learning Projects: A Critical Analysis of the State of the Art. *Journal of Computer Assisted Learning*, 25, pp. 307–31.

Fu, Q-K, and Hwang, G-J (2018) Trends in Mobile Technology-Supported Collaborative Learning: A Systematic Review of Journal Publications from 2007 to 2016. *Computers and Education*, 119, pp. 129–43.

Fukkink, R, Trienekens, N, and Kramer, L (2011) Video Feedback in Education and Training: Putting Learning in the Picture. *Educational Psychology Review*, 23, pp. 45–63.

Gallet, C (2007) A Comparative Analysis of the Demand for Higher Education: Results from a Meta-Analysis of Elasticities. *Economics Bulletin*, 9, 7, pp. 1–14.

Galvis, A (2018) Supporting Decision-Making Processes on Blended Learning in Higher Education: Literature and Good Practices Review. *International Journal of Educational Technology in Higher Education*, 15, 25, p. 38.

Gander, M, Girardi, A, and Paull, M (2019) The Careers of University Professional Staff: A Systematic Literature Review. *Career Development International*, 24, 7, pp. 597–618.

Gao, X, Luo, S, Mu, D, Xiong, Y, Guanjian, L, and Wan, C (2016) Effects of Problem-Based Learning in Paediatric Education in China: A Meta-Analysis. *Journal of Evidence-Based Medicine*, 9, pp. 136–43.

Garrison-Wade, D, and Lehmann, J (2009) A Conceptual Framework for Understanding Students with Disabilities Transition to Community College. *Community College Journal of Research and Practice*, 33, 5, pp. 415–33.

Garzón, J, and Acevedo, J (2019) Meta-Analysis of the Impact of Augmented Reality on Students' Learning Gains. *Educational Research Review*, 27, pp. 244–60.

Gast, I, Schildkamp, K, and Veen, J van der (2017) Team-Based Professional Development Interventions in Higher Education: A Systematic Review. *Review of Educational Research*, 87, 4, pp. 736–67.

Gauntlett, N (2007) *Literature Review on Formative Assessment in Higher Education*. Middlesex University, Mental Health and Social Work Centre for Excellence in Teaching and Learning.

Gay, G (2000) *Culturally Responsive Teaching: Theory, Research and Practice*. New York, Teachers College Press.

Gedrimiene, E, Silvola, A, Pursiainen, J, Rusanen, J, and Muukkonen, H (2019) Learning Analytics in Education: Literature Review and Case Examples from Vocational Education. *Scandinavian Journal of Educational Research*, DOI: 10.1080/00313831.2019.1649718.

Gegenfurtner, A, and Ebner, C (2019) Webinars in Higher Education and Professional Training: A Meta-Analysis and Systematic Review of Randomized Control Trials. *Educational Research Review*, 28, 100293.

Gellin, A (2003) The Effect of Undergraduate Student Involvement on Critical Thinking: A Meta-Analysis of the Literature 1991–2000. *Journal of College Student Development*, 44, 6, pp. 746–62.

Gibbs, P, Cartney, P, Wilkinson, K, Parkinson, J, Cunningham, S, James-Reynolds, C, Zoubir, T, Brown, V, Barter, P, Sumner, P, Macdonald, A, Dayananda, A, and Pitt, A (2017) Literature Review on the Use of Action Research in Higher Education. *Educational Action Research*, 25, 1, pp. 3–22.

Gibson, A (2010) Measuring Business Student Satisfaction: A Review and Summary of the Major Predictors. *Journal of Higher Education Policy and Management*, 32, 3, pp. 251–9.

Gijbels, D, Dochy, F, Van den Bossche, P, and Segers, M (2005) Effects of Problem-Based Learning: A Meta-Analysis from the Angle of Assessment. *Review of Educational Research*, 75, 1, pp. 27–61.

Gikandi, J, Morrow, D, and Davis, N (2011) Online Formative Assessment in Higher Education: A Review of the Literature. *Computers and Education*, 57, pp. 2333–51.

Glass, G (1976) Primary, Secondary and Meta-Analysis of Research. *Educational Researcher*, 5, 10, pp. 3–8.

Goedegebuure, L, Kaiser, F, Maassen, P, Meek, L, Vught, F van, and Weert, E de (eds) (1994) *Higher Education Policy: An International Comparative Perspective*. Oxford, Pergamon Press.

Goldschmid, B, and Goldschmid, M (1976) Peer Teaching in Higher Education: A Review. *Higher Education*, 5, 1, pp. 9–33.

Good, K (2013) Audience Response Systems in Higher Education Courses: A Critical Review of the Literature. *International Journal of Instructional Technology and Distance Learning*, 10, 5, pp. 19–34.

Goradia, T, and Bugarcic, A (2019) Exploration and Evaluation of the Tools Used to Identify First Year At-Risk Students in Health Science Courses: A Systematic Review. *Advances in Integrative Medicine*, https://doi.org/10.1016/j.aimed.201811.003.

Gorard, S, Smith, E, May, H, Thomas, L, Adnett, N and Slack, K (2006) *Review of Widening Participation Research: Addressing the Barriers to Participation in Higher Education*. Bristol, Higher Education Funding Council for England.

Gough, D, Oliver, S, and Thomas, J (2017) *An Introduction to Systematic Reviews*. London, Sage, second edition.

Gralka, S (2018) *Stochastic Frontier Analysis in Higher Education: A Systematic Review*. CEPIE Working Paper, No. 05/18, Dresden, Technische Universität Dresden, Center of Public and International Economics (CEPIE), http://nbn-resolving.de/urn:nbn:de:bsz:14-qucosa2-324599.

Grant, M, and Booth, A (2009) A Typology of Reviews: An Analysis of 14 Review Types and Associated Methodologies. *Health Information and Libraries Journal*, 26, pp. 91–108.

Grant, D, Mergen, E, and Widrick, S (2004) A Comparative Analysis of Quality Management in US and International Universities. *Total Quality Management and Business Excellence*, 15, 4, pp. 423–38.

Gray, M, and Crosta, L (2019) New Perspectives in Online Doctoral Supervision: A Systematic Literature Review. *Studies in Continuing Education*, 41, 2, pp. 173–90.

Gregg, N, and Nelson, J (2012) Meta-Analysis on the Effectiveness of Extra Time as a Test Accommodation for Transitioning Adolescents with Learning Disabilities: More Questions than Answers. *Journal of Learning Disabilities*, 45, 2, pp. 128–38.

Grosemans, I, Coertjens, L, and Kyndt, E (2017) Exploring Learning and Fit in the Transition from Higher Education to the Labour Market: A Systematic Review. *Educational Research Review*, 21, pp. 67–84.

Gu, X, and Blackmore, K (2015) A Systematic Review of Agent-Based Modelling and Simulation Applications in the Higher Education Domain. *Higher Education Research and Development*, 34, 5, pp. 883–98.

Gunn, V, and Fisk, A (2013) *Considering Teaching Excellence in Higher Education: 2007–2013 – A Literature Review since the CHERI Report 2007*. York, Higher Education Academy.

Hafford-Letchfield, T, Pezzella, A, Cole, L, and Manning, R (2017) Transgender Students in Post-Compulsory Education: A Systematic Review. *International Journal of Educational Research*, 86, pp. 1–12.

Haggis, T (2009) What Have We Been Thinking Of? A Critical Overview of 40 Years of Student Learning Research in Higher Education. *Studies in Higher Education*, 34, 4, pp. 377–90.

Hallinger, P (2013) A Conceptual Framework for Systematic Reviews of Research in Educational Leadership and Management. *Journal of Educational Administration*, 51, 2, pp. 126–49.

Hallinger, P, and Chatpinyakoop, C (2019) A Bibliometric Review of Research on Higher Education for Sustainable Development, 1998–2018. *Sustainability*, 11, 2401, 20pp, DOI: 10.3390/su11082401.

Harman, G (2005) Internationalization of Australian Higher Education: A Critical Review of Literature and Research. In P Ninnes and M Helsten (eds) *Internationalizing Higher Education*. Dordrecht, Springer, pp. 119–40.

Harris, M, and Schaubroeck, J (1988) A Meta-Analysis of Self-Supervisor, Self-Peer and Peer-Supervisor Ratings. *Personnel Psychology*, 41, 1, pp. 43–62.

Hart, J, and Metcalfe, A (2010) Whose Web of Knowledge Is It Anyway? Citing Feminist Research in the Field of Higher Education. *Journal of Higher Education*, 81, 2, pp. 140–63.

Hartrey, L, Denieffe, S, and Wells, J (2017) A Systematic Review of Barriers and Supports to the Participation of Students with Mental Health Difficulties in Higher Education. *Mental Health and Prevention*, 6, pp. 26–43.

Harvey, L, and Williams, J (2010a) Fifteen Years of Quality in Higher Education. *Quality in Higher Education*, 16, 1, pp. 3–36.

Harvey, L, and Williams, J (2010b) Fifteen Years of Quality in Higher Education (Part Two). *Quality in Higher Education*, 16, 2, pp. 81–113.

Hattie, J (2009) *Visible Learning: A Synthesis of over 800 Meta-Analyses Relating to Achievement*. London, Routledge.

Hattie, J, and Marsh, H (1996) The Relationship between Research and Teaching: A Meta-Analysis. *Review of Educational Research*, 66, 4, pp. 507–42.

Hattie, J, Biggs, J, and Purdie, N (1996) Effects of Learning Style Interventions on Student Learning: A Meta-Analysis. *Review of Educational Research*, 66, 2, pp. 99–136.

Hayeslip, D (1989) Higher Education and Police Performance Revisited: The Evidence Examined through Meta-Analysis. *American Journal of Police*, 8, 2, pp. 49–62.

Heaslip, V, Board, M, Duckworth, V, and Thomas, L (2017) Widening Participation in Nurse Education: An Integrative Literature Review. *Nurse Education Today*, 59, pp. 66–74.

Heinz, J, and Maasen, S (2019) Co-producing the European Higher Education Area: The (Somewhat Overlooked) Role of the Social Sciences. *Studies in Higher Education*, DOI: 10.1080/03075079.2019.1617684.

Heller, D (1997) Student Price Response in Higher Education: An Update to Leslie and Brinkman. *Journal of Higher Education*, 68, 6, pp. 624–59.

Hemsley-Brown, J, and Oplatka, I (2006) Universities in a Competitive Global Marketplace: A Systematic Review of the Literature on Higher Education Marketing. *International Journal of Public Sector Management*, 19, 4, pp. 316–38.

Henk, W, and Stahl, M (1985) *A Meta-Analysis of the Effect of Notetaking on Learning from Lectures*. Paper presented at the Annual Meeting of the National Reading Conference.

Henning, N, Zhou, C, Adams, P, Moir, F, Hobson, J, Hallett, C, and Webster, C (2017) Workplace Harassment among Staff in Higher Education: A Systematic Review. *Asia Pacific Educational Review*, 18, pp. 521–39.

Henritius, E, Löfström, E, and Hannula, M (2019) University Students' Emotions in Virtual Learning: A Review of Empirical Research in the 21st Century. *British Journal of Educational Technology*, 50, 1, pp. 80–100.

Herbaut, E, and Geven, K (2019) *What Works to Reduce Inequalities in Higher Education? A Systematic Review of the (Quasi-)Experimental Literature on Outreach and Financial Aid*. Washington, DC, World Bank, Policy Research Working Paper 8802.

Hilton, J (2019) Open Educational Resources, Student Efficacy and User Perceptions: A Synthesis of Research Published between 2015 and 2018. *Educational Technology Research and Development*, https://doi.org/10.1007/s11423-019-09700-4.

Hoffler, T, and Leutner, D (2007) Instructional Animation versus Static Pictures: A Meta-Analysis. *Learning and Instruction*, 17, pp. 722–8.

Honicke, T, and Broadbent, J (2016) The Influence of Academic Self-Efficacy on Academic Performance: A Systematic Review. *Educational Research Review*, 17, pp. 63–84.

Horta, H, and Jung, J (2014) Higher Education Research in Asia: An Archipelago, Two Continents or Merely Atomization? *Higher Education*, 68, pp. 117–34.

Horta, H, Jung, J, and Yonezawa, A (2015) Higher Education Research in East Asia: Regional and National Evolution and Path Dependencies. *Higher Education Policy*, 28, pp. 411–17.

Howell, S, and Hoyt, J (2007) *Part-Time Faculty Job Satisfaction in Higher Education: A Literature Review*. Provo, Utah, USA, Brigham Young University.

Hoyt, D (1965) *The Relationship between College Grades and Adult Achievement: A Review of the Literature*. Iowa City, IA, American College Testing Program.

Huang, B, Zheng, L, Li, C, and Yu, H (2013) Effectiveness of Problem-Based Learning in Chinese Dental Education: A Meta-Analysis. *Journal of Dental Education*, 2103, 77, 3, pp. 377–83.

Huang, C, Yang, C, Wang, S, Wu, W, Su, J, and Liang, C (2019) Evolution of Topics in Education Research: A Systematic Review Using Bibliometric Analysis. *Educational Review*, DOI: 10.1080/00131911.2019.1566212.

Huang, J, Van den Brink, H, and Groot, W (2009) A Meta-Analysis of the Effect of Education on Social Capital. *Economics of Education Review*, 28, pp. 454–64.

Huber, C, and Kuncel, N (2016) Does College Teach Critical Thinking? A Meta-Analysis. *Review of Educational Research*, 86, 2, pp. 431–68.

Huisman, B, Saab, N, van den Broek, P, and van Driel, J (2019) The Impact of Formative Peer Feedback on Higher Education Students' Academic Writing: A Meta-Analysis. *Assessment and Evaluation in Higher Education*, 44, 6, pp. 863–80.

Huisman, J (2008) Higher Education Policy: The Evolution of a Journal. *Higher Education Policy*, 21, 2, pp. 265–74.

Hung, J-L, and Zhang, K (2012) Examining Mobile Learning Trends 2003–2008: A Categorical Meta-Trend Analysis Using Text Mining Techniques. *Journal of Computing in Higher Education*, 24, 1, pp. 1–17.

Hutchings, K, Bainbridge, R, Bodle, K, and Miller, A (2019) Determinants of Attraction, Retention and Completion for Aboriginal and Torres Strait Islander Higher Degree Research Students: A Systematic Review to Inform Future Research Directions. *Research in Higher Education*, 60, pp. 245–72.

Hwang, G-J, and Tsai, C-C (2011) Research Trends in Mobile and Ubiquitous Learning: A Review of Publications in Selected Journals from 2001 to 2010. *British Journal of Educational Technology*, 42, 4, pp. E65–E70.

Inceoglu, I, Selenko, E, McDowall, A, and Schlacter, S (2019) (How) Do Work Placements Work? Scrutinizing the Quantitative Evidence for a Theory-Driven Future Research Agenda. *Journal of Vocational Behavior*, 110, pp. 317–37.

Imbulgoda, C (2019) Compliance toward Quality Assurance System in Higher Education: A Systematic Literature Review. Proceedings of the Asia Pacific Quality Network Annual Academic Conference.

Ithnin, F, Sahib, S, Eng, C, Sidek, S, and Harun, R (2018) Mapping the Futures of Malaysian Higher Education: A Meta-Analysis of Futures Studies in the Malaysian Higher Education Scenario. *Journal of Futures Studies*, 22, 3, pp. 1–18.

Ives, J, and Castillo-Montoya, M (2020) First-Generation College Students as Academic Learners: A Systematic Review. *Review of Educational Research*, p. 40, DOI: https://doi.org/10.3102/0034654319899707.

Jackson, J, and Kile, K (2004) Does a Nexus Exist between the Work of Administrators and Student Outcomes in Higher Education? An Answer from a Systematic Review of Research. *Innovative Higher Education*, 28, 4, pp. 285–301.

Jahng, N, Krug, D, and Zhang, Z (2007) Student Achievement in Online Distance Education Compared to Face-to-Face Education. *European Journal of Open, Distance and E-Learning*, p. 12.

Jameson, J (2013) e-Leadership in Higher Education: The Fifth 'Age' of Educational Technology Research. *British Journal of Educational Technology*, 44, 6, pp. 889–915.

Jansen, R, Leeuwen, A van, Jansen, J, Jak, S, and Kester, L (2019) Self-Regulated Learning Partially Mediates the Effects of Self-Regulated Learning Interventions on Achievement in Higher Education: A Meta-Analysis. *Educational Research Review*, 28, 100292.

Jesson, J, Matheson, L, and Lacey, F (2011) *Doing Your Literature Review: Traditional and Systematic Techniques*. London, Sage.

Joda, T, Gallucci, G, Wismeijer, D, and Zitzmann, N (2019) Augmented and Virtual Reality in Dental Education: A Systematic Review. *Computers in Biology and Medicine*, 108, pp. 93–100.

Johnson, R (2019) The State of Research on Undergraduate Youth Formerly in Foster Care: A Systematic Review of the Literature. *Journal of Diversity in Higher Education*, http://dx.doi.org/10.1037/dhe0000150.

Jones, M (2013) Issues in Doctoral Studies. Forty Years of Journal Discussion: Where Have We Been and Where Are We Going? *International Journal of Doctoral Studies*, 8, pp. 83–104.

Jorge, M, and Pena, F (2017) Analysing the Literature on University Social Responsibility: A Review of Selected Higher Education Journals. *Higher Education Quarterly*, 71, pp. 302–19.

Judson, E, and Sawada, D (2002) Learning from Past and Present: Electronic Response Systems in College Lecture Halls. *Journal of Computing in Mathematics and Science Teaching*, 21, 2, pp. 167–81.

Jung, J, and Horta, H (2013) Higher Education Research in Asia: A Publication and Co-Publication Analysis. *Higher Education Quarterly*, 67, 4, pp. 398–419.

Juntunen, M, and Lehenkari, M (2019) A Narrative Literature Review Process for an Academic Business Research Thesis. *Studies in Higher Education*, DOI: 10.1080/03075079.2019.1630813.

Kankaanpaa, I, and Isomaki, H (2013) Productization and Commercialization of IT-Enabled Higher Education Computer Science: A Systematic Literature Review. IADIS Conference.

Kasworm, C (1990) Adult Undergraduates in Higher Education: A Review of Past Research Perspectives. *Review of Educational Research*, 60, 3, pp. 345–72.

Kattoua, T, Al-Lozi, M, and Alrowwad, A (2016) A Review of Literature on E-learning Systems in Higher Education. *International Journal of Business Management and Economic Research*, 7, 5, pp. 754–62.

Kay, R, and LeSage, A (2009) A Strategic Assessment of Audience Response Systems Used in Higher Education. *Australasian Journal of Educational Technology*, 25, 2, pp. 235–49.

Kebritchi, M, Lipschuetz, A, and Santiague, L (2017) Issues and Challenges for Teaching Successful Online Courses in Higher Education: A Literature Review. *Journal of Educational Technology Systems*, 46, 1, pp. 4–29.

Kehm, B, and Teichler, U (2007) Research on Internationalisation in Higher Education. *Journal of Studies in International Education*, 11, 3–4, pp. 260–73.

Kellams, S (1973) Higher Education as a Potential Profession. *Journal of Research and Development in Education*, 6, pp. 30–41.

Kellams, S (1975) Research Studies on Higher Education: A Content Analysis. *Research in Higher Education*, 3, pp. 139–54.

Khalid, M, and Pedersen, M (2016) Digital Exclusion in Higher Education Contexts: A Systematic Literature Review. *Procedia Social and Behavioral Sciences*, 228, pp. 614–21.

Khan, F, Chikkatagaiah, S, Shaffiulah, M, Nasiri, M, Saraf, A, Sehgal, T, Rana, A, Tadros, G, and Kingston, P (2015) International Medical Graduates in the UK: A Systematic Review of Their Acculturation and Adaptation. *International Migration and Integration*, 16, pp. 743–59.

Kilburn, D, Nind, M, and Wiles, R (2014) Leading as Researchers and Teachers: The Development of a Pedagogical Culture for Social Science Research Methods? *British Journal of Educational Studies*, 62, 2, pp. 191–207.

Kim, H, and Lalancette, D (2013) *Literature Review on the Value-Added Measurement in Higher Education*. Paris, Organization for Economic Cooperation and Development.

Kim, K, and Seo, E (2015) The Relationship between Procrastination and Academic Performance: A Meta-Analysis. *Personality and Individual Differences*, 82, pp. 26–31.

Kim, N, Belland, B, Lefler, M, Andreason, L, Walker, A, and Axelrod, D (2019) Computer-Based Scaffolding Targeting Individual versus Groups in Problem-Centered Instruction for STEM Education: Meta-Analysis. *Educational Psychology Review*, https://doi.org/10.1007/s10648-019-09502-3.

Kim, Y, Horta, H, and Jung, J (2017) Higher Education Research in Hong Kong, Japan, China and Malaysia: Exploring Research Community Cohesion and the Integration of Thematic Approaches. *Studies in Higher Education*, 42, 1, pp. 149–68.

Kimball, E, and Thoma, H (2019) College Experiences for Students with Disabilities: An Ecological Synthesis of Recent Literature. *Journal of College Student Development*, 60, 6, pp. 674–93.

King, R, Marginson, S, and Naidoo, R (2011) *Handbook on Globalization and Higher Education*. Cheltenham, Edward Elgar.

Kirkwood, A, and Price, L (2014) Technology-Enhanced Learning and Teaching in Higher Education: What Is 'Enhanced' and How Do We Know? A Critical Literature Review. *Learning, Media and Technology*, 39, 1, pp. 6–36.

Kitchenham, B, Brereton, P, Budgen, D, Turner, M, Bailey, J, and Linkman, S (2009) Systematic Literature Reviews in Software Engineering: A Systematic Literature Review. *Information and Software Technology*, 51, pp. 7–15.

Kluger, A, and DeNisi, A (1996) The Effects of Feedback Interventions on Performance: A Historical Review, a Meta-Analysis, and a Preliminary Feedback Intervention Theory. *Psychological Bulletin*, 119, 2, pp. 254–84.

Kobayashi, K (2005) What Limits the Encoding Effect of Note-Taking? A Meta-Analytic Examination. *Contemporary Educational Psychology*, 30, pp. 242–62.

Koh, G, Khoo, H, Wong, M, and Koh, D (2008) The Effects of Problem-Based Learning during Medical School on Physician Competency: A Systematic Review. *Canadian Medical Association Journal*, 178, 1, pp. 34–41.

Kornhaber, R, Cross, M, Betihavas, V, and Bridgman, H (2016) The Benefits and Challenges of Academic Writing Retreats: An Integrative Review. *Higher Education Research and Development*, 35, 6, pp. 1210–27.

Kosmutzky, A, and Krucken, G (2014) Growth or Steady State? A Bibliometric Focus on International Comparative Higher Education Research. *Higher Education*, 67, pp. 457–72.

Kosmutzky, A, and Putty, R (2016) Transcending Borders and Traversing Boundaries: A Systematic Review of the Literature on Transnational, Offshore, Cross-Border and Borderless Higher Education. *Journal of Studies in International Education*, 20, 1, pp. 8–33.

Kraut, A, Omron, R, Caretta-Weyer, H, Jordan, J, Manthey, D, Wolf, S, Yaris, L, Johnson, S, and Kornegay, J (2019) The Flipped Classroom: A Critical Appraisal. *Western Journal of Emergency Medicine*, 20, 3, pp. 527–36.

Kreber, C (ed) (2001) *Scholarship Revisited: Perspectives on the Scholarship of Teaching*. San Francisco, CA: Jossey-Bass. New Directions for Teaching and Learning, Number 86.

Krull, G, and Duart, J (2017) Research Trends in Mobile Learning in Higher Education: A Systematic Review of Articles (2011–2015). *International Review of Research in Open and Distributed Learning*, 18, 7, p. 23.

Kuder, S, and Accardo, A (2018) What Works for College Students with Autism Spectrum Disorder. *Journal of Autism and Developmental Disorders*, 48, pp. 722–31.

Kulik, C-L, and Kulik, J (1985) Effectiveness of Computer-Based Education in Colleges. Paper presented at the annual meeting of the American Educational Research Association, p. 44.

Kulik, C-L, Kulik, J, and Bangert-Drowns, R (1990) Effectiveness of Mastery Learning Programs: A Meta-Analysis. *Review of Educational Research*, 60, 2, pp. 265–99.

Kulik, C-L, Kulik, J, and Cohen, P (1980) Instructional Technology and College Teaching. *Teaching of Psychology*, 7, 4, pp. 199–205.

Kulik, C-L, Kulik, J, and Shwalb, B (1983) College Programs for High-Risk and Disadvantaged Students: A Meta-Analysis of Findings. *Review of Educational Research*, 53, 3, pp. 397–414.

Kulik, J (2001) Student Ratings: Validity, Utility and Controversy. *New Directions for Institutional Research*, 109, pp. 9–25.

Kulik, J, and Kulik, C-L (1980a) Individualised College Teaching. *Evaluation in Education*, 4, pp. 64–7.

Kulik, J, Cohen, P, and Ebeling, B (1980) Effectiveness of Programmed Instruction in Higher Education: A Meta-Analysis of Findings. *Educational Evaluation and Policy Analysis*, 2, 6, pp. 51–64.

Kulik, J, Kulik, C-L, and Cohen, P (1979a) A Meta-Analysis of Outcome Studies of Keller's Personalized System of Instruction. *American Psychologist*, 34, 4, pp. 307–18.

Kulik, J, Kulik, C-L, and Cohen, P (1979b) Research on Audio-Tutorial Instruction: A Meta-Analysis of Comparative Studies. *Research in Higher Education*, 11, 4, pp. 321–41.

Kulik, J, Kulik, C-L, and Cohen, P (1980a) Effectiveness of Computer-Based College Teaching: A Meta-Analysis of Findings. *Review of Educational Research*, 50, 4, pp. 525–44.

Kuncel, N, Crede, M, and Thomas, L (2005) The Validity of Self-Reported Grade Point Averages, Class Ranks and Test Scores: A Meta-Analysis and Review of the Literature. *Review of Educational Research*, 75, 1, pp. 63–82.

Kuncel, N, Hezlett, S, and Ones, D (2001) A Comprehensive Meta-Analysis of the Predictive Validity of the Graduate Record Examinations: Implications for Graduate Student Selection and Performance. *Psychological Bulletin*, 127, 1, pp. 162–81.

Kuncel, N, Kochevar, R, and Ones, D (2014) A Meta-Analysis of Letters of Recommendation in College and Graduate Admissions: Reasons for Hope. *International Journal of Selection and Assessment*, 22, 1, pp. 101–7.

Kuncel, N, Wee, S, Serafin, L, and Hezlett, S (2010) The Validity of the Graduate Record Examination for Master's and Doctoral Programs: A Meta-Analytic Investigation. *Educational and Psychological Measurement*, 70, 2, pp. 340–52.

Kutscher, E, and Tuckwiller, E (2018) Persistence in Higher Education for Students with Disabilities: A Mixed Systematic Review. *Journal of Diversity in Higher Education*, http://dx.doi.org/10.1037/dhe0000088.

Kuzhabekhova, A, Hendel, D, and Chapman, D (2015) Mapping Global Research on International Higher Education. *Research in Higher Education*, 56, pp. 861–82.

Laat, M de, Lally, V, Simons, R-J, and Wenger, E (2006) A Selective Analysis of Empirical Findings in Networked Learning Research in Higher Education: Questing for Coherence. *Educational Research Review*, 1, pp. 99–111.

Lafuente-Ruiz-de-Sabando, A, Zorrilla, P, and Forcada, J (2018) A Review of Higher Education Image and Reputation Literature: Knowledge Gaps and a Research Agenda. *European Research on Management and Business Economics*, 24, pp. 8–16.

Lambert, S (2020) Do MOOCs Contribute to Student Equity and Social Inclusion? A Systematic Review 2014–2018. *Computers and Education*, 145, 103693.

Lankveld, T van, Schoonenboom, J, Volman, M, Croiset, G, and Beishuizen, J (2017) Developing a Teacher Identity in the University Context: A Systematic Review of the Literature. *Higher Education Research and Development*, 36, 2, pp. 325–42.

Larwin, K, Gorman, J, and Larwin, D (2013) Assessing the Impact of Testing Aids on Post-Secondary Student Performance: A Meta-Analytic Investigation. *Educational Psychology Review*, 25, pp. 429–43.

Lasen, M, Evans, S, Tsey, K, Campbell, C, and Kinchin, I (2018) Quality of WIL Assessment Design in Higher Education: A Systematic Literature Review. *Higher Education Research and Development*, DOI: 10.1080/07294360.2018.1450359.

Laurett, R, and Mendes, L (2019) EFQM Model's Application in the Context of Higher Education: A Systematic Review of the Literature and Agenda for Future Research. *International Journal of Quality and Reliability Management*, 36, 2, pp. 257–85.

Lechtchinskaia, L, Uffen, J, and Breitner, M (2011) Critical Success Factors for Adoption of Integrated Information Systems in Higher Education Institutions: A Meta-Analysis. AMCIS 2011 Proceedings - All Submissions. Paper 53.

Lee, D-C, Jian, M, Sora, G, and Haines, T (2019) Fieldwork Placement Outcomes for International Higher Education Students: A Systematic Literature Review. *Australian Journal of Career Development*, 28, 2, pp. 132–50.

Leonard, D, Metcalfe, J, Becker, R, and Evans, J (2006) *Review of Literature on the Impact of Working Context and Support on the Postgraduate Research Student Learning Experience*. York, Higher Education Academy.

Leslie, L, and Brinkman, P (1987) Student Price Response in Higher Education. *Journal of Higher Education*, 58, pp. 181–204.

Leslie, L, and Brinkman, P (1988) *The Economic Value of Higher Education*. Washington, American Council on Education.

Levett-Jones, T, Cant, R, and Lapkin, S (2019) A Systematic Review of the Effectiveness of Empathy Education for Undergraduate Nursing Students. *Nurse Education Today*, 75, pp. 80–94.

Levinson-Rose, J, and Menges, R (1981) Improving College Teaching: A Critical Review of Research. *Review of Educational Research*, 51, 3, pp. 403–34.

L'Hommedieu, R, Menges, R, and Brinko, K (1990) Methodological Explanations for the Modest Effects of Feedback from Student Ratings. *Journal of Educational Psychology*, 82, 2, pp. 232–41.

Li, H, Xiong, Y, Zang, X, Kornhaber, M, Lyu, Y, Chung, K, and Suen, H (2016) Peer Assessment in the Digital Age: A Meta-Analysis Comparing Peer and Teacher Ratings. *Assessment and Evaluation in Higher Education*, 41, 2, pp. 245–64.

Li, J, and De Luca, R (2014) Review of Assessment Feedback. *Studies in Higher Education*, 39, 2, pp. 378–93.

Light, R, and Pillemer, D (1982) Numbers and Narratives: Combining Their Strengths in Research Reviews. *Harvard Educational Review*, 52, 1, pp. 1–26.

Lin, X (2016) Barriers and Challenges of Female Adult Students Enrolled in Higher Education: A Literature Review. *Higher Education Studies*, 6, 2, pp. 119–26.

Littell, J, Corcoran, J, and Pillai, V (2008) *Systematic Reviews and Meta-Analysis*. Oxford, Oxford University Press.

Little, B, Locke, W, Parker, J, and Richardson, J (2007) *Excellence in Teaching and Learning: A Review of the Literature for the Higher Education Academy*. York, Higher Education Academy.

Liu, L, Du, X, Zhang, Z, and Zhou, J (2019) Effects of Problem-Based Learning in Pharmacology Education: A Meta-Analysis. *Studies in Educational Evaluation*, 60, pp. 43–58.

Liu, M, Kalk, D, Kinney, L, and Orr, G (2012) Web 2.0 and Its Use in Higher Education from 2007 to 2009: A Review of Literature. *International Journal on E-Learning*, 11, 2, pp. 153–79.

Liz-Dominguez, M, Caeiro-Rodriguez, M, Llamas-Nistal, M, and Mikic-Fonte, F (2019) Predictors and Early Warning Systems in Higher Education: A Systematic Literature Review. LASI Learning Analytics in Higher Education conference.

Lloyd, M, and Bahr, N (2016) What Matters in Higher Education: A Meta-Analysis of a Decade of Learning Design. *Journal of Learning Design*, 9, 2, pp. 1–13.

Lo, C-K, and Hew, K-F (2019) The Impact of Flipped Classrooms on Student Achievement in Engineering Education: A Meta-Analysis of Ten Years of Research, *Journal of Engineering Education*, 108, pp. 523–46.

Lombardi, A, Gelbar, N, Dukes, L, Kowitt, J, Wei, Y, Madaus, J, and Lalor, A (2018) Higher Education and Disability: A Systematic Review of Assessment Instruments Designed for Students, Faculty and Staff. *Journal of Diversity in Higher Education*, 11, 1, pp. 34–50.

Lorencová, H, Jarošová, E, Avgitidou, S, and Dimitriadou, C (2019) Critical Thinking Practices in Teacher Education Programmes: A Systematic Review. *Studies in Higher Education*, 44, 5, pp. 844–59.

Lou, Y, Abrami, P, and d'Apollonia, S (2001) Small Group and Individual Learning with Technology: A Meta-Analysis. *Review of Educational Research*, 71, 3, pp. 449–521.

Lou, Y, Bernard, R, and Abrami, P (2006) Media and Pedagogy in Undergraduate Distance Education: A Theory-Based Meta-Analysis of Empirical Literature. *Educational Technology Research and Development*, 54, 2, pp. 141–76.

Lozano, R, Merrill, M, Sammalisto, K, Ceulemans, K, and Lozano, F (2017) Connecting Competencies and Pedagogical Approaches for Sustainable Development in Higher Education: A Literature Review and Framework Proposal. *Sustainability*, 9, p. 1889.

Luiten, J, Ames, W, and Ackerson, G (1980) A Meta-Analysis of the Effect of Advance Organizers on Learning and Retention. *American Educational Research Journal*, 17, 2, pp. 211–18.

Lundin, M, Rensfeldt, A, Hillman, T, Lantz-Andersson, A, and Peterson, L (2018) Higher Education Dominance and Siloed Knowledge: A Systematic Review of Flipped Classroom Research. *International Journal of Educational Technology in Higher Education*, https://doi.org/10.1186/s41239-018-0101-6.

Luzeckyj, A, and Badger, L (2010) *Literature Review for Preparing Academics to Teach in Higher Education*. Strawberry Hills, NSW, Australian Learning and Teaching Council.

Macaro, E, Curle, S, Pun, J, An, J, and Dearden, J (2018) A Systematic Review of English Medium Instruction in Higher Education. *Language Teaching*, 51, 1, pp. 36–76.

Machtmes, K, and Asher, W (2000) A Meta-Analysis of the Effectiveness of Telecourses in Distance Education. *American Journal of Distance Education*, 14, 1, pp. 27–46.

Mackie, S, and Bates, G (2019) Contribution of the Doctoral Education Environment to PhD Candidates' Mental Health Problems: A Scoping Review. *Higher Education Research and Development*, 38, 3, pp. 565–78.

Macleod, J, Yang, H, and Shi, Y (2019) Student-to-Student Connectedness in Higher Education: A Systematic Literature Review. *Journal of Computing in Higher Education*, https://doi.org/10.1007/s12528-019-09214-1.

Maclure, M (2005) 'Clarity Bordering on Stupidity': Where's the Quality in Systematic Review. *Journal of Education Policy*, 20, 4, pp. 393–416.

Mahoney, P, Macfarlane, S, and Ajjawi, R (2019) A Qualitative Synthesis of Video Feedback in Higher Education. *Teaching in Higher Education*, 24, 2, pp. 157–79.

Major, C, and Savin-Baden, M (2010) Exploring the Relevance of Qualitative Research Synthesis to Higher Education Research and Practice. *London Review of Education*, 8, 2, pp. 127–40.

Manatos, M, Sarrico, C, and Rosa, M (2017) The Integration of Quality Management in Higher Education Institutions: A Systematic Literature Review. *Total Quality Management and Business Excellence*, 28, 1–2, pp. 159–75.

Mangan, D, and Winter, L (2017) (In)validation and (Mis)recognition in Higher Education: The Experiences of Students from Refugee Backgrounds. *International Journal of Lifelong Education*, 36, 4, pp. 486–502.

Marambe, K, Vermunt, J, and Boshuizen, H (2012) A Cross-Cultural Comparison of Student Learning Patterns in Higher Education. *Higher Education*, 64, pp. 299–316.

Marsh, H (1987) Students' Evaluation of University Teaching: Research Findings, Methodological Issues and Directions for Future Research. *International Journal of Educational Research*, 11, pp. 253–388.

Marsh, H, and Hattie, J (2002) The Relationship between Research Productivity and Teaching Effectiveness: Complementary, Antagonistic or Independent Constructs. *Journal of Higher Education*, 73, pp. 603–41.

Marsh, H, Bornmann, L, Mutz, R, Daniel, H-D, and O'Mara, A (2009) Gender Effects in the Peer Reviews of Grant Proposals: A Comprehensive Meta-Analysis Comparing Traditional and Multilevel Approaches. *Review of Educational Research*, 79, 3, pp. 1290–326.

Mattingly, J, Mullins, D, Melendez, D, Boyden, K, and Eddington, N (2019) A Systematic Review of Entrepreneurship in Pharmacy Practice and Education. *American Journal of Pharmaceutical Education*, 83, 3, pp. 273–80.

Mayhew, M, Rockenbach, A, Bowman, N, Seifert, T, Wolniak, G, Pascarella, E, and Terenzini, P (2016) *How College Affects Students. Volume 3: 21st Century Evidence That Higher Education Works*. San Francisco, Jossey-Bass.

Means, B, Toyama, Y, Murphy, R, and Bakia, M (2013) The Effectiveness of Online and Blended Learning: A Meta-Analysis of the Empirical Literature. *Teachers College Record*, 115, p. 47.

Means, B, Toyama, Y, Murphy, R, Bakia, M, and Jones, K (2009) *Evaluation of Evidence-Based Practices in Online Learning: A Meta-Analysis and Review of Online Learning Studies*. Washington, DC, U.S. Department of Education Office of Planning, Evaluation, and Policy Development Policy and Program Studies Service.

Medeiros, R, Ramalho, G, and Falcao, T (2018) A Systematic Literature Review on Teaching and Learning Introductory Programming in Higher Education. *IEEE Transactions on Education*, DOI: 10.1109/TE.2018.2864133.

Menges, R, and Brinko, K (1986) Effects of Student Evaluation Feedback: A Meta-Analysis of Higher Education Research. Paper presented at the annual meeting of the American Educational Research Association.

Mercer-Mapstone, L, Dvorakova, S, Matthews, K, Abbott, S, Cheng, B, Felten, P, Knorr, K, Marquis, E, Shammas, R, and Swaim, K (2017) A Systematic Literature of Students as Partners in Higher Education. *International Journal for Students as Partners*, 1, 1, pp. 1–23.

Merchant, Z, Goetz, E, Cifuentes, L, Keeney-Kennicutt, W, and Davis, T (2014) Effectiveness of Virtual Reality-Based Instruction on Students' Learning Outcomes in K-12 and Higher Education: A Meta-Analysis. *Computers and Education*, 70, pp. 29–40.

Miragaia, D, and Soares, J (2017) Higher Education in Sport Management: A Systematic Review of Research Topics and Trends. *Journal of Hospitality, Leisure, Sport and Tourism Education*, 21, pp. 101–16.

Moher, D, Liberati, A, Tetzlaff, J, Altman, D, and the PRISMA Group (2009) Preferred Reporting Items for Systematic Reviews and Meta-Analyses: The PRISMA Statement. *Annals of Internal Medicine*, 151, 4, pp. 264–9.

Moore, J, Sanders, J, and Higham, L (2013) *Literature Review of Research into Widening Participation to Higher Education: Report to HEFCE and OFFA by ARC Network*. Aim Higher Research and Consultancy Network.

Moore, M, Thompson, M, Quigley, A, Clark, C, and Goff, G (1990) *The Effects of Distance Learning: A Summary of Literature*. University Park, PA, American Center for the Study of Distance Education, Pennsylvania State University, Research Monograph No. 2.

Mothibi, G (2015) A Meta-Analysis of the Relationship between E-Learning and Students' Academic Achievement in Higher Education. *Journal of Education and Practice*, 6, 9, pp. 6–10.

Muljana, P, and Luo, T (2019) Factors Contributing to Student Retention in Online Learning and Recommended Strategies for Improvement: A Systematic Literature Review. *Journal of Information Technology Education: Research*, 18, pp. 19–57.

Murdock, T (1987) It Isn't Just Money: The Effects of Financial Aid on Student Persistence. *Review of Higher Education*, 11, 1, pp. 75–101.

Murray, J (2018) Student-Led Action for Sustainability in Higher Education: A Literature Review. *International Journal of Sustainability in Higher Education*, 19, 6, pp. 1095–110.

Mutlu-Bayraktara, D, Cosgun, V, and Altan, T (2019) Cognitive Load in Multimedia Learning Environments: A Systematic Review. *Computers and Education*, 141, 103618, p. 22.

Nabi, G, Linan, F, Fayolle, A, Krueger, N, and Walmsley, A (2017) The Impact of Entrepreneurship Education in Higher Education: A Systematic Review and Research Agenda. *Academy of Management Learning and Education*, 16, 2, pp. 277–99.

Naismith, L, Lonsdale, P, Vavoula, G, and Sharples, M (2004) *Literature Review in Mobile Technologies and Learning*. Bristol, NESTA Futurelab.

Natriello, G (1987) The Impact of Evaluation Processes on Students. *Educational Psychologist*, 22, 2, pp. 155–75.

Nazmi, A, Martinez, S, Byrd, A, Robinson, D, Bianco, S, Maguire, J, Crutchfield, R, Condron, K, and Ritchie, L (2018) A Systematic Review of Food Insecurity among US Students in Higher Education. *Journal of Hunger and Environmental Nutrition*, DOI: 10.1080/19320248.2018.1484316.

Nesbit, J, and Adesope, O (2006) Learning with Concept and Knowledge Maps: A Meta-Analysis. *Review of Educational Research*, 76, 3, pp. 413–48.

Newton, P (2018) How Common Is Commercial Contract Cheating in Higher Education and Is It Increasing? A Systematic Review. *Frontiers in Education*, 3, 67, 18pp.

Neyt, B, Omey, E, Verhaest, D, and Baert, S (2019) Does Student Work Really Affect Educational Outcomes? A Review of the Literature. *Journal of Economic Surveys*, 33, 3, pp. 896–921.

Nichols, S, and Stahl, G (2019) Intersectionality in Higher Education Research: A Systematic Literature Review. *Higher Education Research and Development*, 38, 6, pp. 1255–68.

Nicolaou, M, and Atkinson, M (2019) Do Student and Survey Characteristics Affect the Quality of UK Undergraduate Medical Education Course Evaluation? A Systematic Review of the Literature. *Studies in Educational Evaluation*, 62, pp. 92–103.

Nikula, P-T (2018) Socioeconomic Inequalities in Higher Education: A Meta-Method Analysis of Twenty-First Century Studies in Finland and New Zealand. *Studies in Higher Education*, 43, 12, pp. 2305–20.

Niu, L, Behar-Horenstein, L, and Garvan, C (2013) Do Instructional Interventions Influence College Students' Critical Thinking Skills? A Meta-Analysis. *Educational Research Review*, 9, pp. 114–28.

Noblitt, G (1988) *Meta-Ethnography: Synthesizing Qualitative Studies*. Thousand Oaks, CA, Sage.

Novak, E, Razzouk, R, and Johnson, T (2012) The Educational Use of Social Annotation Tools in Higher Education: A Literature Review. *Internet and Higher Education*, 15, pp. 39–49.

Novak, J, Markey, V, and Allen, M (2007) Evaluating Cognitive Outcomes of Service Learning in Higher Education: A Meta-Analysis. *Communication Research Reports*, 24, 2, pp. 149–57.

Nuske, A, Rillotta, F, Bellon, M, and Richdale, A (2019) Transition to Higher Education for Students with Autism: A Systematic Literature Review. *Journal of Diversity in Higher Education*, http://dx.doi.org/10.1037/dhe0000108.

Ogunyemi, D, Astudillo, Y, Marseille, M, Manu, E, and Kim, S (2019) Microaggressions in the Learning Environment: A Systematic Review. *Journal of Diversity in Higher Education*, http://dx.doi.org/10.1037/dhe0000197.

Olivares-Donoso, R, and Gonzalez, C (2019) Undergraduate Research or Research-Based Courses: Which Is Most Beneficial for Science Students? *Research in Science Education*, 49, pp. 91–107.

Oliver, S, and Tripney, J (2017) Systematic Review and Meta-Analysis. In D Wyse, N Selwyn, E Smith and L Suter (eds) *The BERA/SAGE Handbook of Educational Research*. London, Sage, two volumes, pp. 452–76.

Oliveira Santini, F de, Ladera, W, Sampaio, C, and Silva Costa, G de (2017) Student Satisfaction in Higher Education: A Meta-Analytic Study. *Journal of Marketing for Higher Education*, 27, 1, pp. 1–18.

Onwuegbuzie, A, Daniel, L, and Collins, K (2009) A Meta-Validation Model for Assessing the Score-Validity of Student Teaching Evaluations. *Quality and Quantity*, 43, 2, pp. 197–209.

Organ, D, Dick, S, Hurley, C, Heavin, C, Linehan, C, Dockray, S, Davoren, N, and Byrne, M (2018) A Systematic Review of User-Centred Design Practices in Illicit Substance Use Interventions for Higher Education Students. European Conference on Information Systems, Portsmouth.

Organisation for Economic Cooperation and Development (2018) *Education at a Glance 2018: OECD Indicators*. Paris, OECD.

Osmani, M, Weerakoddy, E, Hindi, M, and Eldabi, T (2019) Graduates Employability Skills: A Review of Literature against Market Demand. *Journal of Education for Business*, 94, 7, pp. 423–32.

Owen, R (2002) *Student and Employee Wellness in Higher Education: A Literature Review*. Morehead, KT, Morehead State University.

Owlia, M, and Aspinwall, E (1997) TQM in Higher Education: A Review. *International Journal of Quality and Reliability Management*, 14, 5, pp. 527–43.

Panadero, E, Jonsson, A, and Botella, J (2017) Effects of Self-Assessment on Self-Regulated Learning and Self-Efficacy: Four Meta-Analyses. *Educational Research Review*, 22, pp. 74–98.

Panadero, E, Klug, J, and Järvelä, S (2016) Third Wave of Measurement in the Self-Regulated Learning Field: When Measurement and Intervention Come Hand in Hand. *Scandinavian Journal of Educational Research*, 60, 6, pp. 723–35.

Pascarella, E, and Terenzini, P (1991) *How College Affects Students: Findings and Insights from Twenty Years of Research*. San Francisco, Jossey-Bass.

Pascarella, E, and Terenzini, P (2005) *How College Affects Students. Volume 2: A Third Decade of Research*. San Francisco, Jossey-Bass.

Payan-Carreira, R, Cruz, G, Papathanasiou, E, and Jiang, L (2019) The Effectiveness of Critical Thinking Instructional Strategies in Health Professions Education: A Systematic Review. *Studies in Higher Education*, 44, 5, pp. 829–43.

Peer, V, and Penker, M (2016) Higher Education Institutions and Regional Development: A Meta-Analysis. *International Regional Science Review*, 39, 2, pp. 228–53.

Penny, A, and Coe, R (2004) Effectiveness of Consultation on Student Ratings Feedback: A Meta-Analysis. *Review of Educational Research*, 74, 2, pp. 215–53.

Permitasari, D, Nurhaeni, I, and Haryati, R (2019) Sustainability of Internationalization of Higher Education in Industrial Revolution 4.0 Era. *Advances in Social Science, Education and Humanities Research*, 343, pp. 88–92.

Phuong, T, Cole, C, and Zarestky, J (2018) A Systematic Literature Review of Faculty Development for Teacher Educators. *Higher Education Research and Development*, 37, 2, pp. 373–89.

Phuong, T, Duong, H, and McLean, G (2015) Faculty Development in Southeast Asian Higher Education: A Review of Literature. *Asian Pacific Education Review*, 16, pp. 107–17.

Pickering, C, Grignon, J, Steven, R, Guitart, D, and Byrne, J (2015) Publishing Not Perishing: How Research Students Transition from Novice to Knowledgeable Using Systematic Quantitative Literature Reviews. *Studies in Higher Education*, 40, 10, pp. 1756–69.

Piggott, B, Muller, S, Chivers, P, Papaluca, C, and Hoyne, G (2019) Is Sports Science Answering the Call for Interdisciplinary Research? A Systematic Review. *European Journal of Sport Science*, 19, 3, pp. 267–86.

Pimmer, C, Mateescu, M, and Grohbiel, U (2016) Mobile and Ubiquitous Learning in Higher Education Settings: A Systematic Review of Empirical Studies. *Computers in Human Behavior*, 63, pp. 490–501.

Pinho, C, Franco, M, and Mendes, L (2018) Web Portals as Tools to Support Information Management in Higher Education Institutions: A Systematic Literature Review. *International Journal of Information Management*, 41, pp. 80–92.

Pino, M, and Mortari, L (2014) The Inclusion of Students with Dyslexia in Higher Education: A Systematic Review Using Narrative Synthesis. *Dyslexia*, 20, pp. 346–69.

Pinto, M, Souza, F, Nogueira, F, Balula, A, Pedro, L, Pombo, L, Ramos, F, and Moreira, A (2012) Tracing the Use of Communication Technology in Higher Education: A Literature Review. Proceedings of INTED 2012 Conference, Valencia.

Poitras, J (2012) Meta-Analysis of the Impact of the Research Setting on Conflict Studies. *International Journal of Conflict Management*, 23, 2, pp. 116–32.

Poropat, A (2009) A Meta-Analysis of the Five-Factor Model of Personality and Academic Performance. *Psychological Bulletin*, 135, 2, pp. 322–38.

Prakhash, G (2018) Quality in Higher Education Institutions: Insights from the Literature. *The TQM Journal*, 30, 6, pp. 732–48.

Puig, B, Blanco-Anaya, B, Bargiela, I, and Crujeiras-Pérez, B (2019) A Systematic Review on Critical Thinking Intervention Studies in Higher Education across Professional Fields. *Studies in Higher Education*, 44, 5, pp. 860–9.

Qasem, Y, Abdullah, R, Jusoh, Y, Atan, R, and Asadi, S (2019) Cloud Computing Adoption in Higher Education Institutions: A Systematic Review. *IEEE Access*, 7, pp. 63722–44.

Qianqian, Z-W (2018) Chinese International Students' Experiences in American Higher Education Institutes: A Critical Review of the Literature. *Journal of International Students*, DOI: 10.5281/zenodo.1250419.

Querol-Julian, M, and Camiciottoli, B (2019) The Impact of Online Technologies and English Medium Instruction on University Lectures in International Learning Contexts: A Systematic Review. *ESP Today*, 7, 1, pp. 2–23.

Radianti, J, Majchrzak, T, Fromm, J, Wohlgenannt, I (2020) A Systematic Review of Immersive Virtual Reality Applications in Higher Education: Design Elements, Lessons Learned and Research Agenda. *Computers in Education*, 147, 103778, p. 29.

Ramis, M-A, Chang, A, Conway, A, Munday, J, and Nissen, L (2019) Theory-Based Strategies for Teaching Evidence-Based Practice to Undergraduate Health Students: A Systematic Review. *BMC Medical Education*, 19, 267, p. 13.

Rao, K, Ok, M, and Bryant, B (2014) A Review of Research on Universal Design Educational Models. *Remedial and Special Education*, 35, 3, pp. 153–66.

Reddy, Y, and Andrade, H (2010) A Review of Rubric Use in Higher Education. *Assessment and Evaluation in Higher Education*, 35, 4, pp. 435–48.

Rey, G (2012) A Review of Research and a Meta-Analysis of the Seductive Detail Effect. *Educational Research Review*, 7, pp. 216–37.

Reyes, D, Dinh, J, Lacerenza, C, Marlow, S, Joseph, D, and Salas, E (2019) The State of Higher Education Leadership Development Program Evaluation: A Meta-Analysis, Critical Review and Recommendations. *The Leadership Quarterly*, https://doi.org/10.1016/j.leaqua.2019.101311.

Rhaiem, M (2017) Measurement and Determinants of Academic Research Efficiency: A Systematic Review of the Evidence. *Scientometrics*, 110, pp. 581–615.

Richardson, M, Abraham, C, and Bond, R (2012) Psychological Correlates of University Students' Academic Performance: A Systematic Review and Meta-Analysis. *Psychological Bulletin*, 138, 2, pp. 353–87.

Riebe, L, Gerardi, A, and Whitsed, C (2016) A Systematic Literature Review of Teamwork Pedagogy in Higher Education. *Small Group Research*, 47, 6, pp. 619–64.

Rinn, A, and Plucker, J (2019) High-Ability College Students and Undergraduate Honors Programs: A Systematic Review. *Journal for the Education of the Gifted*, 42, 3, pp. 187–215.

Robbins, S, Oh, I-S, Le, H, and Button, C (2009) Intervention Effects on College Performance and Retention as Mediated by Motivational, Emotional and Social Control Factors: Integrated Meta-Analytic Path Analyses. *Journal of Applied Psychology*, 94, 5, pp. 1163–84.

Robbins, S, Lauver, K, Le, H, Davis, D, and Langley, R (2004) Do Psychosocial and Study Skill Factors Predict College Outcomes? A Meta-Analysis. *Psychological Bulletin*, 130, 2, pp. 261–88.

Roberts, K, Park, H, Brown, S, and Cook, B (2011) Universal Design for Instruction in Postsecondary Education: A Systematic Review of Empirically Based Articles. *Journal of Postsecondary Education and Disability*, 24, 1, pp. 5–15.

Rogaten, J, Rienties, B, Sharpe, R, Cross, S, Whitelock, D, Lygo-Baker, S, and Littlejohn, A (2019) Reviewing Affective, Behavioural and Cognitive Learning Gains in Higher Education. *Assessment and Evaluation in Higher Education*, 44, 3, pp. 321–37.

Rooij, E van, Brouwer, J, Fokkens-Bruinsma, N, Jansen, E, Donche, V, and Noyens, D (2018) A Systematic Review of Factors Related to First-Year Students' Success in Dutch and Flemish Higher Education. *Pedagogische Studien*, pp. 360–405.

Rosenthal, R, and DiMatteo, M (2001) Meta-Analysis: Recent Developments in Quantitative Methods for Literature Reviews. *Annual Review of Psychology*, 52, pp. 59–82.

Ross, A (1992) Two Decades of Higher Education. *Higher Education*, 23, pp. 99–112.

Roth, A, Ogrin, S, and Schmitz, B (2016) Assessing Self-Regulated Learning in Higher Education: A Systematic Literature Review of Self-Report Instruments. *Educational Assessment, Evaluation and Accounting*, 28, pp. 225–50.

Rovai, A, Gallien, L, and Wighting, M (2005) Cultural and Interpersonal Factors Affecting African American Academic Performance in Higher Education: A Review and Synthesis of the Research Literature. *Journal of Negro Education*, 74, 4, pp. 359–70.

Roy, A, Newman, A, Ellenberger, T, and Pyman, A (2019) Outcomes of International Student Mobility Programs: A Systematic Review and Agenda for Future Research. *Studies in Higher Education*, 44, 8, pp. 1630–44.

Rubin, M (2012) Social Class Differences in Social Integration among Students in Higher Education: A Meta-Analysis and Recommendations for Future Research. *Journal of Diversity in Higher Education*, 5, 1, pp. 22–38.

Rubio-Alcalá, F, Arco-Tirado, J, Fernández-Martín, F, López-Lechuga, R, Barrios, E, and Pavón-Vázquez, V (2019) A Systematic Review on Evidences Supporting Quality Indicators of Bilingual, Plurilingual and Multilingual Programs in Higher Education. *Educational Research Review*, 27, pp. 191–204.

Ryan, G, Toohey, S, and Hughes, C (1996) The Purpose, Value and Structure of the Practicum in Higher Education: A Literature Review. *Higher Education*, 31, pp. 355–77.

Saa, A, Al-Emran, M, and Shaalan, K (2019) Factors Affecting Students' Performance in Higher Education: A Systematic Review of Predictive Data Mining Techniques. *Technology, Knowledge and Learning*, https://doi.org/10.1007/s10758-019-09408-7.

Sackett, P, Kuncel, N, Arneson, J, Cooper, S, and Waters, S (2009) Does Socioeconomic Status Explain the Relationship between Admissions Tests and Post-Secondary Academic Performance? *Psychological Bulletin*, 135, 1, pp. 1–22.

Safipour, J, Wenneberg, S, and Hadziabdic, E (2017) Experience of Education in the International Classroom: A Systematic Literature Review. *Journal of International Students*, 7, 3, pp. 806–24.

Salam, M, Iskandar, D, Ibrahim, D, and Farooq, M (2019) Service Learning in Higher Education: A Systematic Literature Review. *Asia Pacific Education Review*, https://doi.org/10.1007/s12564-019-09580-6.

Samson, G, Graue, E, Weinstein, T, and Walberg, H (1984) Academic and Occupational Performance: A Quantitative Synthesis. *American Educational Research Journal*, 21, 2, pp. 311–21.

Santos, J, Figueiredo, A, and Vieira, M (2019) Innovative Pedagogical Practices in Higher Education: An Integrative Literature Review. *Nurse Education Today*, 72, pp. 12–17.

Sasanguie, D, Elen, J, Clarebout, G, Noorgate, W van den, Vandenabelee, J, and Fraine, B de (2011) Disentangling Instructional Roles: The Case of Teaching and Summative Assessment. *Studies in Higher Education*, 36, 8, pp. 897–910.

Savin-Baden, M, and Major, C (2007) Using Interpretative Meta-Ethnography to Explore the Relationship between Innovative Approaches to Learning and Their Influence on Faculty Understanding of Teaching. *Higher Education*, 54, pp. 833–52.

Savin-Baden, M, McFarland, L, and Savin-Baden, J (2008) Learning Spaces, Agency and Notions of Improvement: What Influences Thinking and Practices about Teaching and Learning in Higher Education? An Interpretative Meta-Ethnography. *London Review of Education*, 6, 3, pp. 211–27.

Schiekirka, S, and Raupach, T (2015) A Systematic Review of Factors Influencing Student Ratings in Undergraduate Medical Education Course Evaluations. *BMC Medical Education*, 15, 30, p. 9.

Schlosser, C, and Anderson, M (1994) *Distance Education: Review of the Literature*. Iowa State University of Science and Technology, Ames Research Institute for Studies in Education.

Schmid, R, Bernard, R, Borokhovski, E, Tamim, R, Abrami, P, Wade, A, Surkes, M, and Lowerison, G (2009) Technology's Effect on Achievement in Higher Education: A Stage 1 Meta-Analysis of Classroom Applications. *Journal of Computing in Higher Education*, 21, pp. 95–409.

Schmid, R, Bernard, R, Borokhovski, E, Tamim, R, Abrami, P, Surkes, M, Wade, A, and Woods, J (2014) The Effect of Technology Use in Postsecondary Education: A Meta-Analysis of Classroom Applications. *Computers and Education*, 72, pp. 271–91.

Schmidt, U, and Gunther, T (2016) Public Sector Accounting Research in the Higher Education Sector: A Systematic Literature Review. *Management Review Quarterly*, 66, pp. 235–65.

Schmidtlein, F, and Milton, T (1990) *A Review of Literature on Higher Education Institutional Planning*. College Park, MD, National Center for Postsecondary Governance and Finance.

Schneider, M, and Preckel, F (2017) Variables Associated with Achievement in Higher Education: A Systematic Review of Meta-Analyses. *Psychological Bulletin*, 143, 6, pp. 565–600.

Schramm, W (1962) Learning from Instructional Television. *Review of Educational Research*, 32, 2, pp. 156–67.

Schreffler, J, Vasquez, E, Chini, J, and James, W (2019) Universal Design for Learning in Postsecondary STEM Education for Students with Disabilities: A Systematic Literature Review. *International Journal of STEM Education*, 6, 8, p. 10.

Schudde, L, and Brown, R (2019) Understanding Variation in Estimates of Diversionary Effects of Community College Entrance: A Systematic Review and Meta-Analysis. *Sociology of Education*, 92, 3, pp. 247–68.

Schuler, H, Funk, U, and Baron-Boldt, J (1990) Predictive Validity of School Grades: A Meta-Analysis. *Applied Psychology*, 39, 1, pp. 89–103.

Schwinger, M, Wirthwein, L, Lemmer, G, and Steinmayr, R (2014) Academic Self-Handicapping and Achievement: A Meta-Analysis. *Journal of Educational Psychology*, 106, 3, pp. 744–61.

Sclater, N, Peasgood, A, and Mullan, J (2016) *Learning Analytics in Higher Education: A Review of UK and International Practice*. Bristol, Jisc.

Scurry, T, and Blenkinsopp, J (2011) Under-Employment among Recent Graduates: A Review of the Literature. *Personnel Review*, 40, 5, pp. 643–59.

Secundo, G, Ndou, V, Del Vecchio, P, and De Pascale, G (2019) Knowledge Management in Entrepreneurial Universities: A Structured Literature Review and Avenue for Future Research Agenda. *Management Decision*, DOI: 10.1108/MD-11-2018-1266.

Seok, S, DaCosta, B, and Hodges, R (2018) A Systematic Review of Empirically Based Universal Design for Learning: Implementation and Effectiveness of Universal Design in Education for Students with and without Disabilities at the Postsecondary Level. *Open Journal for Social Sciences*, 6, 5, pp. 171–89.

Severiens, S, and Ten Dam, G (1994) Gender Differences in Learning Styles: A Narrative Review and Quantitative Meta-Analysis. *Higher Education*, 27, pp. 487–501.

Shahjahan, R, and Kezar, A (2013) Beyond the 'National Container': Addressing Methodological Nationalism in Higher Education Research. *Educational Research*, 42, 1, pp. 20–9.

Sharif, R (2019) The Relations between Acculturation and Creativity and Innovation in Higher Education: A Systematic Literature Review. *Educational Research Review*, https://doi.org/10.1016/j.edurev.2019.100287.

Sharp, J, Sharp, J, and Young, E (2018) Academic Boredom, Engagement and the Achievement of Undergraduate Students at University: A Review and Synthesis of Relevant Literature. *Research Papers in Education*, DOI: 10.1080/02671522.2018.1536891.

Shelley, M, and Schuh, J (2001) Are the Best Higher Education Journals Really the Best? A Meta-Analysis of Writing Quality and Readability. *Journal of Scholarly Publishing*, 33, 1, pp. 11–22.

Shi, Y, Ma, Y, MacLeod, J, and Yang, H (2019a) College Students' Cognitive Learning Outcomes in Flipped Classroom Instruction: A Meta-Analysis of the Empirical Literature. *Journal of Computers in Education*, https://doi.org/10.1007/s40692-019-00142-8.

Shi, Y, Yang, H, MacLeod, J, Zhang, J, and Yang, H H (2019b) College Students' Cognitive Learning Outcomes in Technology-Enabled Active Learning Environments: A Meta-Analysis of the Empirical Literature. *Journal of Educational Computing Research*, DOI: 10.1177/0735633119881477.

Shin, S, Park, J-H, and Kim, J-H (2015) Effectiveness of Patient Simulation in Nursing Education: A Meta-Analysis. *Nurse Education Today*, 35, pp. 176–82.

Shute, V (2008) Focus on Formative Feedback. *Review of Educational Research*, 78, 1, pp. 153–89.

Silverman, R (1982) Journal Manuscripts in Higher Education: A Framework. *Review of Higher Education*, 5, 4, pp. 181–96.

Silverman, R (1985) Higher Education as a Maturing Field? Evidence from Referencing Practices. *Research in Higher Education*, 23, 2, pp. 150–83.

Simpson, V, and Oliver, M (2007) Electronic Voting Systems for Lectures Then and Now: A Comparison of Research and Practice. *Australasian Journal of Educational Technology*, 23, 2, pp. 187–208.

Sisk, V, Burgoyne, A, Sun, J, Butler, J, and Macnamara, B (2018) To What Extent and under Which Circumstances Are Growth Mind-Sets Important to Academic Achievement? Two Meta-Analyses. *Psychological Science*, 29, 4, pp. 549–71.

Skaniakos, T, and Piirainen, A (2019) The Meaning of Peer Group Mentoring in the University Context. *International Journal of Evidence Based Coaching and Mentoring*, 17, 1, pp. 19–33.

Small, L, Shacklock, K, and Marchant, T (2018) Employability: A Contemporary Review for Higher Education Stakeholders. *Journal of Vocational Education and Training*, 70, 1, pp. 148–66.

Smith, K, and Hill, J (2019) Defining the Nature of Blended Learning through Its Depiction in Current Research. *Higher Education Research and Development*, 38, 2, pp. 383–97.

Sneyers, E, and De Witte, K (2018) Interventions in Higher Education and Their Effect on Student Success: A Meta-Analysis. *Educational Review*, 70, 2, pp. 208–28.

Sonderlund, A, Hughes, E, and Smith, J (2018) The Efficacy of Learning Analytics Interventions in Higher Education: A Systematic Review. *British Journal of Educational Technology*, DOI: 10.1111/bjet.12720.

Soufi, N, and See, B (2019) Does Explicit Teaching of Critical Thinking Improve Critical Thinking Skills of English Language Learners in Higher Education: A Critical Review of Causal Evidence. *Studies in Educational Evaluation*, 60, pp. 140–62.

Spady, W (1970) Dropouts from Higher Education: An Interdisciplinary Review and Synthesis. *Interchange*, 1, pp. 64–85.

References

Spante, M, Hashemi, S, Lundin, M, and Algers, A (2018) Digital Competence and Digital Literacy in Higher Education Research: Systematic Review of Concept Use. *Cogent Education*, https://doi.org/10.1080/2331186X.2018.1519143.

Spatoula, V, Panagopoulou, E, and Montgomery, A (2019) Does Empathy Change during Undergraduate Medical Education? A Meta-Analysis. *Medical Teacher*, 41, 8, pp. 895–904.

Spelt, E, Biemans, H, Tobi, H, Luning, P, and Mulder, M (2009) Teaching and Learning in Interdisciplinary Higher Education: A Systematic Review. *Educational Psychology Review*, 21, pp. 365–78.

Spencer, B, Sherman, L, Nielson, S, and Thormodson, K (2017) Effectiveness of Occupational Therapy Interventions for Students with Mental Illness Transitioning to Higher Education: A Systematic Review. *Occupational Therapy in Mental Health*, DOI: 10.1080/0164212X.2017.1380559.

Spooren, P, Brockx, B, and Mortelmans, D (2013) On the Validity of Student Evaluation of Teaching: The State of the Art. *Review of Educational Research*, 83, 4, pp. 598–642.

Springer, L, Stanne, M, and Donovan, S (1999) Effects of Small-Group Learning on Undergraduates in Science, Mathematics, Engineering and Technology: A Meta-Analysis. *Review of Educational Research*, 69, 1, pp. 21–51.

Stanley, T (2001) Wheat from Chaff: Meta-Analysis as Quantitative Literature Review. *Journal of Economic Perspectives*, 15, 3, pp. 131–50.

Starrack, J (1934). Student Rating of Instruction. *Journal of Higher Education*, 5, pp. 88–90.

Steenbergen-Hu, S, and Cooper, H (2014) A Meta-Analysis of the Effectiveness of Intelligent Tutoring Systems on College Students' Academic Learning. *Journal of Educational Psychology*, 106, 2, pp. 331–47.

Steinhardt, I, Schneijderberg, C, Gotze, N, Baumann, J, and Krucken, G (2017) Mapping the Quality Assurance of Teaching and Learning in Higher Education: The Emergence of a Speciality? *Higher Education*, 74, pp. 221–37.

Stes, A, Min-Leliveld, M, Gijbels, D, and Petegem, P van (2010) The Impact of Instructional Development in Higher Education: The State-of-The-Art of the Research. *Educational Research Review*, 5, pp. 25–49.

Stigmar, M (2016) Peer-to-Peer Teaching in Higher Education: A Critical Literature Review. *Mentoring and Tutoring*, 24, 2, pp. 124–36.

Strang, A, Belanger, J, Manville, C, and Meads, C (2016) *Review of the Research Literature on Defining and Demonstrating Quality Teaching and Impact in Higher Education*. York, Higher Education Academy.

Stretton, T, Cochrane, T, and Narayan, V (2018) Exploring Mobile Mixed Reality in Healthcare Higher Education: A Systematic Review. *Research in Learning Technology*, 26, http://dx.doi.org/10.25304/rlt.v26.2131.

Strobl, C, Ailhaud, E, Benetos, K, Devitt, A, Kruse, O, Proske, A, and Rapp, C (2019) Digital Support for Academic Writing: A Review of Technologies and Pedagogies. *Computers and Education*, 131, pp. 33–48.

Subhash, S, and Cudney, E (2018) Gamified Learning in Higher Education: A Systematic Review of the Literature. *Computers in Human Behavior*, 87, pp. 192–206.

Sugrue, C, Englund, T, Solbrekke, T, and Fossland, T (2017) Trends in the Practices of Academic Developers: Trajectories of Higher Education? *Studies in Higher Education*, DOI: 10.1080/03075079.2017.1326026.

Suri, H, and Clarke, D (2009) Advancements in Research Synthesis Methods: From a Methodologically Inclusive Perspective. *Review of Educational Research*, 79, 1, pp. 395–430.

Swanson, E, McCulley, L, Osman, D, Lewis, N, and Solis, M (2019) The Effect of Team-Based Learning on Content Knowledge: A Meta-Analysis. *Active Learning in Higher Education*, 20, 1, pp. 39–50.

Symons, C, and Johnson, B (1997) The Self-Reference Effect in Memory: A Meta-Analysis. *Psychological Bulletin*, 121, 3, pp. 371–94.

Tamim, R, Bernard, R, Borokhovski, E, Abrami, P, and Schmid, R (2011) What Forty Years of Research Says About the Impact of Technology on Learning: A Second-Order Meta-Analysis and Validation Study. *Review of Educational Research*, 81, 1, pp. 4–28.

Tan, A, Muskat, B, and Zehrer, A (2016) A Systematic Review of Quality of Student Experience in Higher Education. *International Journal of Quality and Service Sciences*, 2, pp. 209–28.

Tan, D (1986) The Assessment of Quality in Higher Education: A Critical Review of the Literature and Research. *Research in Higher Education*, 24, 3, pp. 223–65.

Tari, J, and Dick, G (2016) Trends in Quality Management Research in Higher Education Institutions. *Journal of Service Theory and Practice*, 26, 3, pp. 273–96.

Taylor, E, Lalovic, A, and Thompson, S (2019) Beyond Enrolments: A Systematic Review Exploring the Factors Affecting the Retention of Aboriginal and Torres Strait Islander Health Students in the Tertiary Education System. *International Journal for Equity in Health*, 18, 136, p. 19.

Terrion, J, and Leonard, D (2007) A Taxonomy of the Characteristics of Student Peer Mentors in Higher Education: Findings from a Literature Review. *Mentoring and Tutoring*, 15, 2, pp. 149–64.

Tess, P (2013) The Role of Social Media in Higher Education Classes (Real and Virtual): A Literature Review. *Computers in Human Behavior*, 29, pp. A60–A68.

Thomas, G, and Pring, R (eds) (2004) *Evidence-Based Practice in Education*. Maidenhead, Open University Press.

Thomas, G, and Thorpe, S (2019) Enhancing the Facilitation of Online Groups in Higher Education: A Review of the Literature on Face-to-Face and Online Group Facilitation. *Interactive Learning Environments*, 27, 1, pp. 62–71.

Thomas, S, Chie, Q-T, Abraham, M, Raj, S, and Beh, L-S (2014) A Qualitative Review of Literature on Peer Review of Teaching in Higher Education: An Application of the SWOT Framework. *Review of Educational Research*, 84, 1, pp. 112–59.

Thune, T (2009) Doctoral Students on the University-Industry Interface: A Review of the Literature. *Higher Education*, 58, pp. 637–51.

Tight, M (2003) *Researching Higher Education*. Maidenhead, Open University Press.

Tight, M (2004) Higher Education Research: An Atheoretical Community of Practice? *Higher Education Research and Development*, 23, 4, pp. 395–411.

Tight, M (2006) Higher Education Research: A Citation Analysis. *Higher Education Review*, 38, 2, pp. 42–59.

Tight, M (2007) Bridging the Divide: A Comparative Analysis of Articles in Higher Education Journals Published Inside and Outside North America. *Higher Education*, 53, 2, pp. 235–53.

Tight, M (2008) Higher Education Research as Tribe, Territory and/or Community: A Co-citation Analysis. *Higher Education*, 55, pp. 593–608.

Tight, M (2009a) *The Development of Higher Education in the United Kingdom since 1945*. Maidenhead, Open University Press.

Tight, M (2009b) The Structure of Academic Research: What Can Citation Studies Tell Us? In A Brew and L Lucas (eds) *Academic Research and Researchers*. Maidenhead, Open University Press, pp. 54–65.

Tight, M (2010) Are Academic Workloads Increasing? The Post-war Survey Evidence in the UK. *Higher Education Quarterly*, 64, 2, pp. 200–15.

Tight, M (2011a) Student Accommodation in Higher Education in the United Kingdom: Changing Post-war Attitudes. *Oxford Review of Education*, 37, 1, pp. 109–22.

Tight, M (2011b) Eleven Years of Studies in Higher Education. *Studies in Higher Education*, 36, 1, pp. 1–6.

Tight, M (2012a) *Researching Higher Education*. Maidenhead, Open University Press, second edition.

Tight, M (2012b) Higher Education Research 2000–2010: Changing Journal Publication Patterns. *Higher Education Research and Development*, 31, 5, pp. 723–40.

Tight, M (2012c) Levels of Analysis in Higher Education Research. *Tertiary Education and Management*, 18, 3, pp. 271–88.

Tight, M (2013) Discipline and Methodology in Higher Education Research. *Higher Education Research and Development*, 32, 1, pp. 136–51.

Tight, M (2014a) Collegiality and Managerialism: A False Dichotomy? Evidence from the Higher Education Research Literature. *Tertiary Education and Management*, 20, 4, pp. 294–306.

Tight, M (2014b) Working in Separate Silos? What Citation Patterns Reveal about Higher Education Research Internationally. *Higher Education*, 68, 3, pp. 379–95.

Tight, M (2014c) Discipline and Theory in Higher Education Research. *Research Papers in Education*, 29, 1, pp. 93–110.

Tight, M (2014d) Theory Development and Application in Higher Education Research: The Case of Threshold Concepts. In J Huisman and M Tight (eds) *Theory and Method in Higher Education Research, Volume 2*. Bingley, Emerald, pp. 249–67.

Tight, M (2015a) Theory Development and Application in Higher Education: The Case of Communities of Practice. *European Journal of Higher Education*, 5, 2, pp. 111–26.

Tight, M (2015b) Theory Development and Application in Higher Education Research: Tribes and Territories. *Higher Education Policy*, 28, 4, pp. 277–93.

Tight, M (2015c) Theory Development and Application in Higher Education Research: The Case of Academic Drift. *Journal of Educational Administration and History*, 47, 1, pp. 84–99.

Tight, M (2015d) Higher Education Research in the United Kingdom since 1945. In J Case and J Huisman (eds) *Researching Higher Education: International Perspectives on Theory, Policy and Practice*. London, Routledge, pp. 1–19.

Tight, M (2015e) Research on Higher Education Policy and Institutional Management. In J Huisman, M Souto-Otero, D Dill and H de Boer (eds) *Palgrave International Handbook of Higher Education Policy and Governance*. Basingstoke, Palgrave Macmillan, pp. 176–91.

Tight, M (2016a) Phenomenography: The Development and Application of an Innovative Research Design in Higher Education Research. *International Journal of Social Research Methodology*, 19, 3, pp. 319–38.

Tight, M (2016b) Examining the Research/Teaching Nexus. *European Journal of Higher Education*, 6, 4, pp. 293–311.

Tight, M (2018a) Tracking the Scholarship of Teaching and Learning. *Policy Reviews in Higher Education*, 2, 1, pp. 61–78.

Tight, M (2018b) Higher Education Journals: Their Characteristics and Contribution. *Higher Education Research and Development*, 37, 3, pp. 607–19.

Tight, M (2019a) *Higher Education Research: The Developing Field*. London, Bloomsbury.

Tight, M (2019b) Mass Higher Education and Massification. *Higher Education Policy*, 31, 1, pp. 93–108.

Tight, M (2019c) *Documentary Analysis in the Social Sciences*. London, Sage.

Tight, M (2020) Student Retention and Engagement in Higher Education Research. *Journal of Further and Higher Education*, 44, 5, pp. 689–704.

Tight, M (forthcoming – a) Globalization and Internationalization as Frameworks for Higher Education Research. *Research Papers in Education*.

Timmerman, E, and Kruepke, K (2006) Computer-Assisted Instruction, Media Richness and College Student Performance. *Communication Education*, 55, 1, pp. 73–104.

Tinto, V (1975) Dropout from Higher Education: A Theoretical Synthesis of Recent Research. *Review of Educational Research*, 45, 1, pp. 89–125.

Tinto, V (1993) *Leaving College: Rethinking the Causes and Cures of Student Attrition*. Chicago, IL, University of Chicago Press, second edition.

Tipton, E, Pustejovsky, J, and Ahmadi, H (2019) A History of Meta-Regression: Technical, Conceptual and Practical Developments between 1974 and 2018. *Research Synthesis Methods*, 10, pp. 161–79.

Tiruneh, D, Verburgh, A, and Elen, J (2014) Effectiveness of Critical Thinking Instruction in Higher Education: A Systematic Review of Intervention Studies. *Higher Education Studies*, 4, 1, pp. 1–17.

Toor, N, Hanley, T, and Hebron, J (2016) The Facilitators, Obstacles and Needs of Individuals with Autism Spectrum Conditions Accessing Further and Higher Education: A Systematic Review. *Journal of Psychologists and Counsellors in Schools*, 26, 2, pp. 161–90.

Topping, K (1996) The Effectiveness of Peer Tutoring in Further and Higher Education: A Typology and Review of the Literature. *Higher Education*, 32, pp. 321–45.

Topping, K (1998) Peer Assessment between Students in Colleges and Universities. *Review of Educational Research*, 68, 3, pp. 249–76.

Torgerson, C (2003) *Systematic Reviews*. London, Continuum.

Torraco, R (2005) Writing Integrative Literature Reviews: Guidelines and Examples. *Human Resource Development Review*, 4, 3, pp. 356–67.

Trapmann, S, Hell, B, Hirn, J-O, and Schuler, H (2007) Meta-Analysis of the Relationship between the Big Five and Academic Success at University. *Zeitschrift für Psychologie*, 215, 2, pp. 132–51.

Trede, F, Macklin, R, and Bridges, D (2012) Professional Identity Development: A Review of the Higher Education Literature. *Studies in Higher Education*, 37, 3, pp. 365–84.

Trenholm, S, Peschke, J, and Chinnappan, M (2019) A Review of Fully Online Undergraduate Mathematics Instruction through the Lens of Large-Scale Research (2000–2015). *Problems, Resources and Issues in Mathematics Undergraduate Studies*, 29, 10, pp. 1080–100.

Uslu, B, Calikoglu, A, Seggie, F, and Seggie, S (2019) The Entrepreneurial University and Academic Discourses: The Meta-Synthesis of Higher Education Articles. *Higher Education Quarterly*, 73, pp. 285–311.

Uttl, B, White, C, and Gonzalez, D (2017) Meta-Analysis of Faculty's Teaching Effectiveness: Student Evaluation of Teaching Ratings and Student Learning Are Not Related. *Studies in Educational Evaluation*, 54, pp. 22–42.

Van Alten, D, Phielix, C, Janssen, J, and Kester, L (2019) Effects of Flipping the Classroom on Learning Outcomes and Satisfaction: A Meta-Analysis. *Educational Research Review*, 28, https://doi.org/10.1016/j.edurev.2019.05.003.

Van Beveren, L, Roets, G, Busse, A, and Rutten, K (2018) We All Reflect, but Why? A Systematic Review of the Purposes of Reflection in Higher Education in Social and Behavioural Sciences. *Educational Research Review*, 24, pp. 1–9.

Van der Kleij, F, Adie, L, and Cumming, J (2019) A Meta-Review of the Student Role in Feedback. *International Journal of Educational Research*, 98, pp. 303–23.

Van Ginkel, S, Gulikers, J, Biemans, H, and Mulder, M (2015) Towards a Set of Design Principles for Developing Oral Presentation Competence: A Synthesis of Research in Higher Education. *Educational Research Review*, 14, pp. 62–80.

Velez, G, and Giner, G (2015) Effects of Business Internships on Students, Employers and Higher Education Institutions: A Systematic Review. *Journal of Employment Counseling*, 52, pp. 121–30.

Verburgh, A, Elen, J, and Lindblom-Ylanne, S (2007) Investigating the Myth of the Relationship between Teaching and Research in Higher Education: A Review of Empirical Research. *Studies in the Philosophy of Education*, 26, pp. 449–65.

Vernon, D, and Blake, R (1993) Does Problem-Based Learning Work? A Meta-Analysis of Evaluative Research. *Academic Medicine*, 68, 7, pp. 550–63.

Viegas, C, Bond, A, Vaz, C, Borchardt, M, Pereira, G, Seilg, P, and Varvakis, G (2016) Critical Attributes of Sustainability in Higher Education: A Categorization from Literature Review. *Journal of Cleaner Production*, 126, pp. 260–76.

Villano, R, and Tran, C-D (2019) Survey on Technical Efficiency in Higher Education: A Meta-Fractional Regression Analysis. *Pacific Economic Review*, DOI: 10.1111/1468-0106.12310.

Villarroel, V, Bloxham, S, Bruna, D, Bruna, C, and Herrera-Seda, C (2017) Authentic Assessment: Creating a Blueprint for Course Design. *Assessment and Evaluation in Higher Education*, DOI: 10.1080/02602938.2017.1412396.

Virtanen, M, Haavisto, E, Liikanen, E, and Karriainen, M (2017) Ubiquitous Learning Environments in Higher Education: A Scoping Literature Review. *Educational Information Technology*, DOI: 10.1007/s10639-017-9646-6.

Vlachopoulos, D, and Makri, A (2017) The Effects of Games and Simulations on Higher Education: A Systematic Literature Review. *International Journal of Educational Technology in Higher Education*, 14, 22, p. 33.

Vo, H, Zhu, C, and Diep, N (2017) The Effect of Blended Learning on Student Performance at Course-Level in Higher Education: A Meta-Analysis. *Studies in Educational Evaluation*, 53, pp. 17–28.

Volkwein, J, Carbone, D, and Volkwein, E (1988) *Research in Higher Education*: Fifteen Years of Scholarship. *Research in Higher Education*, 28, 3, pp. 271–80.

Vrielink, R, Jansen, E, Hans, E, Hillegersberg, J (2017) Practices in Timetabling in Higher Education Institutions: A Systematic Review. *Annals of Operations Research*, DOI: 10.1007/s10479-017-2688-8.

Wachtel, H (1998) Student Evaluation of College Teaching Effectiveness: A Brief Review. *Assessment and Evaluation in Higher Education*, 23, 2, pp. 191–232.

Wagner, E, and Szamoskosi, S (2012) Effects of Direct Academic Motivation-Enhancing Intervention Programs: A Meta-Analysis. *Journal of Cognitive and Behavioral Psychotherapies*, 12, 1, pp. 85–101.

Wallin, A, Nokelainen, P, and Mikkonen, S (2019) How Experienced Professionals Develop Their Expertise in Work-Based Higher Education: A Literature Review. *Higher Education*, 77, pp. 359–78.

Wang, J, Xu, Y, Liu, X, Xiong, W, Xie, J, and Zhao, J (2016) Assessing the Effectiveness of Problem-Based Learning in Physical Diagnostics Education in China: A Meta-Analysis. *Scientific Reports*, 6, 36279, 7pp.

Watts, L, Wagner, J, Velasquez, B, and Behrens, P (2017) Cyberbullying in Higher Education: A Literature Review. *Computers in Human Behavior*, 69, pp. 268–74.

Webb, S, Burke, P, Nichols, S, Roberts, S, Stahl, G, Threadgold, S, and Wilkinson, J (2017) Thinking with and Beyond Bourdieu in Widening Higher Education Participation. *Studies in Continuing Education*, 39, 2, pp. 138–60.

Weightman, A, Farnell, D, Morris, D, Strange, H, and Hallam, G (2017) A Systematic Review of Information Literacy Programmes in Higher Education: Effects of Face-to-Face, Online and Blended Formats on Student Skills and Views. *Evidence Based Library and Information Practice*, 12, 3, pp. 20–54.

Weimer, M, and Lenze, L (1991) Instructional Interventions: A Review of the Literature on Efforts to Improve Instruction. In J Smart (ed) *Higher Education: Handbook of Theory and Research*, 7. New York, Agathon, pp. 294–333.

Weiss, M, and Barth, M (2019) Global Research Landscape of Sustainability Curricula Implementation in Higher Education. *International Journal for Sustainability in Higher Education*, 20, 4, pp. 570–89.

Wekullo, C (2019) International Undergraduate Student Engagement: Implications for Higher Education Administrators. *Journal of International Students*, 9, 1, pp. 320–37.

Whiting, W, Pharr, J, Buttner, M, and Lough, N (2019) Behavioral Interventions to Increase Condom Use among College Students in the United States: A Systematic Review. *Health Education and Behavior*, 46, 5, pp. 877–88.

Whitley, B (1998) Factors Associated with Cheating among College Students: A Review. *Research in Higher Education*, 39, 3, pp. 235–74.

Whittemore, R, and Knafl, K (2005) The Integrative Review: Updated Methodology. *Journal of Advanced Nursing*, 52, 5, pp. 546–53.

Wihlborg, M, and Teelken, C (2014) Striving for Uniformity, Hoping for Innovation and Diversification: A Critical Review Concerning the Bologna Process – Providing an Overview and Reflecting on the Criticism. *Policy Futures in Education*, 12, 8, pp. 1084–100.

Wilger, A (1997) *Quality Assurance in Higher Education: A Literature Review*. Stanford University, National Center for Postsecondary Improvement.

Williams, J, Ireland, T, Warman, S, Cake, M, Dymock, D, Fowler, E, and Baillie, S (2019) Instruments to Measure the Ability to Self-Reflect: A Systematic Review of Evidence from Workplace and Educational Settings Including Healthcare. *European Journal of Dental Education*, 23, pp. 389–404.

Wimpenny, K, Beelen, J, and King, V (2019) Academic Development to Support the Internationalization of the Curriculum: A Qualitative Research Synthesis. *International Journal for Academic Development*, DOI: 10.1080/1360144X.2019.1691559.

Winberg, C, Adendorff, H, Bozalek, V, Conana, H, Pallitt, N, Wolff, K, Olsson, T, and Roxa, T (2018) Learning to Teach STEM Disciplines in Higher Education: A Critical Review of the Literature. *Teaching in Higher Education*, DOI: 10.1080/13562517.2018.1517735.

Winzer, R, Lindberg, L, Gulbrandsson, K, and Sidorchuk, A (2018) Effects of Mental Health Interventions for Students in Higher Education Are Sustainable over Time: A Systematic Review and Meta-Analysis of Randomized Control Trials. *PeerJ*, 6, p. e4598, DOI: 10.7717/peerj.4598.

Wirihana, L, Welch, A, Williamson, M, Christensen, M, Bakon, S, and Craft, J (2017) The Provision of Higher Education in Regional Areas: An Integrative Review of the Literature. *Journal of Higher Education Policy and Management*, 39, 3, pp. 307–19.

Wright, S, and Jenkins-Guarnieri, M (2012) Student Evaluations of Teaching: Combining the Meta-Analyses and Demonstrating Further Evidence for Effective Use. *Assessment and Evaluation in Higher Education*, 37, 6, pp. 683–99.

Wrigley, T (2018) The Power of 'Evidence': Reliable Science or a Set of Blunt Tools? *British Educational Research Journal*, 44, 3, pp. 359–76.

Wu, W-H, Wu, Y-C, Chen, C-Y, Kao, H-Y, Lin, C-H, and Huang, S-H (2012) Review of Trends from Mobile Learning Studies: A Meta-Analysis. *Computers and Education*, 59, pp. 817–27.

Wu, Y-C, and Shen, J-P (2016) Higher Education for Sustainable Development: A Systematic Review. *International Journal of Sustainability in Higher Education*, 17, 5, pp. 633–51.

Xu, P, Chen, Y, Nie, W, Wang, Y, Song, T, Li, H, Li, J, Yi, J, and Zhao, L (2019) The Effectiveness of a Flipped Classroom on the Development of on Chinese Nursing Students' Skills Competence: A Systematic Review and Meta-Analysis. *Nurse Education Today*, 80, pp. 67–77.

Yadav, R, Tiruwa, A, and Suri, P (2017) Internet-Based Learning in Higher Education: A Literature Review. *Journal of International Education in Business*, 10, 2, pp. 102–29.

Younger, K, Gascoine, L, Menzies, V, and Torgerson, C (2018) A Systematic Review of Evidence on the Effectiveness of Interventions and Strategies for Widening Participation in Higher Education. *Journal of Further and Higher Education*, DOI: 10.1080/0309877X.2017.1404558.

Zawacki-Richter, O, Marin, V, Bond, M, and Gouverneur, F (2019) Systematic Review of Research on Artificial Intelligence Applications in Higher Education: Where Are the Educators? *International Journal of Educational Technology in Higher Education*, 16, 39, https://doi.org/10.1186/s41239-019-0171-0.

Zhai, K, Gao, X, and Wang, G (2019) Factors for Chinese Students Choosing Australian Higher Education and Motivation for Returning: A Systematic Review. *SAGE Open*, April–June, pp. 1–11.

Zhang, J, and Cui, Q (2018) Collaborative Learning in Higher Nursing Education: A Systematic Review. *Journal of Professional Nursing*, 34, pp. 378–88.

Zhang, L-C, and Worthington, A (2018) Explaining Estimated Economies of Scale and Scope in Higher Education: A Meta-Regression Analysis. *Research in Higher Education*, 59, pp. 156–73.

Zhang, Q, Kang, N, and Barnes, R (2016) A Systematic Literature Review of Funding for Higher Education Institutions in Developed Countries. *Frontiers of Education in China*, 11, 4, pp. 519–42.

Zhao, Y, Lei, J, Yan, B, and Tan, S (2005) What Makes the Difference? A Practical Analysis of Research on the Effectiveness of Distance Education. *Teachers College Record*, 107, 8, pp. 1836–84.

Zhou, M, and Lam, K (2019) Metacognitive Scaffolding for Online Information Search in K-12 and Higher Education Settings: A Systematic Review. *Educational Technology Research Development*, https://doi.org/10.1007/s11423-019-09646-7.

Index

academic development 47–8, 216–20
academic drift 206
academic work 215–23
    women academics 221–2
achievement. *See* success and achievement
action research 76–7
active learning 76–7
advance organizers 46
assessment 119–31
    authentic 130–1
    formative and summative 120–1
    peer, self and teacher 121–4
    previous and current 128
audience response systems 57–8
authentic assessment 130–1

blended learning 93–8
Bologna Process 197–8

cheating 129
computer-assisted instruction 61–3
computer-based scaffolding 64
course design 51–154
critical thinking 146–9
curriculum 103–17
cyberbullying 173

databases 24–6
digital literacy 99, 172
discipline 100–1, 220
distance learning 81–101
    effectiveness 83–6
    success 86–8

economies of scale and scope 207
educational development 47–8, 216–20

e-learning 81–101
employer engagement 115–16
English medium instruction 65
entrepreneurship 75, 150–1, 206–7
evaluation. *See* student evaluation of teaching

faculty development 47–8, 216–20
feedback 124–8
Feldman, Kenneth 134, 179
flipped classrooms 59–61
food insecurity 173
formative assessment 120–1

game-based learning 55–7
globalization 194–5
group-based learning 68–70, 98

Hattie, John 19
Hawthorne effect 116
higher education research 229–30
Horta, Hugo 27

information literacy 150
innovative pedagogical practices 65
institutional management 203–14
    efficiency 211–12
    information and knowledge management 208–9
instructional animation 63–4
intelligent tutoring systems 64
interdisciplinary and innovative learning 43–4
internationalization 195–6

journals 24–5, 31, 37, 67, 82, 103, 119, 133, 155, 177, 194, 203, 215, 225

knowledge and research 225–30
Kulik, James 61–62

leadership 47, 99, 116, 209–11
    e-leadership 99
    student leadership 116
    transformational instructor 47
learner-centred initiatives 78–9
learning 38–44. *See also* teaching
        and learning
    active 76–7
    analytics 107–9
    approaches, patterns and styles 38–41
    blended 93–8
    design 104–5
    distance 81–101
    e-learning 81–101
    game-based learning 55–7
    group 68–70, 98
    interdisciplinary and innovative 43–4
    interventions 105–7
    mobile 90–3
    online 81–101
    problem-based 70–3
    self-regulated 41–3
    service 77–8
    types of 67–80
    ubiquitous 91–8
    virtual 88–90
    and work 73–6
literature reviews 3, 14–15

management. *See* institutional management
marketing 212–13
massification 196
meta-analyses 3, 17–19
    definition 14
methodology 48
mobile learning 90–3
mobility 116
motivation 46
    motivation enhancement 46
multilingual provision 65

non-traditional students 199–201
note-taking 63

online learning 81–101
oral presentations 150
outcomes 133–54

Pascarella, Ernest 134–5
peer
    assessment 121–4
    instruction, mentoring and tutoring 52–5
    review 228
persistence 99, 152–3, 168–9
placements and internships 73–5
policy. *See* system policy
positivity 236
postgraduate study 109–11, 167–8
problem-based learning 70–3
professional development 149–50
professional staff 223

quality 177–92
    assurance 188–9
    management 189–91

reading 113–14
reflection 151
retention 99, 152–3, 168–9
research 225–30
    student 79
    syntheses 3, 9–21, 23–34
research/teaching nexus 225–8
rubrics 127–8

scholarship of teaching and learning 46
search engines 6
self-assessment 121–4
self-regulated learning 41–3
service learning 77–8
social capital 201–2
students
    boredom 172
    bullying 173–5
    burnout 174
    characteristics 160–4
    class 161–2
    disability 164–6
    diversity 166–7
    drug abuse 173

employment 76
ethnicity 156–7
evaluation of teaching 178–85
experience 155–75
   first-year 171
   LGBTQ+ 162–3
   mental health 169–70
   mobility 116
   nationality 157–9
   non-traditional 199–201
      research 79
   older 160–1
   postgraduate 167–8
   price response 170–1
   satisfaction 185–7
   sexual assault 174
   support 168–70
   types 156–66
   women 160
study skills 140–1
success and achievement 134–52
   generic studies 136–7
   psychological attributes 139–40
   student characteristics 137–9
   study skills 140–1
   subsequent achievement 142
summative assessment 120–1
supervision 99–100
support services 168–70
sustainability 111–13, 205–6
syntheses 3, 9–21, 23–34
   countries of authors 31–3
   country studies 26–7
   discipline studies 27
   generic studies 26
   journals of publication 31
   scale 34
   strengths and weaknesses 19–21

   topic studies 27–34
   trends in publication 30–1
   varieties 9–13
system policy 193–202
   international and comparative 194–8
   national 198–9
   thematic studies 199–202
systematic reviews 3, 14–17
   definition 14

teaching 45–6
   evaluation 178–85
   excellence 45
teaching and learning 37–49
Terenzini, Patrick 134–5
textbooks 3
themes 28–30, 33. *See also* topics
   sub-themes 33
third mission 204–5
third wave 4
threshold concepts 115
Tight, Malcolm 5–6, 26
timetabling 213–14
Tinto, Vincent 153
topics 33–4. *See also* themes
transnational higher education 196–7
types of instruction 51–65
types of learning 67–80
types of students 156–66

ubiquitous learning 91–8

verbal redundancy 64
virtual learning 88–90

work 73–6
work-integrated learning 75–6
writing 114